Charles Comfort

Take Comfort – The Career of

Charles Comfort

La carrière de Charles Comfort

MARY JO HUGHES

ESSAYS BY / ESSAIS PAR

ROSEMARIE TOVELL

ROSEMARY DONEGAN

LAURA BRANDON

ANNA HUDSON

THE WINNIPEG ART GALLERY

LE MUSÉE DES BEAUX-ARTS DE WINNIPEG

Library and Archives Canada Cataloguing in Publication

Hughes, Mary Jo
Take Comfort : the career of Charles Comfort = la carrière de Charles Comfort / author: Mary Jo Hughes ; contributing writers: Rosemarie Tovell ... [et al].

Curated by Mary Jo Hughes.
Text in English and French.
Catalogue of an exhibition held at the Winnipeg Art Gallery, Winnipeg, Man., Feb. 10-Apr. 28, 2007, Confederation Art Centre, Charlottetown, P.E.I., Jun. 17-Sept. 2, 2007, and Museum London, Ont., Oct. 6-Dec. 16, 2007.
Accompanied by a CD-ROM.
Includes bibliographical references.

ISBN 978-0-88915-237-3

1. Comfort, Charles Fraser, 1900-1994—Exhibitions. I. Tovell, Rosemarie L. II. Winnipeg Art Gallery III. Confederation Art Gallery and Museum IV. Museum London (London, Ont.) V. Title.

ND249.C59H83 2007 759.11 C2006-905913-6E

Catalogage avant publication de Bibliothèque et Archives Canada

Hughes, Mary Jo
Take Comfort : the career of Charles Comfort = la carrière de Charles Comfort / author: Mary Jo Hughes ; contributing writers: Rosemarie Tovell ... [et al].

Conservatrice: Mary Jo Hughes.
Acc. d'un CD-ROM.
Texte en anglais et en français.
Catalogue d'une exposition présentée à la Winnipeg Art Gallery, Winnipeg, Man., 10 fév.-28 avril 2007, au Confederation Art Centre, Charlottetown, Î-P.-É., 17 juin-2 sept. 2007 et au Museum London, Ont., 6 oct-16 déc. 2007.
Comprend des réf. bibliogr.

ISBN 978-0-88915-237-3

1. Comfort, Charles Fraser, 1900-1994—Expositions. I. Tovell, Rosemarie L. II. Winnipeg Art Gallery III. Confederation Art Gallery and Museum IV. Museum London (London, Ont.) V. Titre.

ND249.C59H83 2007 759.11 C2006-905913-6F

Printed in Canada

TOUR

The Winnipeg Art Gallery, Winnipeg, Manitoba, February 9 – April 28, 2007.

Confederation Art Centre, Charlottetown, Prince Edward Island, June 17 – September 2, 2007.

Museum London, London, Ontario, October 6 – December 16, 2007.

ITINÉRAIRE

Le Musée des beaux-arts de Winnipeg (Winnipeg, Manitoba), 9 février – 28 avril 2007.

Le Musée des beaux-arts du Centre de la Confédération (Charlottetown, Île-du-Prince-Édouard), 17 juin – 2 septembre 2007.

Museum London (London, Ontario), 6 octobre – 16 décembre 2007.

CONTENTS / SOMMAIRE

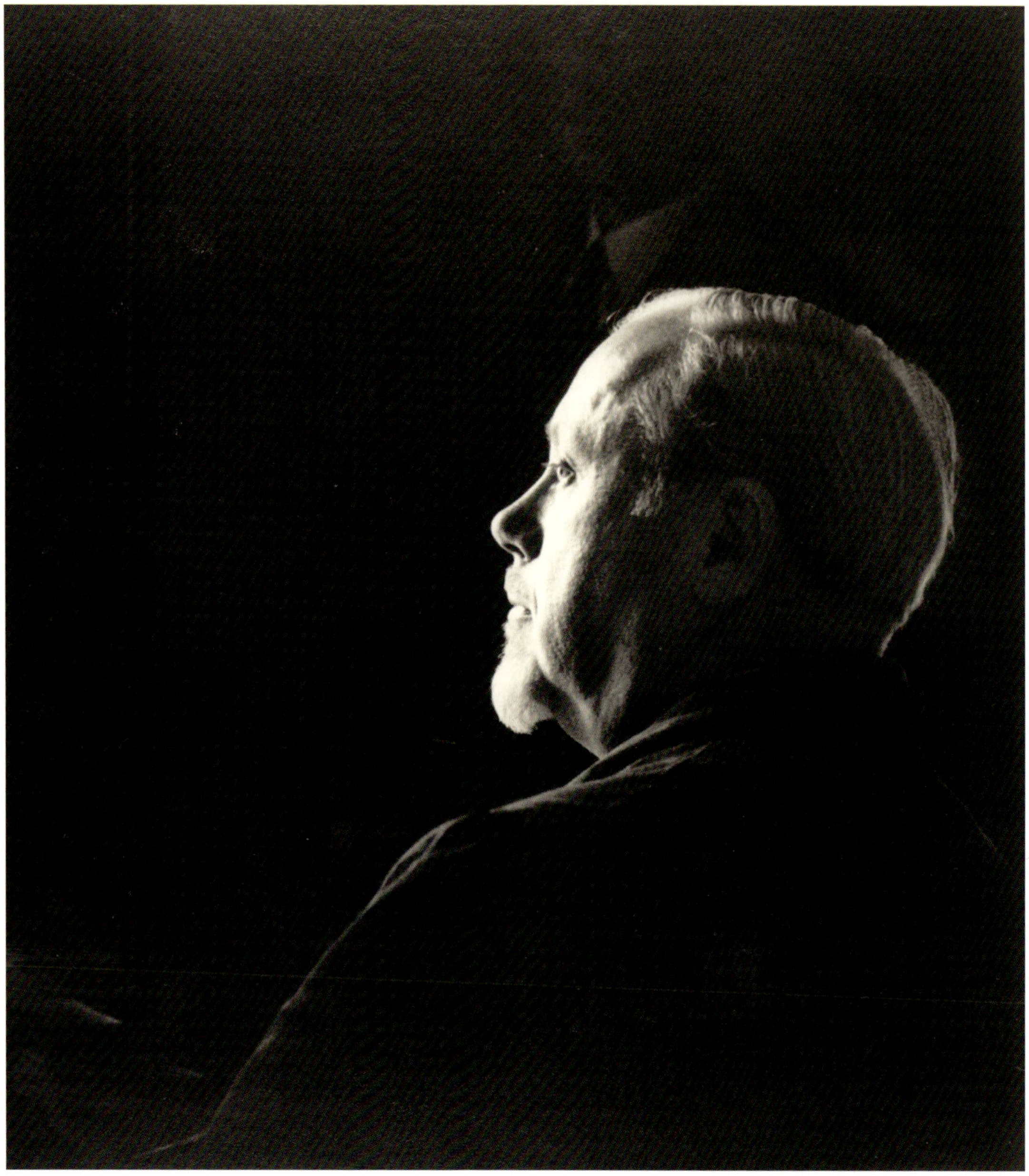

ALFRED UPTON, **Charles Fraser Comfort, R.C.A.**, 1972
Photography, Library and Archives Canada/PA186001

Director's Foreword

Take Comfort is a retrospective that presents a broad view of Charles Comfort's long and fruitful career over more than five decades of artistic activity and cultural interaction, beginning in Winnipeg in 1914. The Winnipeg Art Gallery has played a significant part in Charles Comfort's prestigious art career. In 1922 the Gallery presented Comfort's first one-man exhibition. Fifty years later we held a retrospective, *Charles Comfort – Fifty Years*. *Take Comfort* will be the first exhibition since that time devoted to this artist, the first opportunity to critically examine his contribution to Manitoba and Canadian art history.

With the perspective of time and the availability of Comfort's personal papers, the exhibition's curator, Mary Jo Hughes, presents his multi-faceted career within several contexts. In this publication the first essay, "Rare Feast," is an introduction to Comfort's life and career, exploring his development, goals, and contributions to Canadian culture in the context of his sincere enthusiasm for art's ability to contribute to the human experience. In the second essay, "A Promising Talent: The Making of a Painter in Watercolour," Rosemarie Tovell explores Comfort's early watercolours and the development of his stylistic and technical skills. In "Muscled Workers, Speeding Trains, and Composite Figures: Charles Comfort's Murals," Rosemarie Donegan discusses the intersection of his murals with his commercial career. Anna Hudson in "Charles Comfort's Moment in the Relationship of Art and Life, 1935–1945" expands upon the notion of Comfort as part of the generation of artists who moved Canadian painting forward in the 1930s and 40s by developing a common symbolic language. In "Veracity and Expectation in Charles Comfort's War Art, 1940–48: The Hitler Line in Perspective," Laura Brandon explores his artistic approach as a war artist during the Second World War. *The Comfort Guestbook, 1931–1939*, a CD-ROM located at the back of the publication, acts as another chapter that allows us a glimpse into the group of artists and cultural figures with whom Louise and Charles Comfort interacted during the period when he was emerging as an artist.

This project is a result of hundreds of people over several years contributing their time, interest, and expertise. On behalf of the Gallery and the curator, I sincerely thank the Comfort family and George Falconer for their assistance with the research of this exhibition. We are grateful to all the private lenders and institutions who have contributed to the exhibition by allowing their works to tour. Special thanks go out to the four guest writers whose insights, as noted earlier, are essential to this project. Without the work and ideas of The Winnipeg Art Gallery staff, this exhibition would not be possible. I send my warm appreciation to all of those who were involved in many capacities. Mary Jo would like to extend special thanks to the Hucals, researcher and co-writer of the CD-ROM, Andrew Kear, and to all the kind people who helped her with research and loans, especially Charles C. Hill, Rosemarie Tovell, and other National Gallery of Canada staff; Library and Archives Canada staff, particularly Mary Margaret Johnston-Miller, Lynne Amstrong, Jim Burant, and Karen Clack; and Georgiana Unlyarik, Dennis Reid, and Sylvie Latham at the Art Gallery of Ontario. I would like to extend a special thank you to Library and Archives Canada for their partnership in providing the digital photography for the Comfort Guestbook CD-ROM.

I acknowledge with appreciation the generous financial support that this project has received from the Department of Canadian Heritage through its Museum Assistance Program; The Winnipeg Art Gallery Foundation; the Heritage Grants Program, Manitoba Culture, Heritage and Tourism; Inco Limited; Princess Auto; Western Paint; and the Winnipeg Free Press. Finally I wish to express my congratulations and heartfelt thanks to Mary Jo Hughes, Curator, Historical Art, for her energetic and thoughtful management of this project.

Pierre Arpin
Director

Avant-propos du directeur

La carrière de Charles Comfort est une rétrospective qui présente une vue d'ensemble de la longue et fructueuse carrière de Charles Comfort, une carrière qui, débutant à Winnipeg en 1914, s'est étendue sur plus de cinq décennies d'activité artistique et d'interactions culturelles. Dans cette prestigieuse carrière artistique, le

Musée des beaux-arts de Winnipeg a joué un rôle de premier plan. En 1922, en effet, le musée a accueilli la première exposition solo de Comfort et cinquante ans plus tard, nous avons présenté une rétrospective justement intitulée *Charles Comfort – Fifty Years*. L'exposition actuelle, *La carrière de Charles Comfort* est la première que nous lui consacrons depuis ce temps et aussi la première occasion qui nous est offerte de procéder à un examen critique de sa contribution tant au Manitoba qu'à l'histoire de l'art au Canada.

Avec suffisamment de recul et la possibilité d'accéder aux documents personnels de Charles Comfort, Mary Jo Hughes, conservatrice de l'exposition, nous décrit la carrière à facettes de l'artiste dans différents contextes. « Une rare célébration » premier essai dans cette publication nous fait entrer dans la vie et la carrière de Comfort par l'examen de sa progression, de ses objectifs et de sa contribution à la culture canadienne, et ceci dans le contexte de son sincère enthousiasme pour la manière dont l'art est capable d'enrichir l'expérience humaine. Dans un deuxième essai, intitulé « Un talent prometteur : la formation d'un aquarelliste », Rosemarie Tovell analyse les débuts de l'artiste dans l'aquarelle et le développement de ses capacités techniques et stylistiques. Se penchant sur « Travailleurs musclés, trains rapides, personnages composites : les murales de Charles Comfort», Rosemarie Donegan traite de la manière dont s'entrecroisèrent ses œuvres murales et sa pratique de l'art commercial. Dans « Le Moment psychologique de Charles Comfort dans le rapport entre l'art et la vie, 1935–1945 », Anna Hudson s'étend sur l'idée d'un Comfort faisant partie de la génération d'artistes qui ont fait avancer la peinture canadienne dans les décennies 1930 et 1940 en mettant au point un langage symbolique commun. Pour Laura Brandon, sous le titre «Véracité et attentes dans l'art militaire de Charles Comfort de 1940 à 1948 : La ligne Hitler en rétrospective», elle étudie sa démarche artistique en tant que peintre de guerre au cours de la Deuxième Guerre mondiale. Enfin *Le Livre d'or de Comfort, 1931–1939*, cédérom encarté au dos de cette publication, constitue un autre chapitre offrant un aperçu sur un groupe d'artistes et de personnalités culturelles qui interagissaient avec Louise et Charles Comfort à l'époque où il commençait à se distinguer en qualité d'artiste.

Ce projet est l'aboutissement des efforts de centaines de personnes qui, plusieurs années durant, y ont consacré leur temps, leur intérêt et leurs compétences. Au nom du Musée et de la conservatrice, j'exprime ma sincère gratitude à la famille Comfort et à George Falconer pour leur appui à la recherche en vue de cette exposition. Notre reconnaissance s'adresse aussi à tous les prêteurs privés et aux institutions qui ont contribué à l'exposition en permettant que leurs œuvres soient présentées en tournée : un remerciement tout spécial à nos quatre collaboratrices invitées dont les essais d'une pénétrante vision, comme je l'ai signalé, ont été essentiels à la réalisation du projet. Sans le travail et les idées du personnel du Musée des beaux-arts de Winnipeg, ce projet n'aurait pu se concrétiser. Ma profonde gratitude s'adresse également à tous ceux et celles qui ont prêté leur concours à sa réalisation à divers titres. Mary Jo tient à remercier tout spécialement les Hucal, Andrew Kear qui s'est chargé de la recherche pour le cédérom et a collaboré à sa rédaction, ainsi que toutes les personnes qui l'ont aimablement aidée dans ses recherches et ont prêté des œuvres, particulièrement Charles C. Hill, Rosemarie Tovell, et d'autres membres du personnel du Musée des beaux- arts du Canada. Nous remercions aussi la Bibliothèque et Archives Canada ainsi que son personnel, spécialement Mary Margaret Johnston-Miller, Lynne Armstrong, Jim Burant et Karen Clack, sans oublier Georgiana Uhlyarik, Dennis Reid, et Sylvie Latham du Musée d'art de l'Ontario. J'adresse un merci tout particulier à l'équipe de Bibliothèque et Archives Canada qui ont agi en partenaires pour réaliser la photographie numérique du cédérom *Le Livre d'or de Comfort*.

Je tiens à témoigner ma reconnaissance au ministère du Patrimoine canadien pour son généreux soutien financier accordé dans le cadre de son programme d'aide au musées, ainsi qu'à la Fondation du Musée des beaux-arts de Winnipeg, au Programme de subventions destinées au Patrimoine, à Culture, Patrimoine et Tourisme du Manitoba, à Inco Limited, Princess Auto, Western Paint, et à Winnipeg Free Press. Je voudrais enfin adresser mes félicitations et mes sincères remerciements à Mary Jo Hughes, conservatrice, Art historique, qui a conçu et administré ce projet avec toute son attention et son énergie.

Pierre Arpin
Directeur général

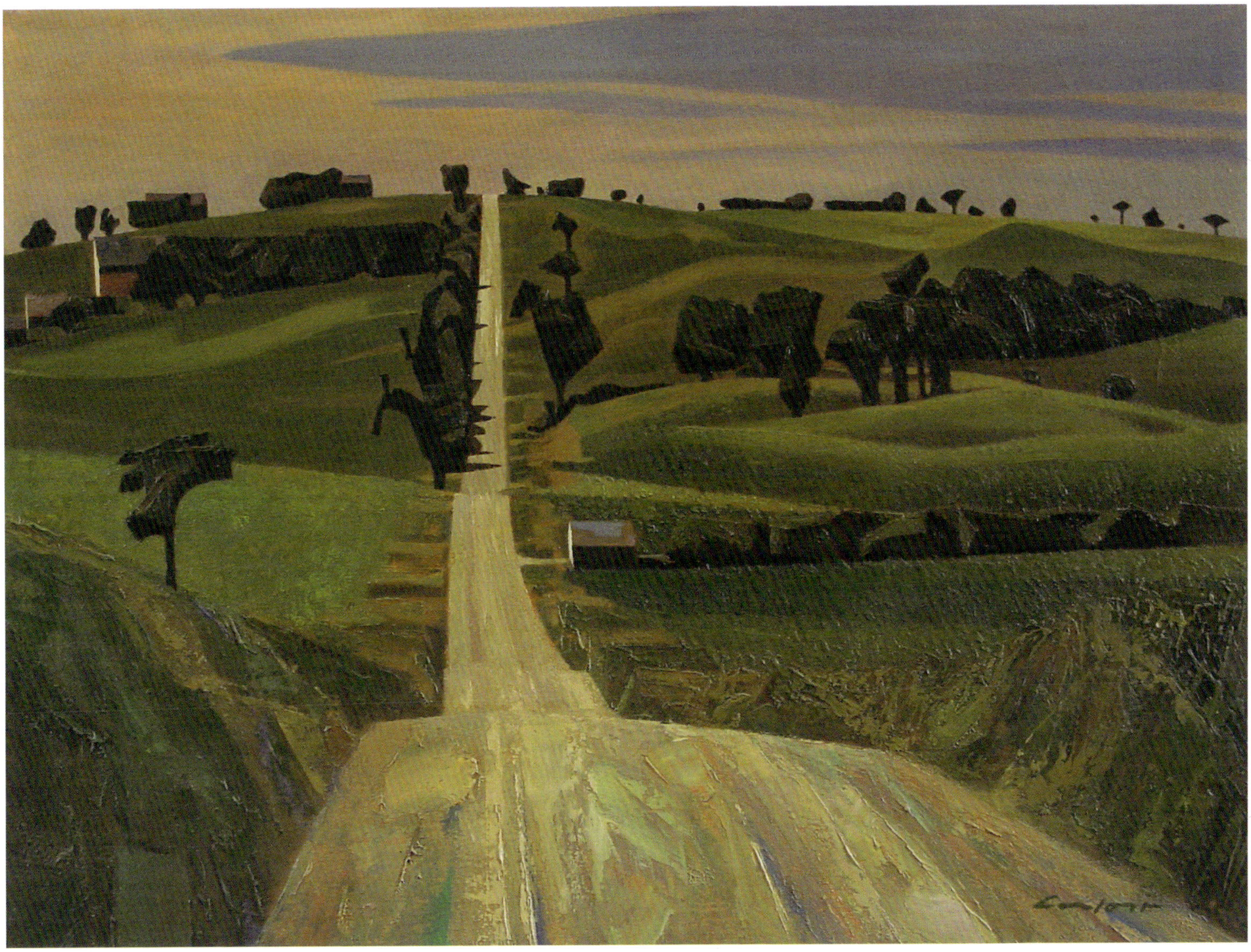

80. **Seventh Line, Tecumseh Township, Simcoe County**, 1970

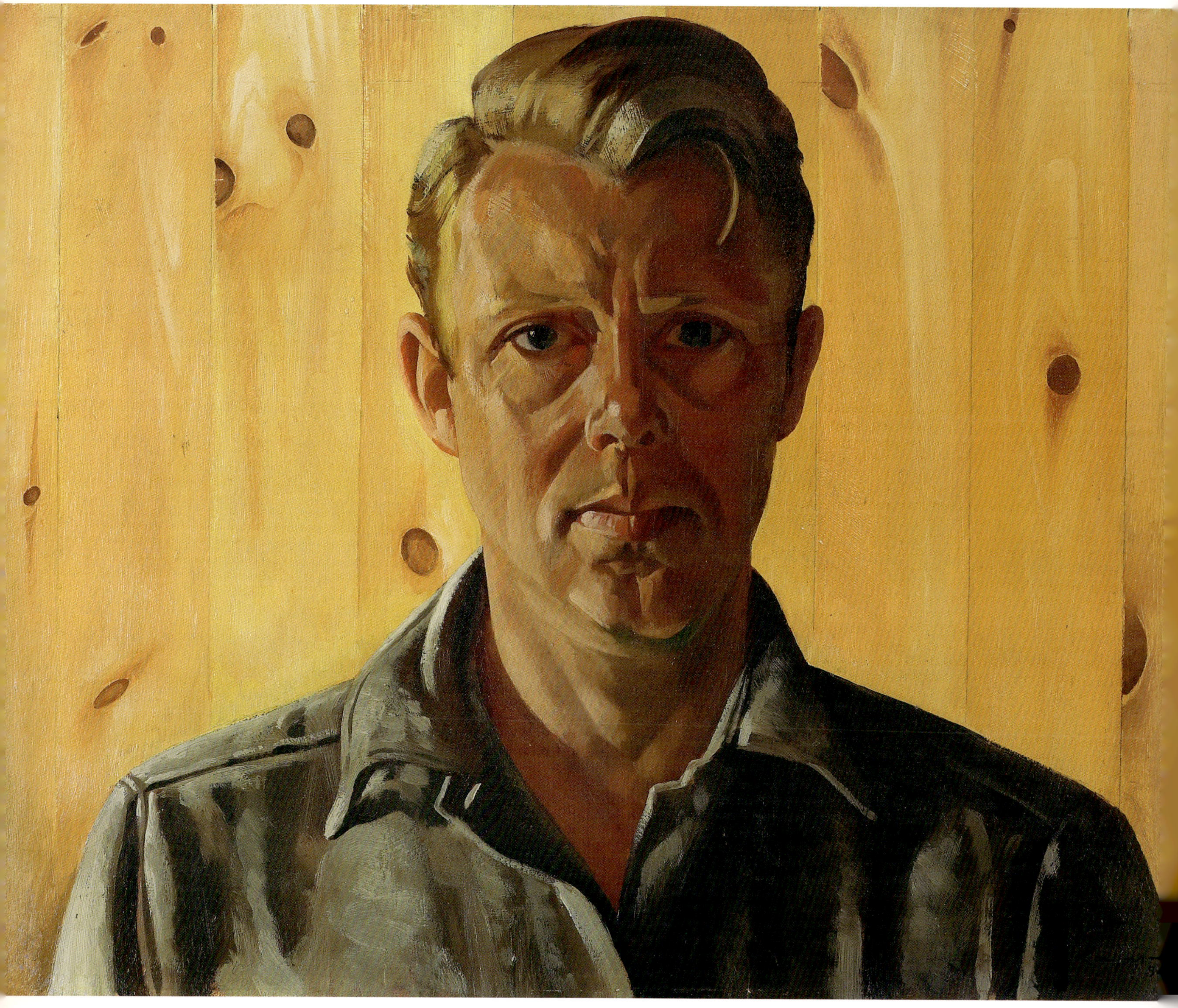

51. **Portrait in August**, 1934

MARY JO HUGHES

Rare Feast – Charles Comfort's Life and Career

TAKE COMFORT – THE CAREER OF CHARLES COMFORT considers an artist whose contribution to Canadian culture is extensive. Comfort emerged into prominence in the 1930s and 1940s between the two big breaks with tradition in Canadian art – the celebrity of the Group of Seven and the excitement of the ensuing generation who introduced abstraction as the dominant form. As a result, Comfort and his contemporaries have suffered from lack of critical analysis.[1] Their shared goals are too often overlooked; particularly because they emerged gradually and amicably from the Group of Seven without an overt rejection of their predecessors. Condescension toward commercial art contributes to this attitude, especially in the case of Comfort whose career, like many of his contemporaries, sprang from a background in commercial art and whose work often blurred the lines. For Comfort, commercial art contributed elements to his artistic work, particularly in his efforts to establish new ways for art to speak to people. Misunderstanding of these intentions has occasionally led to trivialization of his work. Because he had a long career and did not merely disappear after the 1940s but continued to experiment with different ways of communicating his artistic concerns, he is often derisively labeled as "eclectic."

Our goal is to contribute a nascent understanding of a considerable career spanning nearly seven decades. In his commercial art, public art, landscape and portrait painting, art education, cultural policy-work and administration, Comfort is concerned with the humanist goal of art in service of society. "...the arts are among the most important manifestations of a culture, inasmuch as they contribute to the enrichment of the human mind," he declared.[2]

> I was born into what appeared to be a civilized and composed world, its faults discreetly hidden behind its manifest accomplishments. I am ending my useful days in a world of violence and confusion which brazenly and openly admits of its revolutionary purpose, in spite of the magnitude of its accomplishments. Yet, if I were offered the opportunity of choosing the century and the period of history in which to live my life, I would most definitely choose the first eight decades to the twentieth century.[3]

Charles Fraser Comfort (1900–1994) was highly aware of the time and place in which he lived. He was conscious of the breadth of his lifetime, spanning almost the entire twentieth century, witnessing horse and buggies progress through to rocket travel. He experienced both World Wars.

During the first, he supported his mother and seven siblings, while his father served; during the second, he served as a war artist; in between, he struggled to support his own family as a commercial artist. While he managed to achieve opportunities in various facets of the Canadian cultural scene, nothing came easily to Comfort. From his working-class roots, he developed a strong work ethic that he applied to every aspect of his life and which fed his socially conscious inclinations.

Continually in awe of what he witnessed and eager to express it through his art, Comfort divulged in his journals and unpublished biography how he constantly set his experience within a context of the outside world. His dedicated journals, travelogues, and correspondence make Comfort's life perhaps one of the best documented of all Canadian artists of the twentieth century. Furthermore his unpublished autobiography, *Sketches from Memory*, details his childhood in Britain, his formative years in Winnipeg, and his early adulthood in Toronto. In the foreword to it, he described this obsession with documentation; "I have been a compulsive note-maker all my life, filling endless notebooks... A day without a readable page committed to paper is a day lost. I just have to do it..."[4] These self reflections are valuable in bringing to life his modest but rich background coloured by his self-deprecating humour.[5]

Beginnings

Comfort's early life foreshadows the hardworking artist and dedicated cultural supporter that he became. He was the eldest child of Charles Sr. (1879–1945) and Jean (1879–1949) Comfort, born in Edinburgh, Scotland on July 22, 1900. When he was three, he was sent to live with his maternal grandmother and maiden aunts in England because of family finances. He claimed the six years with his grandmother were the most carefree and happy of his life, setting the foundation for his interest in culture and providing him with experiences he would not have had living in the impoverished parental home.

His grandmother, Christina Annan, was a widow who ran the laundry for Hadham Hall, an Elizabethan estate between London and Cambridge. There Comfort's interests in aesthetic and historical concerns were sparked. Four adults raised him with the utmost attention and consideration. "They nourished my mind... (and were) determined to cultivate in me a respect for things of the spirit."[6] Unlike his brothers and sisters, Charles had his own room; he was read to and taken to art galleries and architectural monuments.

Back in Edinburgh in the fall of 1909, he was upset about leaving the only family he knew for one he barely remembered. Not only was he thrust into a crowded household but the physical environment of the city challenged him. "Disappointed, even shocked, I found that Springvalley Gardens supported no growing thing, not a blade of grass, not a flower, not a tree."[7] Within weeks of his returning home, his father suggested he get a job to help support the family. Although Comfort never intimated this suspicion, it seems likely that the need for more money motivated his return to the family home.

Winnipeg

In April 1912, the impoverished family departed for Winnipeg in search of better fortune. Within weeks of his arrival Comfort found a temporary job delivering yeast samples, and the following summer he carried water for an asphalt gang to help with family finances. At school his many friends included Robert Ayre, future art critic, with whom he remained friends throughout adulthood in Toronto.

At this time Winnipeg was a frontier city interested in building formal institutions that promoted culture.[8] Community leaders were keen on fostering a fully rounded environment with a healthy arts scene and a strong economy. The year of Comfort's arrival, The Winnipeg Art Gallery opened its doors at the Industrial Bureau, an organization promoting the betterment of the community to attract growth in industry. The Gallery stood as the city's prime public cultural symbol. At every opportunity Comfort visited it to examine its modest collection and traveling exhibitions. No doubt the emphasis put on developing culture in Winnipeg affected Comfort throughout his life as he continued his involvement with various galleries, viewing them as valuable social institutions.

The establishment of the Winnipeg School of Art in 1913 allowed Winnipeg to foster home-grown artists to draw upon for design, commercial art, and fine-art purposes. That year Comfort won first prize in the painting section at the YMCA's "Boy's Hobby Exhibition." Toronto artist Frederick Brigden, who judged the exhibition, was in Winnipeg setting up a western branch of Brigdens Limited (a family-owned commercial art firm). Impressed with the boy's talents, Brigden approached Comfort's parents to allow him to work as a studio apprentice the following year.

Art Prodigy

Initially founded in Toronto, Brigdens Limited was one of Canada's oldest graphic art firms. It opened in Winnipeg specifically to produce the western Canadian version of the Eaton's mail-order catalogue. Brigdens of Winnipeg gave talented artists a reason to stay in Winnipeg while working in an art-related field and enjoying a stimulating environment where creative people worked together. Its apprenticeship program offered preliminary artistic training supplemented by courses that employees were encouraged to take in the evenings at the School of Art. As one of the largest employers of artists in the city, Brigdens had a significant effect on the developing art scene between the two World Wars.

Art historians have drawn parallels between the development of advertising art and fine art in Canada.[9] The late historian Angela Davis saw Brigdens as a "breeding ground" for many artists who contributed significantly not only to Winnipeg but also to the larger national cultural scene. She wrote: "... the graphic arts industry holds a place in Canadian social and cultural history unlike that of any other industry. The people whom it employed, and the material that it produced, became essential ingredients in both the formation of 'Canadian Art' and the expansion of popular mass communication."[10]

Certainly when Comfort moved to Toronto, many of the artists whom he befriended had their roots in commercial art including members of the Group of Seven. Out of this similar milieu at Brigdens of Winnipeg many artists developed national reputations, like Charles Comfort, Caven Atkins, Philip Surrey, and Fritz Brandtner. Others such as master printmaker Eric Bergman had flourishing local careers. Certainly in Comfort's case, design work at Brigdens in Winnipeg and Toronto; Rapid, Grip & Batten Ltd.; and in his own commercial studio in the 1930s supported his family while his fine-art career developed. Furthermore, Brigdens' relentless catalogue schedule instilled discipline in him and, as will be discussed later, influenced the style and iconography of his mural and easel painting.

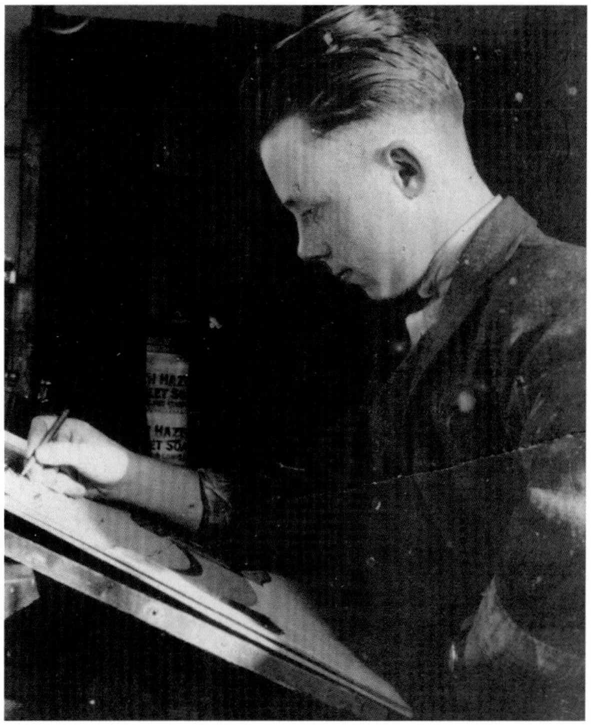

Fraser (Charles) making layouts at Brigdens
20 March 1917
Charles Comfort Collection / Library and Archives Canada / e002505478

In October 1914 Comfort began his art career at Brigdens of Winnipeg, working under Thomas McLean and Fred Brigden's cousin, Arnold Brigden, who managed the branch. Comfort's serious adherence to Frederick Brigden's advice – to practice sketching everyday and to take night classes – made him into one of the company's best draughtsman within a few years. He first studied through Kelvin Technical School (1914–1916) under Valentine Fanshaw and then at the School of Art (1916–1919) under Alexander Musgrove. "The result was that my very natural gift of drawing was being buffed and polished into a promising accomplishment which might prove useful professionally."[11] Although indebted to their technical drawing instruction, Comfort felt neither teacher contributed greatly to his ability to produce a work of fine art.

Nonetheless, interaction with artists at Brigdens stimulated Comfort to consider art seriously: "These multi-faceted new contacts, occurring as they did in an emotional and cerebral environment so vastly removed from the domestic simplicity of my home life and the crude vulgarities of the asphalt plant, performed an almost magical transformation ... [and]

awakened in me an abiding interest in thoughtful reflection and an irresistible desire to improve myself and develop an attitude of inquiry about all the arts."

He attended as many musical concerts, operas, and theatrical events as he could during his teens, developing an insatiable love of all things cultural. Arnold Brigden shared his private collection of Japanese and European prints, including etchings by Rembrandt and engravings by William Blake, which opened Comfort's eyes to historical art. The sketching trips he took with other artists into the wilderness regions of Manitoba and northwestern Ontario fostered his love of nature and his ability to paint landscape.[12]

But the First World War loomed and in October 1916 his father departed to fight overseas, leaving Charles as the head of the family to provide for his mother and seven other children. While Charles took part in militia training and hoped to be recruited, he was turned down repeatedly.

Making Connections

> I always say that my physical birth took place in Scotland, but my spiritual birth took place in the Arts and Letters Club in Toronto. There is where I received my education under the greatest of circumstances, because I had access to poets, writers, readers, university professors, painters.[13]

When his father returned in 1919, Comfort accepted a brief transfer to the Brigdens office in Toronto. Its art director, Tom McLean, helped Comfort make connections, taking him to the Arts & Letters Club, a men's club where members involved or interested in theatre, visual arts, literature, architecture, and music, gathered to escape the banalities of the everyday business world. Today, it is perhaps best known for the role it played in fostering the careers of the Group of Seven artists. There Comfort met a mix of younger avant-garde types like the future Group artists and older, conservative artists like George A. Reid, principal of the Ontario College of Art. Comfort also took life classes sponsored by the Royal Academy under Frederick Challener, Charles W. Jefferys, and Gustav Hahn.

This brief sojourn helped Comfort decide to become a painter.[14] On his way home to Winnipeg, he visited art museums in Chicago and Minneapolis and met the Curator of Prints and Drawings to discuss Rembrandt etchings. Such initiatives demonstrate Comfort's passion for art and his sincere desire to meet scholars through whom he could feed his hunger for knowledge.

He returned to Toronto in late spring, and stayed for a year with the help of $100 he won from Eatons in a Catalogue Cover Competition;[15] he lunched almost every weekday at the Arts & Letters Club. Just before his 20th birthday, he was asked to become a member through the sponsorship of Frederick Brigden and Tom McLean. He also joined the Canadian Society of Graphic Art where he took further informal life drawing classes and interacted with other artists.[16]

The Group of Seven's inaugural Toronto exhibition in late spring 1920 was pivotal for Comfort. In their work he recognized the first signs of vitality that he had ever witnessed in Canadian art and the possibility of reflecting Canada through a more modern style.[17] He returned to Winnipeg in 1921, rented his own room, and worked night and day on catalogue drawings while yearning to apply his talents to more creative pursuits. Despite his relentless schedule, by early 1922 he had exhibited four watercolours in the Winnipeg Sketch Club's annual exhibition, one of which was *The Green Canoe* (cat. 2).[18]

Comfort was encouraged by developments in Winnipeg when Group of Seven member Franz Johnston assumed the directorship of The Winnipeg Art Gallery and the School of Art in 1922. Johnston offered Comfort a joint exhibition with F.T. Moore Beatty at the Gallery that fall,[19] which earned him his first significant public notice: "...the exhibition that had just come to a close of two pupils of the Winnipeg Art Gallery School... is a glorious shadow of the progress of art in Western Canada and reflects great praise upon both the pupils themselves as well as the School of Art ...some hundreds of visitors visited the galleries daily, but the exhibition in our minds merited a much wider audience... Mr. Comfort, likewise, has hung some two score paintings, landscape, genre and portraits. We think Mr. Comfort's forte is his portrait work. These show great character and breadth as well as color-harmony that instantly commands interest and attention…"[20]

Another interesting project materialized that year when Arnold Brigden recommended Comfort to illustrate a book on the lives of pioneer women of the region, *Women of Red River*.[21] While the author, provincial librarian W. J. Healy, interviewed the elderly women, Comfort drew freehand ink portraits that were eventually reproduced in the book (cat. 89).[22] The portraits reveal his ability to capture character and expression in faces and postures in a seemingly effortless quick sketch.

Despite his successes, Comfort recognized that he needed more progressive training and, with the encouragement of Tom MacLean and Walter Huntley, he applied to the New York Arts Students' League with the hope of studying with Robert Henri, the most respected teacher of his time, a man who also began his career as an illustrator. Before Comfort departed, he met Louise Irene Chase at a party in October 1921 and, as Comfort wrote, she soon became "an indispensable factor in my life." Louise supported his desire to leave for school; the absence intensified their relationship.

New York

In October 1922 he arrived at the New York Art Students' League for a short but intense immersion into formal training. With his grandmother's sister living nearby and connections with George Fawcett and his son Robert, both from Winnipeg, the transition was easy. The Fawcetts were commercial artists in the city and George offered him piecemeal commercial work. The fast pace of the crowded studios at the school, the museums and galleries, theatre and opera kept Comfort absolutely entranced.

At school, Robert Henri encouraged him to look more closely at the Old Masters such as Hals and Velasquez, thus igniting his life-long passion for the analysis of technique. His other teacher, Euphrasius Tucker, had been involved in the organization of the famous 1913 Armory Exhibition and piqued Comfort's interest in producing a living art in touch with the modern experience. Tucker encouraged him to read art critic Clive Bell's books to grasp an understanding of modern principles. Comfort also wrote about being influenced in his own teaching career by Tucker's pedagogical theories, which included an emphasis on formal analysis. Tucker was guided by the statement "Art has to be learned, it cannot be taught."[23] The only extant work from this period is a watercolour of the New York skyline (cat. 3), wherein the prevailing greyness of the smog obscuring the buildings is enlivened by white patches of snow that jump out almost like abstract patterning.

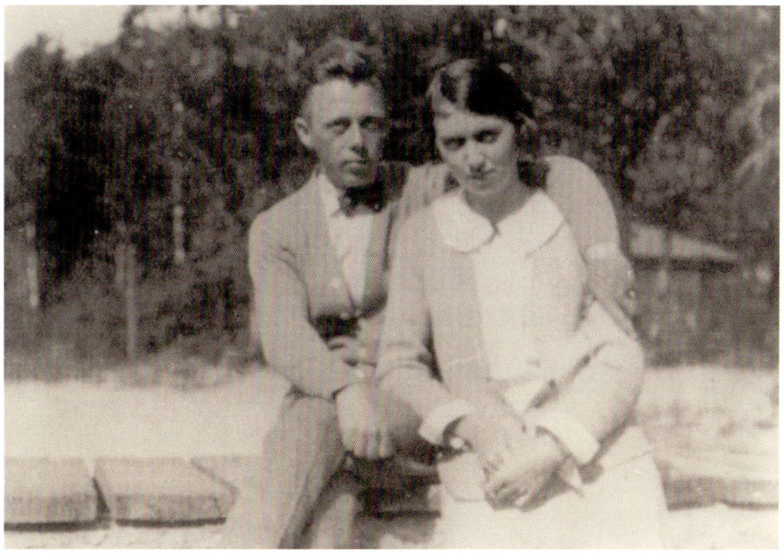

Louise and Charles Comfort, Summer 1924
Charles Comfort Collection / Library and Archives Canada / e002505482

Settling Down

In March 1923 Comfort left behind the euphoria of New York and returned to Brigdens of Winnipeg. The city's sedate environment was offset by his reunion with Louise. In the spring of 1924 they married and had a rustic honeymoon in the Minaki region on the Winnipeg River. That summer they also visited Point au Chenes, Louise's family cottage on Lake of the Woods.[24] From there Comfort enjoyed expeditions with artist friends such as Eric Bergman and produced a number of watercolours. These works (see cat. 5 and 6) suggest new formal interests awakened in New York that moved his work beyond the traditional picturesque approach. He sought expression of the unexpected in the landscape composition. Tension between foreground and background in *Lake of the Woods, Route Bay* (cat. 6) for example, establishes ambiguity through contrasts of form, light, and space. A pyramidal rock, verging on the abstract, dominates the foreground and contrasts the pastoral landscape in the background.

Always seeking to expand his experience, Comfort

designed costumes and sets for the Winnipeg Community Players during his last year in Manitoba. There he met L.L. FitzGerald and W. J. Phillips, both well-known for their theatre designs. It was probably at this time that he studied woodblock engraving with Phillips (see cats 14-18).[25] Comfort's driving ambitions prompted Louise and Charles to leave Winnipeg in April 1925 and settle in Toronto.

Toronto: Launching of Painting Career

In Toronto Comfort continued to work at Brigdens. He spent increasing time sketching with Harold Ayres and Will Ogilvie. Ogilvie had just arrived from South Africa in 1925. Unmarried until decades later, he became Louise and Charles' fondest friend and spent countless evenings and holidays in their home.[26] Later in the year Comfort began work on his first attempts at major oil paintings including *Prairie Road* (formerly *Out West*) (cat. 19). He experimented with intense colour and broad brushwork, no doubt inspired by the looser handling and rawer use of pigment that he saw in the Group's painting. Lawren Harris encouraged Comfort to submit it to the Royal Canadian Academy (RCA) exhibition at the Art Association of Montreal in late 1925. When it was shown again at the 1928 Group of Seven exhibition, the work earned Comfort rave reviews, signaling his emergence as an artist. Reviewer Jeanne Adeney wrote: "Outside of the Group of Seven the strongest Canadian painter is, undoubtedly, Charles Comfort. No less modern than theirs, his work bears a living message and is warmly appreciated by public and critics alike. Because it fell to the lot of the Group of Seven to break with old traditions in Canada, and because Charles Comfort painted after this break and outside the Group, it may be his destiny to reap a harvest of their sowing. At any rate he seems to see his way clearly before him, unclouded by doubts, and his painting is a joy to the beholder. What can one say of that barren road in *Out West*, changed to a riot of glory by the setting sun?"[27]

At Fred Brigden's recommendation, Comfort joined the Canadian Society of Painters in Water Colour (CSPWC) in 1926 where he exhibited regularly. He joined the exhibition committee that visited Ottawa to organize a watercolour exhibition for the National Gallery of Canada (NGC) in which he exhibited four works including *Stoney Lake* and *Mountain Lake* (cats. 11 and 12). The following year, he became a member of the Ontario Society of Artists (OSA), another exhibiting society in which he played an active administrative role in the following decades.

The spring of 1927 was a pivotal moment for modern art in Toronto. Through Katherine Dreier, founder of the *Société Anonyme* which promoted modern art, Lawren Harris arranged for an exhibition at the Art Gallery of Toronto (AGT), which shocked the placid Toronto art appreciators with the works of modern artists Wassily Kandinsky, Kassimir Malevich, Joan Miro, and Piet Mondrian, and greatly stimulated Comfort and his circle. Comfort, Hortense Gordon, Edna Taçon, Bertram Brooker, Gordon Webber, Lawren Harris, and Lowrie Warrener were honoured when AGT Board Chair Albert Robson asked them to act as docents during the run of the exhibition.

This ground-breaking exhibition had an impact on various aspects of Comfort's practice. He claimed to have been most affected by Joseph Stella's *Brooklyn Bridge*. Certainly in many of his commercial projects and in his mural *Romance of Nickel* (cat. 85) Comfort's abstract backgrounds share Stella's emphasis on man-made structural elements. The first direct influence of this exhibition on his easel painting appeared in *Louise* (cat. 43), completed in the fall of 1927. In it, the elegant figure sits in an undefined background of greens, which radiate from her body like auras of energy akin to the work of the Futurists, conveying not only motion, but also potential spiritual energy. Furthermore, the gentle tilt of Louise's head and the smooth, simplification of her skin is an overt reference to Brancusi's *Muse* which he also admired in the exhibition. This iconographic link suggests the role his wife, Louise, played as muse at that time; he drew hundreds of sketches of her (cat.40, 41, and 49). Throughout their seven-decade marriage, she was his greatest supporter and critic. Her practical, administrative, and moral support made Comfort's panoply of accomplishments possible. "Louise is not only my wife and the mother of my children, she is Traffic Manager, Vice-President and Treasurer, as well as Secretary. She relieves me of all the business aspects of my career as a professional artist. Quite frankly, I could not operate without her."[28]

The painting represents Comfort's first major foray into portraiture, something that would develop more fully in the next decade. It won Comfort second prize in the prestigious Willingdon Art Competition and was chosen by Bertram Brooker to be illustrated in *Yearbook of the Arts in Canada 1928–29* as an example of original Canadian art.

Through the late 1920s and early 30s, Comfort's oil sketches made on trips around Toronto betray his admiration for the Group of Seven. He focused on wilderness landscapes defined in wide, thickly applied strokes, rhythmically drawn across the board to produce bold simplified forms. *Tawny, (York Mills)* (cat. 20) for example is reminiscent of the patterning of snow and soil found in A. Y. Jackson's sketches. Comfort drew attention to the two-dimensionality of the board through the daring placement of a vertical trunk, which cuts the composition in half visually and tilts the hillside parallel to the surface. *Winter Woods* (cat. 24) demonstrates an abstract play of light and shadow, paying homage to other Group members such as J.E.H. MacDonald; the decorative screen effect was made famous by Group precursor Tom Thomson.

A shift towards further experimentation with landscape was introduced to Comfort's work towards the end of the twenties. In the study for *Wilderness* (cat. 21) Comfort engaged with a more monumental view than his previous wood interiors. From a hilltop, Comfort painted a broad expanse of water with the cloud and sky reflected in it. The flatness of the reflections plays against the modeled quality of the trees, which appear to cut backwards into a deep and distant space. In the large finished canvas of the same title (cat. 22) the flatness of the pool's reflection is emphasized; the smoother paint surface contrasts the impasto rock in the foreground. The forest, into which the river slices, appears like one solid mass in the finished work, unlike the less substantial painterly indication of trees in the sketch. In this work Comfort introduced a harder edge to his organic forms, foreshadowing his precisionist landscapes of the 1930s in which natural forms are further simplified into smooth, ordered elements.

Innovation

The Depression further shifted Comfort's approach to various philosophical and practical issues. In the early 1930s more than 1.5 million Canadians were dependent on government relief or were transient. Growing fear of Communist plots led to controls over freedom of thought, political criticism, and assembly, which deeply disturbed artists. As commercial work dried up, private collectors stopped buying, and public collections slashed acquisition budgets, artists were also hit economically. Just prior to the Stock Market Crash, Comfort left Brigdens and signed a lucrative two-year contract with Rapid, Grip & Batten Ltd. which they honoured despite the economic downturn.[29] In 1931, with no other opportunities in sight, Comfort launched his own commercial business with Harold Ayres and Will Ogilvie.[30]

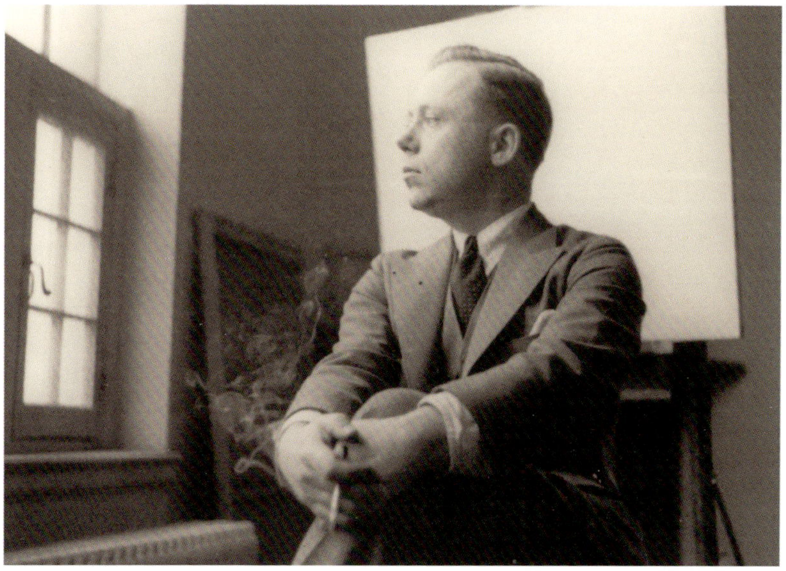

Charles in the Studio Building, May 1938
Charles Comfort Collection / Library and Archives Canada / e002505479

Certainly his freelance illustration work engaged more of Comfort's skills than were being used at Brigdens. The Eaton's catalogue images he produced at Brigdens were required to have a uniform consistency: artists could not stand out as individuals. In the work Comfort was doing independently for clients such as Inco he signed his images, gaining recognition for his commercial talents. In this body of work he experimented with the effects of line and texture, applying design elements found in contemporary art to build drama and express character and narrative, appealing to a popular audience.

As Rosemary Donegan explores in her essay, Comfort took the lessons he learned in commercial art about the need to speak to one's intended audience and applied them to his mural production. Comfort broke into the field in 1932 with the North American

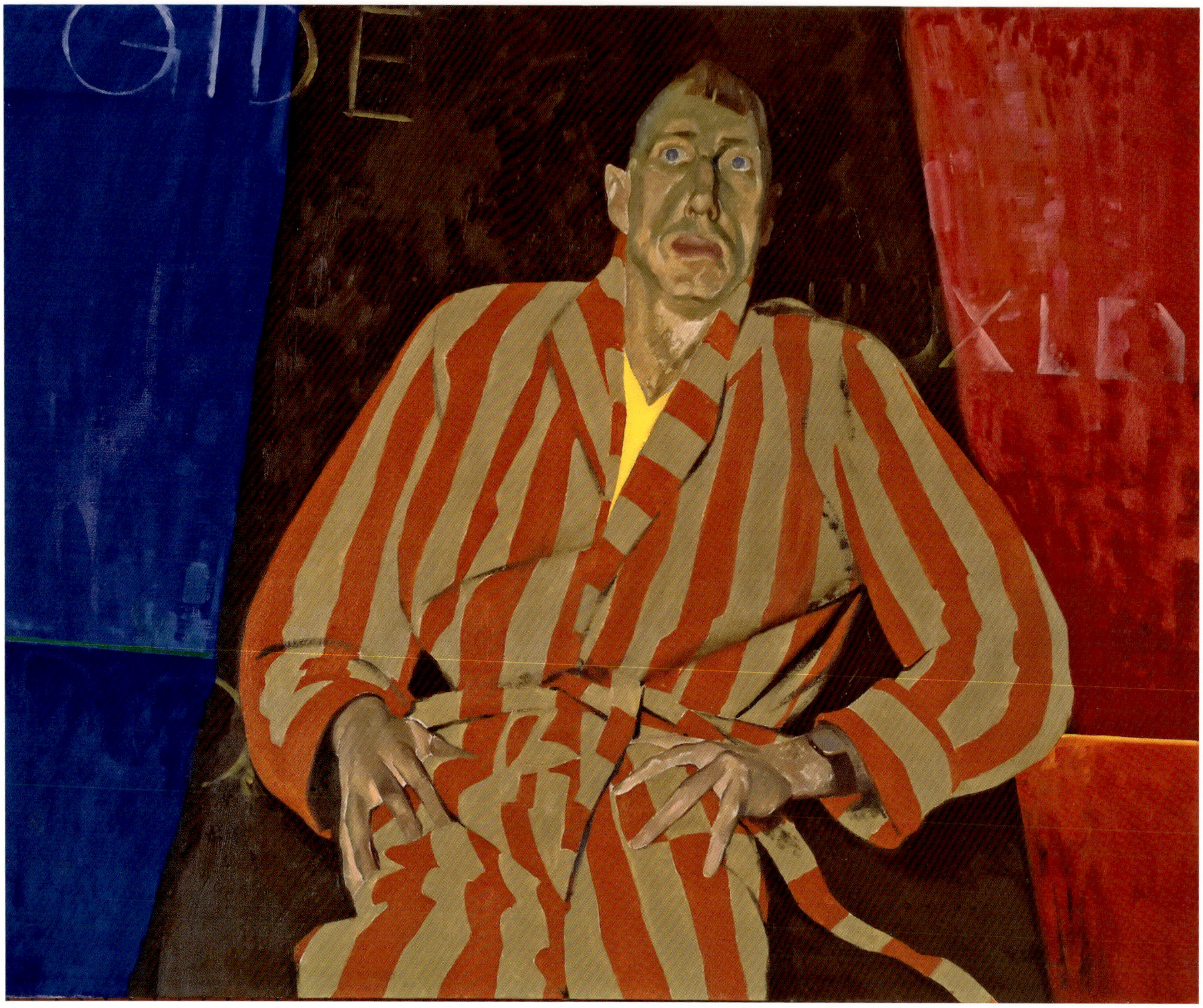

CHARLES COMFORT, **The Dreamer**, 1929
Oil on canvas, 101.7 x 122.1
Art Gallery of Hamilton; Gift of the Hamilton Spectator, 1957

Life Assurance Company mural in Toronto which he installed with the help of artist Carl Schaefer. Before the end of the decade, he had completed several projects including the Toronto Stock Exchange murals and exterior friezes (1936–37); *Romance of Nickel* (cat. 85), commissioned by Inco for the Paris World's Fair 1937; and *Captain Vancouver's voyage to the Pacific Northwest* mural commissioned by the Canadian National Railway for the Hotel Vancouver. In 1938 he expanded his art practice to include stone relief for the program at Gare Centrale in Montreal.[31]

As Canada's best known muralist by the end of 1935, Comfort was offered a job as head of the new department of Mural Painting at the Ontario College of Art.[32] However, by 1937, utterly exhausted from working so hard to eke out a living, he was feeling the Depression's residual effect. He considered moving to the United States when his friend Robert Fawcett, then a successful illustrator, sent him $500 and encouraged him to forget about "making it" as an artist in Canada. Fawcett suggested Comfort move to New York where steady commercial work was available.[33] The idea of giving up his fine art for advertising repelled him and he decided to stay.

Despite its poor financial returns, his easel painting was showing promise. He began painting large-scale symbolic portraits, exploring not only character but also social issues. In *The Dreamer*, 1929, Comfort painted Norman Robinson: during his sittings, his friend discussed literary figures including Andre Gidé and Aldous Huxley, both humanists concerned with contemporary society's moral issues. The portrait shows a delirious pajama-clad man in an abstract background over which the words "GIDE" and "HUXLEY" float. This unconventional portrait suggests Comfort's own questioning of the moral state of society.[34]

Comfort's further experimentation with capturing the essence of character and environment resulted in portraits such as *Chuhaldin*, 1931 (cat. 47) *Young Canadian*, 1932 (cat. 48) and *Professor Felix Walter*, 1933 (cat. 50). Because of their unusual size, each approaching about a metre in height, these portraits gained him attention. Watercolours were popular with Comfort and his contemporaries in the Depression because they were inexpensive to produce and offered expressive possibilities, resulting from the necessity to work quickly. *Young Canadian*, Comfort's portrait of his friend, artist Carl Schaefer, was exhibited widely over the decade and has stood the test of time as an iconic image of the artist's struggle during the Depression. All three of these works emphasize the figures' hands and heads; the background reflects the sitters' interests.

By the late 1920s and the 1930s, as the reign of the Group of Seven wound down and the Canadian Group of Painters (CGP) arose from its roots, Comfort straddled the various streams of landscape painting. He maintained an interest in and popularity for his works such as *The Great Rock*, (cat. 23), *Black Spruce, Pickerel River* (cat. 26), *Clearing, Big Stone Bay, Lake of the Woods* (cat. 28), *Saugenay River* (cat. 29), and *Distant View of Manitoulin*, 1936 (cat. 33). All of them reflect the wilderness and rural aesthetic à la Group of Seven.[35] At the same time, like many of his generation, his iconography shifted towards an awareness of social issues depicted through ordered landscapes, emphasizing the mark of its inhabitants. The Depression wrought societal changes and both local and international havoc.[36]

As Robert Ayre wrote in his review of the first CGP exhibition: "Not only are we moving toward human life, away from landscape, which in the long run must be sterile, but in growing up we are beginning to show the effects of the profound disturbance in human affairs which have shaken the world; social implications are creeping in." He singled out Comfort as making one of the most significant strides in this regard.[37]

In works such as *Tadoussac* (cat. 31), *Smelter Stacks* (cat. 34), *Lake Superior Village* (cat. 35) and *Pioneer Survival* (cat. 36) Comfort was most successful in achieving an ordered landscape reflecting the human aspect of Canada. *Tadoussac* clearly demonstrates a streamlining of the landscape, drawing upon the influence of the American Precisionist Charles Sheeler, whom Comfort met while visiting Robert Fawcett's Ridgefield, Connecticut home in 1933.[38] *Smelter Stacks* and *Lake Superior Village* represent Comfort's developing interest in less picturesque subjects. Industrial imagery was not unique to Comfort, as both Lawren Harris and Yvonne Housser were also working with similar subjects. It was perhaps a natural result of Comfort's work with Inco and the railroads, creating images for their advertisements. In fact, he gathered

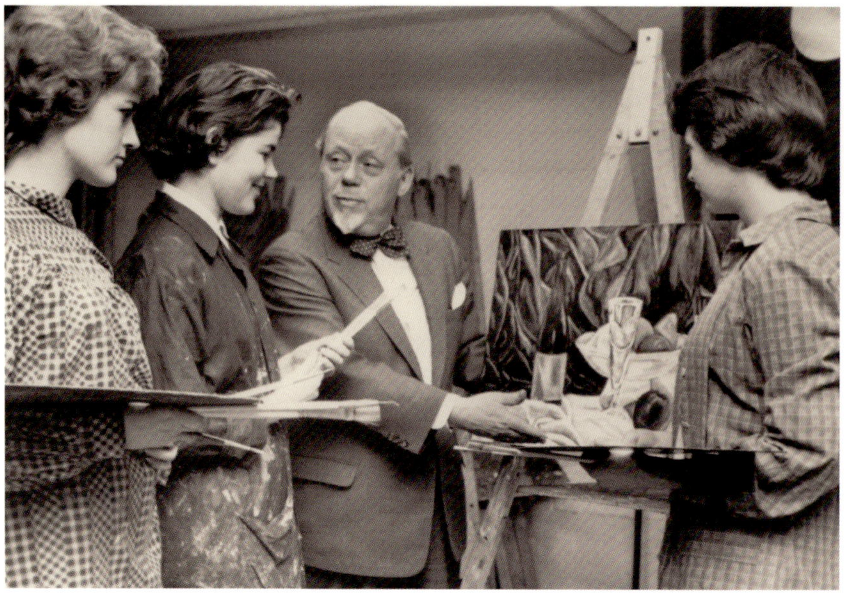

Charles with Students (U. of T.),
February 8, 1960
Charles Comfort Collection / Library and Archives Canada / e002505480

sketches for these paintings while traveling to Sudbury to work for Inco. By the time these works were completed, he had undertaken the murals and friezes for the Toronto Stock Exchange, which included mining and lumber subjects.

In *Smelter Stacks*, Comfort provided a distant view of the smelter's operations, with the sky dominating and the industrial landscape relegated to the lower section of the canvas, similar to his prairie watercolour compositions (cats. 1 and 7). Like the structures in *Tadoussac*, buildings and smoke stacks have a simplified geometric solidity. However, the billowing exhaust takes on a life of its own, spewing forth into the brilliant blue sky and melding with the wispy cloud cover. The visually disturbing straight line of exhaust, continuing up the left side of the stack, underlines Comfort's desire to bring order to the chaotic operation. Comfort is not aggrandizing the industrial operation, as he did in his commercial work (see p. 124). Instead, he offered these non-traditional painting subjects as valid aesthetic considerations and symbols of contemporary existence. Rather than criticize his paintings as too commercial, which was often done, I propose that the validity in Comfort's bold application of subject and stylistic tendencies from his commercial practice onto his fine art is comparable to our acceptance of contemporary artists borrowing style and iconography from advertising and pop culture.

Lake Superior Village, 1937, painted from sketches done in 1935 in Rossport, Ontario (cat. 32) represents the synthesis of Comfort's talents and his initiation as a painter on the international scene.[39] This painting was entered in the Great Lakes Exhibition, which toured cities in Canada and U.S. It won first prize and earned Comfort public notice.[40] Of the winning painting, Robert Ayre wrote: "I feel that it is essentially Canada and it is the more important because it is not the much-painted Canada of swirling Laurentians, monumental Rockies, or the blazing pageantry of autumn forests. ...It is solidly built, well-ordered, and the small figures of men reveal the bigness of scale that must always be Canada."[41] Like other works that year, such as *The Observatory* (cat. 37), *Lake Superior Village* maintained Comfort's precisionist hard-edged style, while reintroducing a more tactile texturing of paint. It was held up as a prime example of modern painting in Canada[42] and its popularity led to an offer from the Albright Gallery in Buffalo for a one-man exhibition in 1939. Unfortunately, the unfolding events of the war forced Comfort to cancel his commitment for his first solo international exhibition.[43]

Teacher and Cultural Activist

In 1936 Charles Comfort was encouraged by his appointment as an Associate to the Royal Canadian Academy and obtained a studio in the famed Studio Building next to that of A.Y. Jackson. Comfort's disparate artistic endeavours began to pay off. He was appointed Associate Professor at the University of Toronto, teaching historical painting techniques, a subject of great interest to him throughout his life. Furthermore, he was able to give up his commercial art practice and concentrate on painting and on academic interests.[44] Except during 1943 and 1946, he held this teaching position continuously until 1960.

In May 1939, following his first year at the University, he travelled to Italy to strengthen his scholarship, absorbing as much art as possible and taking photographs to use in his lectures. He studied mural projects like the work of Michelangelo in the Sistine Chapel, the frescoes of Cimabuie and Giotto in Assisi, and the mosaics of Pompeii, and he examined contemporary Italian art and architecture, noting the success with which modern artists employed the traditions of ancient technique.[45] Comfort's journals from this period indicate his enthusiasm for new experiences and his passion for art had not waned. He described his reaction to the Sistine Chapel: "In such an experience all critical judgment fails one. I knew I was there, the fearful beauty of the place possessed me immediately. I found myself in that same spiritual ecstasy which begat the renaissance. ... I walked out as I came in blind to all else..."[46]

Comfort's teaching career monopolized his time for the next couple of years. At the university Comfort taught a variety of studio courses, including mural painting, fresco, oil, tempera, drawing, design, architectural design, anatomy, and even camouflage painting. In addition to regular sessions, he taught at the Banff Summer School in 1941. Over the years his methodical teaching philosophy maintained his two-pronged approach: he encouraged studying and understanding past technical practice, followed by persistent practice.[47] Some of the most notable of his former students included art historians and arts administrators such as Russell Harper, Canadian Art curator; Dr. Gerald Finley, art historian, Queen's University; and Jean Sutherland Boggs, Degas scholar who succeeded Comfort as Director of the National Gallery.

The late thirties and forties were important for Comfort and his circle for their art activism. By the time the Second World War was underway, many Canadian artists were vocal about the state of the artist in Canadian society. At the Kingston Conference, held at Queen's University, June 1941, they assembled along with museum directors and art historians. Cognizant of Roosevelt's Works Progress Administration that provided many American artists with work on public art projects during the 1930s, artists wanted to present the government with recommendations for establishing a support system. They also held professional development workshops on technique.[48] Comfort was involved in the organization of the conference and introduced the keynote speaker, American muralist Thomas Hart Benton. The conference represented the largest public assembly of Canadian artists to date and the climax of all the rumblings and informal assemblies of the 1930s.

The conference goal was to establish and reinforce the notion of the artist as legitimate worker in society. At the conference, the artists decided to form the Federation of Canadian Artists (FCA) with Andre Biéler as president to take the ideas of the conference forward with concrete attempts to improve the state of the arts. The first meeting of the Federation was held in Comfort's studio that fall. The establishment of a government war-art program to employ artists was one of their recommendations. While it came to fruition shortly, the other goals were longer term. The call for government support of artists would involve committee and lobbying work for many of the artists, most notably Comfort's good friend Elizabeth Wyn Wood. Their lobbying, along with that of other cultural interest groups, eventually led to the formation of the Massey Commission in 1949, which produced the 1951 Massey Report. The Commission highlighted concerns about the dangers of Canadian reliance on American culture and the need for the protection of our national cultural identity through state-sponsored cultural development. The Canada Council for the Arts, still a vital support to Canadian artists, emerged from their advocacy.

Because of his consistent involvement in Canadian culture over the years and his articulation of art-related topics in his roles as teacher, guest lecturer, and an executive member of various art societies, Comfort was asked to contribute an essay on the state of painting in Canada to the Massey Report. Comfort called for government support, modeled roughly on the British Arts Council, to "ensure standards and production in the visual arts in the interests of national consciousness and unity."[49] He also championed openness toward varied aesthetic expression; he outlined the reasons for art legitimately shifting towards abstraction in a world changed exponentially since World War I. While he championed the Group of Seven as a positive force for the country's nascent cultural identity, he emphasized that art expression must be allowed to change and grow, with abstraction seen as a valid form of Canadian art. The conservative picture of him that emerged through the media during his tenure at the National Gallery in the 1960s, contrasts with Comfort's writings from the thirties through the fifties. From this paper, he appears as a strong, open-minded proponent of modernism. So too do his often-cited articles "The Painter and his Model" (1931) and "1938–48: Observations on a Decade" (1948).[50]

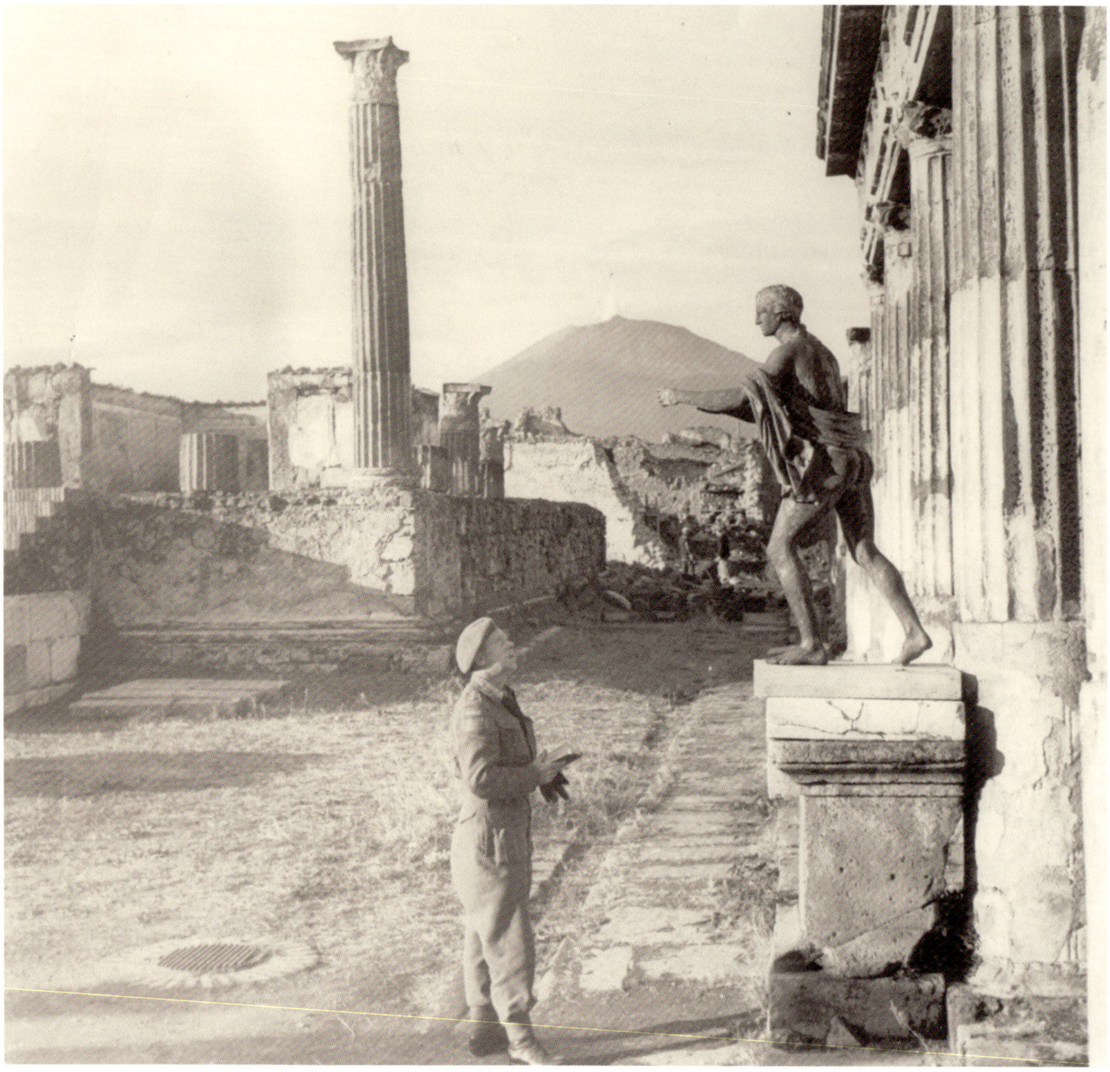

Charles, Apollo and Vesuvius Pompeii
Charles Comfort Collection / Library and Archives Canada / e002505476

War Artist

For Comfort the War marked a high point in his career despite the fact that he was separated from his family and was forced to witness destruction and human suffering worse than anything he had ever imagined. His war art and his subsequent book *Artist at War* were great personal and professional successes. In 1946 he returned to Canada as a highly respected Canadian artist. As a friend and as an art critic, Robert Ayre summarized his war activity when the book was released. "He would have made an efficient soldier, and perhaps a distinguished one, but Canada was wise enough to realize that he would be more valuable as an observer and recorder than as a combatant."[51]

Although his official instructions were to record the activities of Canadian soldiers at war, many of Comfort's works evoke a subtle emotional expressionism, raising them above pure documentation. From on-site sketches, he later produced finished oils like *Campobasso* (cat. 67) which initially appears as a lovely view of the ancient city seen through a screen of trees; further study identifies tanks and soldiers moving across the foreground.

Some of his most powerful works are watercolours completed directly in the field, such as *Wrecked Buildings, Ortona* (cat. 62), which depicts buildings ripped apart to skeletal shreds, thereby commenting on the state of civilization. They show the influence of the British artist John Piper whom Comfort met in 1943 at a party hosted by Sir Kenneth and Lady Clark.[52] One bittersweet irony of his stay in Italy: he had the opportunity to examine and in some cases re-examine masterworks of Italian art he had come across in the various campaigns. In fact, the soldiers were encouraged to admire the culture of the region in which they were stationed and were given brochures on art appreciation entitled "Soldier's Guide to Rome."[53]

Post-War

Upon his return to Canada, Charles Comfort was stationed in Ottawa while he completed his large war-art paintings. Over the course of the next several months he rode the wave of the post-war interest in the war. War art exhibitions were held at the National Gallery in Ottawa and Hart House in Toronto that spring and he gave numerous lectures. In July he was released from military service and reunited with his family in Toronto. That summer he spent an extended amount of time with his family, Will Ogilvie, and friends Doris and Gordon Davies on Cedar Lake in Algonquin Park. For the first time ever, his journals were strangely void of talk of painting as he decompressed from his war experience, "I have no great urge to paint, a desire for nothing but uninterrupted idleness fills me."[54]

When he resumed his teaching position, Comfort struggled to adjust to regular life without the fanfare associated with being a war artist. A deflation of mood is evident from his journals, as people turned their backs on the past and moved forward into a much changed society. To compound this feeling, he was close to being destitute. In fact, when his mother died in late 1947, he considered not attending the funeral in Winnipeg because he did not have the money.[55] He ended his 1947 journal, "I have never been so poor and ragged since I was a boy."[56]

Though continuing to struggle financially during the next two decades, Comfort soon became incredibly busy. Still teaching, he continued his research into technique when he won a Royal Society Fellowship for study in the Netherlands in 1955. Louise and he spent a year travelling and studying Flemish and Dutch painting. He also undertook numerous corporate commissions during the fifties: as part of their series on the cities of Canada, Seagram's Distilleries commissioned him to paint Edmonton. The Canadian Club in New York asked him to paint the Parliament Buildings. His public commissions included the massive mural for the Toronto Dominion Bank in Vancouver in 1951 (cat. 87); a smaller mural of the Bow Valley, Banff National Park for the inside of one of the Canadian Pacific Railway Parks Cars, 1954;[57] a Veterans Affairs mural in Ottawa in 1955; and a mural of the history of medicine for the Neurosurgical Unit at the Toronto General Hospital in 1958. Furthermore through this period until the mid-1970s he completed numerous official portraits of political and military officials.

Comfort was also deeply involved with the art society and gallery activities. Since he first moved to Toronto, he had been dedicated to the Art Gallery of Toronto: he was elected to their board in 1946, served on their Canadian Collection committee (acquisitions) from 1949 until late 1959, and was on their exhibition committee from 1946 to 1949.[58] He was also on the Hart House Gallery advisory committee for purchasing works of art. In 1950 he was elected president of the Canadian Group of Painters while simultaneously holding office as president of the Canadian Society of Painters in Watercolours. From 1957 through 1960 he was the President of the Royal Academy of Arts. Mount Allison University recognized his accomplishments with an honourary doctorate in 1958; the University of Alberta awarded him a Gold Medal for Painting in 1963; and he received the *Medaglio al Merito Culturale* that same year for his contributions to the sharing of culture between Italy and Canada.

He exhibited widely immediately after the war at the OSA, RCA, CSPWC, and CGP exhibitions. Initially he submitted the works expressing his war experience or older works such as *Tadoussac* and *Young Canadian*. He also was represented in international exhibitions in France, New Zealand, and the United States.

Modest private sales and some significant public sales helped to place his important works across the country: *Lake Superior Village* to the Art Gallery of Ontario in 1950; *Aura Lee* to The Winnipeg Art Gallery in 1952, *Chuhaldin* and *The Dreamer* to the Art Gallery of Hamilton in 1954 and 1957, and *Smelter Stacks* to the National Gallery in 1957. By this time, he had attained the status of a significant senior artist. Consequently, in 1948 Robert Ayre was hired by Ryerson Press to write a monograph on his career for their Canadian Artist Series putting Comfort in the company of Cornelius Krieghoff, Tom Thomson, A.Y. Jackson, and other well known artists. However, insulted by Ayre's characterization of him as "a funny little man who writes diaries,"[59] Comfort refused to allow the book to be published. Because of his disagreement with Ayre, a focused study of his work was not published until the 1970s, possibly jeopardizing some of the recognition he may have received for his painting in the intervening years.

Comfort's reinvigorated painting production resumed within a couple of years. He produced new portraits such as those of Ogilvie (cat. 68) and Schaefer honouring their war service. By the late 40s he was also exhibiting new landscapes, mostly based on studies he completed each summer either at Cedar Lake or later at Go Home Bay where he was a guest of the Jackmans who had recently purchased the famous MacCallum cottage. The Comforts holidayed there each summer for the next few decades, often joined by A.Y. Jackson and Will Ogilvie. Interested in moving his work into new areas of inquiry, Comfort began combining symbolic elements with various degrees of abstraction in these landscapes. *Aeons Ago* (cat. 70), completed as part of a series at Cedar Lake has a surrealistic sensibility where seemingly disparate representational elements – driftwood, a primitive mask, a waning balsamic moon (symbolic of a time of death and rebirth), and the disembodied foot (reminiscent of Picasso's anti-war painting *Guernica*) – intermingle with an abstract background. Herein, Comfort struggled to express ideas about the history of civilization, its movement through dark times, and his hope for the future. Stylistically, Comfort revisited the influences of the British artists he had met overseas such as Henry Moore and John Piper.

Over the course of the next two decades, the development of recurring symbolic iconography makes Comfort's work interesting. As Anna Hudson will discuss in her essay, Comfort and his contemporaries were experimenting with common symbolic elements in their paintings.[60] Various Toronto artists, perhaps beginning with Bertram Brooker, used the tree root and the subsequent well-worn driftwood as symbols. Inspired by L.L. FitzGerald, in the early 1930s, Brooker began drawing biomorphic trees. In 1945 he painted an oil of a piece of driftwood – the base of a tree trunk, with truncated roots morphing into animal faces, with which Comfort would have been familiar as a friend. Beginning with *Pioneer Survival* (cat. 36) from 1938 Comfort utilized uprooted tree stumps, dominating the foreground, as symbolic of the displaced human spirit struggling during the Depression. He continued his usage of uprooted stumps and driftwood throughout numerous paintings, consistently exploring the formal and symbolic meanings of tree remains. In *Transfiguration* (cat. 71), 1948 Comfort extended the symbolism to burnt stumps following a forest fire, with the surrounding new vegetation promising regrowth. *Aura Lee* (cat. 73) an oil painting of two years later, has a pile of driftwood screening the small island that appears to float like a ship through the solid, Cedar Lake landscape. Comfort was not merely painting the landscape for itself, his work communicated his concern for the human condition – in this case of deterioration, death, and the promise of renewal.

The shifting rock face of the Canadian Shield was another recurring symbolic element of transformation adopted by Comfort. *Rocky Site*, 1952 (cat. 74), shows the result of shifting geological plates, forming shattered debris below and exposed rock faces above, upon which the windblown pines cling. His thick paint application reveals his interest in achieving novel technical effects. He dragged brilliant pigment – oranges, blues, yellows, and greens – through the more naturalist browns and beiges of the rock. This approach is recognizable from some of his war oils such as *Hitler Line*, acknowledging the influence of John Piper who worked with similar effects in his early 1940s oils. Throughout the 1950s Comfort's paint surface is a luscious whipped-up impasto that indicates not only texture, but a literal transformation. *Wherewhen*, (cat. 76) perhaps represents the culmination of this trend; it is a monumental work that presents what he referred to as a "derelict tree" washed up on shore. The simplified, almost abstract shore, lake, and rock islands of Georgian Bay express a stark barrenness evocative of loneliness and neglect, counteracted by Comfort's rich application of textured paint. The sky formed by various blues in intersecting planes is reminiscent of Canadian Shield formations. The prevailing earth tones of the tree bark are enlivened with strokes of bright blue, red, and yellow. Furthermore, the first quarter moon that hangs in the sky, symbolic of the evolution of new forms even in the face of resistance, suggests the painting as a harbinger of hope.

Interwoven with Comfort's experimentation with representational symbolism during this decade are his further forays into abstraction. In its emulation of

John Piper's mixed-media collages from the mid 1930s, *Thrush Song*, 1948/49 (cat. 72) is the most literal example of Comfort's admiration for modern British art. Although abstract, it uses the Canadian Shield as an inspiration from which his forms emerge. In 1957 he pushed his exploration of the landscape to a new level in such works as *Pre-Cambrian Legend* (cat. 77).[61] Like *Wherewhen*, it is inspired by the Georgian Bay landscape and includes bold splashes of expressionistic colour. However, herein Comfort rejects the heavy impasto of multicoloured oil pigment in favour of a flatter articulation of interacting rock planes.[62]

In 1959 Comfort was approached to apply for the position of Director of the National Gallery and it was necessary for him to put serious painting on hold until 1965.

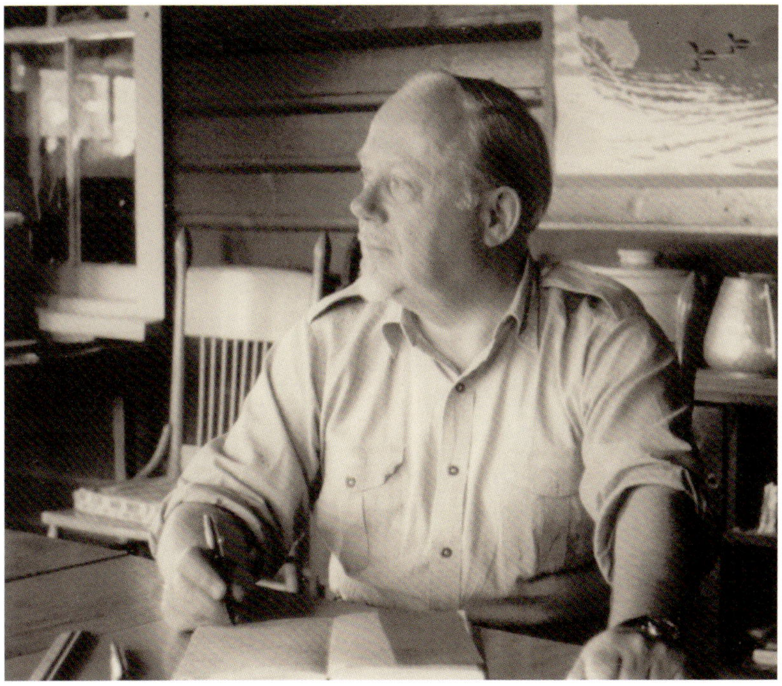

Charles at Westwind Cottage, August 5, 1965
Charles Comfort Collection / Library and Archives Canada / e002505477

Art Administrator

Being considered for such a prestigious position verified all Charles Comfort had worked towards in his Canadian cultural endeavours over the previous four decades. His connections to the NGC beginning in the 1920s and his committee work with other societies and art galleries dealing with exhibitions, acquisitions, and policy aptly prepared him for the task. Furthermore, he had had personal and professional relationships with the previous three former directors: Eric Brown, H.O. McCurry, and Alan Jarvis. Nonetheless, Louise and he approached the decision with trepidation. In his journals he described it as a time of soul searching and agonized about being associated with an institution whose last director fell, in Comfort's opinion, under criticism for his emphasis on modern art. When Comfort finally accepted the position, he noted Louise's observation: "Well, up until now our life has been one of happiness and adjustment. I cannot help but feel that phase has definitely ended and that we will now be plagued with pressures and hostility."[63] Even NGC board member Harry Jackman discouraged him from taking the position.[64] Despite the bleak foreshadowing, Comfort acted against instinct and accepted the position with the hope that he would make a difference, as the first artist to hold the position.

Comfort was effective in his roles as ambassador and spokesperson for the Gallery, giving speeches at openings and touring dignitaries through the gallery. His strong passion for art and knowledge of international and Canadian art practice, both historical and contemporary, made him an excellent statesman for the institution. However, before the first year was over, speculation about Comfort's relationship with staff arose when several key people resigned. By the end of the year, the responsibilities had taken its toll on his previous enthusiastic life view, "After a year's exposure I am a sadder and a wiser man. ... It has been a year of unending labour with not a great deal to show for it yet, but earnest, conscientious labour cannot go unrewarded forever."[65] One journalist noted that "...a period of calm has settled on the National Art Gallery, giving rise to the hope that politics and paintings have been divorced. ... In any event, the gallery has been free of controversy since his appointment."[66]

By 1962 this could no longer be said. An exhibition ironically titled "The Controversial Century: 1850–1950," which included works purported to be by artists like Degas, Renoir, Cezanne, and van Gogh from the collection of Walter Chrysler, erupted into an international controversy. A month before the exhibition was to arrive at the NGC, Comfort received a call from Evan Turner, Director of the Montreal Museum of Fine Arts. Turner told him that while he had been in New York, he'd heard that many of the paintings in the Chrysler collection had been uncovered as fakes.

The newly formed Art Dealers Association of America (ADAA) was investigating the Provincetown, Massachusetts collection in an effort to remove forgeries from the marketplace. Never having seen the work, Comfort trusted the research of his Associate Director, William Dale, who had negotiated what had seemed like a rare opportunity. Even though Comfort went to the Department of Justice with the concern, he downplayed it as a rumour, especially since the ADAA never contacted him directly.

When the ADAA discovered that the show had opened in Canada, they leaked the story to the press. Comfort was inundated by calls from *Time Magazine*, *Newsweek*, and *Life Magazine*. *The New York Times* art critic John Canaday recanted his previous glowing review of the exhibition. When the local press learned about it, opposition Liberal MP Judy LaMarsh brought the issue up in Parliament and Comfort was asked to justify his position before the Gallery Board. Ultimately, the board voted that they had confidence in Comfort's professional integrity but the ordeal left him battered and depressed, "Dark thoughtless depression has filled my mind... No one seemed to understand, or recognize that I had done all that I could have be (sic) done short of canceling the exhibition when it began to grow so big."[67] The highly publicized incident cast shadows across the remainder of Comfort's tenure as director as he predicted, "...the 'Controversial Century' will remain as a lurid incident in personal and Gallery history."[68]

Exhausted by this issue and his ongoing perception that staff and board were disrespectful, Comfort looked forward to his retirement. Unfortunately, a few months before this event, another publicized controversy hounded him. As Director of the national institution, he was responsible for signing import papers allowing works of art to cross the border duty free when coming in for exhibition. When he refused to sign off on Andy Warhol's soup can and Brillo Pad works because he couldn't define a "multiple" as an original work of art, he was "lampooned as an artistic square."[69] He was quoted: "I don't classify these processed cartons and tin cans as sculpture."[70] In being criticized for these particular objects, Comfort pointed to the fact that the National Gallery had held two American Pop Art exhibitions in recent years. To justify his actions, he recounted his desire to bring issues surrounding the status of the recent phenomenon of multiples to the forefront of discussion. However, he felt the media's opportunistic ridiculing of the outgoing director overshadowed his point.

Retirement was bittersweet. He left behind a positive legacy of increased attendance at the Gallery through high-profile exhibitions. He also increased the National Gallery's tour-exhibition program and encouraged major additions to the collection of historical European masterworks, as well as works of Canadian modern painters like Jean Paul Riopelle, Paul-Émile Borduas, and Harold Town. Comfort was also instrumental in the development of the National Conservation Research Laboratory and the founding of the Canadian Art Museum Directors Organization, still in existence today. CAMDO plays a large role in the professional development of museums across Canada. Despite these accomplishments, Comfort found it difficult to shake the dark cloud that made him feel he had lost the respected stature he had once held. In his parting speech to the staff he likened his departure to the time when he left military service: "I am giving up rank, surrendering the weapons I have had to learn to use in what Sir John Rothinstine (sic) has described as 'The unpredictable, relentlessly cruel, jungle-warfare of the art world.' I am giving it up to be repatriated, to recover my identity and my reputation as Charles Comfort."[71]

Return

Indeed, focusing on the bright side, Comfort acknowledged that he would finally have the opportunity for the first time in his life to paint full-time. Immediately, he accepted portrait commissions and began the murals for the National Library Reading Room.

Over the next two decades he continued to experiment with increased degrees of abstraction in his landscape paintings. His later career demonstrates his dedication to delving deeper and looking to the ever-changing world and his shifting place within it for inspiration. As a self-proclaimed humanist, his world view was centred on life as one big opportunity to seek knowledge and make new discoveries. In 1974 he wrote the following artist statement in the third person:

> "As an artist he is a humanistic realist whose paintings are characterized by a spirit of ordered freedom and technical conservatism. For him, the visible world is the valid point of departure for a work of art. This does not mean that his purpose is to imitate nature, but rather to recreate it, remoulding and harmonizing it to agree with his own idiomatic mannerisms and his own personal concepts. He envisages his world as being inexhaustibly inspiring and meaningful."[72]

In his representational works, Comfort delved into themes concerning the epic search for meaning in life. *Seventh Line, Tecumseh Township* (cat. 80) and *Edge of the World, Georgian Bay* (cat. 81) from the 1970s suggest his interest in life as a journey, questioning what comes afterward. Both are beautifully painted: his elegant and multilayered handling of the medium, sure colour sense, and simplification and ordering of forms through which he pursued landscape as metaphor, continued.

At the same time, Charles Comfort returned to pure abstraction, possibly to quash the conservative reputation he had gained as Gallery director. Works such as *Epic Theme* (cat. 78) demonstrate his assured handling of abstraction and impart his admiration of Borduas' earlier black and white palette-knife works. Like in *Pre-Cambrian Legend*, painted nearly a decade earlier, Comfort introduced a bold splash of colour over the prevailing monotone grid-like structure. The painting's overlapping forms suggest his abiding interest in abstracting the natural forms of the Canadian Shield and as the title implies, exploring the monumental themes of life. His self-conscious need to reassert his identity as a modern painter is telling; in his *Self-Portrait* (cat. 54), commissioned by the National Gallery, he depicted himself dressed in a painter's smock, with a painting similar to *Epic Theme* in the background.

That same year he produced the "Newspeak Series," horizontal hard-edged abstracts that represented the farthest he had strayed from natural forms (cat. 79).[73] Here the expressionistic grid, drawn from the rock formations in his previous paintings, becomes more strictly geometric. His explanation of this shift in approach reveals his continued search for new ways of expressing his ongoing concern for society through formal aspects of painting:

> "My *Newspeak Series* ... [is a] new development in my work as a formal deliberative, rectilinear organisation, parallel to nature, in which the operative word is 'equivalence.' The solid and spatial world of naturalism still has vital significance for me, but my 'horizontal events' offer a new device through which to express aspects of order at a point of crisis in the evolution of our society."[74]

The statement reveals his dedication to art in service to society. This dedication was publicly recognized when he was made an Officer of the Order of Canada in 1972. Decades earlier, he had spoken of the artist's role to "...contribut[e] to the cultural life of the community with honesty, sincerity, and deep integrity toward his work, and in relation to his generation."[75]

In this context, we can make sense of Comfort's widely varied artistic approach that emerged over several decades. These later works represent the final ordering of the landscape, something he started in the late 1920s, becoming most evident in the 1930s. Until the end of his career, he continued to experiment enthusiastically with further manipulation of landscape forms. He had the courage to abandon his popular and established approach for newer more abstract approaches, allowing him to pursue the visual equivalents which provided landscape with deeper meaning. His goal in art, after all, was not the creation of an identity or of one recognizable style by which he could be associated, rather it was about finding new ways for his art to explore the world and express its fascinating and ever-transforming nature.

> A human lifetime is such a brief, transient moment in the scale of time that, having been afforded the privilege of living through what may prove to be "the hinge" that connects the conclusion of a mature civilization and the "blast-off" into a completely new and, as yet unknown, cultural identity, I rise from the table, address myself to my host and say, "Thank you for this rare feast."[76]

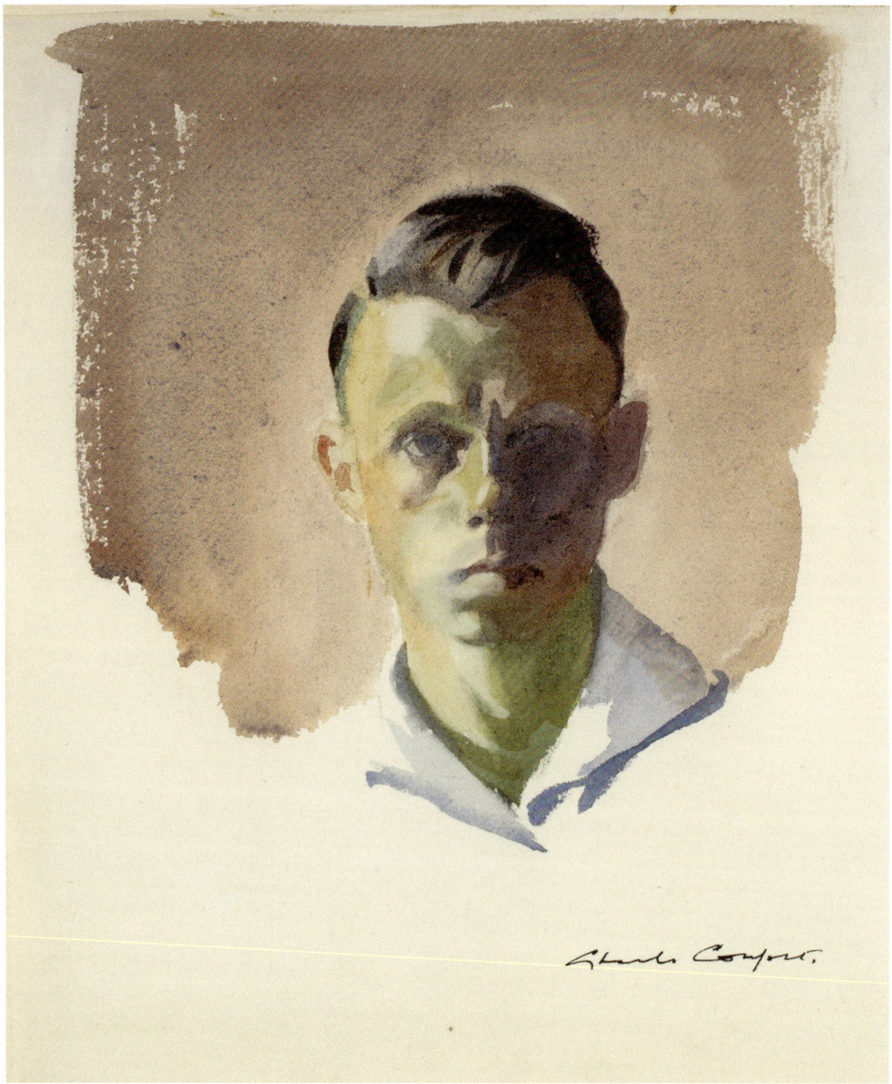

39. **Self-portrait**, 1920–1921

1. The following provide a general overview of the period: Charles Hill *Canadian Painting in the Thirties* (Ottawa: The National Gallery of Canada, 1975) and Christine Boyanoski, *The 1940s: A Decade of Painting in Ontario*, (Toronto: Art Gallery of Ontario, 1984).

2. Charles Comfort, *Sketches From Memory*, unpublished manuscript, c 1984, Charles Fraser Comfort Fonds (CFC Fonds), Library and Archives Canada, Ottawa, MG30, D81 volume 8, V.

3. *Sketches*, III.

4. *Sketches*, I.

5. I have accepted facts from this autobiography carefully. Inherent to such retrospective documents, is a tendency for sentimentality, personal bias, and faulty dating.

6. *Sketches*, 7.

7. *Sketches*, 37.

8. For a discussion of the development of Winnipeg's cultural scene see Marilyn Baker, *The Winnipeg School of Art*, (Winnipeg: University of Manitoba Press, 1984).

9. Some examples include Angela E. Davis, *Art and Work: A Social History of Labour in the Canadian Graphic Arts Industry to the 1940s* (Montreal and Kingston: McGill-Queen's University Press, 1995) and Robert Stacey and Hunter Bishop, *J.E.H. MacDonald: Designer* (Ottawa: Archives of Canadian Art: An imprint of Carleton University Press, 1996).

10. Angela E. Davis, *Business, Art and Labour: Brigden's (sic) and the Growth of the Canadian Graphic Arts Industry 1870–1950* (Doctoral Thesis, The University of Manitoba, Winnipeg, 1986), 3.

11. *Sketches*, 111.

12. His unpublished essay titled *The Walk*, 1917, CFC Fonds, describes a sketching trip to Minaki by foot with Walter Huntley.

13. Charles Hill interview with Comfort, October 3, 1973, (typescript in The Winnipeg Art Gallery Archives), unpaginated.

14. Hill interview.

15. He was awarded tenth prize. Letter from M. Leison to Comfort, March 16, 1920. CFC Fonds, *Correspondence*, 1920–1938.

16. This Society grew from the Graphics Art Club founded in 1904/05 by professional artists working in the commercial field such as Frederick Brigden and C.W. Jeffreys to encourage original printmaking, drawing, commercial art, and textile design.

17. *Sketches*, 165.

18. The exhibition was January 7–21, 1922 at The Winnipeg Art Gallery.

19. It opened October 21. There is no extant list and Comfort does not mention what was included.

20. "Art Notes." *The Winnipeg Free Press*, n.d. (1922), pasted in Minute Book, CFC Fonds, vol. 22.

21. W.J. Healy, *Women of Red River: Being a Book Written from the Recollections of Women Surviving from the Red River Era* (Winnipeg: The Women's Canadian Club, 1923).

22. Comfort exhibited some of these ink drawings in 1924 at the AGT Canadian Graphic Art exhibition.

23. *Sketches*, 192.

24. *Portrait in August* (cat. 51) was painted there.

25. See Tovell essay.

26. "I met a handsome young South African who had just arrived in Canada ... this young man would become a close life-long friend ... I was aware immediately of his attractiveness and his loneliness." *Sketches*, 210.

27. Jeanne Adeney. "The Group of Seven: Their 5th Annual Exhibition." cited in Charles Hill, *The Group of Seven: Art for a Nation* (Ottawa: National Gallery of Canada, 1995), 328.

28. Speech given at Sarnia Public Library and Art Gallery, January 23, 1976, *Lectures and Speeches Binder "NG"* 1972–1976, CFC Fonds.

29. At Grip, Comfort was greatly respected and he was allowed to take time off to teach art classes, "I cannot emphasize too emphatically that you will be working with me and not for me." Macnamara to Comfort, December 5, 1929, CFC Fonds, Vol. 31, *Correspondence 1920–1938*.

30. They received accounts through advertisement agencies such as Cockfield, Brown and J.J. Gibbons where Brooker worked. Hill interview.

31. See Donegan's essay for details on these projects.

32. As early as 1928 Comfort was teaching. He provided art classes on the side such as a ten-week session on watercolour to employees of Darling and Pearson Architects. Letter to Barry Cleveland from Comfort, October 29, 1928, CFC Fonds, Vol. 31, *Correspondence 1920–1938*.

33. Robert Fawcett to Comfort, July 18, 1938. Volume 31, *correspondence* 1938–1940.

34. For an analysis of this painting see Christopher Jackson, *The Dreamer*, (Hamilton: Art Gallery of Hamilton, 1996).

35. While Jeanne Adeney panned the 1928 OSA exhibition for lacking vitality, she was excited by Comfort's landscapes: "But having wandered, uneventfully, for the most part, through three of the rooms, it was startling to come suddenly upon 'The Great Rock', by Charles Comfort, hanging between 'Wilderness', by the same artist, and 'Waterfall', by Lawren Harris. After the first shock, however, one began to share the feeling of awe suggested by the mighty crag." "The 56th O.S.A. Exhibition," *The Canadian Bookman* (March 1928), 79–80.

36. For a thorough discussion of the shift to "ordered" landscape see Anna Hudson, *Art and Social Progress: the Toronto community of Painters, 1933–1950*, Doctoral thesis (Toronto: University of Toronto, 1997).

37. Robert Ayre "Canadian Group of Painters," *The Canadian Forum*, 14 (December, 1933), 100.

38. Hill interview.

39. See Christine Boyanoski, *Charles Comfort – Lake Superior Village*, (Toronto: Art Gallery of Ontario, 1991).

40. "Artist's Work Wins Acclaim," *Globe and Mail* (October 29, 1938); "Canadian Wins Prize for Art" *London Free Press* (Oct. 29, 1938).

41. Robert Ayre, "Tributes to Canadian Artist Who Achieved Wide Acclaim At Great Lakes Exhibition," *Montreal Standard*, (Nov. 12, 1938).

42. Robert Hubbard, Assistant Director of the National Gallery, in his 1947 discussion of modern painting chooses Comfort's work as his first example of modernism evident in Canadian representational painting: "...the industrial landscapes and murals of Charles Comfort.... have a precision and a simplification of form which suggest the mechanical efficiency of our age. And those modern forms are inseparable from his very tangible subject matter." Robert Hubbard, *Modern Painting in Canada*, reprint # 48 (Ottawa: National Gallery of Canada, 1947), 1.

43. Comfort to Edwin J. Wiess, Sept. 11, 1939, CFC Fonds, vol. 31, *Correspondence 1938–1940*.

44. He also continued teaching his mural class at OCA in 1938.

45. "Toronto Artist Impressed By Art Of Modern Italy," *Toronto Telegram*, (August 19, 1939).

46. Travel Journal, May 25, 1939, CFC Fonds, Vol. 1.

47. *Teaching Notes*, CFC Fonds, Vol. 5, 1938–1960.

48. See Michael Bell. *The Kingston Conference Proceedings – A reprint of the Proceedings of the 1941 Kingston Artists' Conference*. (Kingston, Ontario: Agnes Etherington Art Centre, 1991).

49. "The Visual Arts in Canada 1950," CFC Fonds, vol. 42, *Massey Commission 1949–1951*.

50. See "The Painter and His Model " in William Arthur Deacon and Wilfred Reeves eds., *Open House* (Ottawa: Graphic Publishers Limited, 1931), 213-218 and "1938–1948: Observations on a Decade," *Journal, Royal Architectural Institute of Canada* (Jan. 1948), 3-9.

51. Robert Ayre, "Charles Comfort-The Soldier's Eye," *The Montrealer*, December 1956, 61.

52. See Boyanoski, *The 1940s: A Decade of Painting in Ontario*, 23. Piper's watercolours were on display during the event. The party was also attended by Graham Sutherland, Henry Moore, and Paul Nash.

53. "This brochure has been written for the use of the Allied troops by the Monument and Fine Arts Sub-Commission of the Allied Control Commission. It was designed and produced by the Psychological Welfare Branch, AFHQ, Italy." Introduction to "Soldier's Guide to Rome," CFC Fonds, Vol. 9, *War Art Printed Material: army n.d., 1942/43*.

54. *Journal*, July 10, 1946, CFC Fonds.

55. Ogilvie and Louise Comfort pooled money to buy him a ticket.

56. *Journal* 1947, Memoranda page.

57. Originally, Comfort planned to paint a modern version of Manet's *Le Déjeuner sur l'herbe* set in the Rockies but his sketch was rejected and he was forced to paint a conventional landscape. See Ian Thom, *Murals from a Great Canadian Train* (Outremont, Quebec: Libre Expression and Via Rail Canada, 1986), 115-123.

58. AGT/AGO List of Committee Member, Art Gallery of Ontario Library.

59. *Journal* May 16, 1948.

60. See Hudson's essay.

61. In 1958 this painting was in the *Australian-British-Canadian Art Exhibition* through the Women's Auxiliary, Vancouver.

62. Ayre described an example of this series as a "...studied, almost scientific investigation of colour and form..." praising the "...passage of colours that moves diagonally across the neutral background – like a rock face- a procession in a pageant." Robert Ayre, "Canadian Group of Painters on Display at the Museum," *The Montreal Star* (Nov. 9, 1957), 27.

63. *Journal*, December 11, 1959.

64. *Journal*, Dec. 21, 1959.

65. *Journal*, April 1, 1961.

66. Ralph Hyman, "Gallery of Canadians: Excellence the Only Standard" undated, unnamed source, CFC Fonds, Vol. 20, *Clippings 1961*.

67. *Journal*, Dec. 9, 1962.

68. *Journal*, November 6, 1962. It would seem that these works were forgeries. They have never emerged since and were not among the works later donated by Chrysler to the Chrysler Museum in Norfolk, Virginia. See AADA website for their description of the incident. They claimed that the controversy cost Comfort his job. http://www.artdealers.org/who.history.html.

69. Gerald Waring, "Ottawa's Hunt for a New Art Czar." Date and source cut off. Vol. 45, *Retirement National Gallery* 163–65.

70. Jay Walz, "Canada Rules out Art-in-a-Can 'Art,'" *New York Times* March ?, 1965, 34.

71. Remarks to Members of Staff on the occasion of his retirement, July 21, 1965, CFC Fonds, Vol. 4, *Lectures and Speeches Binder, Oct 1964 – Oct. 1965*.

72. *Curriculum Vitae* c. 1974, CFC Fonds.

73. "Newspeak" refers to the fictional language in George Orwell's book *1984* where words had such a limited and literal meaning that there was no opportunity for them to inspire thought. One wonders whether Comfort was criticizing the idea that abstraction could have no room for deeper meaning beyond formal concerns.

74. Robertson Gallery, Ottawa exhibition handout for exhibition of *Georgian Bay* and *Newspeak Series*, May 5–20, 1967, CFC Fonds, Vol. 57.

75. Comfort, University of Toronto Extension Department Lecture, Art Gallery of Toronto, October 23, 1946, handwritten speaking notes, CFC Fonds, Vol. 4, *Lectures and Speeches*.

76. *Sketches*, III.

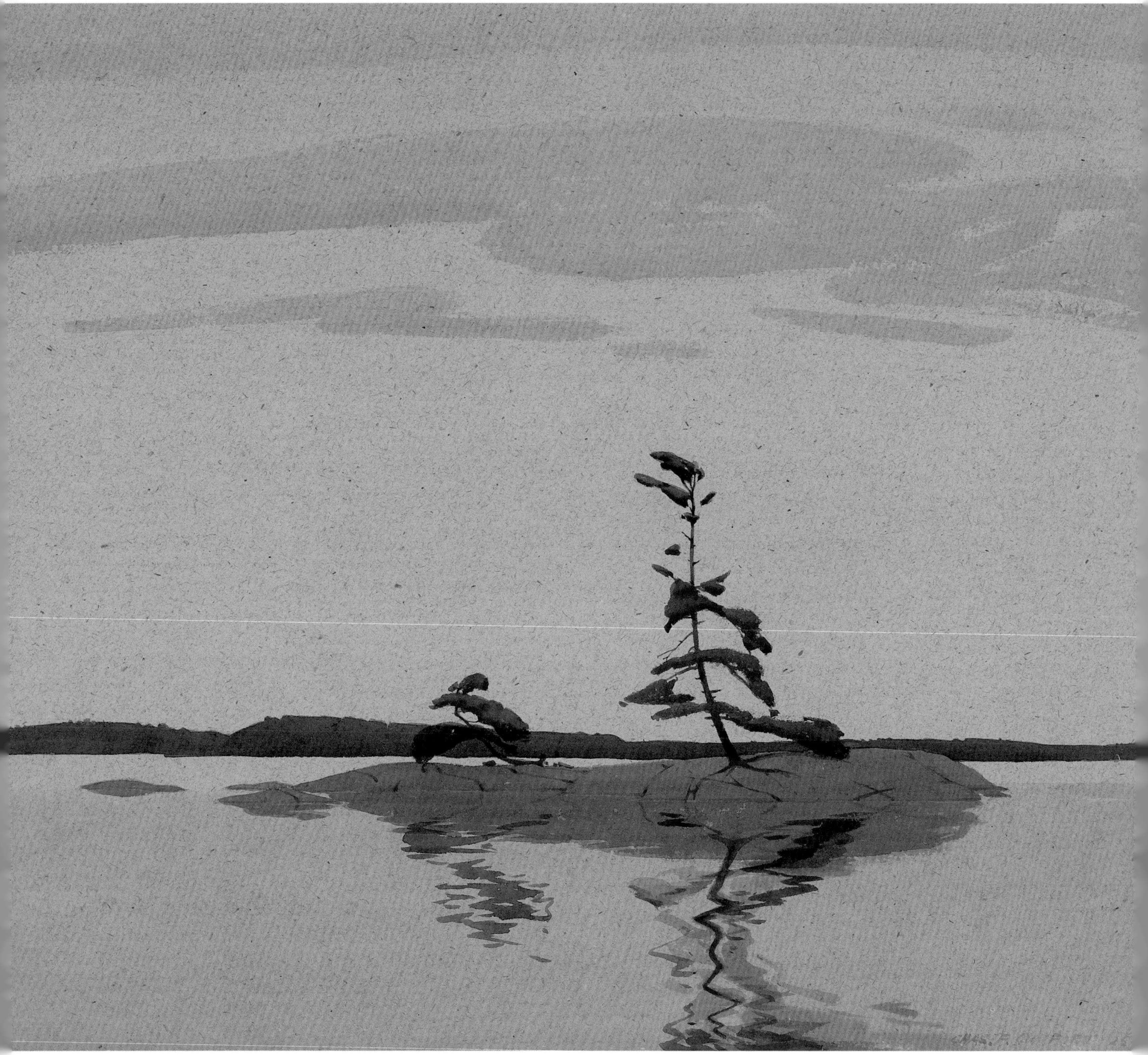

11. **Stoney Lake**, 1925

ROSEMARIE L. TOVELL

A Promising Talent: The Making of a Painter in Watercolour

CHARLES COMFORT'S PUBLIC DEBUT at the Y.M.C.A.'s 1913 summer exhibition was the turning point in his life. The watercolours he submitted attracted the attention of the sole jury member, F.H. Brigden, who not only awarded Comfort first prize, but also offered him an apprenticeship with the newly established Winnipeg branch of Brigdens Limited, which he was managing. While these works are now lost, we have examples of Comfort's first watercolours made a few years earlier, when he was just an eight- and nine-year old boy. Despite their being juvenilia, these flower studies show he had an inherent talent for the medium, displaying a knack for composition and for laying down washes of pure, bright colours.[1]

When Comfort accepted the offered apprenticeship, he may have expected to receive some training from Brigden himself – one of Canada's most distinguished painters and watercolourists. But while Brigden kept an eye on Comfort's activities, he left the training to others. In the firm's art department, he came under the supervision of T.W. MacLean, originally from Toronto, a long-time member of the Graphic Arts Club and well-known to that city's leading art circles, and. T.G. Greene, another well-connected Toronto artist. These contacts would prove useful when Brigden assigned Comfort to their Toronto shop a few times, beginning in 1919. H. Eric Bergman, a professional wood engraver newly arrived from Germany, was among the other employees Comfort befriended. To augment his training at Brigdens, Comfort took drawing classes from Valentine Fanshaw at Kelvin Technical High School and later from Alexander Musgrove at the Winnipeg School of Art. It is interesting to note that in all these instances Comfort received training only in drawing with an emphasis on technique and process. He received little, if any, reference to aesthetics – the creative side of art making. With no one at this time to truly guide him, Comfort was dependent on his own acumen while viewing the paintings and watercolours at the Winnipeg Museum of Fine Arts (later The Winnipeg Art Gallery) and at Richardson Brothers, the only art dealer in town. British contemporary art dominated the gallery walls along with works by local artists and touring exhibitions by the Royal Canadian Academy. Cyril Barraud and Walter J. Phillips, both able watercolourists and recent immigrants from England, were the two most significant local artists at the time.[2] At best, what Comfort was seeing could be described as an already out-of-date conservative Impressionism and Post-impressionism.

Comfort's *Self-Portrait* of 1920–21 (cat. 39) was painted during his second sojourn in Toronto, when his interest in watercolours began to take hold. Yet, without known antecedents dating to his first Winnipeg years, it is difficult to determine how his exposure to and involvement in Toronto's active art scene furthered his art.[3] The early watercolours of his first teachers, Fanshaw and Musgrove, bear no similarity to his *Self-Portrait* in either technique or choice of colours. This tender, rather old-fashioned vignette-formatted work is rendered in layered washes of brown, green, and mauve, applied with sponge and brush. This palette, which would persist for a number of years, similar to the preferred palette of W. J. Phillips, strongly suggests that Comfort was already a keen observer of Phillips' watercolours and colour woodcuts. However, his use of pine green, now faded to a sage green, as the principle facial colouring, perhaps witnesses Comfort's excitement at experiencing the colour and dynamism on display at the first Group of Seven exhibition.[4] *Kildonan Skyline Across the Red River* of 1922 (cat. 1) brings into play the vigorous brushwork Comfort admired in the Group of Seven's paintings, while he retains the colours used in *Self-Portrait*. A year later in New York, Comfort rendered a January snowstorm over Manhattan (cat. 3) in the abstract, near monochromatic tonality of the Impressionist style characteristic of the Glasgow School[5] with no apparent assimilation of the latest avant-garde styles despite Comfort's assertion that Euphrasius Tucker, one of his instructors at the Art Students League, had awakened his interest in art trends beyond Impressionism and Post-impressionism.[6]

Upon his return to Winnipeg in March 1923, Comfort began to apply the lessons learnt from Tucker, closely exploring the work being created by his fellow artists, Bergman and Phillips in particular. His best friend and sketching partner, Eric Bergman, had taken up watercolour in 1922[7] and was investigating the technical possibilities of the medium. In 1924,[8] W.J. Phillips was giving Comfort private instruction in Japanese colour woodcuts – a printing technique that was technically and aesthetically akin to watercolours. Not only was Comfort observing Philips' and Bergman's work, he was also collecting their colour woodcuts and watercolours, now in the collection of the National Gallery of Canada. Comparing Bergman's watercolour *Near Blindfold Rapids, Lake of the Woods* (NGC 23891) with Comfort's *Lake of the Woods, Route Bay* (cat. 6), both apparently painted on the same sketching trip, we see each artist experimenting with the same varied modes of watercolour technique on the same sheet. Comfort used the blotting-out technique to soften the colours and contours of the clouds; the application of gum arabic to the trees in the middle distance to emphasise the richness of the greens; and finally, the brusquely layered brown-over-purple washes to replicate the roughness of the foreground rock. However, the compositional model for Comfort's watercolour must have been Phillips' *Lake of the Woods* (NGC 23539) with its large mass of bare ground, created by a brown-over-purple wash, dominating the lower half of the composition.

Indeed Bergman's influence on Comfort's watercolours is not as pronounced as Phillips'. Comfort's preference for creating compositions emulating Phillips' Orientalism is evident in the bird's-eye view and calligraphic brush work of *Blindfold Rapids, Lake of the Woods* (cat. 5) or the low horizon of *Suburban Cottages, Winnipeg* (cat. 7). With the latter, Comfort extends his debt to Phillips in the streaky brushwork of the sky which is similar to Phillips' treatment of skies in his colour woodcuts. As already noted, there is little difference between Comfort's and Phillips' colour choices.

By this date Comfort was acquainted with L.L. FitzGerald through the Winnipeg Little Theatre. His response to FitzGerald's work, however, was limited to little more than a similarity of subject matter. For example, Comfort's 1924 watercolour *Near Headingly, Manitoba*[9] (coll. AGO # 89/53), has the low horizon, cloud-filled sky, and telephone poles lining the road leading into the distance, which are common motifs in FitzGerald's art.

By the time Comfort left Winnipeg for Toronto in early 1925, his abilities as a watercolourist and printmaker were on solid ground. The first year in Toronto he refined his art to make it wholly his own.

"For me, Toronto was an attractive city, built in a forest bordering on a great lake, furrowed with wooded ravines which led to two pleasant watercourses, which in turn meandered toward their estuaries through romantic valleys rich in flowers and forestry."[10] This was Comfort's subject matter. *Don Valley Brick Yard* (cat. 10), painted in May 1925, illustrates that he was not able to entirely shake off his Winnipeg way of seeing; it shares its palette and composition with *Suburban Cottages, Winnipeg* (cat. 6) – now reversed. The effect of light had been a constant in Comfort's earlier art and with *Bridge over the Don*, (cat. 8) he uses a blotting technique to masterfully capture the dappled spots of sunshine shining through the unseen trees above. *In the Valley* (cat. 9) is the culmination of his Toronto ravine subjects: painted in August 1925, the watercolour captures the distant trees, rendered in a soft purple, shimmering in the humidity of a Toronto summer.[11]

A trip to the Kawartha Lakes in the company of Harold and Elizabeth Ayres provided the final step in Comfort's realization as a fully accomplished watercolourist. Comfort admired their watercolours "which they employed with breadth and richness of colour"[12] and his own work on this trip, like *Kawartha Lakes*[13] (cat. 13) showed a new boldness in his choice of palette and brushwork. When he worked up his Kawartha Lakes watercolour sketches into the large, calligraphic and now very faded *Stoney Lake* (cat. 11), he retained the bright blues. We can only guess whether he employed any other rich colours.

By the end of 1925 Charles Comfort had become a founding member of the Canadian Society of Painters in Water Colour, joining the ranks of Canada's leading watercolourists. He was also active with the Canadian Society of Graphic Art, serving as its secretary, and in autumn that year he briefly joined the other members in their experimentation with various printmaking techniques like etching and colour linocuts. He did not return to colour woodcuts. By the end of the decade, Comfort was a firmly established professional artist. His work could be seen at all the major society exhibitions and his watercolour *Stoney Lake* had been purchased by the National Gallery of Canada.

Notes

1. *Sketchbook*, 1908–09, Library and Archives of Canada (# 1991-306-142).

2. Comfort mentions seeing an exhibition of English watercolours from James McDiarmid's collection at the Winnipeg Museum of Fine Art. *Sketches*, p. 122. There is no record of such an exhibition nor can it be determined what watercolours McDiarmid had in his collection at the time. However, as McDiarmid was an early patron of both Barraud and Phillips, surely their watercolours would have been on display. The annual reports of the Fine Arts Committee of the Winnipeg Industrial Bureau (1913 to 1916) and a number of catalogues attest to the fact that Comfort had access to an impressive number of Canadian and international exhibitions.

3. Comfort's membership in the Graphic Art Club (1919) and the Arts and Letters Club (1920), brought him into contact with Toronto's most important artists.

4. *Sketches*, 164.

5. In September 1914 an exhibition of Modern Scottish Artists was shown at WMFA in the Winnipeg Industrial Bureau. "Report of the Fine Arts Committee," *Annual Reports* (Winnipeg: Winnipeg Industrial Bureau, 1914), 37.

6. There is some problem with Comfort's dating of watercolours. He dates the New York watercolour January 1922 whereas his stay in New York spanned October 1922 to March 1923.

7. "H. Eric Bergman biographical form," received 12 February 1927, Artists documentation files, National Gallery of Canada Archives.

8. Comfort talks about taking private instruction at Phillips' home in July, 1921. Sketches, 176-177. One would expect that these lessons would involve creating a very finished colour woodcut. However, *At Headingly, Manitoba*, Library and Archives Canada (#1994-210-77), his only known exhibition-quality colour woodcut, was first exhibited in Toronto at the February 1925 annual exhibition of the Canadian Society of Graphic Art. During the previous years, he had exhibited only drawings. Additionally, his first Christmas cards, executed as colour woodcuts, began in 1924. These facts suggest that Comfort took instruction in 1924, not 1921. That same year Bergman studied Japanese colour woodcuts with Phillips. (ref. "H. Eric Bergman biographical form.")

9. Fitzgerald's painting of Headingly's grain elevators is similar to but not the same as Comfort's colour woodcut of the same title.

10. *Sketches*, 207.

11. *Ibid*, 208. During his first summer in Toronto, Comfort first experienced the "devastating heat and an enervating humidity unknown to us in the west."

12. *Ibid*, 209.

13. Comfort titled the work as *Lake of the Woods* and dated it 1925 at a later date, probably not recognizing the subject as having been painted at the Kawartha Lakes. There is no record of Comfort being in Lake of the Woods during the summer.

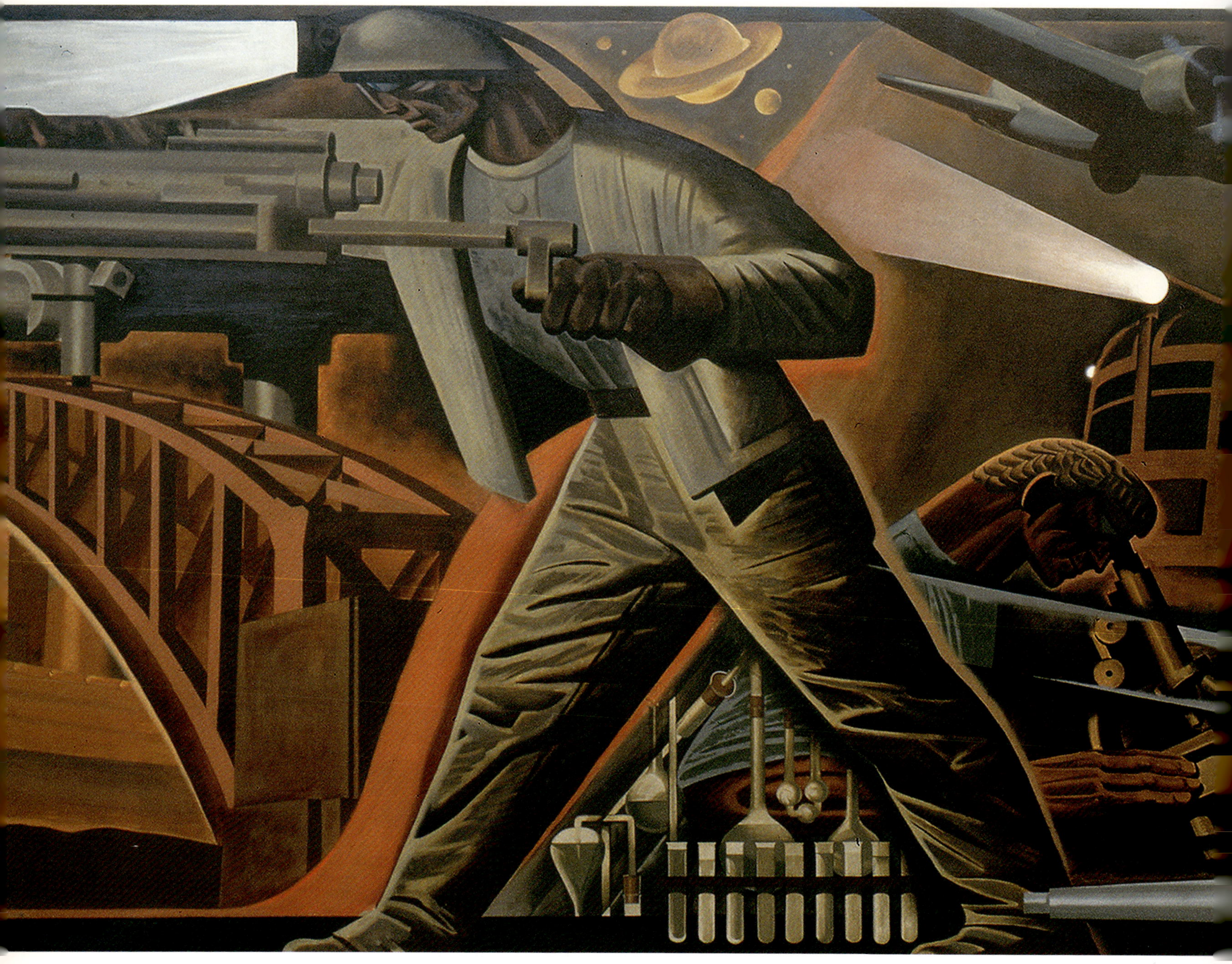

85. **The Romance of Nickel**, (detail), 1937

ROSEMARY DONEGAN

Muscled Workers, Speeding Trains, and Composite Figures: Charles Comfort's Murals

THROUGHOUT THE 1920s CHARLES COMFORT worked hard to establish his career as an independent painter and to earn a living as a commercial artist. He carefully positioned himself between the commercial arts industry and the visual arts community, exhibiting regularly with the various art societies (as discussed in other essays). However, the series of murals that he produced in the 1930s would bring these elements of his work together and shift his practice from the commercial arts to the fine arts as a muralist, art teacher, and administrator, culminating in his being appointed the Director of the National Gallery of Canada in 1960.[1]

When Comfort moved to Toronto from Winnipeg in 1925, he continued to work for Brigdens as an art director and production supervisor. By late 1929 he was so well established in the Toronto industry that he was able to leave Brigdens and negotiate a contract with Rapid-Grip Ltd. for $9,000.00 a year, a large sum for the times.[2] However, with the Stock Market Crash in November 1929 and its reverberating effects on Canada, Comfort was out of work by early 1932. He attempted to return to Brigdens, but with the Depression in full force, there were no salaried positions available. Later that year he opened up an office with Will Ogilvie and Harold Ayers in the Studio Building on Severn St. and undertook various illustration and advertising contracts. He managed to put together a living as a free-lancer, combining illustration work, private teaching, art direction, painting contracts, and public lectures. Successful in attracting clients, he did work for *The Canadian National Railway Magazine, Saturday Night* magazine, Imperial Oil, and the International Nickel Company of Canada (Inco) among others.

Comfort's advertising career provided the philosophical underpinnings of his mural work; he believed that the commercial artist should never lose sight of the client. As he articulated in a lecture given in 1931:

> A good rule is to be a little ahead of the crowd, but not too far ahead lest you also get ahead of the buying public. Be original but not as original as can be. Some enthusiasts take up a new idea like modernism and run away with it. They lose sight of the primary purpose of advertising, and the main fact that art when applied to advertising is, after all, merely a means to an end, and that end is the selling of goods. Photographs or paintings, realistic or modern. It is never a question of what you or I like best in art, but always of how effective this drawing will be in attracting and finally compelling the public to like and buy your goods.[3]

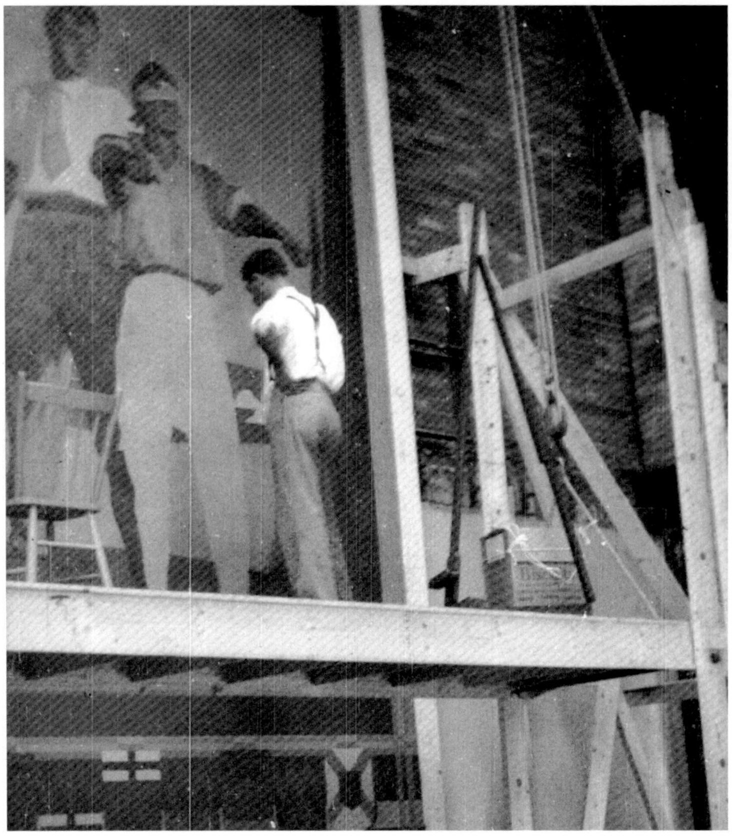

Will Ogilvie inspects the North American Life Mural, August 1932
Charles F. Comfort /Library and Archives Canada/PA-175351

Comfort brought the same pragmatic approach to his mural work, an understanding of advertising and the client, which he adapted through a synthesis of form and style to the architectural scale and public role of mural painting.

II.

His first mural project was a temporary decoration for Toronto's Arts & Letters Club in 1926 with a humorous and incongruous twist on the capture of General Wolfe in Quebec.[4] In 1932 he was commissioned to produce a wall-painting for the lobby of the North American Life Assurance Building by the architect F. Marani.[5] Comfort's early murals were rooted in older traditions of wall-painting in Canada.[6] In Quebec, Catholic churches and religious orders often displayed large wall- or easel paintings. In contrast in English Canada, the Arts and Crafts movement had introduced wall-paintings into private homes and public places such as hotels, libraries, theatres, department stores, and schools. Most of these murals were narrative, painted on canvas and installed on interior wall surfaces; they were usually decorative in nature.

Without doubt, the strongest impetus for mural painting in the 1930s was the Mexican fresco murals of Diego Rivera, David Siqueiros, and José Clemente Orozco. After his mural commissions at the San Francisco Stock Exchange, the Detroit Institute of Art, and the notorious destruction of his Rockefeller Center mural in New York in 1934, Rivera had become an international art celebrity. The Mexican muralists had created a new visual history of the Mexican people, valorizing and celebrating the indigenous peoples in accordance with the government's policy of *mexicanidad* ('Mexicanness').[7] Their powerful narrative – a highly symbolic rendering of a national history in fresco, with their intense spatial organization, colour, and vibrancy – inspired many Canadian and American artists to explore a new approach to mural painting.

The new mural movements espoused the re-union of painting and architecture, separated since the development of easel painting in the Renaissance. Some even claimed that mural painting would save the artist from the isolation of the studio, the limitations of the canvas edge, and the inward looking, private language of abstraction. Modern architecture, particularly modern institutional architecture, was seen as the perfect scale and location for artists to find a wider general public. The faith in murals, as a social and political form, was widely advocated and was an aspect of the larger concept of the artist in society.[8] As Arthur Lismer commented in an article in the *Royal Architectural Institute of Canada Journal*, dated 1933, murals "...are signs that our democracy, which is still adolescent, is slowly achieving a new renaissance through more coordinated activity in the designing of structure and its decoration."[9]

Within this context of mural painting Charles Comfort was asked by Samuel Maw, associate architect with the firm of George & Moorhouse, and a fellow member of the Arts & Letters Club, to design an exterior stone frieze for the new Toronto Stock Exchange on Bay Street. The major objective of the new Toronto Exchange was to create an image of stability, rekindling faith in the stock market after the disastrous crash of 1929. Comfort's design for the exterior frieze depicted a procession of Canada's industries marching together in a strong forward movement.[10] There were 31 life-size figures moving in a tightly structured geometric pattern from right to left in a bank 22 metres long and over 1 1/2 metres high. Comfort produced a full-scale cartoon, which was then attached to the wall, perforated and drawn on the surface, relying on stylized figures in low relief contrasted with etched-line details, creating shadows and depth. The design was cut, rather than carved, with a combination of pneumatic work and hand-chiseling on the Indiana limestone.

Comfort's Stock Exchange frieze symbolically integrated the capitalist, represented by the figure of the stockbroker, as a productive element alongside the labourer, the salesman, the white collar worker, the farmer, the scientist and the miner, as part of *the natural order of things* in the world of work. As a symbol of the lifting of the Depression, it represented the public image of the power of industry, with both capital and labour working together to exploit Canadian resources. A rather ironic detail in the frieze over the north doorway is the top-hatted stockbroker whose hand appears to be in a worker's pocket. According to Comfort, the juxtaposition of the two figures was unintentional.[11] However over the years, it became an insiders' joke among the exchange brokers and is part of Toronto's popular mythology.

Although the murals in the interior of the Stock Exchange were originally to be commissioned from four different artists, by the time the contract was awarded in January 1937, Comfort had been selected to design and paint all eight mural panels (each 11.2 x 4.9 metres). The murals depicted the industries of Canada whose stocks were traded on the Exchange floor: construction and engineering, mining, smelting, refining, oil, pulp and paper, agriculture, transportation and communications. Muscled workers, speeding trains, pouring vats, electrical towers, and industrial structures unify the tightly constructed vertical panels. For the human figures, Comfort re-used the stylized figures from the exterior murals, which created a strong forward movement in the horizontal frieze. In the vertical interior murals, the strong graphic lines of the figures, their repeated stance, the reach, and the warm, rich, earthy colours, all serve to unify the individual vertical panels into a whole. Within the overall space, Comfort's murals complemented the scale and the detailing of the Trading Floor, neither dominating nor competing with the architectural style (which we would now refer to as Art Deco). As the vertical murals were designed to be seen from below, the individual panels have a tendency to break down into pure planes and forms when observed in isolation.

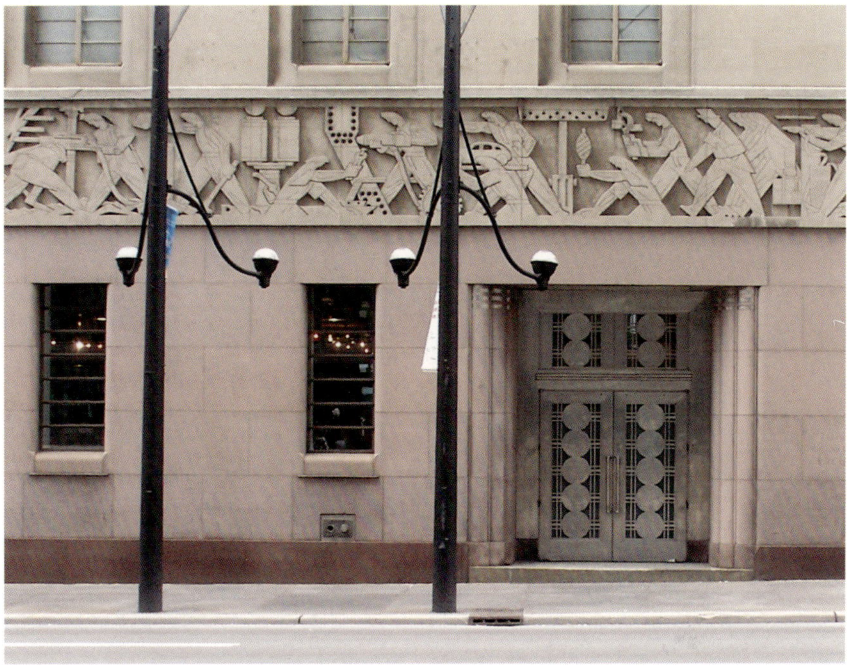

Toronto Stock Exchange, exterior stone bas relief (in situ at the Design Exchange, Toronto)
Photography: George Lobb

In between his completion of the exterior and interior murals for the Stock Exchange, in the fall of 1936 Comfort was commissioned by Inco to paint a mural for their mining display in the Canadian Pavilion at the upcoming 1937 International World's Fair in Paris.[12] The final 6.1 metre long *Romance of Nickel* (cat. 85) depicts the process of nickel and copper production, merging them into a seamless landscape of the New Ontario. The mural is dominated by the inverted Y-form of a heroic hard-rock miner, whose aggressive stance emphasizes the power and thrust of machines and miners. A second figure of an earnest scientist gazing into his microscope is surrounded by the icons of modern life: skyscrapers, bridges, crank shafts, streamlined trains and automobiles, radio towers, and airplanes representing the rational objectives of technology and industry. The mural combines symbols of technology with French *moderne* design, and elements of what one could call Stalinist heroic realism, industrial futurism, and corporate beneficence. It speaks of progress, the future, and jobs at a time when Canada and the mining industry, which had been particularly hard hit by the 1929 Crash, had just crawled out of the worst of the Depression.

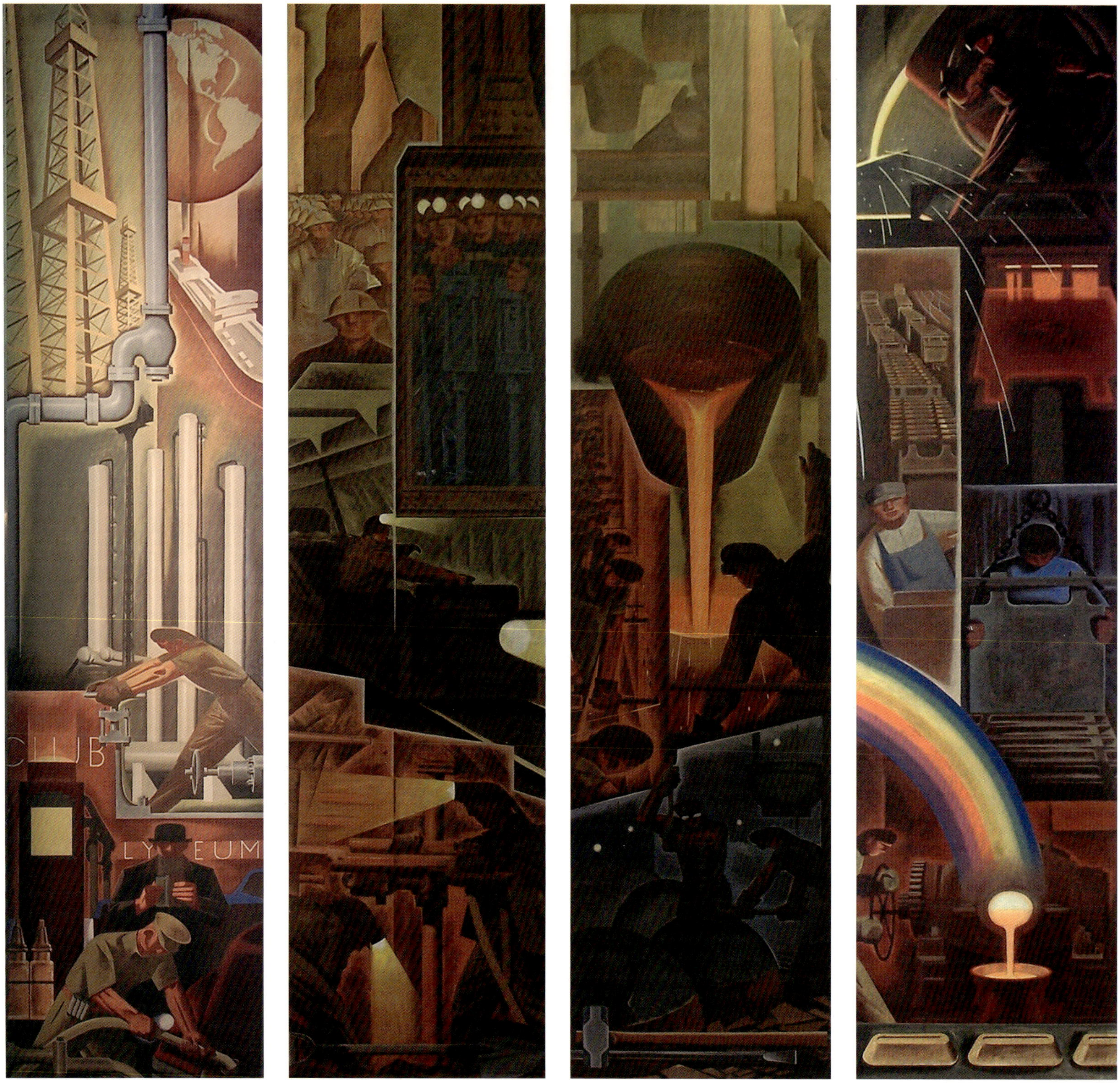
CLUB
LY EUM

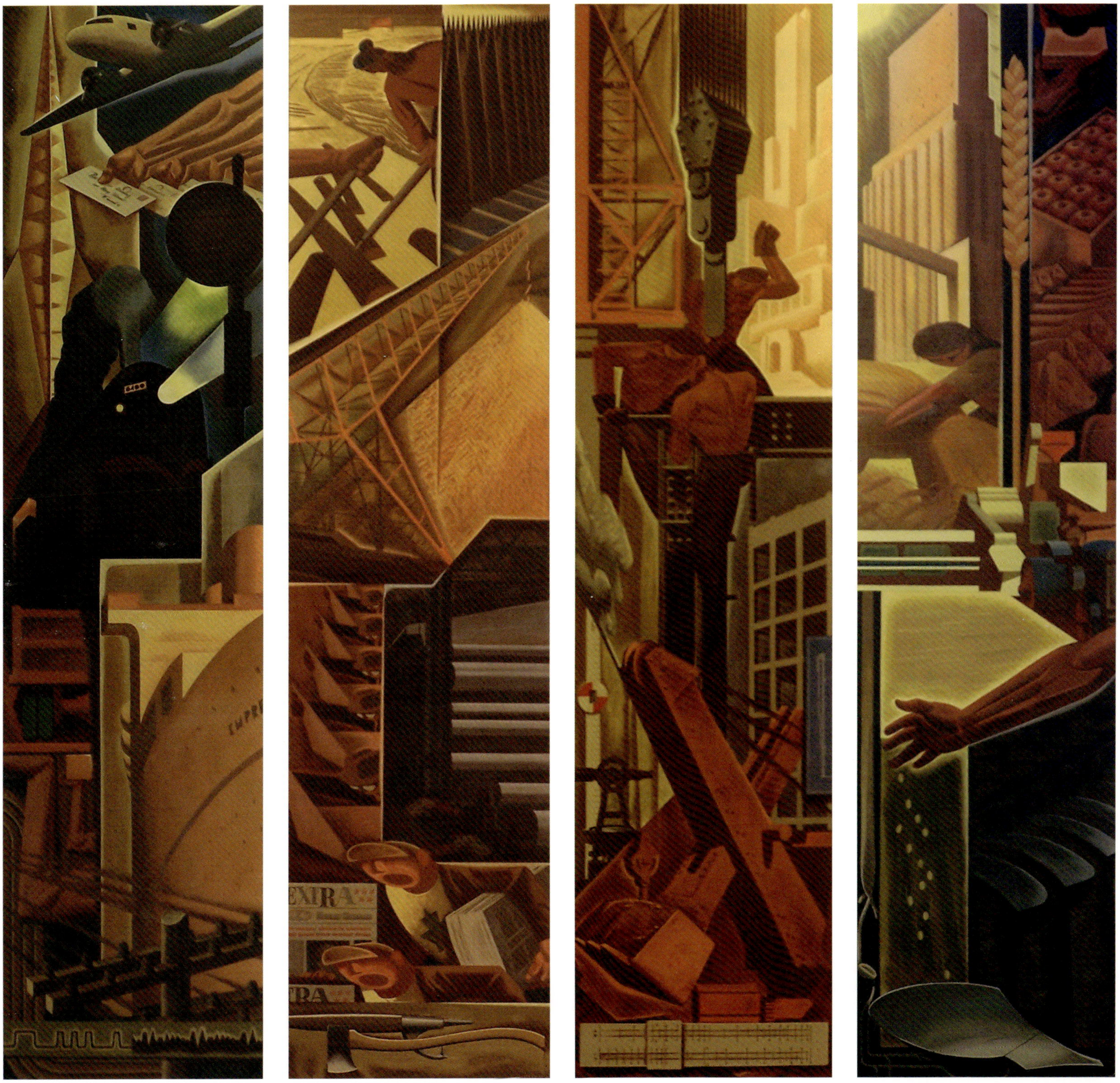

Toronto Stock Exchange, interior mural paintings Photography: George Lobb

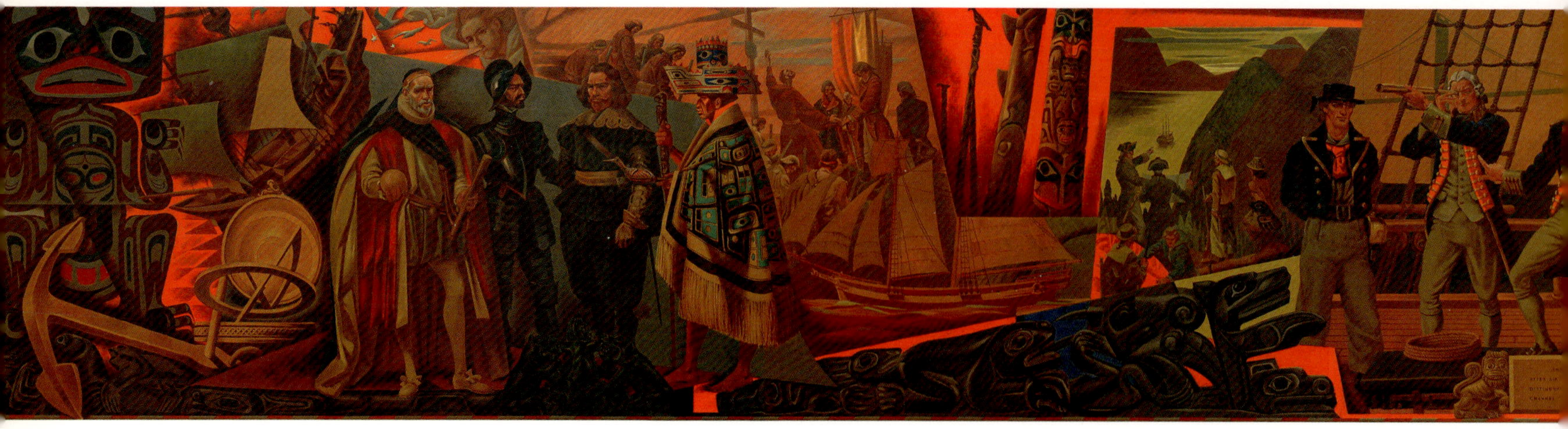

III.

Although the Stock Exchange murals and the Inco commission for the Canadian Pavilion at the Paris World's Fair were a great success, Comfort had serious financial problems in the late 1930s. He was having trouble finding commercial work and was more interested in murals and teaching. Money was such an issue that Comfort resigned from the Arts & Letters Club, as he was unable to pay his fees and was in arrears. This was acutely embarrassing for Comfort, as he had been active in the Club since the early 1920s. Many of his contacts for professional work had come through associates at the Club, and it was a symbolic centre of Toronto's cultural and intellectual community in the 1930s. It was during this period that he took over teaching a course in mural decoration and kindred uses at night and on Saturdays at the Ontario College of Art. In 1938 he started teaching part-time at the University of Toronto, which allowed him to stay in Canada and not to take up a position in commercial art in New York. Comfort, who was primarily self-educated, was a conscientious teacher and spent a considerable time researching the history of murals, painting techniques, and later art history.[13]

Over the next 25 years, Comfort continued to search out mural work. In early 1939, through a rather circuitous route, he was hired by the CNR to paint a mural for the lobby of the new Hotel Vancouver for a fee of $1,800.00.[14] The design, approved by CN, focused on Captain Vancouver and his subalterns being received with Potlach gifts by three natives in the foreground. Comfort commented ironically that in the mural Captain Vancouver "...is being peacefully and ceremoniously received by the natives of the district (a circumstance about which there is much doubt)."[15] When completed in May 1939, the mural was installed in the Hotel Vancouver lobby with favourable notice and remained there until 1968, when the hotel was renovated. In 1942 he received a large public commission to design exterior stone bas-reliefs and interior murals for the Dorchester St. Central Station in Montreal, focusing on the history of transportation.

In 1951 Comfort painted an almost 20-metre long mural *British Columbia Pageant* for the Dominion Bank at the corner of Granville and Pender in downtown Vancouver. This rather heroic allegory of British Columbian history started with the Spanish explorers, included Captain Vancouver and crew, various aboriginal and Euro-Canadian figures, plus Emily Carr, and was spatially organized using various West Coast aboriginal motifs, such as Tlingit totems and Haida poles. In 1951 when the mural was unveiled, Paul Duval described Charles Comfort as "the nation's top mural artist..." and saw him playing "...a leading position in this vital, though neglected, field of architectural art."[16]

In 1955 Comfort, along with fellow veterans, Will Ogilvie and Andre Biéler, were invited by the Department of Veterans Affairs to produce three murals for the new Veterans Affairs building on Wellington Street in Ottawa. Comfort's mural depicts the three branches of the Canadian military during the war: the Navy in the midst of a night time naval battle; the Army involved in a ground battle of men

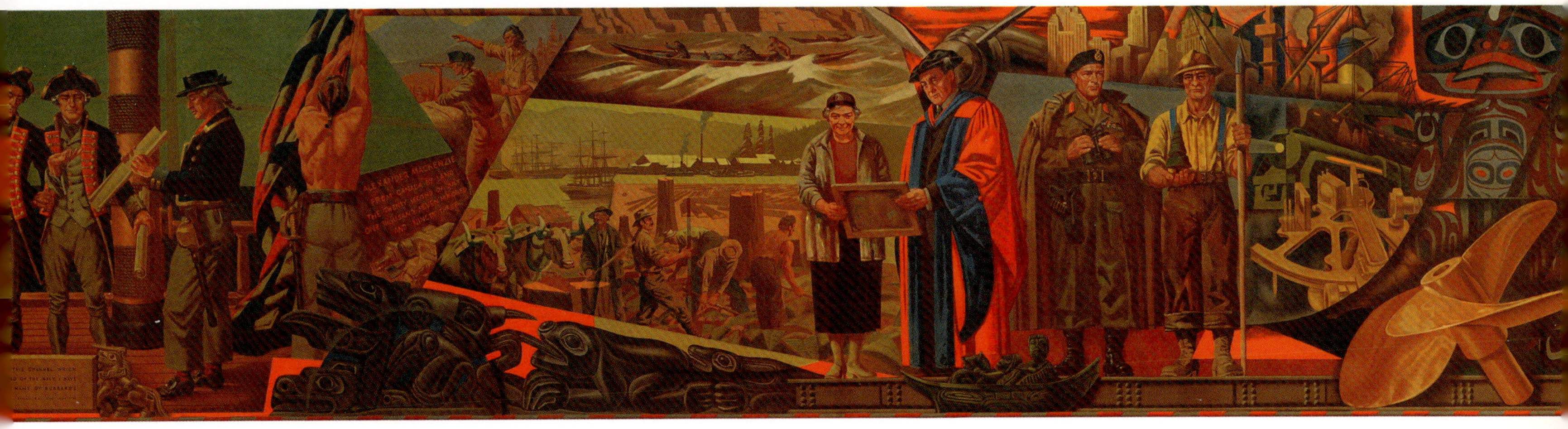

British Columbia Pageant mural, 1951
Courtesy of Simon Fraser University, Burnaby

and tanks; and the Air Force Lancaster bombers in night-time raids over central Europe. These are accompanied by five smaller panels which are layered over the larger scenes at the lower edge of the mural. Reading like photographic capsules, these vignettes capture the contemporary role of Veterans Affairs in the 1950s: demobilized soldiers; a military group portrait including a nursing sister; a meeting of the veterans' pension board; and a classic advertising image of a father returning to his suburban bungalow greeted by his wife and child, with his new car in the driveway.

The Veterans Affairs mural, although largely unknown, has a number of interesting aspects. Comfort grappled with time and abstraction by creating a series of floating scenes and vignettes, while seriously constrained by the limitations of the architectural space. The mural is highly narrative and figurative in style. Rather than introducing highly symbolic figures like his historical murals, his utilization of photographic framing and visual quotations from contemporary life in the 1950s adds intriguing elements to the highly formal piece.

His last major mural commission was for the new National Library of Canada which opened in 1967. The two paintings, *Legacy* and *Heritage*, at either ends of the Reading Room, were designed to be low key and not distracting to the readers, while providing a historical context for both intellectual history and Canadian arts and letters. The murals focus on a series of historical figures illustrated in a soft grisaille technique floating in a soft green/grey visual field.

IV.

As a public art form, art and ideology overtly intersect in murals through their content and style, as well as through the vision of the patron commissioning the work. And although the mural revival of the 1920s and 30s was hailed as a new form of public art and in many instances a political educational tool, public response over the years toward the murals has proved to be somewhat contradictory and invariably complicated.[17]

In Canada, like the US, murals tended towards historical themes of famous thinkers, explorers, founding fathers, dead politicians, classical heroes, early transportation, etc. Virtually all of the murals commissioned in Canada avoided contemporary issues, particularly the devastation of the economic and agricultural depression of the 1930s.[18] The occasional futuristic themes of economic prosperity through technological invention such as Comfort's work were limited. Most importantly these figurative murals were designed to be legible so they could be read as a narrative. By the mid 1950s, figurative historical murals would be eclipsed by the interest in abstraction, exemplified in the dynamic expressionistic mural that Harold Town completed for the St. Lawrence Generating Station in Cornwall, Ontario as part of the St. Lawrence Seaway Project in 1958.

Like many Canadian artists in the 1920s and 30s Comfort used his murals to search for and construct a symbolic Canadian culture. As the Mexican muralists attempted to create a *mexicanidad* (a national people's history), Comfort and his friends in the Group of

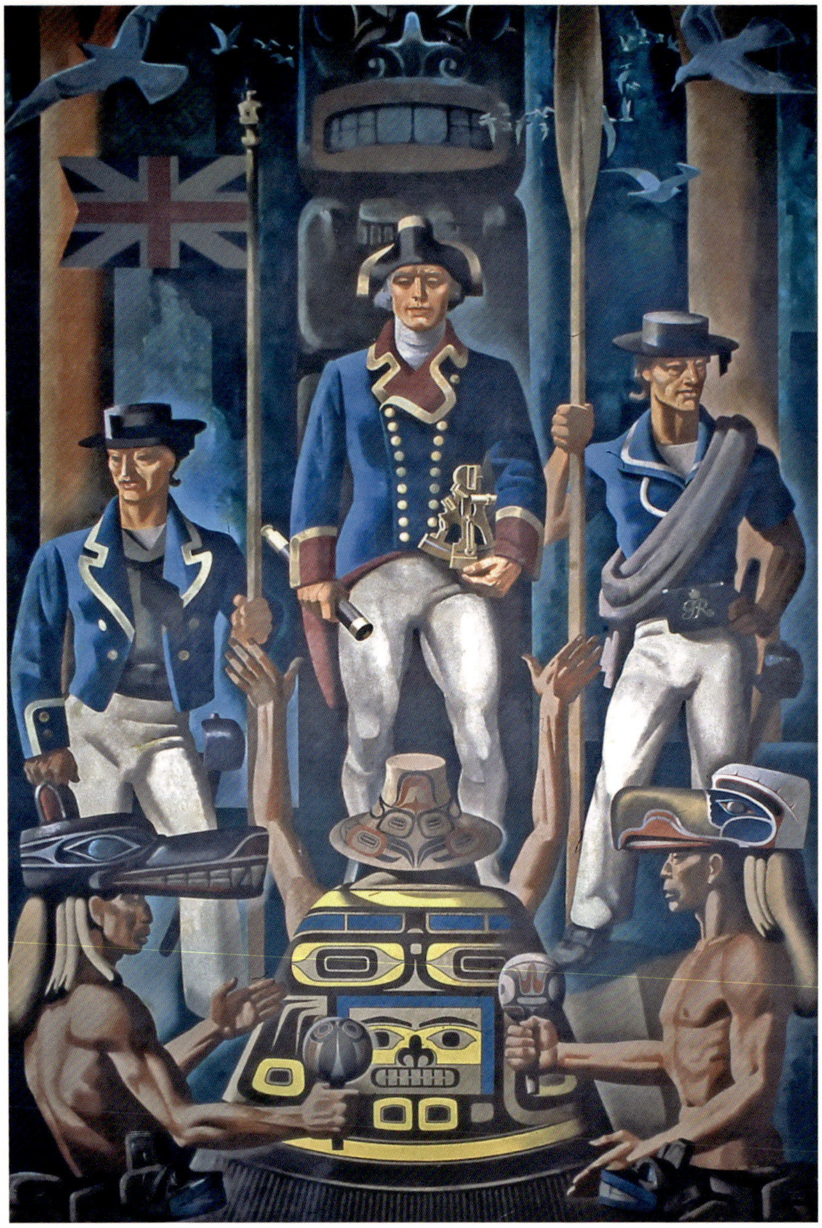

Captain Vancouver mural for Hotel Vancouver, 1939
Confederation Centre Art Gallery, CAG 73.12

Seven sought to develop a modern iconography of the Canadian landscape. Comfort's advertising background made him comfortable with commissioned work; he perceived his mural decorations as allegories, rather than documentaries to be read by the public in the historical sense.[19]

In their time Comfort's murals were virtually all received positively with little discussion of their content as their meaning appeared to be self-evident. More recently, the symbolic content of his historical murals, specifically the Hotel Vancouver mural of Captain Vancouver and the Dominion Bank *British Columbia Pageant* mural, have been hotly debated.[20] The historical figures and generic composite characters of aboriginal peoples developed by Comfort, representing his attempt to construct a symbolic history, have become contentious as new approaches to First Nations and post-colonial history have evolved.

Comfort's strongest murals – the exterior frieze and interior murals of the Toronto Stock Exchange and the *Romance of Nickel* – dealing with contemporary industry, technology, and the future, are visually coherent, stylistically mature and ideologically clear. In contrast, his historical murals today read like didactic scroll paintings, muddled clichés of historical figures. In his industrial images he adopted a two-dimensional Cubist approach to space that is much more formally and stylistically ambitious. His use of layered forms, floating planes, plus shapes and colours, avoids the perspectival accuracy of traditional figurative painting, while allowing the scale of objects and figures to be adjusted to the narrative and spatial limitations of the composition. These murals are an unabashed glorification of industry, an attempt to create new symbols of the businessman, the scientist, and the worker. They symbolize the power of modern industry and implicitly of capitalism, particularly the resource-extraction industries, rising phoenix-like from the ashes of the Depression. Charles Comfort brought his clarity of industrial imagination and his belief in the future to these murals in the 1930s: both vitally corresponded to the search for an image of a modern industrial Canada and in some manner, still do to this day.

With thanks to David Wallace, Charles Hill, Scott James, Dot Tuer, and Jerry Zaslove.

Appendix: Charles Comfort Murals

1932 – North American Life Assurance Co., Toronto (destroyed)

1936 – Toronto Stock Exchange, Bay St., exterior stone bas relief (in situ in the Design Exchange, Toronto)

1936 – *The Romance of Nickel*, Canadian Pavilion, Paris World's Fair, 1937 (on loan to the National Gallery of Canada, Ottawa)

1937 – Toronto Stock Exchange, interior mural paintings (in situ in the Design Exchange, Toronto)

1938 – Central Station, Dorchester Station, Montreal (partially destroyed, remnants re-installed in the Montreal Train Station, Place Ville Marie)

1939 – Hotel Vancouver/Captain Vancouver mural (now in the Confederation Art Centre, Charlottetown, PEI)

1948 – Sunnybrook Hospital, Toronto (destroyed)

1951 – *British Columbia Pageant*, Dominion Bank, Granville and Pender Sts., Vancouver (now in the collection of Simon Fraser University, Burnaby)

1955 – *The Canadian Armed Forces*, Ottawa (in situ in the Department of Justice, in the former east wing of the Veterans' Memorial Building, Ottawa)

1958 – Neurological Division, Toronto General Hospital (now in the collection of the University Health Network, Toronto)

1967 – National Library and Archives Building, Ottawa (in situ in the National Library Reading Room)

1968 – Academy of Medicine, Toronto (presumed destroyed)

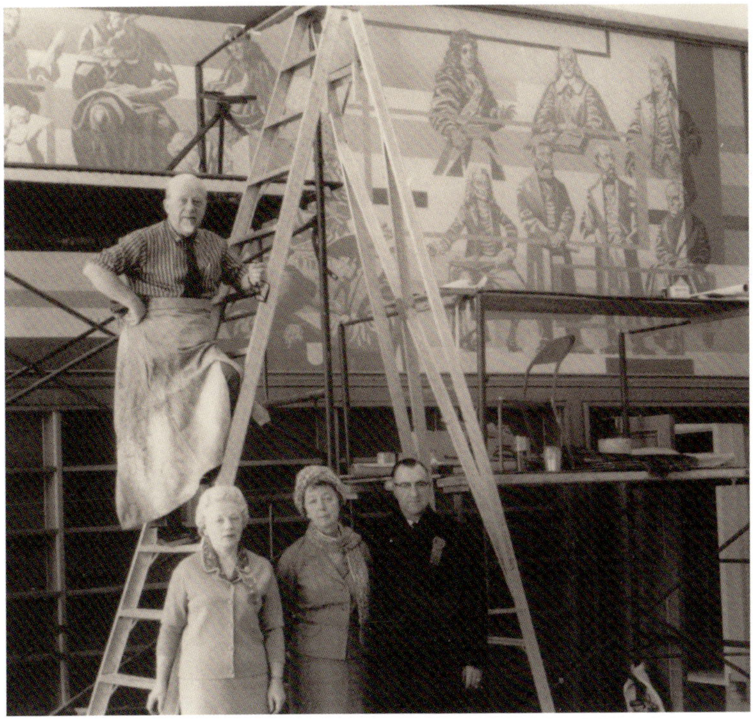

Comfort working on National Library Reading Room Murals, March 9, 1967 Charles Comfort Collection / Library and Archives Canada / e002505481

Notes

1. Comfort was the first artist appointed as Director of the National Gallery; once appointed, he omitted any mention of his commercial arts career from his resume.

2. Contract Charles Comfort and Rapid-Grip Corporation, Toronto, Nov. 28, 1929, CFC Fonds, *Correspondence* 1920–1938, box. 31.

3. Comfort "A Value for Art in Advertising," 1931, CFC Fonds, vol. 34.

4. See *The Journal Royal Architectural Institute of Canada*, (Nov.–Dec. 1926), 252.

5. See *The Journal Royal Architectural Institute of Canada* (July 1933), 132.

6. See Marylin McKay, *A National Soul: Canadian Mural Painting 1860s –1930s* (Montreal/Kingston: McGill-Queen's University Press), 2002.

7. See Laurance P. Hurlburt, *The Mexican Muralists in the United States* (Albuquerque: University of New Mexico Press, 1989).

8. See Christine Boyanoski, *The 1940s: A Decade of Painting in Ontario*, 10-19.

9. Arthur Lismer, "Mural Painting," *The Journal Royal Architectural Institute of Canada* (July 1933) 127-135.

10. Comfort used a strikingly similar spatial design with the inverted Y figure and narrative structure on both the horizontal exterior stone frieze and the eight interior vertical murals of the Toronto Stock Exchange and in the mural *Romance of Nickel*. See Rosemary Donegan "Legitimate Modernism: Charles Comfort and the Toronto Stock Exchange," *Designing the Exchange: Essays Commemorating the Opening of the Design Exchange* (Toronto: The Design Exchange, 1994) and "Mural Roots: Charles Comfort and the Toronto Stock Exchange" *Canadian Art*, vol. 4, no.2 (Summer 1987), 64-69.

11. Irvin Lutsky "Designer denies that frieze depicts a worker rip-off," *Toronto Star*, Oct. 19, 1977. Interestingly, although Comfort lived in Toronto until 1960 he did not see the interior Stock Exchange murals installed until 1977.

12. After the 1937 World's Fair, Comfort's mural the *Romance of Nickel* appears to have been rolled up and returned to the Department of Mines in Ottawa where it was stored for many years. It was first exhibited publicly in Canada in 1987 in the exhibition *Industrial Images/Images Industrielles*, Art Gallery of Hamilton, 1987. The mural is presently on long-term loan to the National Gallery of Canada.

13. See CFC Fonds, *Murals in Teaching Notes binder*, 1938–1951 file.

14. See Letter Feb. 13, 1939, CFC Fonds, vol. 60, *Vancouver Mural*, 1939–1975 file.

15. See Letter Feb. 7, 1939, CFC Fonds, vol. 60. *Vancouver Mural*, 1939–1975 file.

16. Paul Duval, "BC Mural: Sixty Feet of Progress" *Saturday Night* (Oct. 6, 1951), 31.

17. See: Karl Ann Marling *Wall-to-Wall America: A Cultural History of Post Office Murals in the Great Depression* (Minneapolis: University of Minnesota Press, 1982) in which she discusses the difficulties and complications in the process of commissioning mural designs, producing the paintings in situ and the public reception to the paintings in post offices across the United States.

18. Other major historic mural projects such as Edwin Holgate's commission for the 1939 New York World's Fair or the Orville Fischer, Paul Goranson, E.J. Hughes mural for the Golden Gate Exposition in San Francisco in 1939, celebratory in nature, were not exhibited in Canada. The one exception would be Miller Brittain's murals for the St. John Tuberculosis hospital designed in the early 1940s but never produced. Brittain examined some of the causes and effects of tuberculosis in contemporary society. See Barry Lord, *The History of Painting in Canada: Towards a People's Art* (Toronto: NC Press, 1974), 183–189. Also see forthcoming thesis by Kirk Niergarth "Art and Democracy: New Brunswick Artists and Canadian Culture between the Depression and the Cold War," University of New Brunswick, 2007.

19. "Notes re: Vancouver Hotel Mural, Mar 3, 1939," CFC Fonds, vol. 60, *Vancouver Mural* file.

20. In 1972 when the Hotel Vancouver mural was donated to the University of British Columbia, a series of heated interchanges regarding the murals historically inaccurate and stereotypical treatment of aboriginal people as subserviently kneeling at the feet of Vancouver was initiated. To avoid further controversy, the mural was later donated to the Confederation Centre for the Arts in Charlottetown, Prince Edward Island. The Dominion Bank mural *British Columbia Pageant*, recently donated to Simon Fraser University, has also been seriously criticized at public forums for its inaccurate and insensitive portrayal of First Nations peoples. It is to be the subject of a forthcoming issue of *West Coast Line* in 2007.

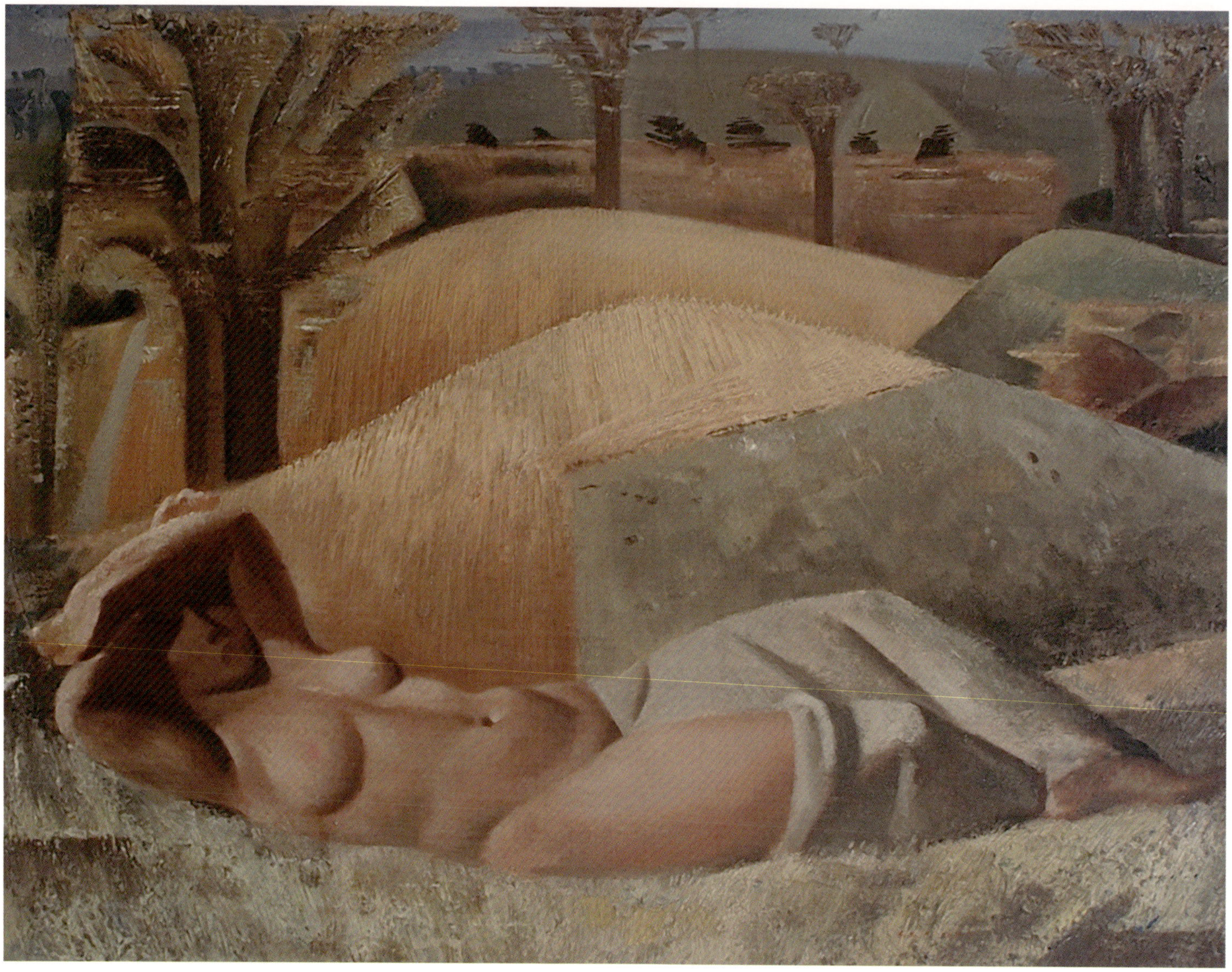

CHARLES COMFORT, **Primavera**, 1941
Oil on canvas, 60 x 75
Women's Art Association of Canada, Toronto
Photography: George Lobb

ANNA HUDSON

Charles Comfort's Moment in the Relationship of Art and Life, 1935–1945

TADOUSSAC, 1935, (CAT. 31): BLUE, SMOOTH, STILL, AND GRACEFUL. Charles Comfort worked the Saguenay village, a popular summer tourist destination, into mesmerizing visual focus. High on mescaline, a mesmerized Aldous Huxley apprehended the world through uninhibited vision. Our experience of *Tadoussac* is similarly euphoric.

Huxley, a British writer who settled in California in 1937, used psychedelic drugs to open "the doors of perception."[1] These doors were like gates to Eden, behind which, wrote Huxley, "I was seeing what Adam had seen on the morning of his creation – the miracle, moment by moment, of naked existence."[2] Comfort painted *Tadoussac* in brilliant contrast to the blindness we ordinarily experience in our busy daily lives. We tend to forget what we see. A memorable visual experience is, by comparison, full of potential meaning. Huxley's quest to regain his sight was a search for meaning in his life. His efforts parallel the working process of a visual artist like Comfort. As Herbert Read wrote:

> Aldous Huxley has recently shown that under the influence of the drug called mescalin [sic] a heightened sense of reality, of the '*isness*' of things, is induced: forms are more clearly defined, colors are more intense, etc., and this heightened sense of reality is due, according to his theory, not to an extension of normal faculties but rather to a relaxing of the inhibitions that normally reduce consciousness to manageable proportions.[3]

Read, a British philosopher of art whose work was widely published in English Canada, was careful to differentiate *isness* from the separate reality of art. Seeing, he clarified, "is the revelation or creation of an objective world, not the representation of one."[4]

The relationship of *isness* and representation frames a generation obsessed with the union of art and life. Roger Fry, an English artist and critic, described it in terms of *Vision and Design*, as he titled his influential collection of essays published in 1920. We can trace its roots to John Ruskin, William Morris, and the Arts and Crafts movement. In Canada this British tradition took hold with the Group of Seven, who visualized a self-conscious promotion of art in national life through wilderness landscapes painted during the 1920s. Charles Comfort was among those younger artists whom the Group gathered as invited contributors to their exhibitions. He was a key member of a Toronto community of painters who emerged with the formation of the Canadian Group of Painters (CGP) in Toronto in 1933. This community – including Comfort, Paraskeva Clark, and Carl Schaefer – aimed, as stated in the first CGP catalogue, "[t]o extend the creative faculty beyond the professional meaning of art and to make of it a more common language of expression...."[5] The problem, exacerbated by the economic depression, was how? How would art and life be united?

Paraskeva Clark would be sure to remind her Toronto colleagues of state support for the arts in Leningrad (now St. Petersburg), where she grew up and trained in the "Free Studios." President Roosevelt's New Deal for the Arts in the United States, set an immediate example of art operating within national life. By contrast, the misperception of art as a luxury, about which Toronto's cultural cognoscenti complained, was perhaps symptomatic of a less enlightened society. Comfort described his 1932 watercolour portrait of Carl Schaefer, *Young Canadian* (cat. 48), as "symbolic of the futility and discouragement suffered and endured during the Depression by youth of that memorable decade; it is a document recording the hopelessness and despair felt... by a whole generation...."[6] Schaefer is seated in the foreground of the painting, staring out from a farm field typical of Hanover (Ontario), his childhood home. He appears fixed on the essential order and pattern of the furrows. As Comfort noted, "Regularity in a landscape is invariably a sign of men."[7] Schaefer isolated the *isness* of the rural landscape experience in his paintings of the 1930s. Comfort emphasized the importance of visual communication and sought his own "formal idioms through which a new content might be more broadly understood."[8]

Charles and Louise Comfort celebrated their thirteenth wedding anniversary by purchasing Virginia Woolf's popular 1937 novel, *The Years*. Inside the front cover they inscribed:

From Us
to
Ourselves
after 13 years
May 22nd 1937[9]

Woolf's story of the Pargiter family sets every fact of their ordinary lives in the context of Britain's rapid social change from 1908 through the First World War until the 1930s. "No fact is too little to let slip through one's fingers," argued Woolf.[10] Comfort's meticulous diaries, which he kept throughout his life, are likewise obsessive.

Like so many writers of the interwar years, Woolf's description of "*all* of what was happening" revealed a schism between the inner self and outer life.[11] This schism, concurrently described in modern psychology, was most profoundly felt during a so-called "psychological moment."[12] In *The Years*, Woolf elicits such moments at the beginning of each of the eleven chapters, capturing the years through vivid descriptions of nature, which interrupt the otherwise banal course of daily events. And so, in 1911:

> The sun was rising. Very slowly it came up over the horizon shaking out light. But the sky was so vast, so cloudless, that to fill it with light took time.[13]

Comfort's *Tadoussac* potently represents the same incredible contradiction on which Woolf's novel turns: an intense visual experience holds time captive. Among the perpetual sequence of scenes that daily cross our vision, all too rarely does one image become a powerful extended moment. The experience, even in memory, portends an expansion of awareness. When time is stopped like this, human limits – which the Pargiter family so cogently demonstrated in Woolf's novel – are lifted to reveal the largeness of being, or as Huxley called it, the *isness*. The specifics of time and place then become irrelevant, spiritually speaking. "If the doors of perception were cleansed everything would appear to man as it is, infinite," quoted Huxley from William Blake's poem, *The Marriage of Heaven and Hell* (1790–92).

In the confusion of world war and the breakdown of religious order in Western society, secular life – the popular subject matter of the arts of the 1920s through 1950s – gathered a spiritual imperative. In anxious anticipation of a further unraveling of social and political order, the *moment* was rarefied. Woolf's character, Lady Kitty Lasswade, savours it:

> A deep murmur sang in her ears—the land itself, singing to itself, a chorus, alone. She lay there listening. She was happy, completely. Time had ceased.[14]

In 1938 Comfort pressed his painting into strict service of what Fred Housser, author of *A Canadian Art Movement: The Story of the Group of Seven*, identified in

1926 as the need "to re-plant our fields so that we may harvest food for our souls as well as for our bodies."[15] For a world on the brink of a second world war, the spiritual stakes of "a more common language of expression" were high. No artist in Toronto could avoid Paraskeva Clark's passionate appeal – made in reference to the Group of Seven – to "Come Out From Behind the Pre-Cambrian Shield." But the question remained: of what consequence is painting as a fine art?[16] "Art and the function of the artist are subjects very difficult to discuss with understanding and simplicity," reasoned Clark, who admonished her colleagues to engage their art with society. Through the CGP, in contrast to the older and stuffier Royal Canadian Academy of Arts (RCA) and the Ontario Society of Artists (OSA), the Toronto community of painters sought a contemporary relevance for the Western tradition of painting (as inherited from the Renaissance and advanced through the academies of Europe). Walter Abell, an American art educator and philosopher who was active in Canada from 1928 to 1943, explained that the key to this relevance was design.[17]

As Abell argued in his 1936 publication, *Representation and Form: A Study of Aesthetic Values in Representational Art*, an analysis of design in the art of any period of Western art reveals "ultra-pictorial bonds with current thought and feeling, bonds which we ourselves hardly recognize because they are so intimately a part of life as we accept it."[18] In his estimation an artist utilizes design to control the psychology of vision.[19] What we see and what we know, as Woolf and Huxley believed, are tied in memory. "Art is a mode of knowledge," confirmed Herbert Read, "and the world of art is a system of knowledge as valuable to man as the world of philosophy or the world of science."[20] The artist anticipates this connection and choreographs our response. This level of control worried the Montreal art critic Robert Ayre, who suspected Comfort's unfaltering hand, honed through years of commercial work at Brigdens Limited in Winnipeg and Toronto, seemed "too easy."[21] But Comfort had perfected a design sensibility through his commercial art. He mastered symbolic representations which were, in essence, broadly resonant distillations of psychological moments of *isness*. Comfort pushed the combination of symbolic design and academic painting practice in his diploma piece for the RCA, *Pioneer Survival* of 1938 (cat. 36).

The image is a reworking of the rural landscape theme, which distinguished CGP exhibitions of the 1930s and the work of Carl Schaefer in particular. Comfort echoed his colleague's isolation of the generous rhythms and patterns of farmland in southern Ontario. But the sunny balance of a rolling sweep of patterned landscape, enveloped by a generous expanse of sky, turned stormy in Comfort's hands. Paraskeva Clark had reworked Schaefer's signature rural landscape motifs more than a year earlier. The simultaneous exhibition of Clark and Schaefer's parallel images of wheat fields punctuated the 1937 CGP exhibition with a remarkable synchronicity. Artists were speaking to one another and in their visual dialogue a symbolic language emerged. When Comfort entered the painterly conversation, throwing jagged stumps into the foreground of an historic "pioneer" landscape, the language of fine art turned academic. His painting gained authority by referencing the history of art in Canada. Images of pioneer life in Ontario by Homer Watson, the president of the RCA from 1918–1922, were equally dramatic evocations of Ontario's past. Comfort's self-conscious reference to his predecessor was made in deference to tradition and to a gathering interest in the discipline of art history. When Comfort began teaching in the Department of Fine Art at the University of Toronto, he emboldened his painting with canonicity. *Pioneer Survival* introduced academic rigor into the design of a painting. The psychological moment therein approached cognition of the *isness* of art.

In 1938 Comfort stayed in Toronto to teach mural design and historical techniques instead of taking a more lucrative commercial art job in the United States. The decision, he explained, would allow more time to paint. But he struggled for job security and adequate pay for contractual teaching at the Ontario College of Art and the University of Toronto. Only in 1946 after the war, when he returned from duty as an official Canadian War Artist with the Canadian Army, did the university hire Comfort on faculty as an Associate Professor in the newly amalgamated Department of Art and Archeology. The forty-six year old artist developed his practical courses to complement the study of art history. Since his early thirties, Comfort had been expanding his professional network to include art historians. John Alford, a Courtauld graduate and the founding Chair of Fine Arts at the University of Toronto in 1934, whom Comfort valued as a friend, and Peter Brieger, an art historian trained in Germany whom the university hired in 1936, guided the artist's study of art history.[22] Just before the war broke out in 1939, Alford and Brieger plotted Comfort's extended trip through Italy, with shorter stops in Paris and London.[23] Comfort consumed the iconic works of Western art history along with the food, wine, and accommodations, knowing that an impending war would destroy so much art and architecture. Only memory would preserve his experience.

Art history is the collective memory of art. Comfort's thinking about his role in society evolved alongside the development of art history as a discipline in Canada, led by the University of Toronto. He considered the value of art education, which Arthur Lismer of the Group of Seven famously established as a prerogative of the Art Gallery of Toronto. Comfort would "encourage a respect for western culture which is the very basis of the western democratic way of life."[24]

> Art as a way of thinking and as a human conception has never been a more inspiring, a more helpful, yes a more salutary function in life than it is to-day.[25]

In the context of the German novelist Thomas Mann's above quote, from the 1942 CGP exhibition catalogue, Comfort's *Primavera* is a humanist painting. Humanism in the twentieth-century might be best understood as an intellectual idealism that uniformly swept up artists, writers, philosophers, and even scientists in the allied countries – Canada, the United States and Britain – between 1920 and 1950. While every self-proclaimed humanist, it seems, held individual views, humanists in general feared Fascism, Communism, and Nazism as anti-democratic ideologies. Many humanists of this period were spiritual but incredulous of religion. They recognized how dramatically theories of evolution opposed art and science. Above all, humanists believed in education and on building knowledge from the foundation of human history. Art history, as a discipline within the humanities, thus found its place as a humanist field of study and Comfort's refashioning in *Primavera* of Titian's fifteenth-century *Venus of Urbino*, evoked the Italian Renaissance as a cultural fountainhead.

In *Primavera* Venus strikes a casual pose in the rolling fields of an Italian *campagna*. She is unmistakably a work of art, more stone than flesh, manifesting for Comfort a democratic cultural legacy. Her future, however, seems imperiled. In Comfort's original version of the painting,[26] wheat stooks morph into tanks advancing through the Italian countryside. *Primavera* pictures the reality of cultural destruction Comfort feared. His art inspires action with a prescient call to arms, extended in the spirit of humanism, for the protection of Western civilization. As the British writer and philosopher Bertrand Russell passionately avowed, art comes to life when "a sense of the whole human race as one cooperative unit" supersedes national, let alone individual, identity.[27] Comfort was tapping into an imagined international cultural community.

Imagine thirty years of insecurity, "of anxious and pessimistic uncertainty" as the American philosopher John Dewey described the outcome of the First World War.[28] "Our world is a mad world," claimed Russell. "Ever since 1914 it has ceased to be constructive." For North Americans like Comfort the problem was intensified by the lack of an "instinctive sense of the community which exists in the older countries."[29] In his search for that union of art and life which would solidify civilization, Herbert Read found Jungian theory. He explored Jungian archetypes and collective, hereditable patterns of perception which shape our perception of reality.[30] These patterns, Read discovered, were embedded in art. Comfort tested the extent to which symbols enriched by art historical reference afforded a more common or archetypal language of expression. He was playing with fire; he risked cliché. If forms in art are significant by virtue of their archetypal quality, and therefore of fixed or predetermined meaning, is the art not rendered pedantic?[31]

The difference between art and advertising or propaganda, which vexed artists and writers between 1920 and 1950, boiled down to the question of freedom – of expression and of interpretation. The experience of art should retain something of that euphoric psychological moment when one inexplicably communes with the universal. For the American philosopher of art Susanne Langer who published *Philosophy in a New Key* in 1942, "familiar signs and abbreviated symbols have to be supported by a vast intellectual structure in order to function so smoothly that we are almost unaware of them...."[32] Once "exhumed from stock of our buried knowledge" this language of art presents an intellectual game which operates enigmatically. The idea fit comfortably with the goal of the Department of Art and Archaeology at the University of Toronto "to teach the student a vocabulary of expression." Comfort's practice demonstrated its operation.

Langer spoke of our need to share "a few, historic, 'charged' symbols that have about the same wealth of meaning for everybody." She also identified the dearth of such symbols in an increasingly fragmented modern world.[33] Comfort's decision to mine the history of art for the footings of what Langer called "mental anchorage" was self-conscious.[34] Could he invest old forms with "that rich, confused, historic accretion of meanings" described by Langer? Would he succeed in recreating those charged symbols "to which we seem to respond instinctively"?[35] A driving need for a united front during the Second World War urged artists in both Allied and Axis countries towards symbolism. Comfort embraced the role of a cultural soldier defending democracy. In 1945, as an official war artist, he completed *Canadian Armour Passing Through Ortona*. Rolling fields are here replaced by the heaps of rubble, representing the destroyed buildings at Piazza Plebiscito in Naples. The admonishing *putti* in the bottom foreground of the painting is "Art" reminding us of our history. The tank at the left signals the present.

Mircea Eliade, a controversial religious historian of Comfort's generation, charged "the *completely* profane world, the wholly desacralized cosmos, is a recent discovery in the history of the human spirit."[36] The schism of inner self and outer life about which psychologists obsessed, manifest in the separation of art and life, was for Eliade the simple fact of a loss of faith. The result was our singular experience of secular time, which passed into unrecoverable history with existential anguish. Sacred time, by comparison, circled to link the past, present and future in a state of universal oneness. How close this comes to explaining that rarefied psychological moment by which writers and artists gave meaning – symbolically – to ordinary life. The moment of war could hardly merit the same veneration. As Eleanor Pargiter concluded in Woolf's novel:

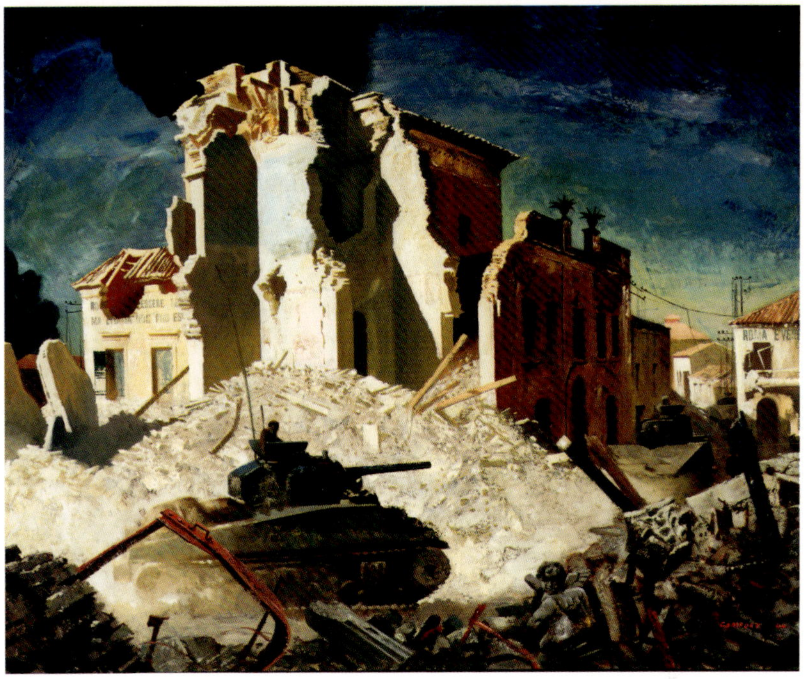

CHARLES COMFORT, Canadian Armour Passing Through Ortona,
November 1944, Oil on canvas, 102 x 121.9
Beaverbrook Collection of War Art, Canadian War Museum, 19710261-2152

> There must be another life, she thought, sinking back into her chair, exasperated. Not in dreams; but here and now.... There must be another life, here and now, she repeated. This is too short, too broken. We know nothing, even about ourselves.... she wanted to enclose the present moment; to make it stay; to fill it fuller and fuller, with the past, the present and the future, until it shone, whole, bright, deep with understanding.[37]

Between 1935 and 1945, from *Tadoussac* to *Canadian Armour Passing Through Ortona*, Comfort invited viewers into an increasingly self-conscious contemplation about art and its relationship to life. In his search for a more common language of expression, his art grew steadily symbolic and, as a result, self-referential. Perhaps art and life were driven further apart as a result. The art historian R.H. Wilenski anticipated as much in 1927. After all, he explained, "The modern movement is based not on service to religion but on service to a consciously-held idea of art."[38]

Notes

1. "If the doors of perception were cleansed everything would appear to man as it is, infinite." William Blake, *The Marriage of Heaven and Hell* (1790–92), as quoted in Aldous Huxley, *The Doors of Perception*, (London: Chatto & Windus Ltd., 1954), 6.

2. Aldous Huxley, *The Doors of Perception*, (1954; rpt. London: Granada Publications Limited/Panther Books, 1977), 15.

3. Herbert Read, *Icon and Idea: The function of art in the development of human consciousness*, (London: Faber and Faber, 1955), 130.

4. *Ibid*, 130.

5. "Foreword," *Catalogue of an Exhibition of Paintings by [the] Canadian Group of Painters* (Toronto: Canadian Group of Painters, 1933), unpaginated.

6. "Three hundred years of Canadian art", Lecture III — The Twentieth Century: 1900–1950, National Gallery of Canada, May 2, 1967, CFC Fonds, Vol.2.

7. *Teaching Notes* Binder: "Camouflage" 1942, CFC Fonds, Vol.5.

8. "1929 marks the end of an important phase in Canadian art," stated Comfort. "Art is obviously not always a direct and simple reflection of society or social events, but no matter how purely aesthetic the result, it remains always a social phenomenon. The depression was a cataclysmic economic event which affected social relationships and, consequently, the relationship of art and society." *Speech: Montreal Arts Club, 50th Anniversary Banquet*, May 12, 1962, CFC Fonds, Vol.2.

9. Inscription in Charles and Louise Comfort's copy of: Virginia Woolf, *The Years*, London: Hogarth Press, 1937. SCS1 COMF1 W66 1937, National Gallery of Canada Library and Archives, Ottawa.

10. Virginia Woolf, *The Common Reader*, 95; as quoted in, C.E.M. Joad, *Guide to Modern Thought*, (1933; rpt. London: Faber and Faber, 1948), 246.

11. "The inner life," wrote Joad – who was well known for his participation in the BBC wartime broadcast, *Brain's Trust*, "it is increasingly realized, may be more important than the outer, and the strife between conflicting elements in the same person more vivid than strife between persons." Joad, 244

12. According to Joad, who explored the relationship of modern psychology to contemporary literature, the inner life of thought and feeling was paramount; hence, the true subject of the novelist is the "stuff" of psychology. The truth about life, he continued, is to be found neither in a biography, nor in the contents of a mind, nor in its development, nor even in a psychological mood, "but in a psychological moment." Here's where modern psychology makes itself felt for "an individual is not, when you examine him, a personality at all, he is merely a succession of fleeting persons, each of whom endures for a psychological moment." Joad, 249–251.

13. Virginia Woolf, *The Years*, (1937; rpt. London: The Hogarth Press, 1979), 206.

14. *Ibid*, 300.

15. Fred Housser, *A Canadian Art Movement: The Story of the Group of Seven*, (Toronto: The Macmillan Company of Canada Limited, 1926), 32–33.

16. Paraskeva Clarke [sic] (as told to G. Campbell McInnes), "Come Out From Behind the Pre-Cambrian Shield," *New Frontier* 1 (April 1937), 16.

17. Abell argued that design was the "one quality so important in art that an understanding of it could be called a 'key' to art." Walter Abell, "A Key to Art: summary of a lecture," Carnegie Corporation – Individuals: Abell, Walter (1934–1937), Box 296, file 13 – 7.4c, National Gallery of Canada Library and Archives, Ottawa.

18. Walter Abell, *Representation and Form: A Study of Aesthetic Values in Representational Art*, (New York: Charles Scribner's Sons, 1936), 102.

19. Abell labeled a perfected design in art "representational form." Form, he explained, is not essentially tangible or physical or plastic in its nature. "It is rather a life informing a body, an organizing principle which brings elements into significant relationship with each other. Its beauty results from the quality of the relationship rather than from the nature of the elements related." "Such form [representational form] alone is capable of pressing formal beauty to the maximum range and richness attainable in the visual arts." Walter Abell, 165.

20. Herbert Read, *Art and Society*, 3d ed. rev. (1936; London: Faber and Faber, 1956), 7.

21. Robert Ayre, "Canadian Art Series: Charles Fraser Comfort, RCA," undated manuscript, CFC Fonds, Vol. 54.

22. See: E. Lisa Panayotidis, "The Department of Fine Art at the University of Toronto, 1926–1945 – Institutionalizing the 'Culture of the Aesthetic'," *Journal of Canadian Art History*, XXV (2004), 100-121.

23. Comfort left for Europe on May 12, 1939 from New York, landing in Italy and traveling on to Spain, Switzerland, Paris and Normandy before returning to New York on June 26. *Travel Journal (Europe) 1939*, CFC Fonds, Vol.1.

24. "In studying the art of the past and the present," added Comfort in 1948, "the student is made to understand the function of the arts in human life." *Teaching Notes: University of Toronto*. 1946–59, "Talk on Department of Art and Archaeology — 20 October 1948," CFC Fonds Vol.5.

25. Thomas Mann (1875–1955), as quoted in the catalogue foreword, *Canadian Group of Painters* (Toronto: Art Gallery of Toronto, 1942), 3.

26. Comfort repainted *Primavera* in 1972. The later version of the painting is in this exhibition.

27. Russell described "the cultivation of a vivid sense of citizenship of the world," as the most vital need. Bertrand Russell, *Education and the Social Order*, (1932; rpt. London: Unwin Paperbacks, 1977), 19.

28. John Dewey, *Reconstruction in Philosophy*, (1920; rpt. New York: Mentor Books, 1950), 8.

29. Russell, 152.

30. David Thistlewood, *Herbert Read – Formlessness and Form: An introduction to his aesthetics*, (London: Routledge & Kegan Paul,1984), xiii.

31. Read gave this paradox a lot of thought during the 1950s. Archetypes, he reasoned, were undoubtedly "indispensable as social condensers," but ineffective if deliberately employed. Picasso's 1937 painting, *Guernica*, exemplified how an artist's handling or *facture* kept archetypal forms from becoming outmoded and therein losing their aesthetic appeal. Thistlewood, 153–154.

32. Susanne K. Langer, *Philosophy in a New Key: A Study of the Symbolism of Reason, Rite, and Art*, 3rd ed. (1942; rpt. Cambridge, Mass: Harvard University Press, 1957), 281.

33. In modern civilization there are two great threats to mental security: the new mode of living, "which has made old nature-symbols alien to our minds, and the new mode of working, which makes personal activities meaningless,..."Langer, 291.

34. "If we are able to look upon tradition as successful experiment," explained Comfort in 1949, "it becomes a living element in our creative work, living because it is ever changing and growing, and because its change and growth are our own." Charles Comfort, "Painting: An Essay Prepared for the Royal Commission on National Development in the Arts, Letters, and Sciences, 1949–51," 414; CFC Fonds, Vol.8.

35. Langer, 287–288.

36. Mircea Eliade, *The Sacred and the Profane: The Nature of Religion*, trans. Willard R. Trask (1957; New York: Harcourt Brace Jovanovich, 1959), 13.

37. Woolf, *The Years*, 461–462.

38. R.H. [Reginald Howard] Wilenski, *The Modern Movement in Art*, (New York: Frederick A. Stokes Company, 1927), 51–52.

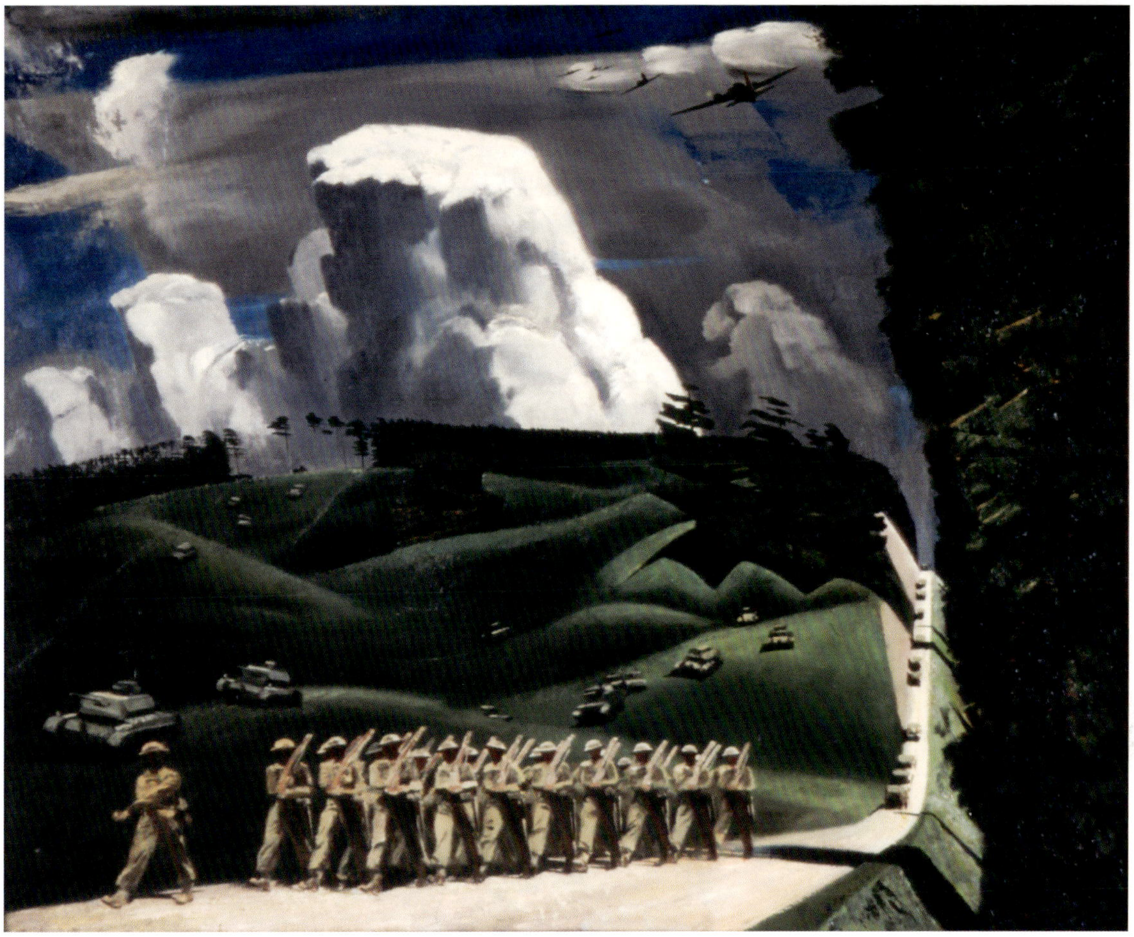

55. **Ontario Summer**, 1940

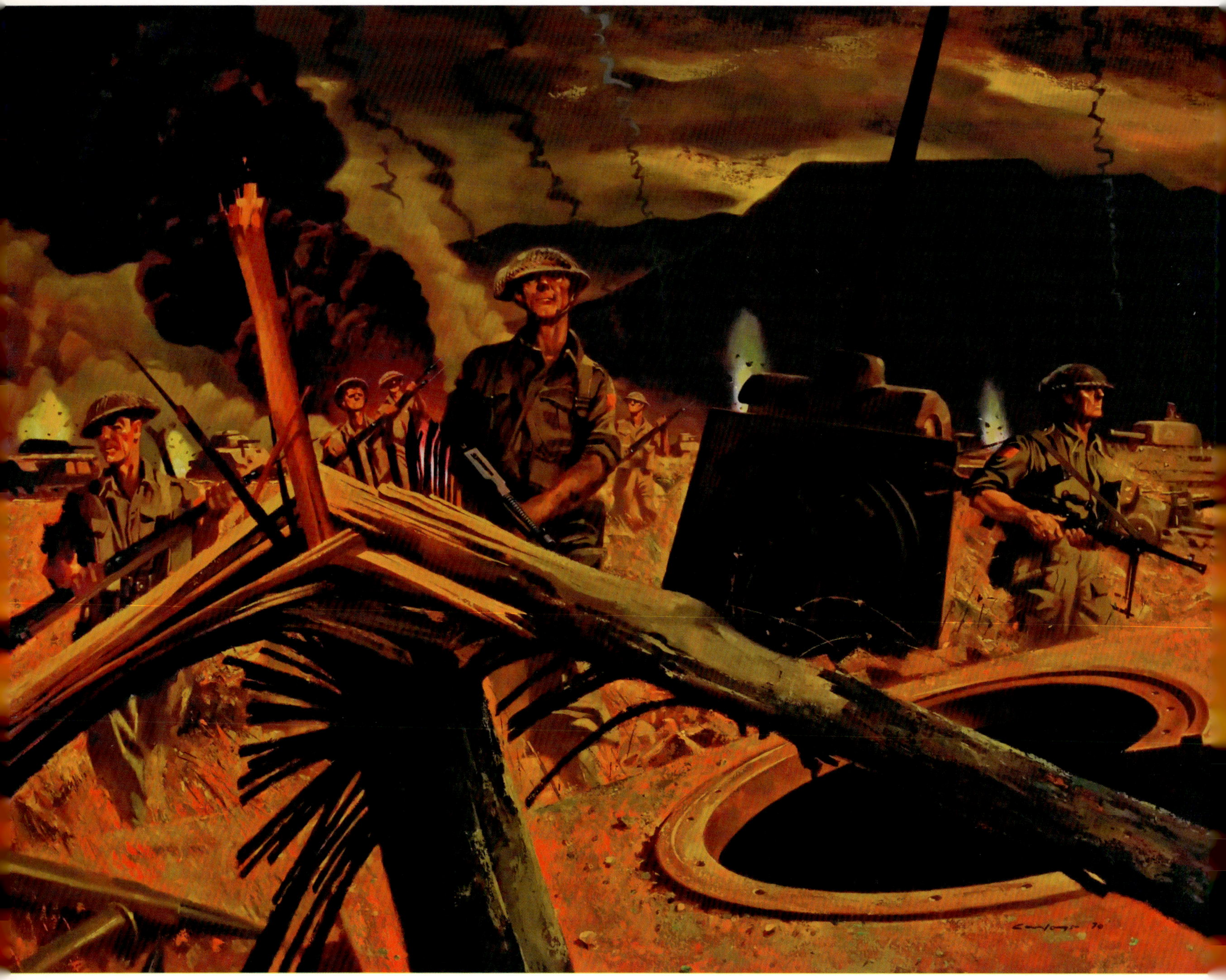

69. **Hitler Line II**, 1944/1970

LAURA BRANDON

Veracity and Expectation in Charles Comfort's War Art, 1940–48: The Hitler Line in Perspective

ONE OF THE MOST RECOGNIZED IMAGES of Canadian involvement in the Second World War is Charles Comfort's *The Hitler Line* (1944).[1] He considered it his best work.[2] An approximately one metre-square canvas, it depicts a group of Canadian soldiers in Italy moving forward in a fiery-hued landscape of hills, smashed trees, destroyed artillery, and billowing black smoke. The scene is carefully composed. The foreground third of the canvas is marked by a destroyed so-called *panzerturm* (here with its gun replaced by a large black hole in a piece of rusted metal), and a horizontal splintered tree trunk, whose innards fan out like dark palm fronds against the garish red-orange middle third of the painting.[3] In this section, six men progress diagonally in a line across the width of the composition. Behind them, an almost black mountain peak dominates the background third of the picture. Two vertical elements also divide the painting in three. On the left, the base of the shattered tree links with smoke from a conflagration of some kind in the middle ground. To the right, a vertical *panzerturm* dissects the canvas. Further a grey and a white plume of smoke emphasizes the work's vertical construction.

The figurative elements are curiously delineated. The six soldiers are expressionless, sometimes almost faceless, with steel-helmeted heads perched on long necks atop gun-toting muscular bodies. Robot-like, they are curiously unbelievable as human beings in an otherwise believable war-torn landscape. The reason for their alien appearance sheds light not only on one problem associated with depicting war in general, but also on Charles Comfort's own approach to war art.

Quite clearly, this painting was composed the way it was to create an impact on viewers. The breaking of the Hitler Line in May 1944 was, after all, a significant Canadian achievement that was worthy of recognition.[4] The government used the artwork almost immediately in a poster designed to encourage support for the 8th Victory Bond campaign.[5] Four years later, influential military historian C. P. Stacey included it in his book *The Canadian Army* (1948) and posited that the soldier in front was the section leader.[6] In 1970 Comfort agreed to copy it for a soldier-friend who had participated in the battle. It is this copy that is included in the current exhibition (cat. 69).[7] More recently, it was used as the Second World War chapter-heading illustration in *Canvas of War: Painting the Canadian Experience* (2000).[8] These are only a few examples of its many appearances since it was originally painted.

It is important to note, however, that *The Hitler Line* is not a carefully observed scene completed in the field of conflict. Rather, it is a studio work. The violent circumstances of battle that comprise the image rule out any basis in a contemporary field sketch as well. But Comfort was there on the

23rd and 24th of May 1944. He listened to eyewitness reports during the battle, he heard the noise of conflict, and he visited the battlefield afterwards. He recorded what he learned, what he saw, and what he heard in his war diary.[9] An examination of this document and an analysis of some aspects of the official Second World War art program, in the context of the times, help to explain Comfort's approach to *The Hitler Line*. This exploration also raises an important question about war art: is the perceived veracity of an image predicated on observation or expectation?

Comfort, like many of his peers, depicted military subjects long before there was an official program. Based on his 1939–1943 experience as an infantry rifle instructor with the University of Toronto's Canadian Officer Training Corps, *Ontario Summer, 1940* (cat. 55) is the same size as *The Hitler Line* and depicts troops moving through a bucolic landscape of green trees below billowing white clouds. The military content is almost incidental: a postscript to the picturesque essay on nature in summer. Just over two years later, in February 1943, the Canadian War Records Committee (CWRC) hired Comfort as an official war artist attached to the Army. (He was discharged in July 1946). Formally established in January 1943, the Ottawa-based committee consisted of National Gallery director H. O. McCurry and senior military personnel from the three services.[10] Recognized mature artists, including Comfort, advised the group. In this capacity Comfort drew up a recommended list of required artist supplies based on the production requirements outlined in the instructions that CWRC gave newly appointed artists. In Britain, High Commissioner Vincent Massey was the guiding light; senior officers in the services handled the mechanics of the program.

The CWRC hired thirty-two official war artists who received officer rank, pay, supplies, and instructions. The committee divided them approximately evenly between the three services. The instructions they received when first appointed suggest they had little room to manœuvre from an artistic point of view.[11] "The intention is that your productions shall be worthy of Canada's highest cultural traditions, doing justice to History, and as works of art, worthy of exhibition anywhere at any time."

The directions specified the size and quantity of the paintings as well as their subjects. In the field, the artists sketched the equipment, vehicles, uniforms, machines, and the men and women who looked after them. Battle scenes were extremely rare. Larger watercolour paintings were done in the field and also away from battle. The time, date, location, event, or the names of the units depicted were carefully noted on the back of the works. Historical officers attached to the same units as the artists assessed the compositions for accuracy and any breach of censorship requirements before the pieces were forwarded to headquarters in London. Once the war in Europe was over, the artists were sent back to Canada, where they were provided with studio space to complete a predetermined number of canvases based on watercolours that they had produced in London.

For the most part, the artists, trained in a landscape-painting tradition, were poorly equipped to deal pictorially with the reality of war. Thus Comfort's large and dramatic painting *Campobasso* (cat. 67),[12] which is based on his initial experiences in Italy, perhaps says more about his appreciation for the landscapes of the Renaissance artist Giovanni Bellini, than it does about his interest in the Canadian Army. It also explains why an artist with an extensive art-history teaching background but no overseas military service, found it difficult to escape military expectations for stirring scenes of drama and heroism, as opposed to his own eyes, when it came to war art.

Comfort served initially in England, where he depicted scenes in West Sussex at Selsey on the south coast. Much like the woodenness of *Ontario Summer, 1940*, the staged feeling of the parted camouflage netting revealing the gun beyond in *Bofors Gun Site in a Field* (cat. 56) demonstrates how compositional balance took precedence over the military content for Comfort. A few months later, he was in Cornwall, where the Royal Canadian Engineers were building airstrips in preparation for the invasion of Europe the following year. St. Eval, whose church he depicted (cat. 57), was their base. *Sappers Quarrying* (cat. 58) is the preliminary watercolour for *Sappers Drilling in Preparation for Secondary Blasting* (cat. 59). In this latter composition, the artist focused on the two figures in the foreground, providing them with a muscularity and purpose not apparent in the watercolour sketch. This figural style aligns this work with the approach he had adopted in his murals of the previous decade.

Based on the evidence of his watercolours from October 1943 in Italy, Comfort continued to search for an effective means to depict what he was seeing and what he was expected to record. He first visited the battlefield at Casa Berardi, scene of an important battle on 14 December 1943. In *Battle Scene (Fantasy)* (cat. 60) he lets the paint fly; his gestural application of watercolour evokes an imagined action-scene of anti-aircraft fire and exploding bombs in combination. *Battlefield near Berardi Crossroads* (cat. 61) could be the same location; certainly it is close by. However in this case, the two crosses to the left of the composition, the static quality of the trees, and more distant explosions imply that here the battle is over. Following the vicious battle for Ortona on the Adriatic coast of December 21 to 27, 1943, Comfort applied himself to depicting the consequences of the successful Canadian-led assault on the town four months later. In *Wrecked Buildings, Ortona* (cat. 62), he used the same trio of vertical and horizontal elements that he later implemented in *The Hitler Line* to construct his composition. In *San Pietro in Vaticano*, painted after the Canadians helped liberate Rome on 4 June 1944, Comfort downplayed the military content to a frieze that contrasts with the stunning beauty of Bernini's *Triumph of the Cathedra Petri* (1657), depicted above it. He constructed similar frieze-like compositions in *Ontario Summer* and *Campobasso*.

On a return visit to the Hitler Line, Comfort painted the compelling *Dead German on the Hitler Line* (cat. 63). Depicting the dead was not something war artists often did. On the back of the watercolour, Comfort noted, "I am not given to painting lugubrious subjects of this kind, but at least one horror picture is not inept (sic) in this situation."

His preferred subjects were, in fact, portraits of the living, as in the extraordinary *Sergeant P. J. Ford* (cat. 66), whose deep blue eyes speak about long years of war-weariness. Two weeks earlier, Comfort had painted himself (cat. 64), but without the weapon he provided Ford. Comfort looks at us; Ford looks away. It was not until 1948 that the now civilian artist completed his portrait of fellow war artist Will Ogilvie, perhaps his greatest friend (cat. 68) Here, the landscape of the Sicilian countryside, which Ogilvie documented as a war artist in 1943, frames the uniformed portrait of the soldier-artist, the two here indelibly linked and the gaze neither engaged nor disengaged in relation to the viewer, but a combination of the two.

The paintings, as discussed above, demonstrate that Comfort's compositional interests took precedence over military subject matter, except when it came to depicting people, whom he portrayed sympathetically and directly for the most part. There can be no doubt, however, that the artist was a finely tuned visual witness to the war. His meticulous diaries attest to acute powers of observation. This is apparent in his record of the breaking of the Hitler Line. Familiar with the battlefield (he had reconnoitered it the day before from a distance) he wrote from nearby on 23 May 1944: "Drama upon drama has been affected this afternoon. Faced with the insurmountable obstacles of 96 tks. [tanks] we continued to press across the AQUILO – PONTECORVO Rd. Apparently we had not enough infantry to protect this mass of armour."[13]

During the early hours of the next day he noted that "Heavy ack ack [anti-aircraft] fire roused me at 0310 hrs. I looked out to see the night brilliant with German flares. ... The flak was intense. The sky seemed full of aircraft, the stars paled behind the amazing red fire play of thousands of tracer shells."[14]

Later that day he recorded that "The destruction of trees in full foliage leaves a more sinister impression than those wracked in winter. No tree, shrub, or bush along this road has escaped. They are striped[sic], shorn, and shattered."

Add to this a later comment from his published war diary regarding an upright gun, and the necessary content for *The Hitler Line* has all been carefully taken on board. "One gun created a fantastic sight, sticking perpendicularly up into the air, like a gigantic pylon memorializing the disasters of war. A direct hit had detonated its magazine, the resulting blast tearing the whole turret from its casement and tossing it in the air. There it was, a vast, inert steel probe, blindly challenging the heavens."[15] Comfort also sketched the gun.[16] Notably absent in his documents are depictions of fighting soldiers. Comfort did not see them on the battlefield and one can only assume he was told of the acts of heroism and sheer stoicism. From these stories he no doubt imagined the soldiers in *The Hitler Line*. He certainly had no personal experience of battle. As he remarked in a 1977 interview, "I didn't go in with the troops, non-combatants were not permitted in action areas."[17]

Context must also be taken into account. Comfort knew he was a spectator to important events and that, as an official war artist, he was responsible for capturing the nature of these events in paint. The men who surrounded him and history itself told him that it was the soldiers who counted. What he saw and heard for himself, however, was not men in action but the power of technology. It is the tension between what he saw and what he was expected to portray that creates the friction in *The Hitler Line* and accounts for the curious lack of believable humanity in so many other works. It is only recently that war historians such as the Australian Robin Prior have emphasized the argument that war is about technology and not people. He writes that "all the virtues of the warrior – courage, persistence, morale, physical prowess – count for nothing in the face of unsubdued firepower."[18]

As his diaries and many watercolour sketches attest, Comfort witnessed the Second World War version of this firepower and its consequences on the battlefield. Depicting the humanity of war, he painted portraits of soldiers behind the lines, or after they were long dead. In *The Hitler Line* he was unable to portray the event without including the presence of the infantry as leading players, hence their inclusion. In so doing, he produced a popular work of art that met commonly held expectations about the nature of battle, but minimized his own experience of it. Furthermore, he laid his art open to criticism as a document of history even if, as art, it exceeded expectation.

Notes

1. Charles Comfort, *The Hitler Line*, 1944, oil on canvas, 101.6 x 121.7 cm, Beaverbrook Collection of War Art, Canadian War Museum, (#19710261–2203).

2. Joan Murray interview with Comfort, 14.

3. The *panzerturm* was a tank turret with a gun mounted on a concrete base, which the Germans used defensively in the war.

4. See Daniel G. Dancocks, *The D-Day Dodgers: The Canadians in Italy, 1943–1945* (Toronto: McClelland and Stewart, 1991).

5. Charles Comfort, *They Also Buy Victory Bonds*, 1945, offset lithograph on wove paper, Library and Archives Canada (# 1994–210–114). When the National Defense Headquarters in Ottawa requested to use the painting it was on exhibit at the National Gallery, London. E. T. Heathcote, *Weekly Progress Report* (1 Feb. 1945), Library and Archives Canada, RG 24, vol. 20, 299, file 937.013 (D1).

6. C. P. Stacey, *The Canadian Army, 1939–1945* (Ottawa: King's Printer, 1948), 140.

7. It was painted in 1970 at the request of Albert E. Shepherd who was a chancellor at the University of Western Ontario. During sittings for his official portrait painted by Comfort, he had expressed an interest in obtaining his own copy of *The Hitler Line*.

8. Dean F. Oliver and Laura Brandon, *Canvas of War: Painting the Canadian Experience* (Vancouver: Douglas and McIntyre, 2000), 72–3.

9. Comfort's war diaries are in CFC Fonds, vol. 36, files 6–12.

10. For more detailed information see Laura Brandon, *Art or Memorial? The Forgotten History of Canada's War Art* (Calgary: University of Calgary Press, 2006).

11. The instructions are reprinted in full in *Art or Memorial?*.

12. Campobasso was captured in late October 1943.

13. *War Diaries*, CFC Fonds, vol. 36, file 9, 23 May 1944.

14. *War Diaries*, 24 May 1944.

15. Charles Comfort, *Artist at War*, 2nd. ed. (Pender Island, B.C.: Log House Books, 1995), 134. This gun is also visible in Canadian Army Newsreel 33, Library and Archives Canada, J. P. Rigby fonds, 1973–0162/33109.

16. Charles Comfort, *Destroyed Panzerturm, Hitler Line*, 21 June 1944, watercolour on paper, Beaverbrook Collection of War Art, Canadian War Museum (# 19710261–2182).

17. Murray interview, 4.

18. Robin Prior, "The Heroic Image of the Warrior in the First World War," *War and Society* (Sept. 23, 2005), 21.

WORKS OF ART

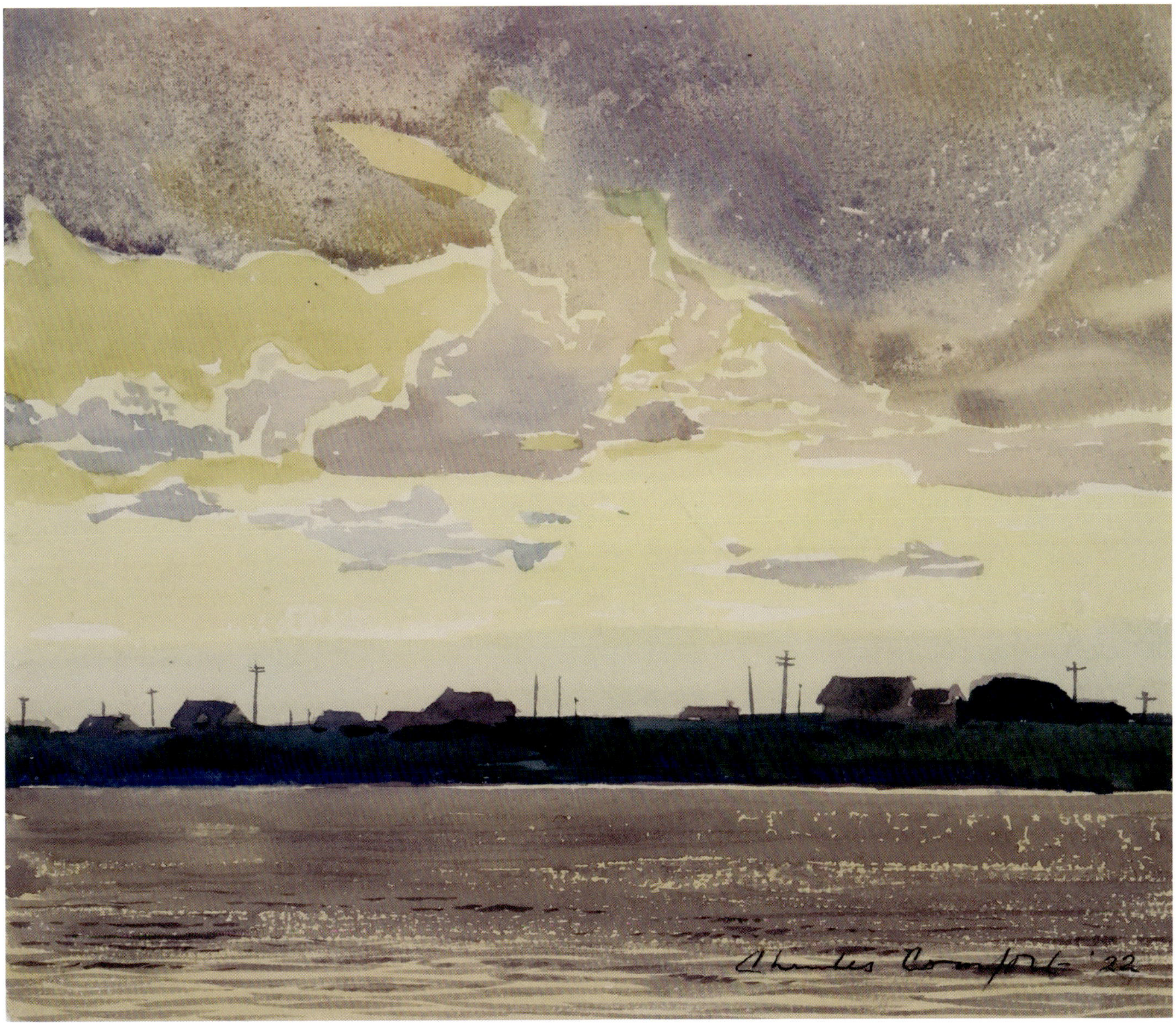

1. **Kildonan Skyline Across the Red**, 1922

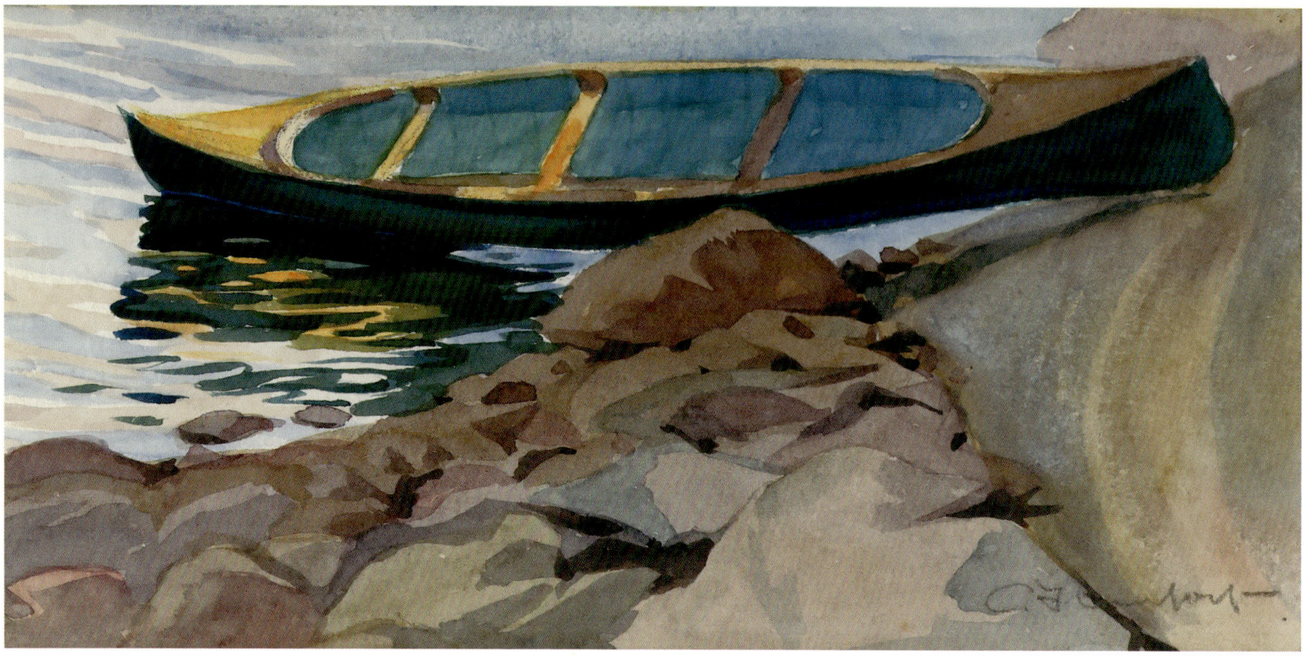

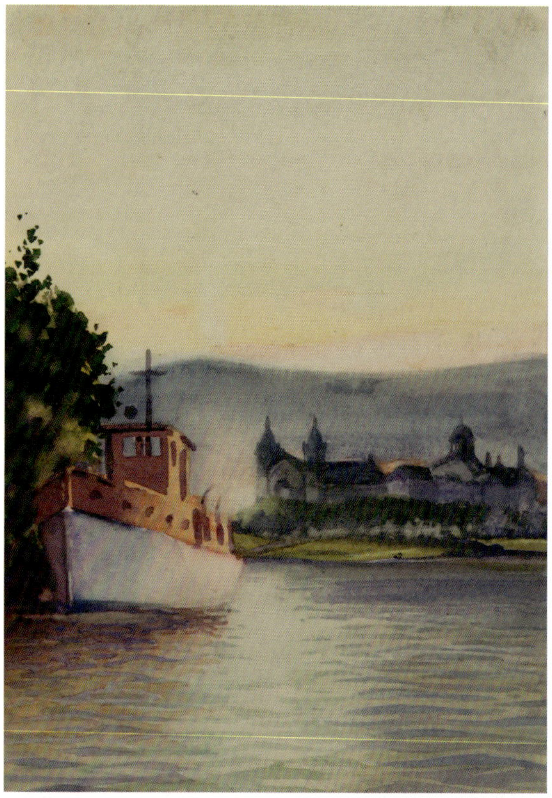

2. **Green Canoe**, 1922 | 4. **Red River and the St. Boniface Cathedral**, c.1923 | 3. **New York**, 1923

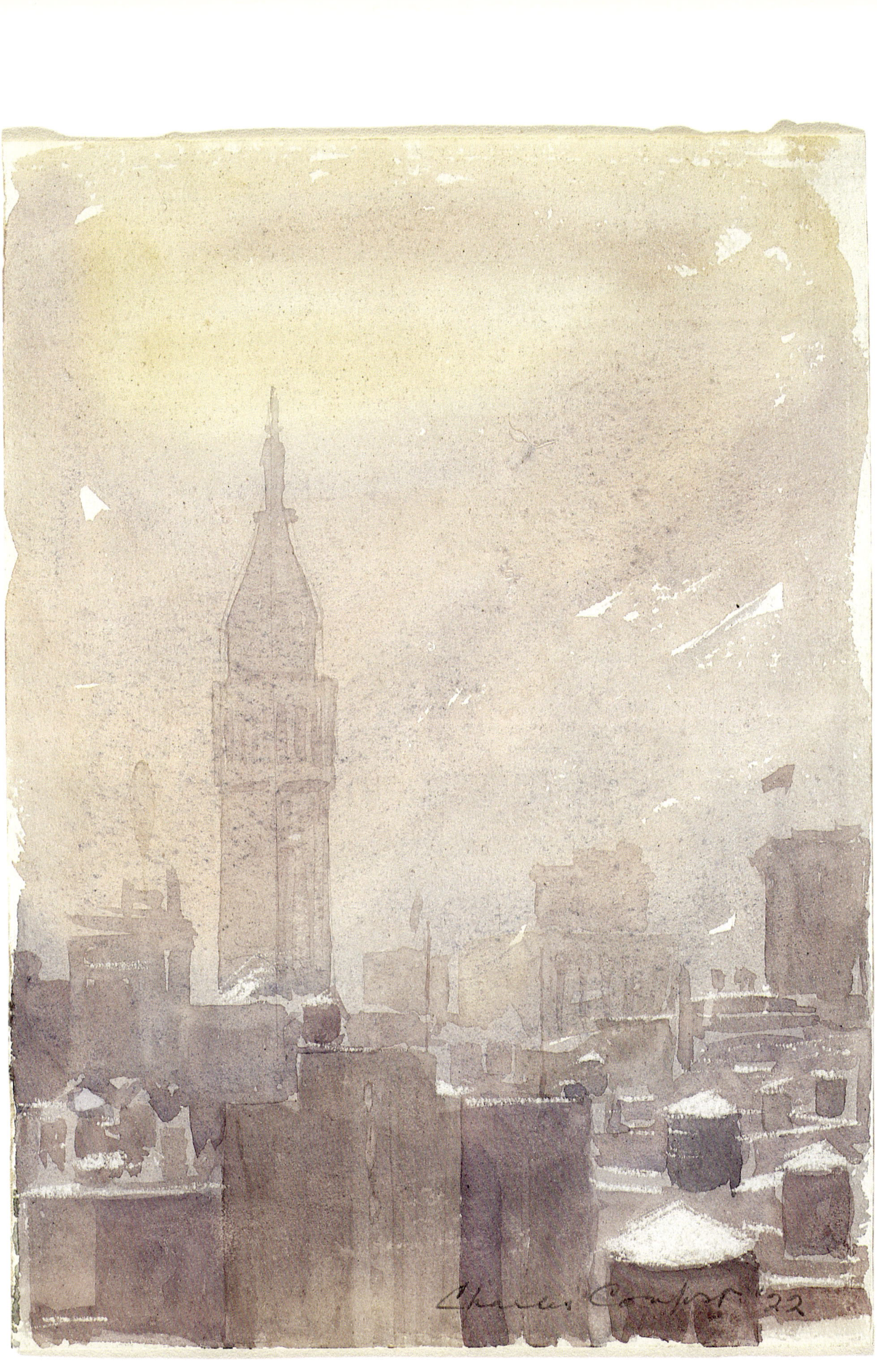

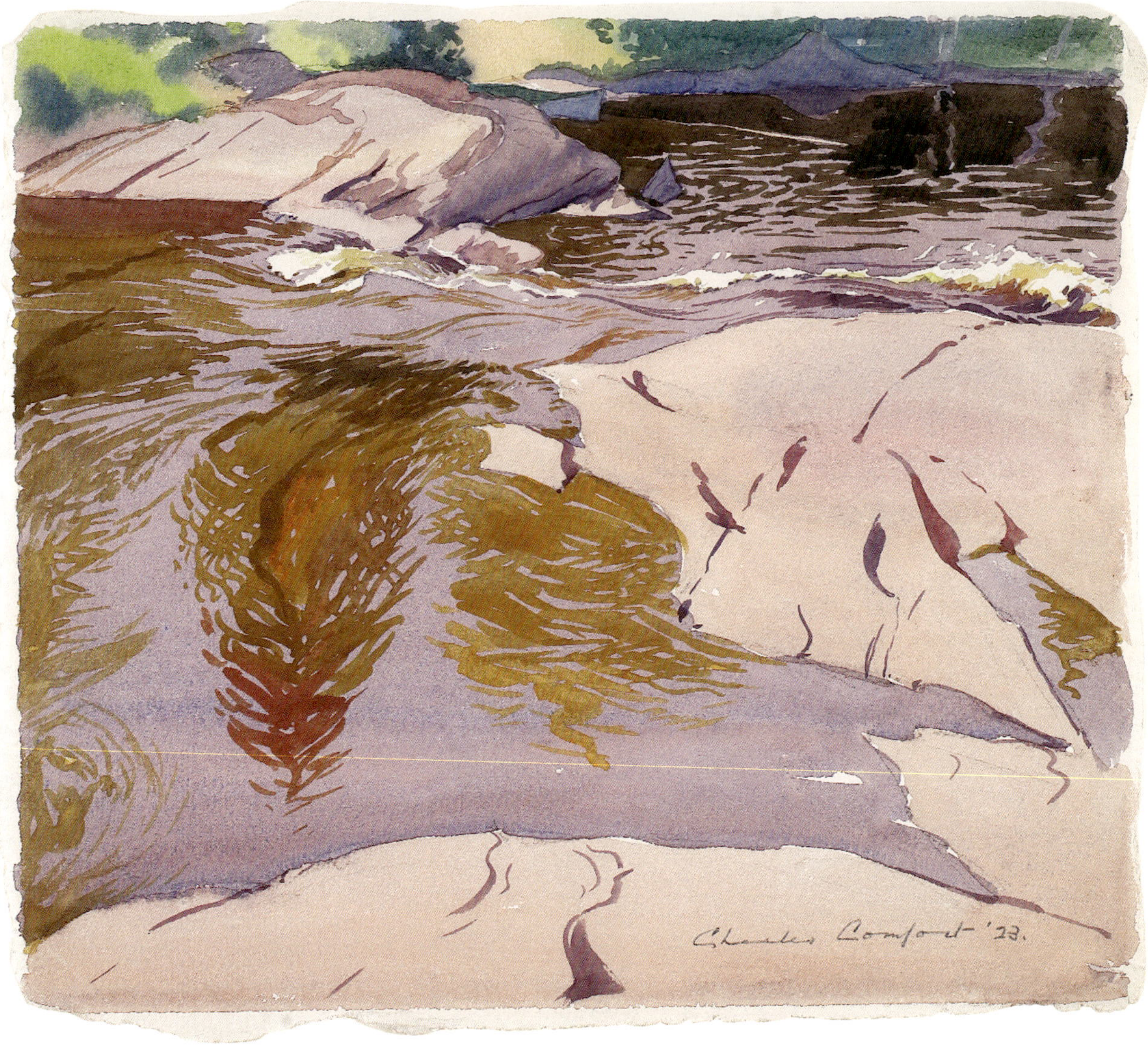

5. **Blindfold Rapids, Lake of the Woods**, 1923

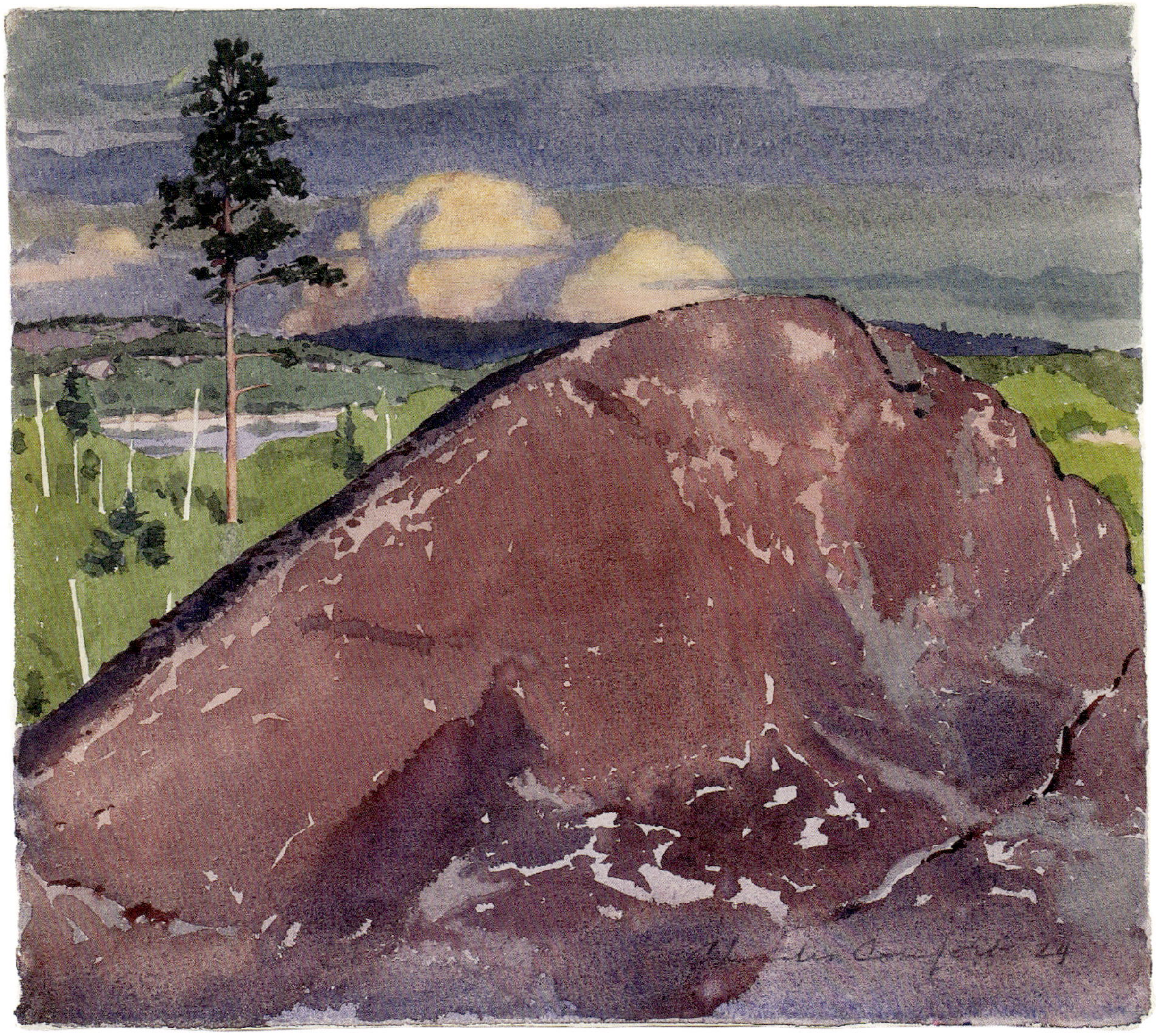

6. **Lake of the Woods, Route Bay**, 1924

7. **Suburban Cottages, Winnipeg**, 1924

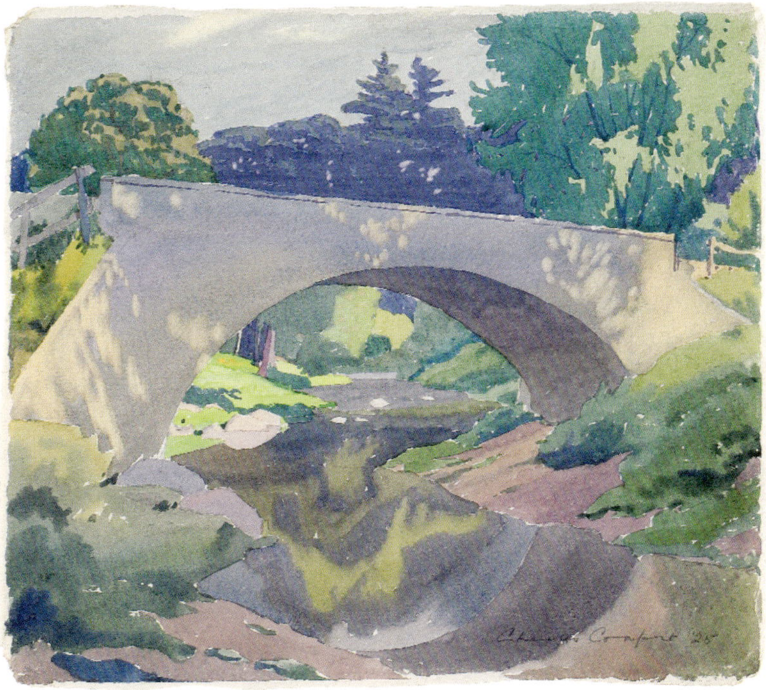

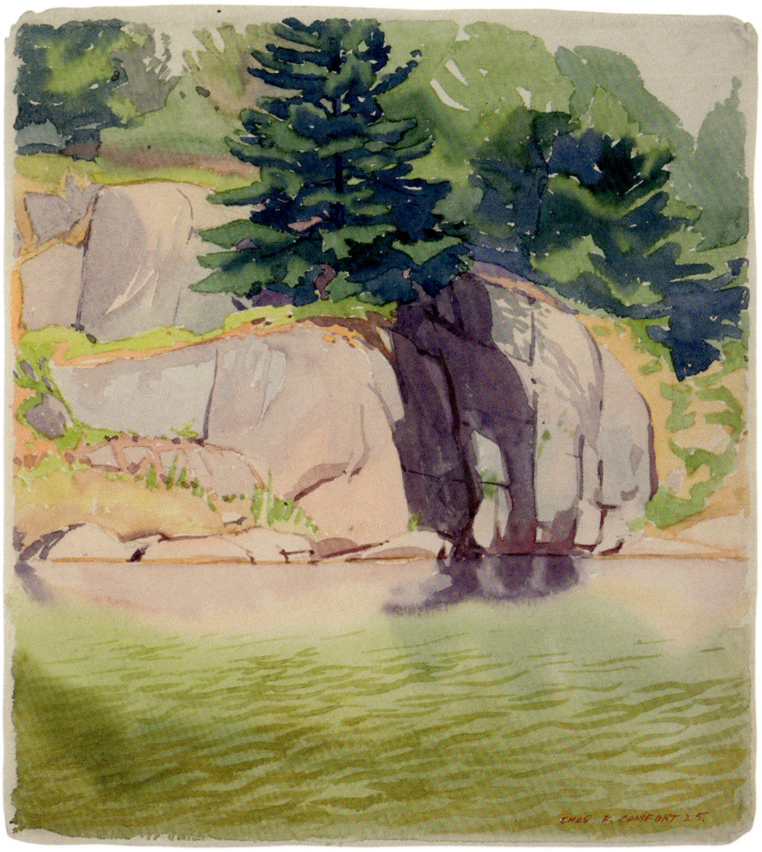

8. **Bridge Over the Don**, 1925 | 13. **Kawartha Lakes**, 1925

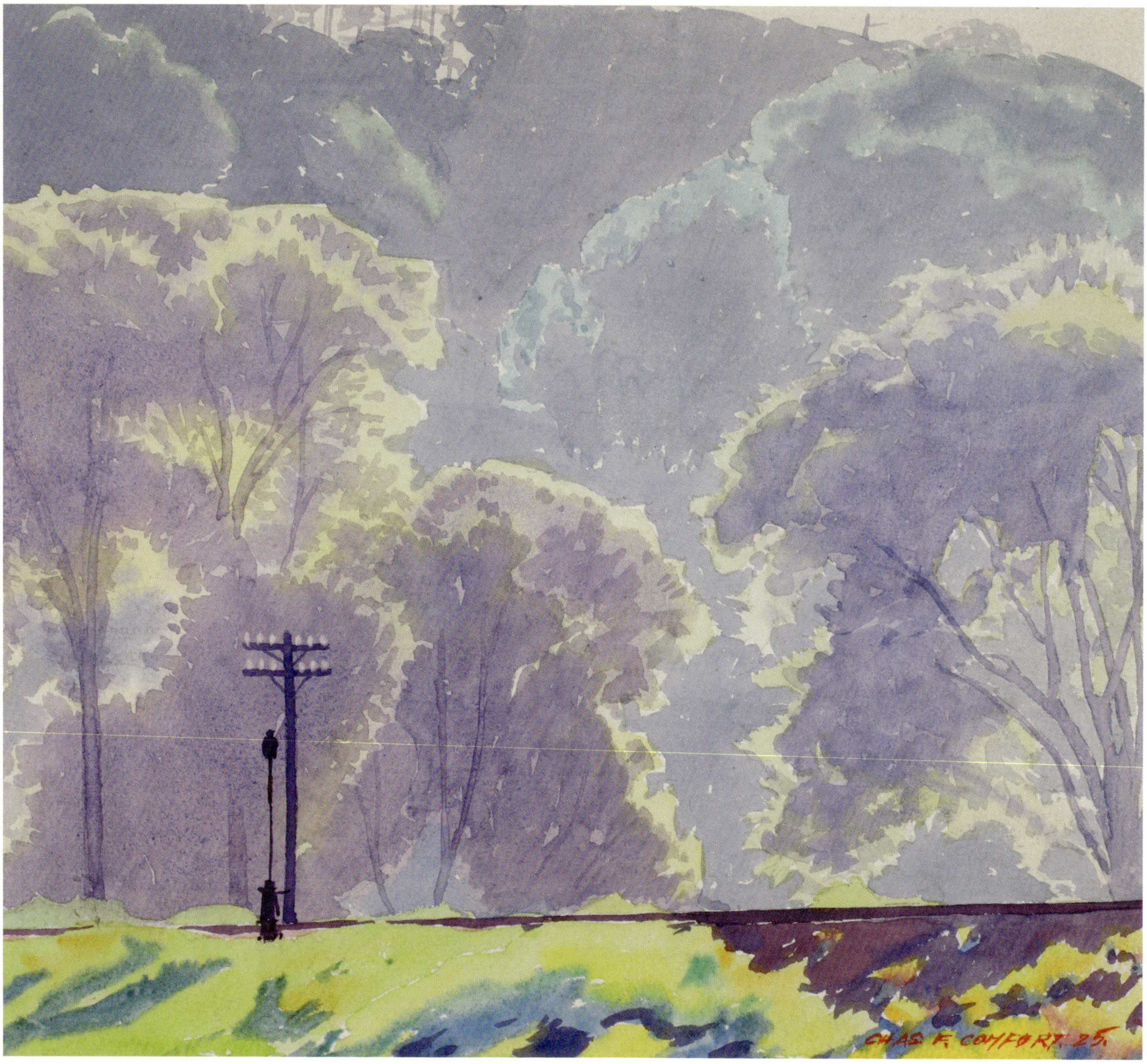

9. **In the Valley**, 1925

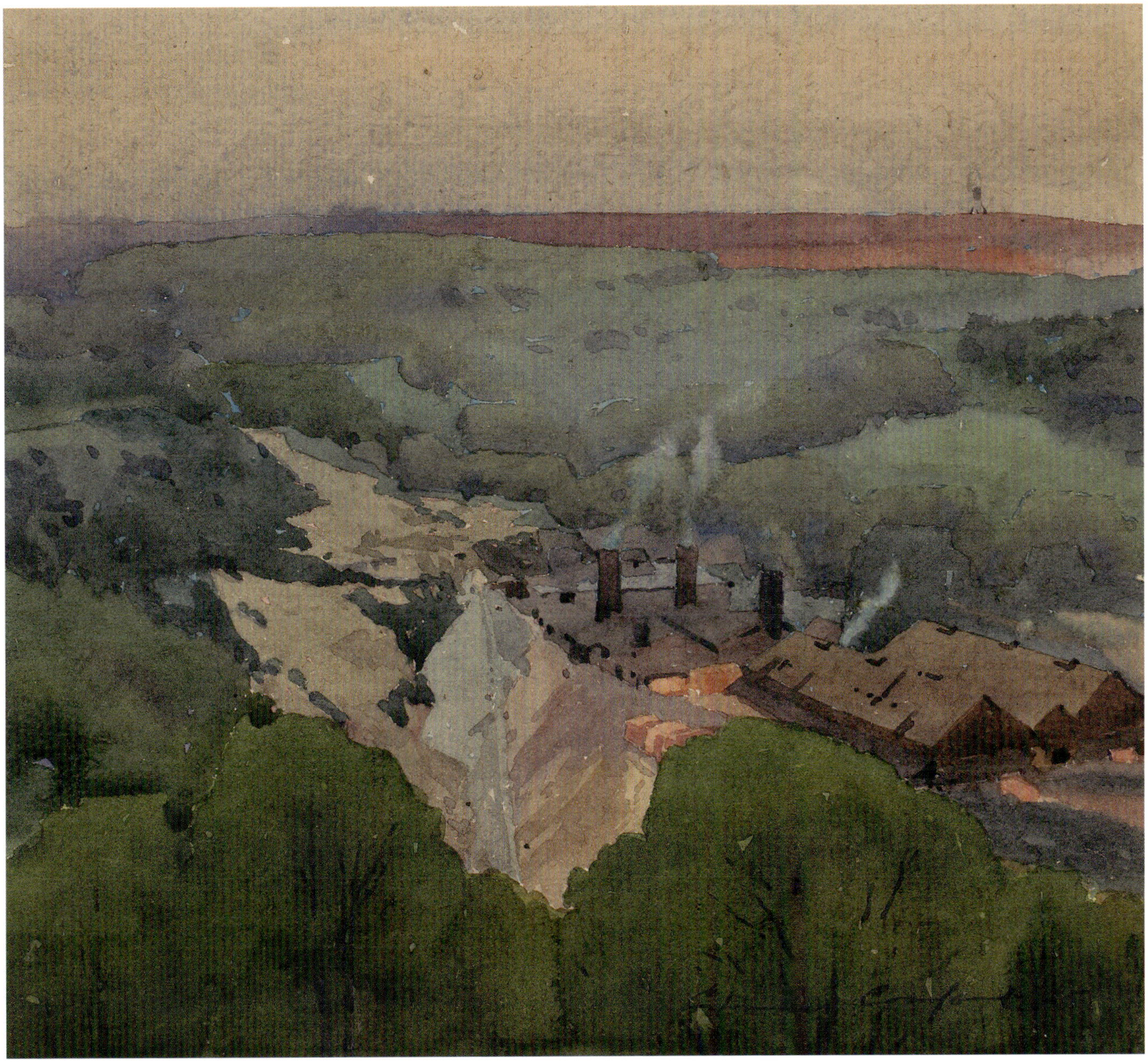

10. **Don Valley Brickyard**, 1925

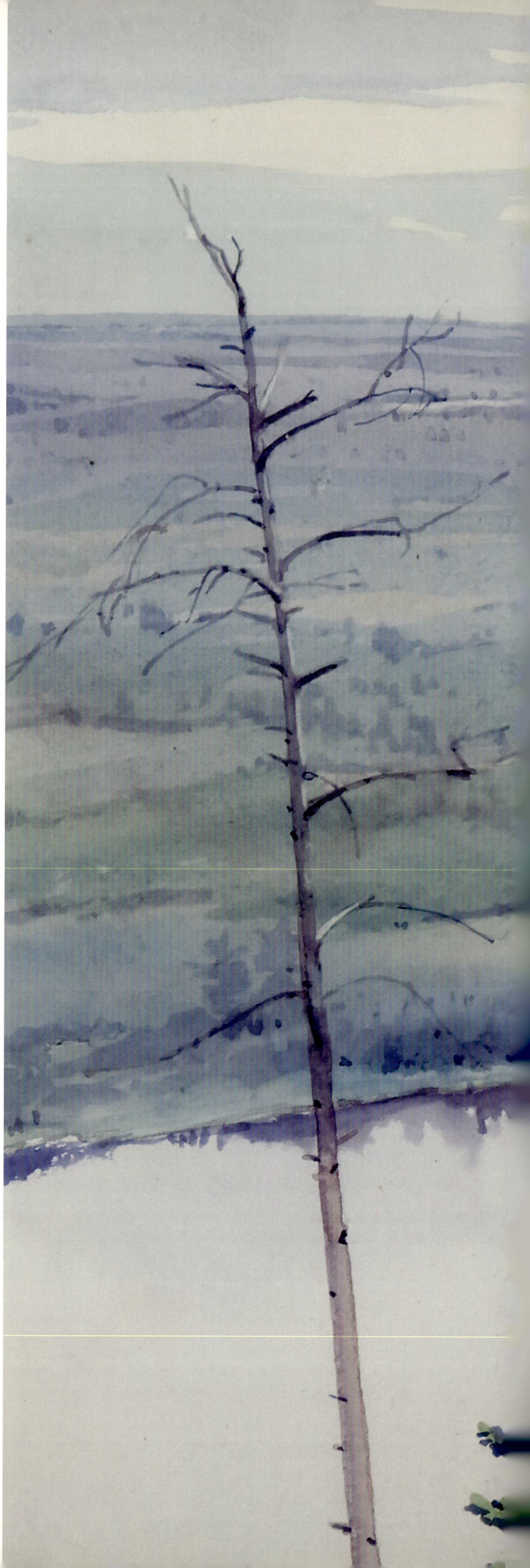

12. **Mountain Lake (Kawartha Lake)**, 1925

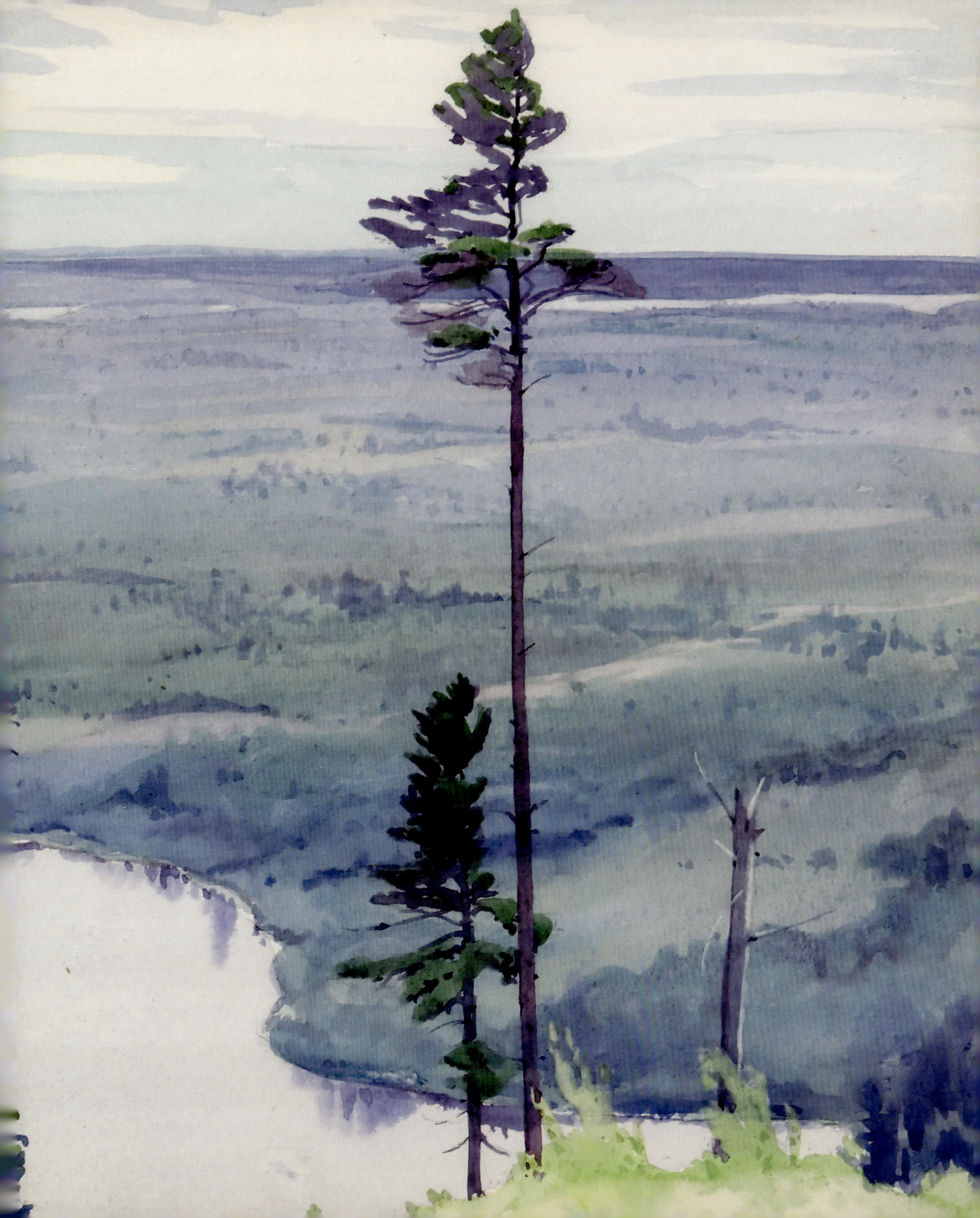

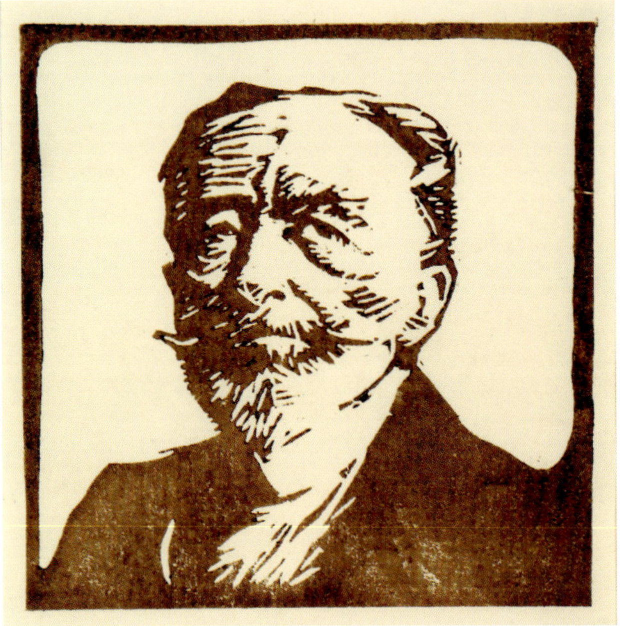

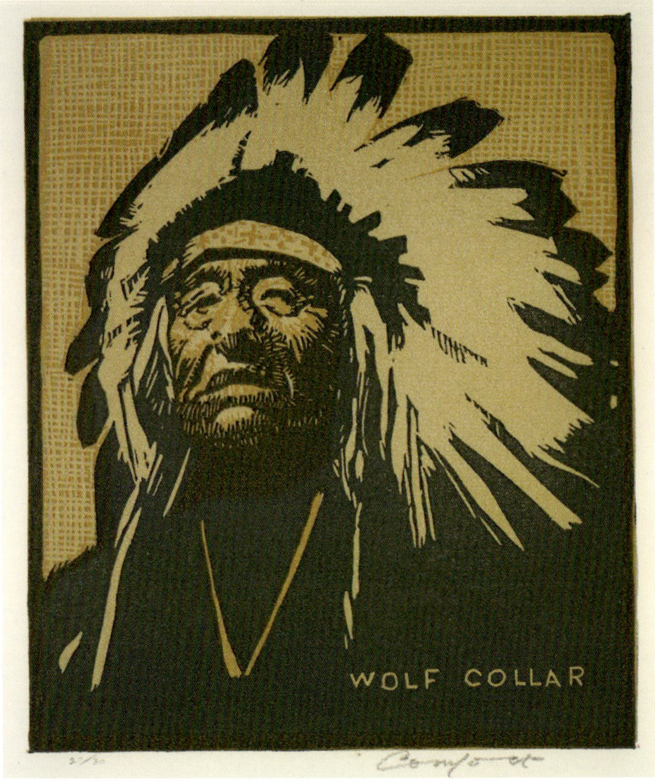

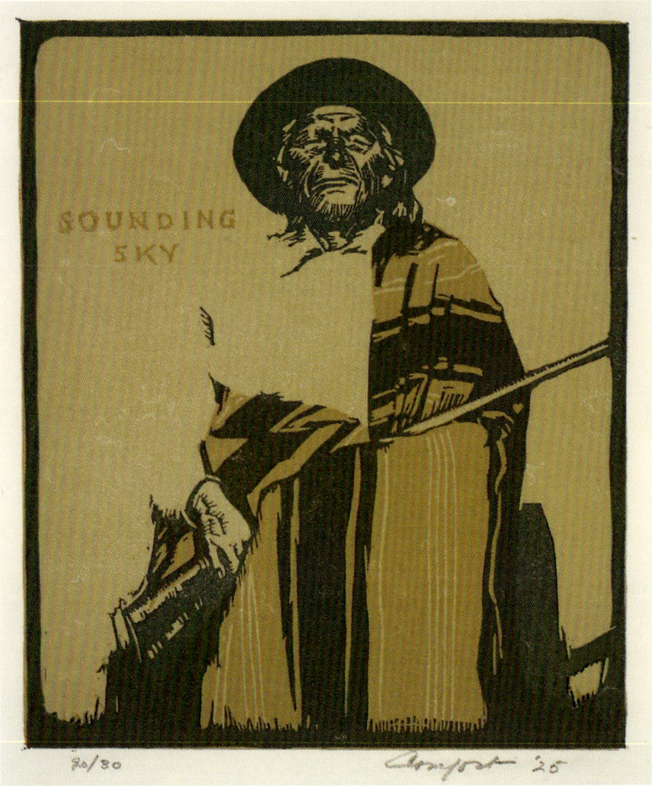

16. **Andre Lapine**, c. 1925 | 14. **Wolf Collar**, 1925 | 15. **Sounding Sky**, 1925

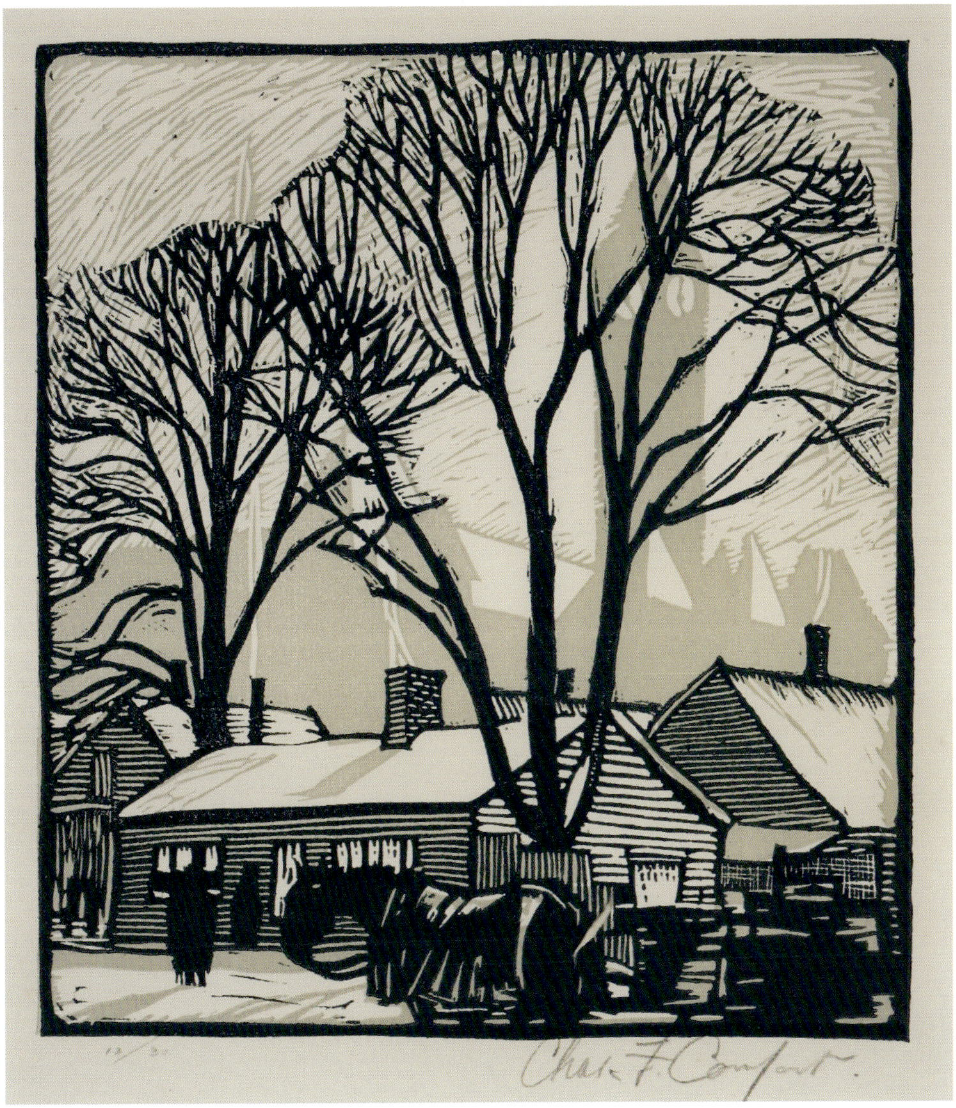

18. **December**, c. 1926

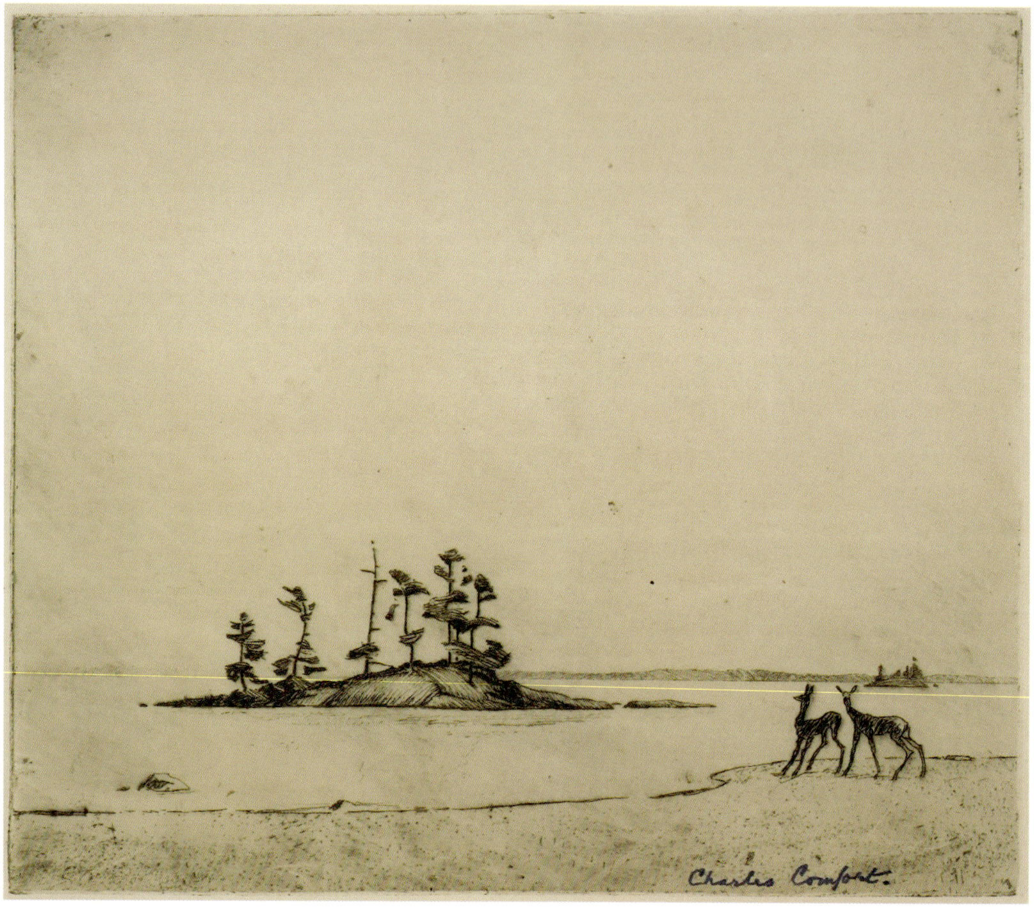

18. **Boschink**, c. 1925–26

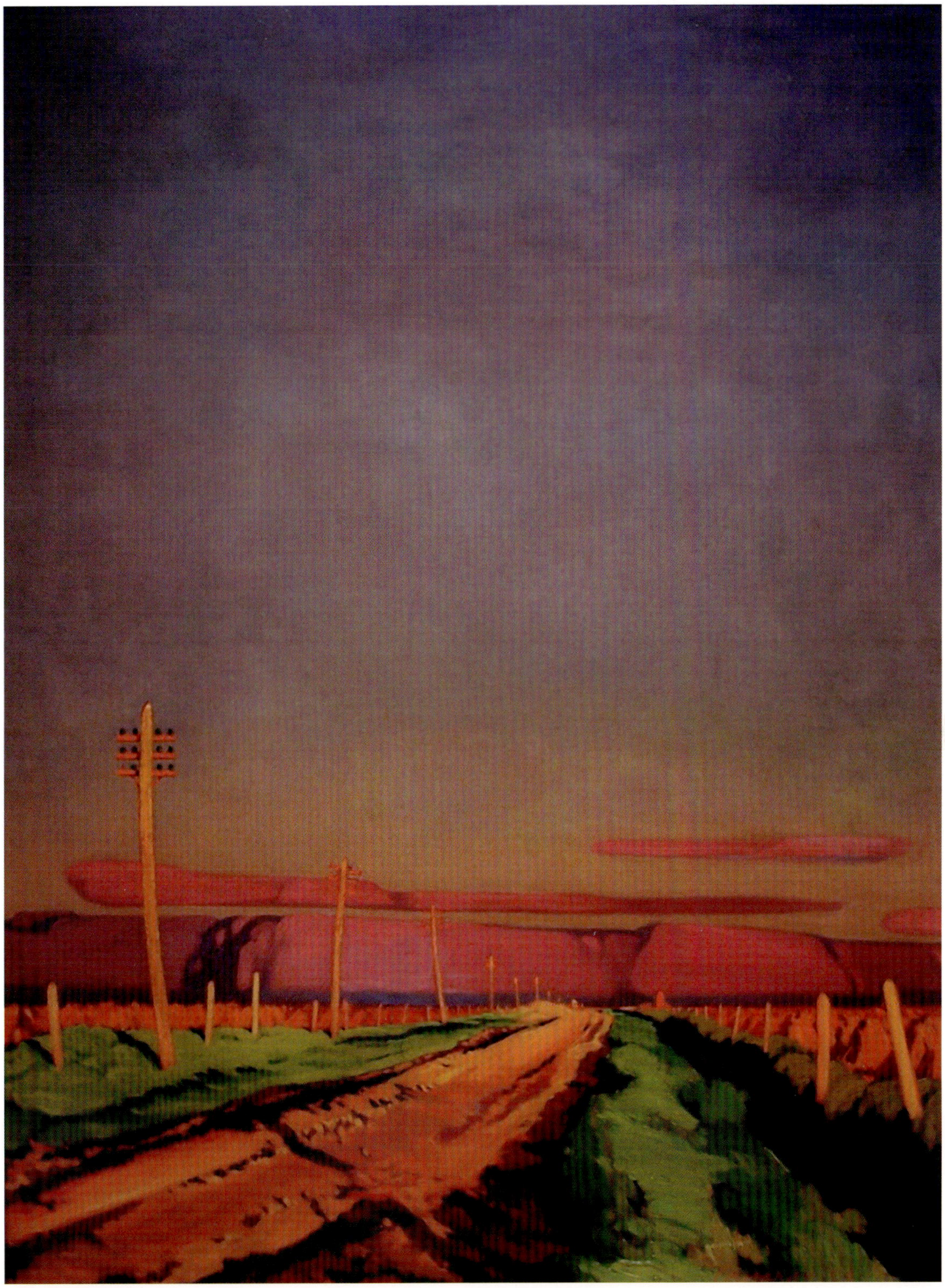

19. **Prairie Road (Out West)**, 1925

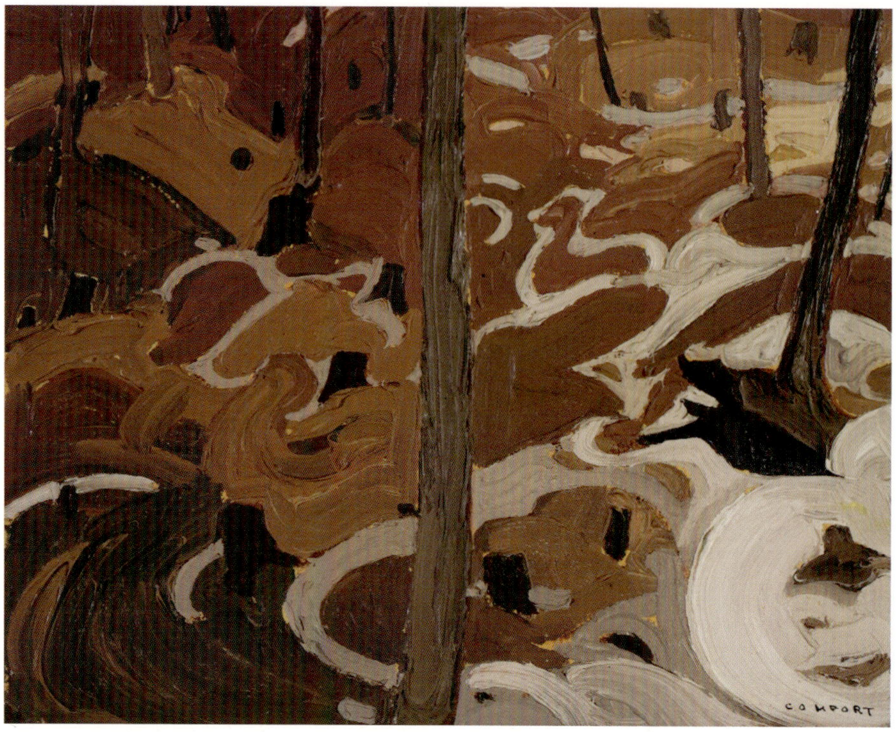
COMFORT

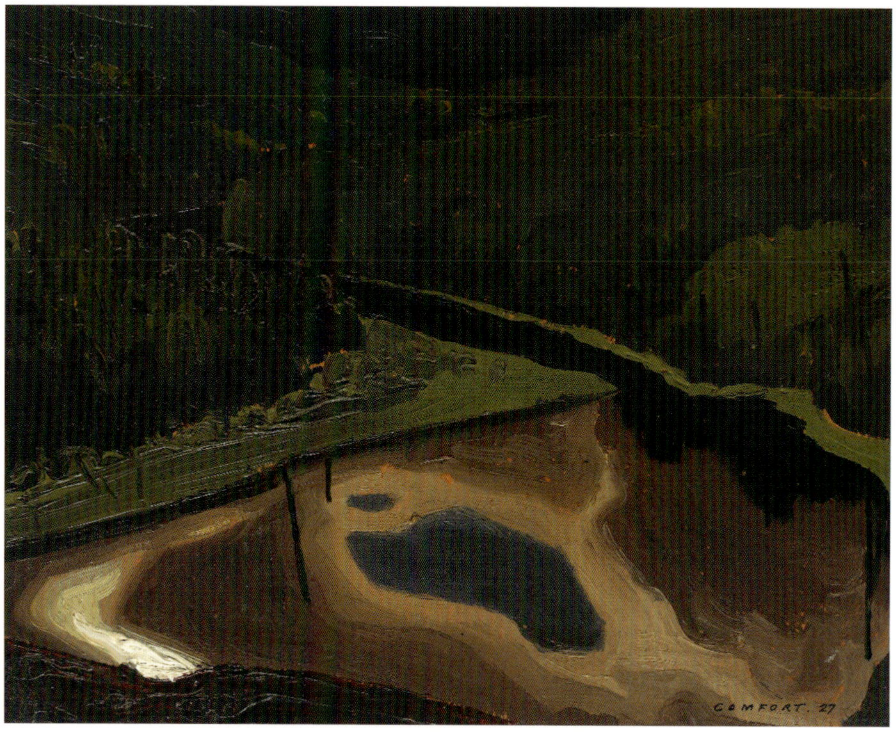
COMFORT. 27

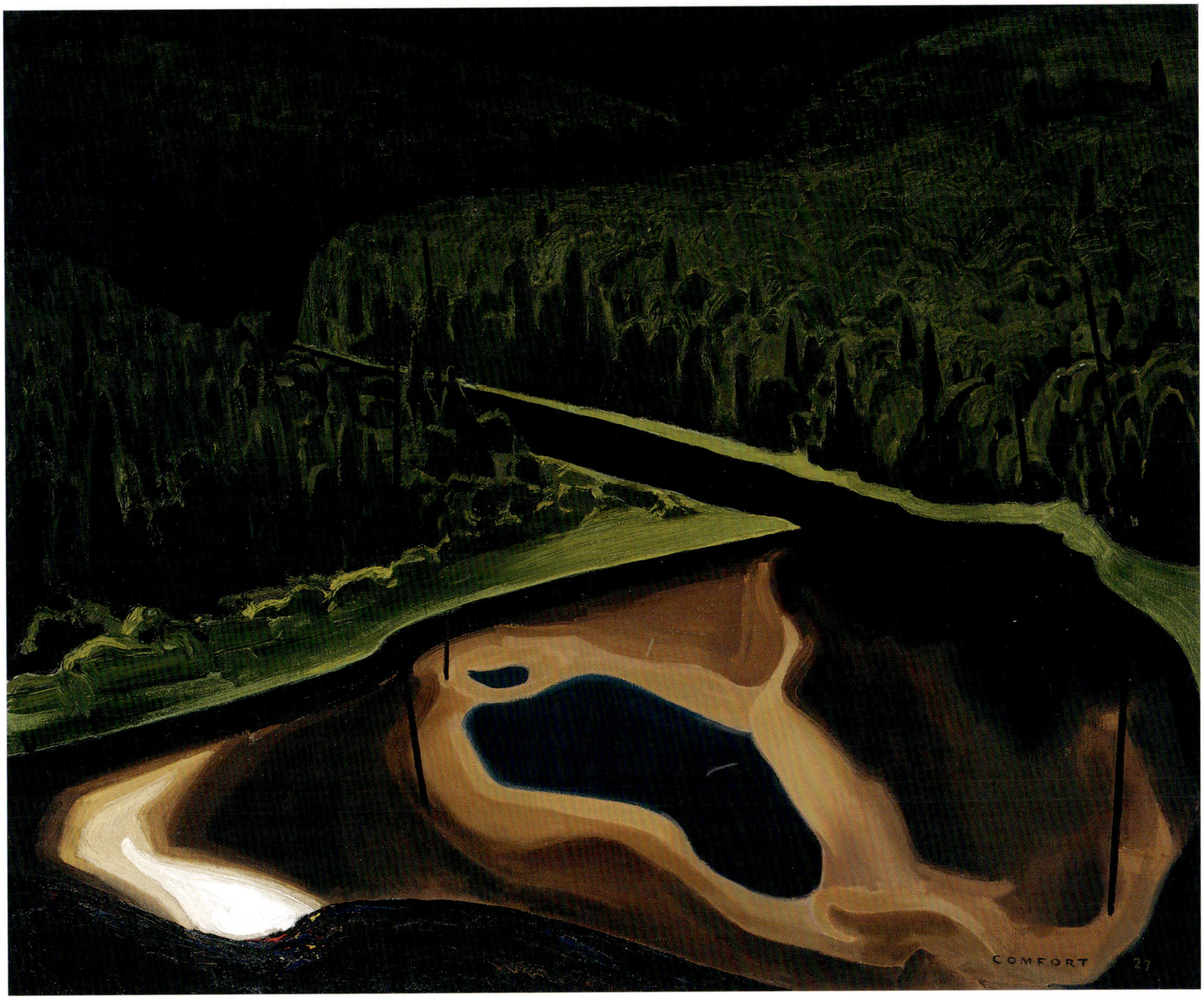

20. **Tawny, (York Mills)**, 1927 | 21. **Study for Wilderness**, 1927 | 22. **Wilderness**, 1927

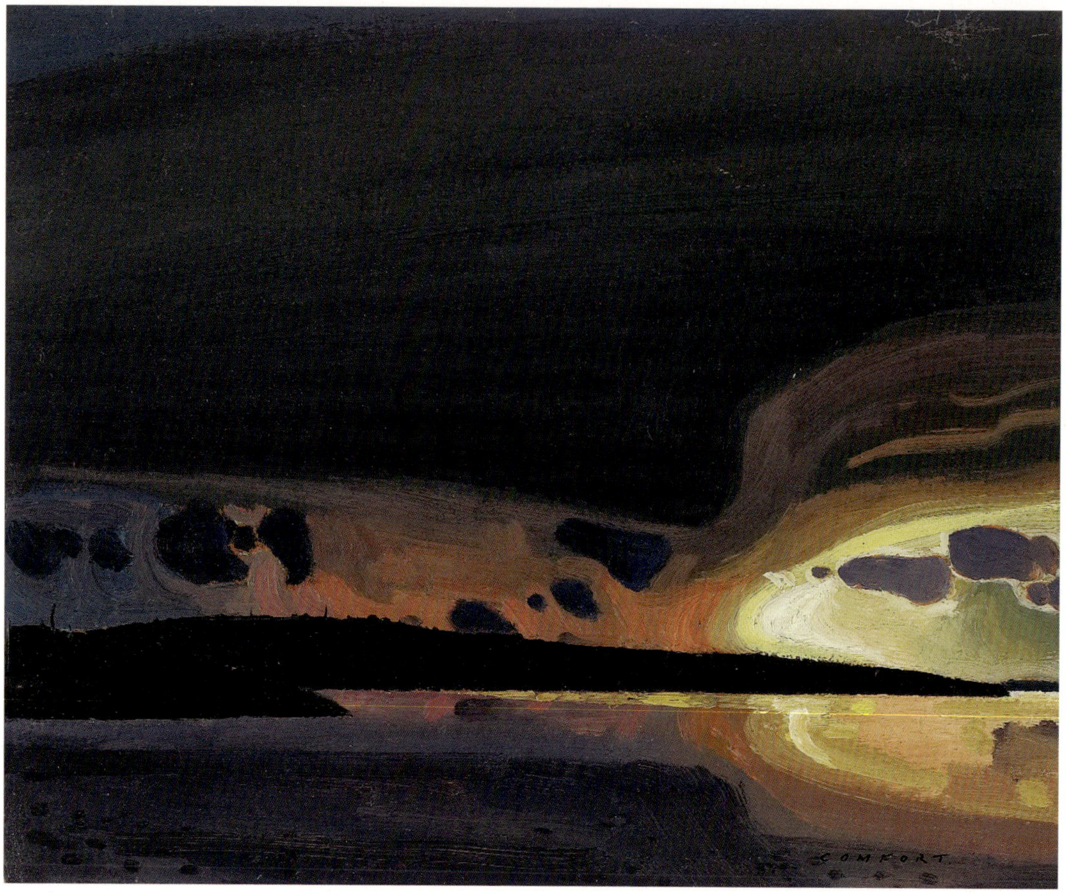

28. **Clearing, Big Stone Bay, Lake of the Woods**, 1934

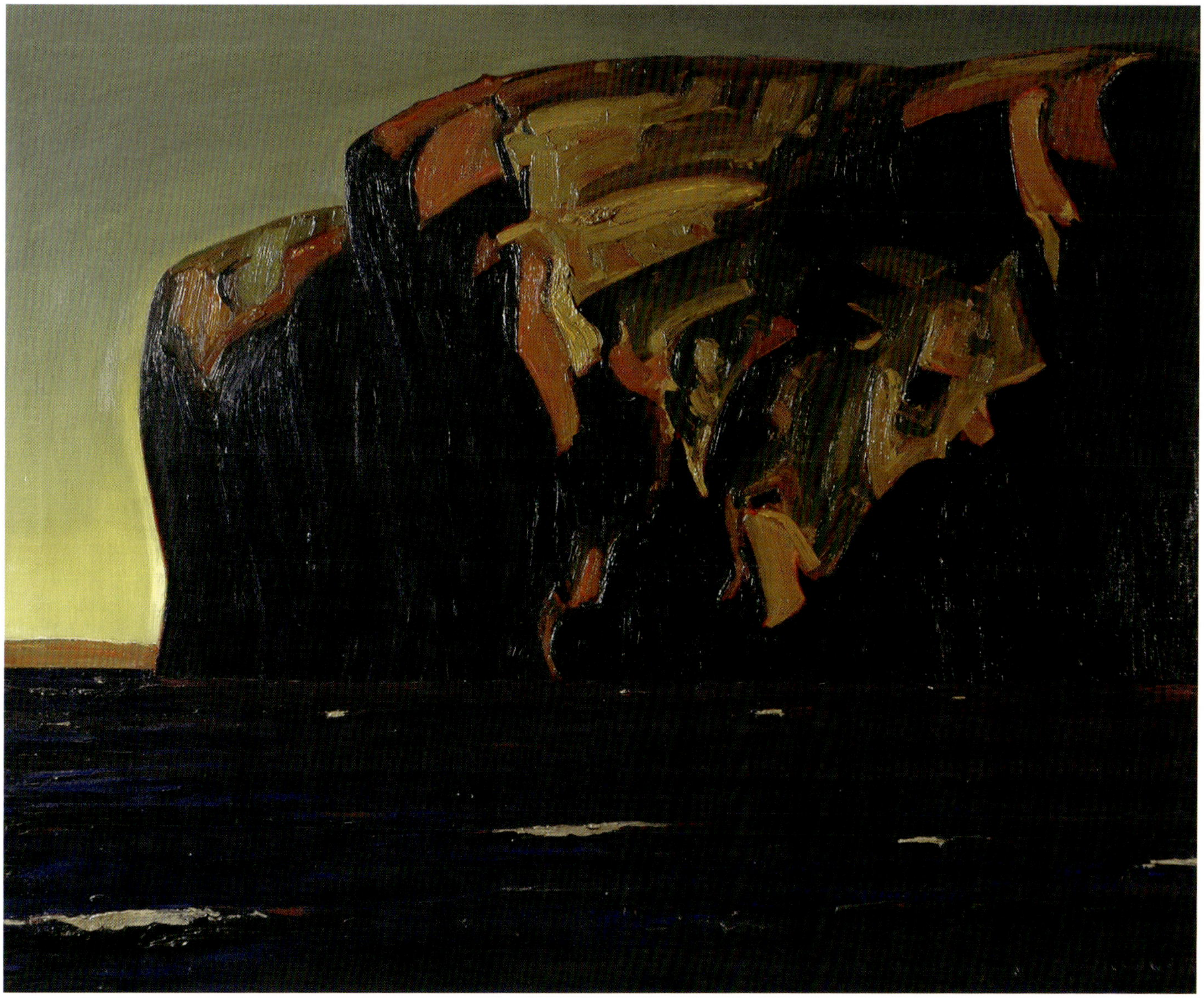

23. **The Great Rock, Bon Echo**, 1928

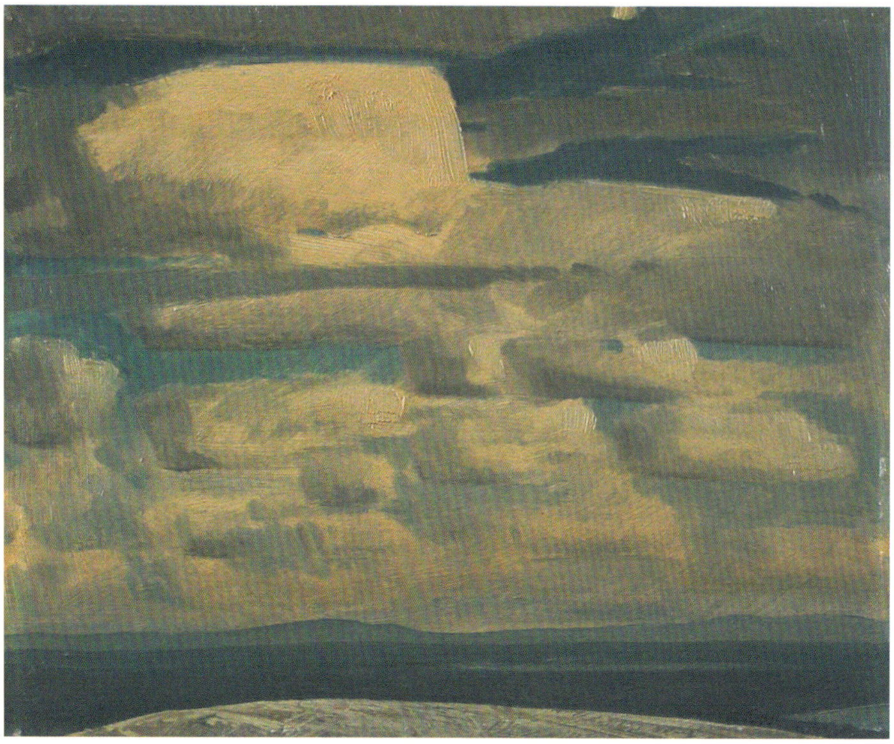

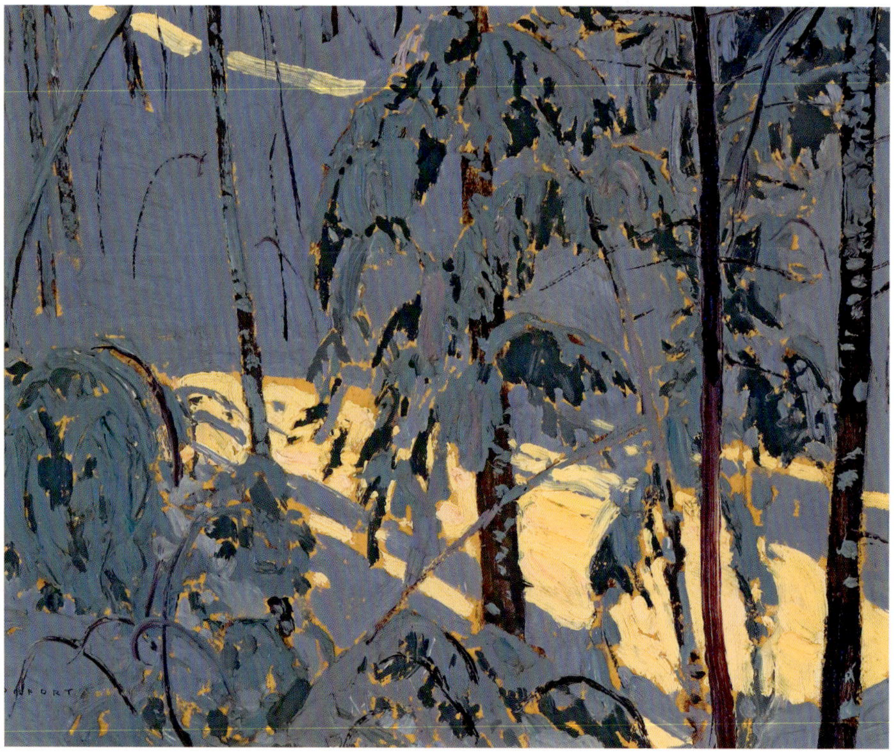

33. **Distant View of Manitoulin**, 1936 | 24. **Winter Woods**, 1928 | 26. **Black Spruce, Pickerel River**, 1932

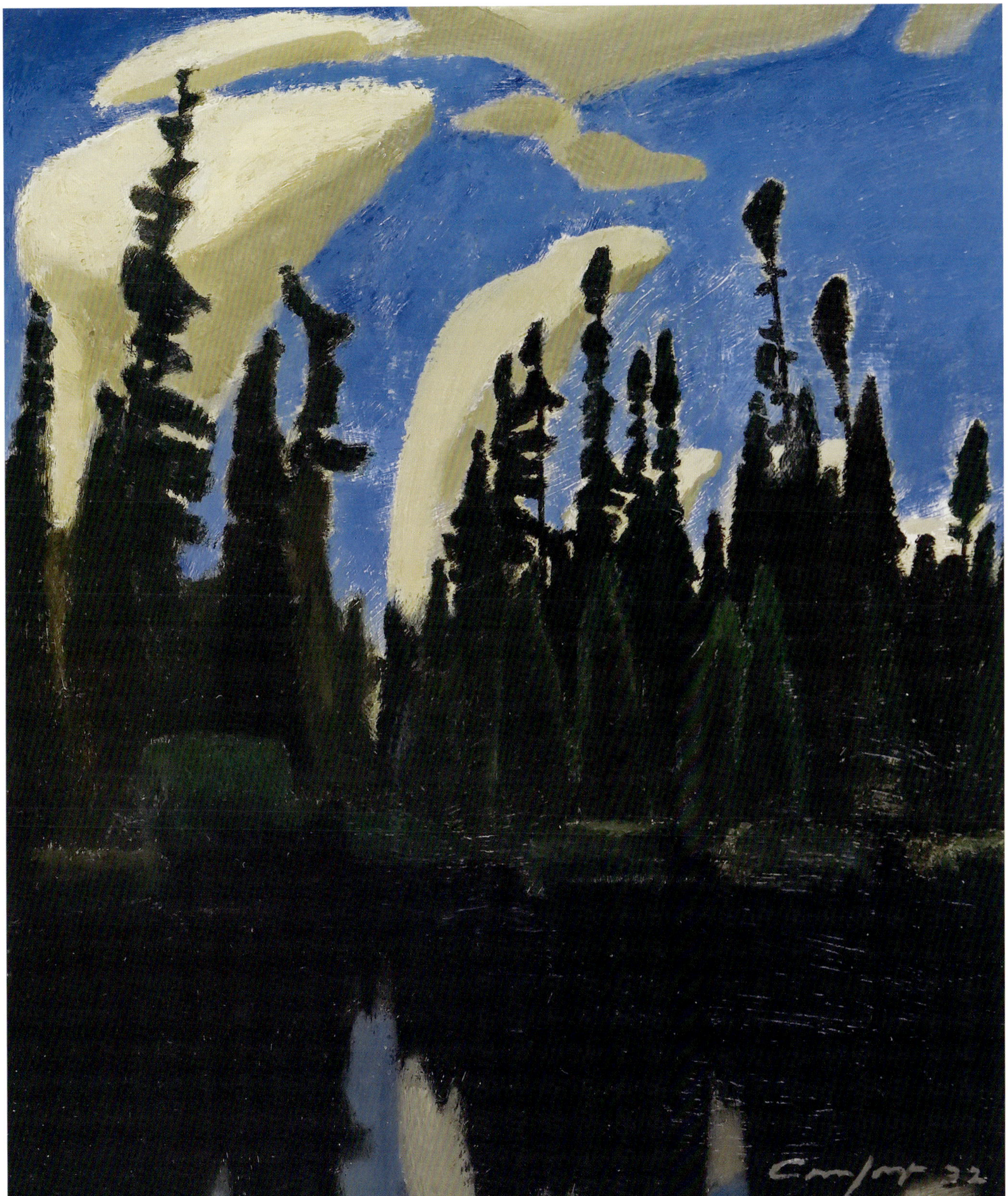

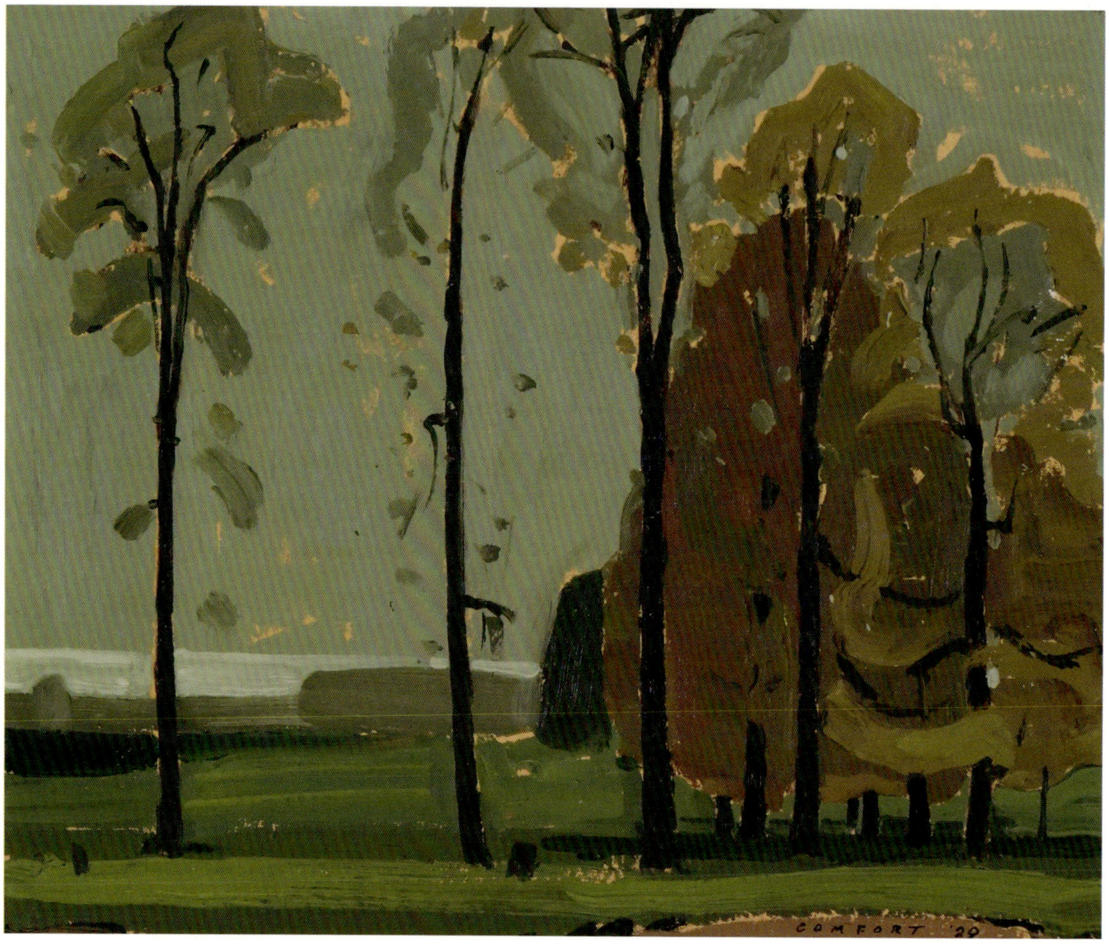

25. **Pastoral, Duncan, Ontario**, 1929

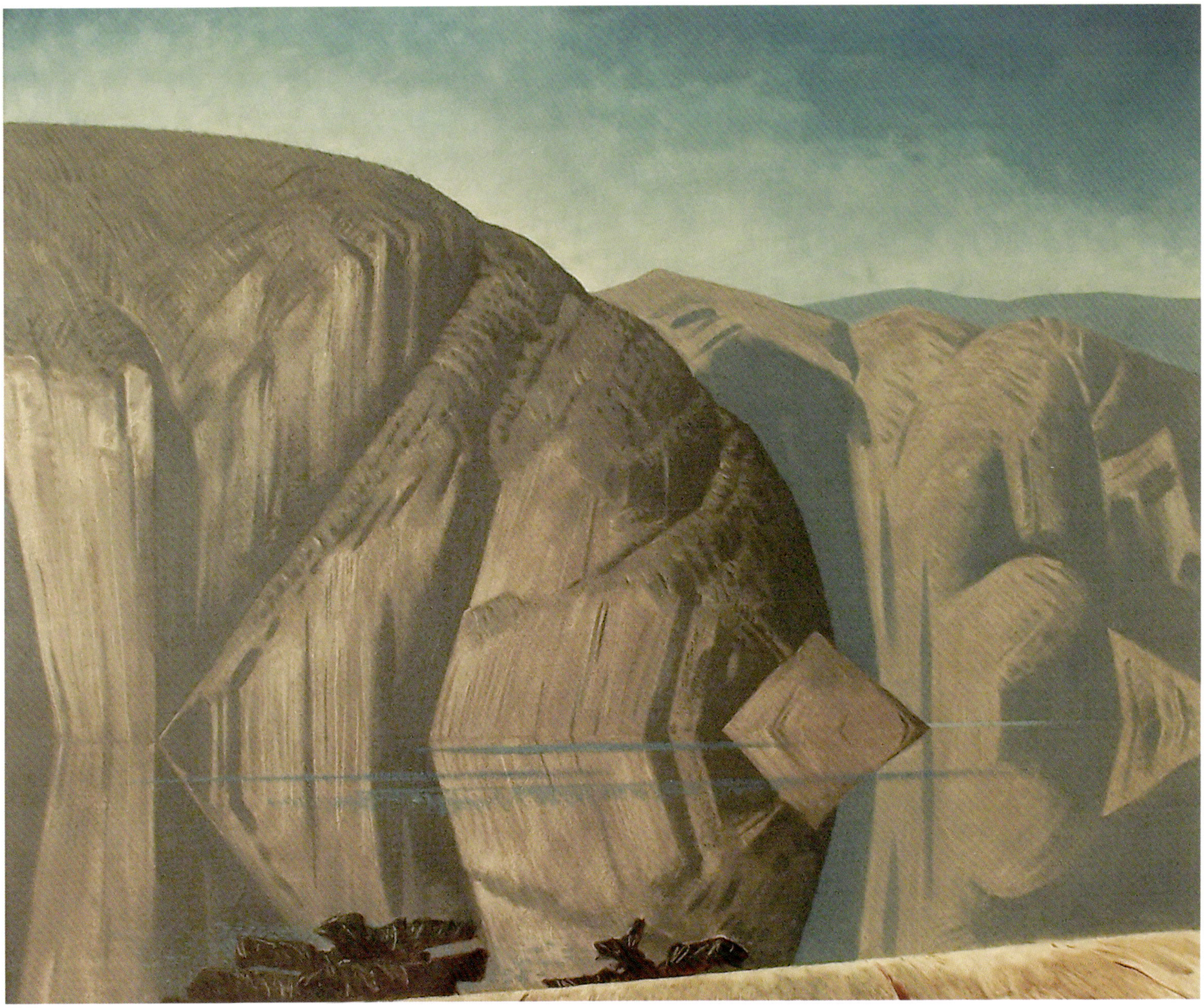

29. **Saugenay River**, 1935

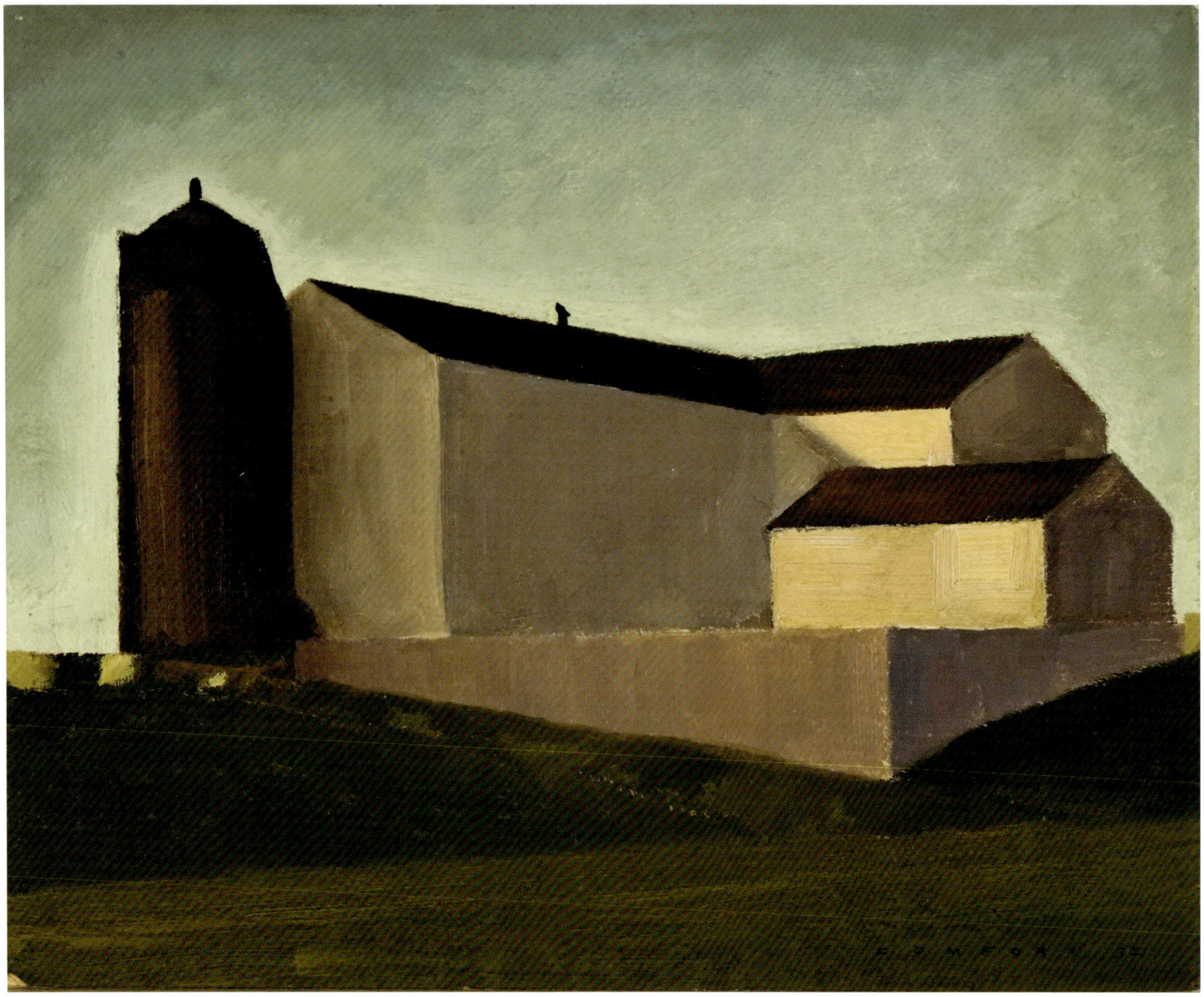

27. **Barns Near Wexford on the Lawrence Ave. Line**, 1932

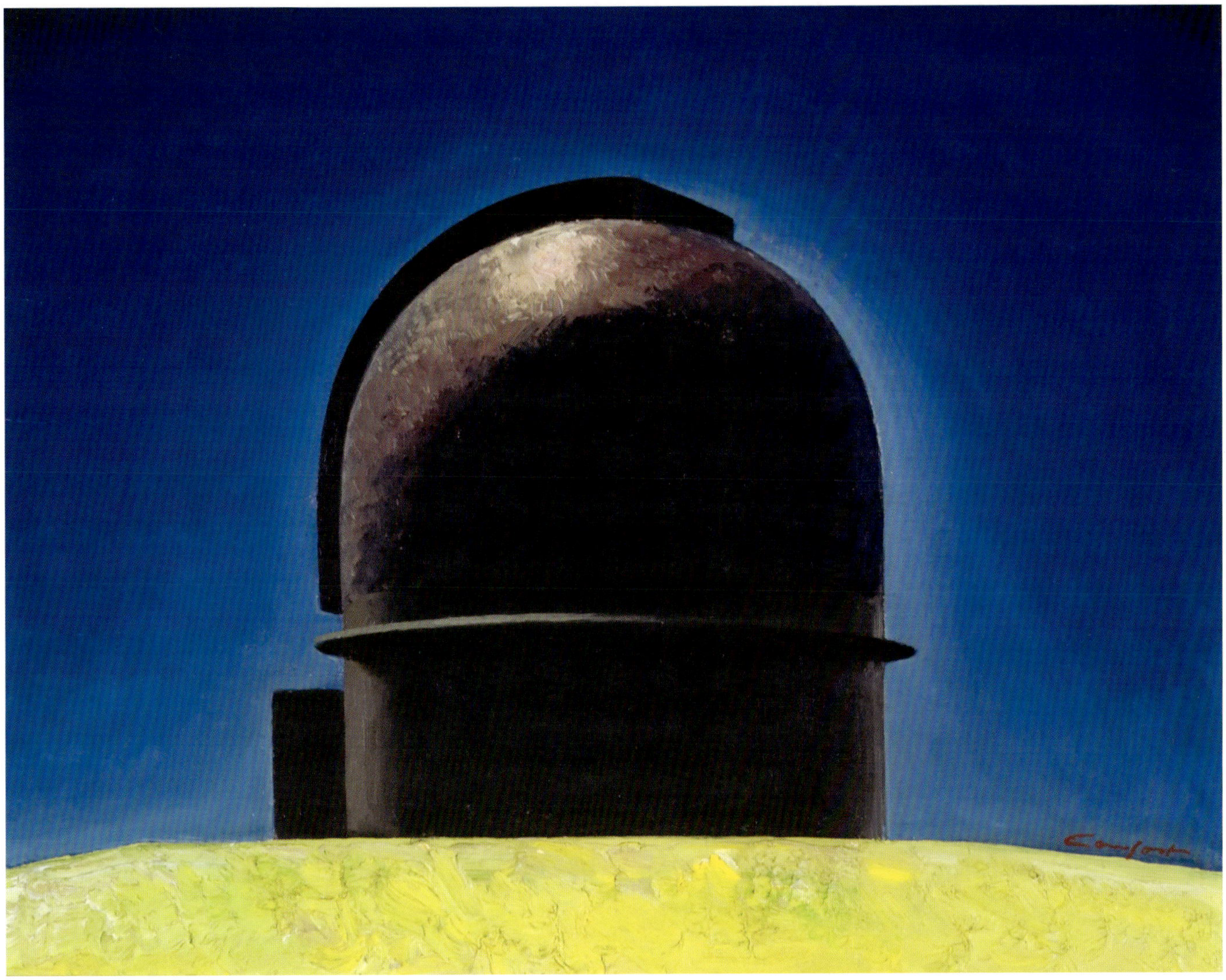

37. **Observatory**, 1938

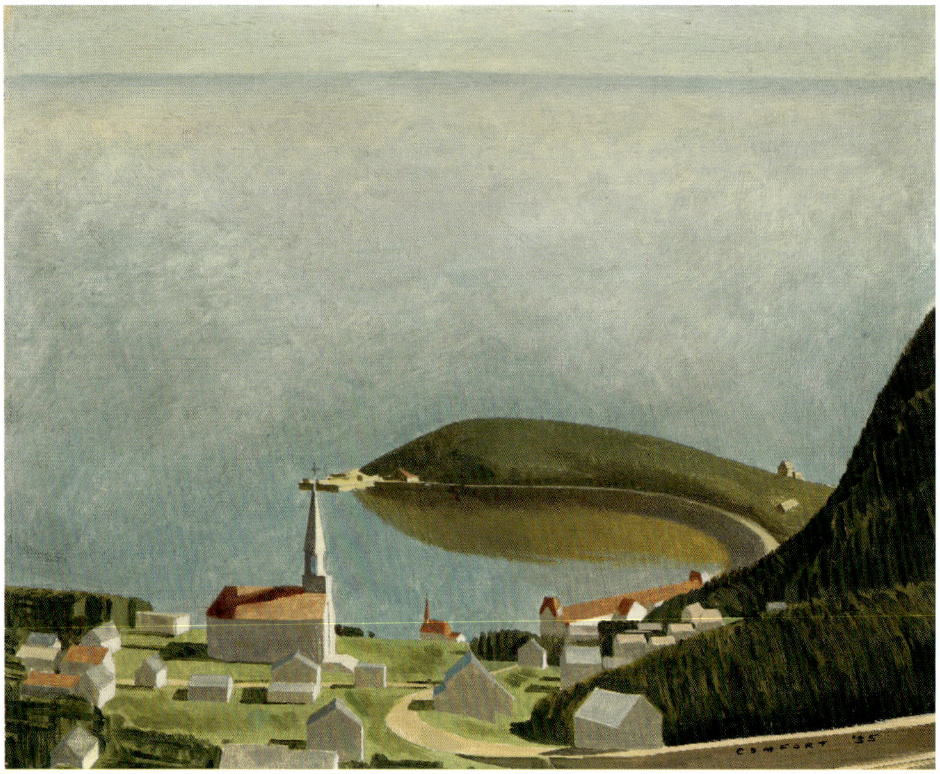

30. **Tadoussac**, (sketch), 1935 | 31. **Tadoussac**, 1935

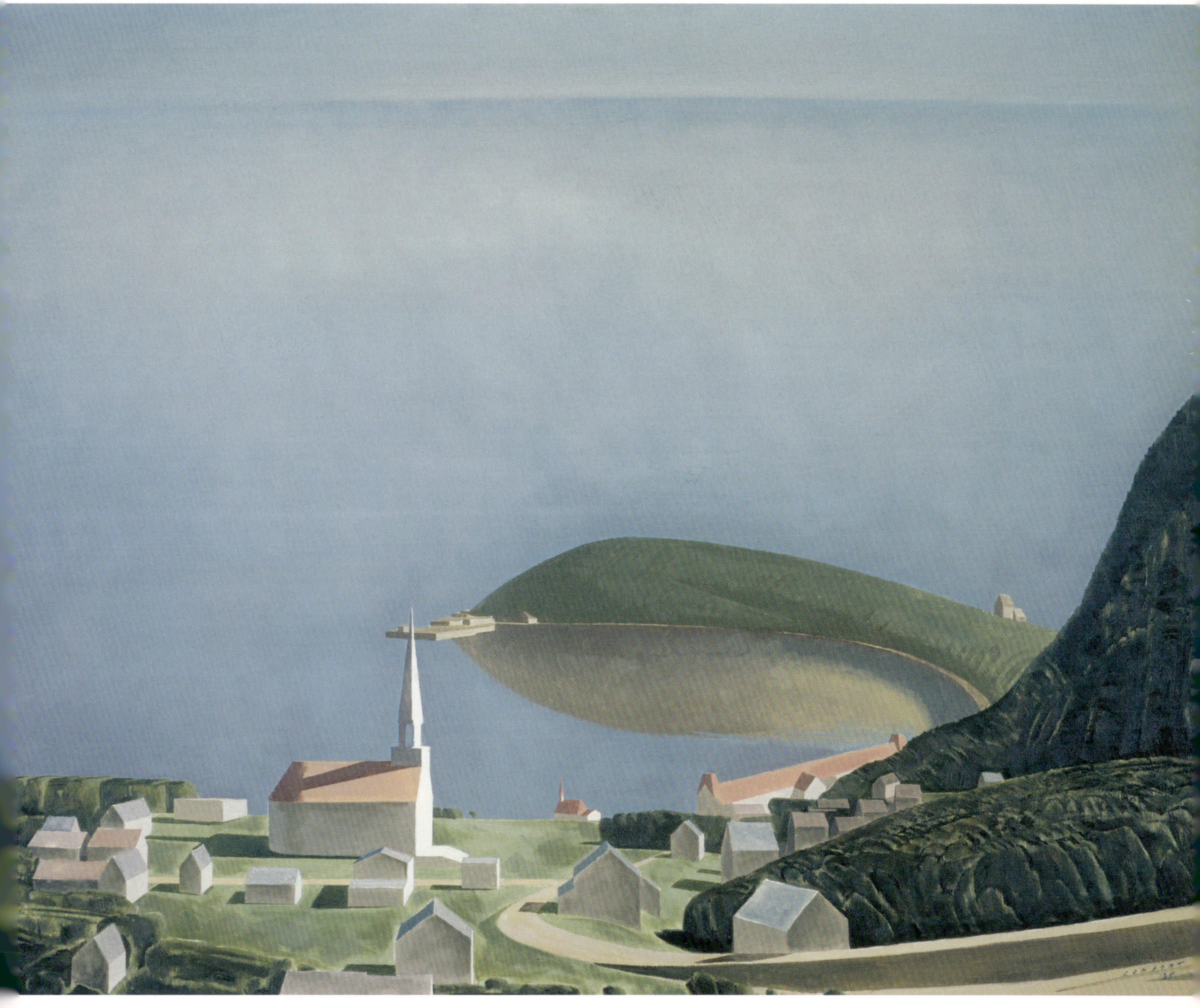

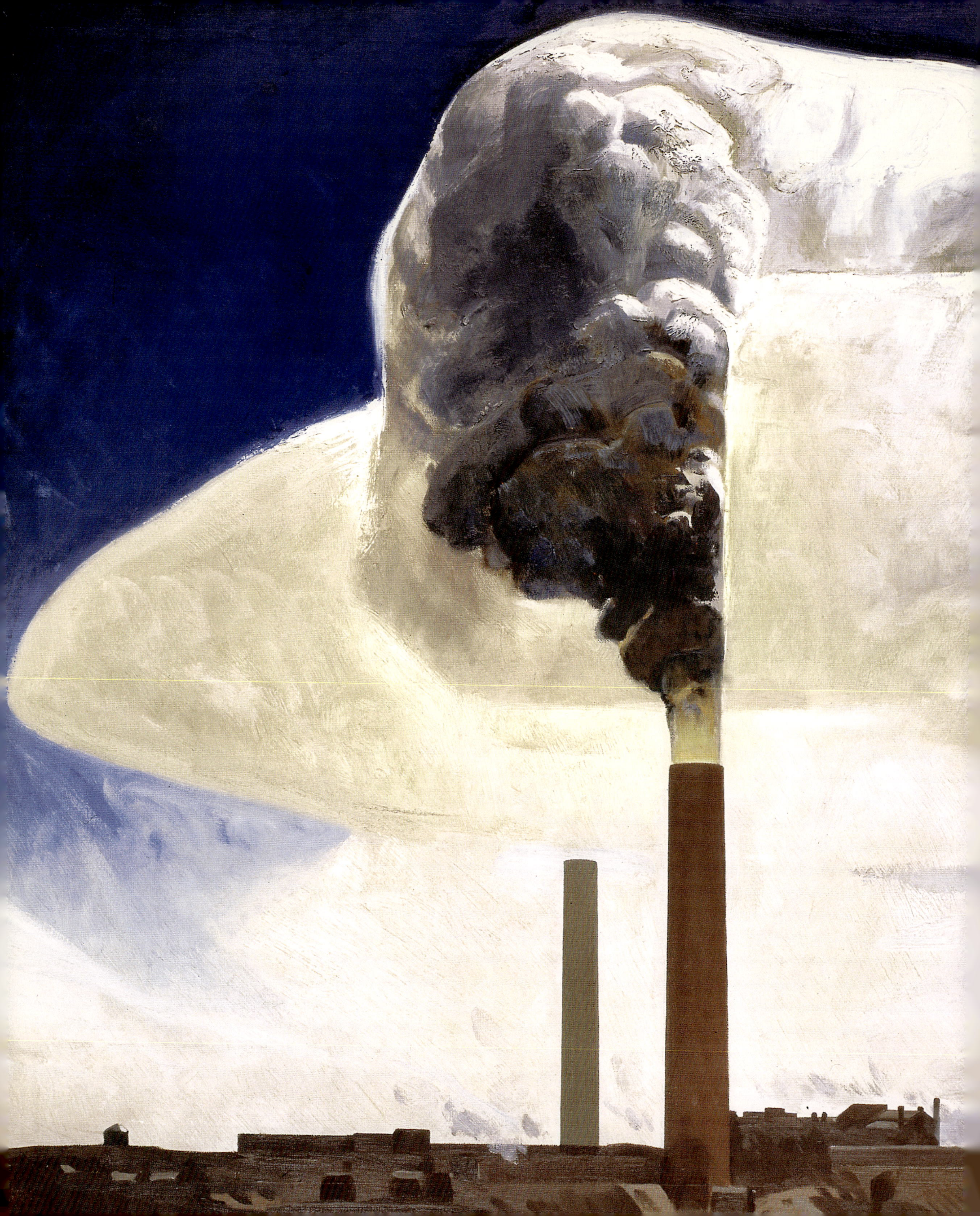

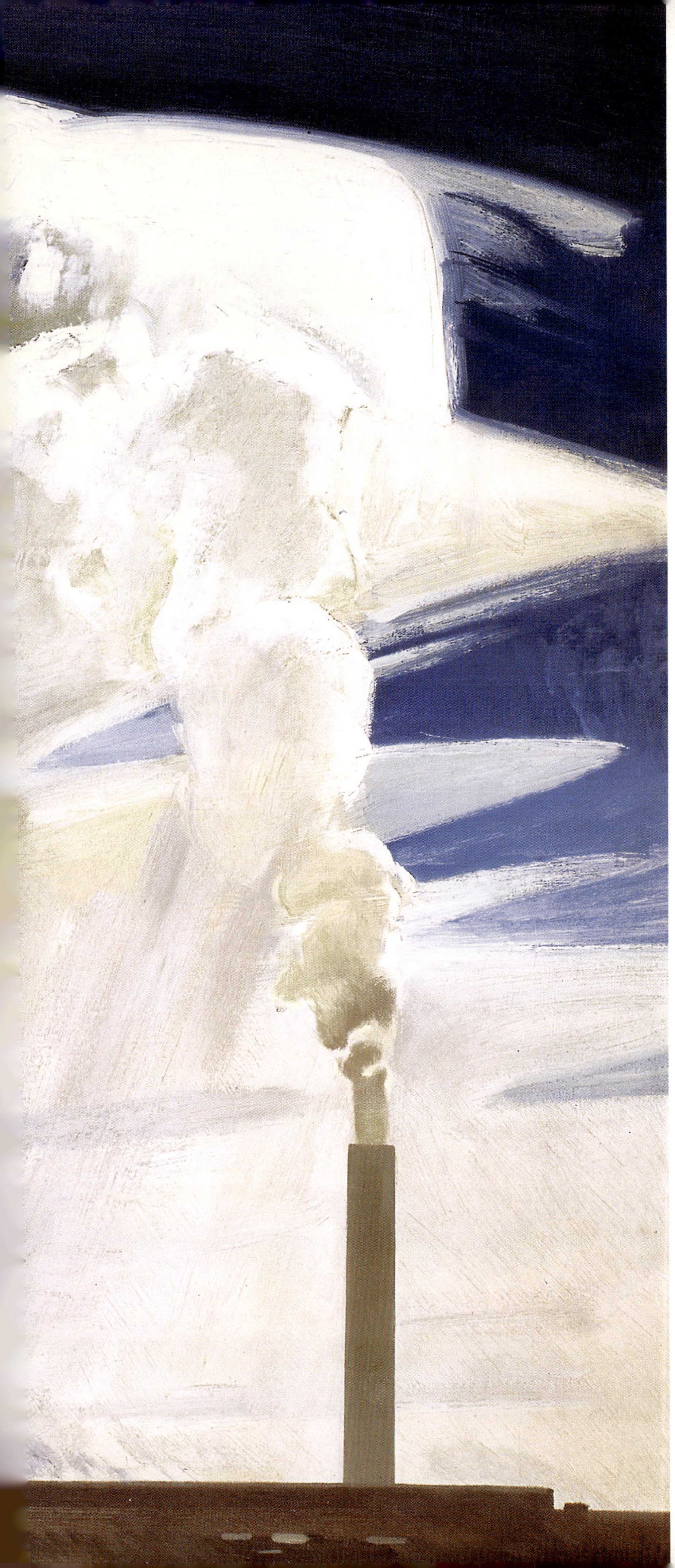

34. **Smelter Stacks, Copper Cliff**, 1936

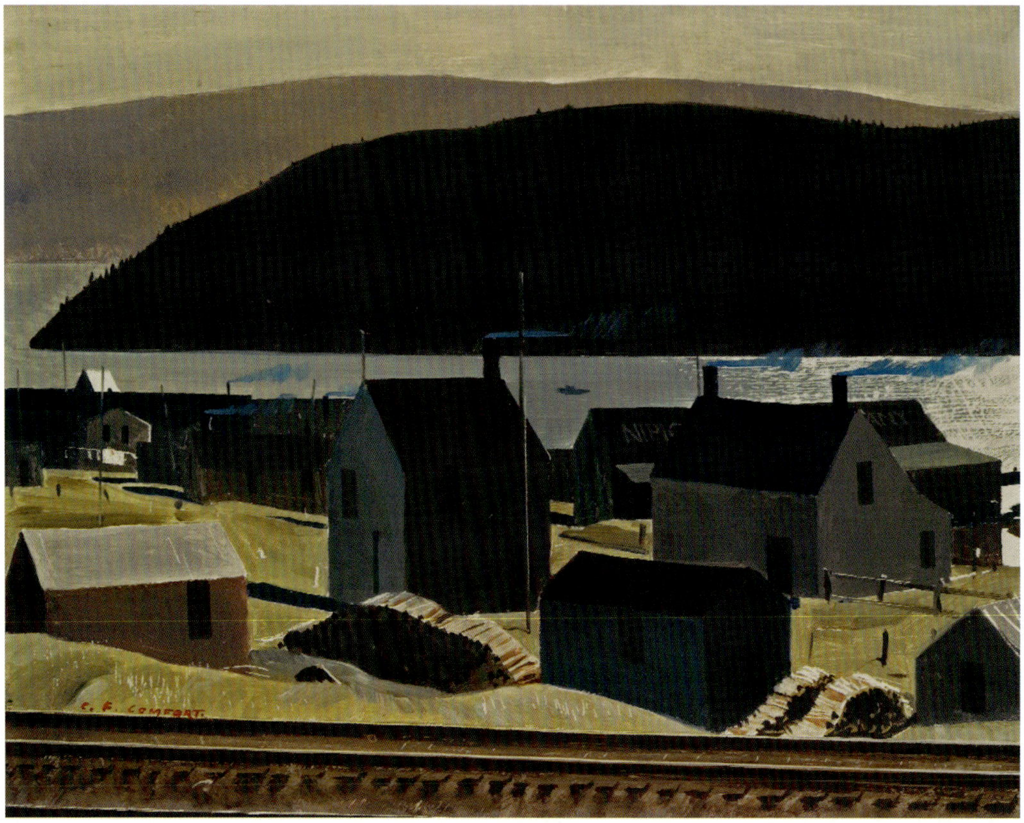

32. **Rossport, Lake Superior**, 1935

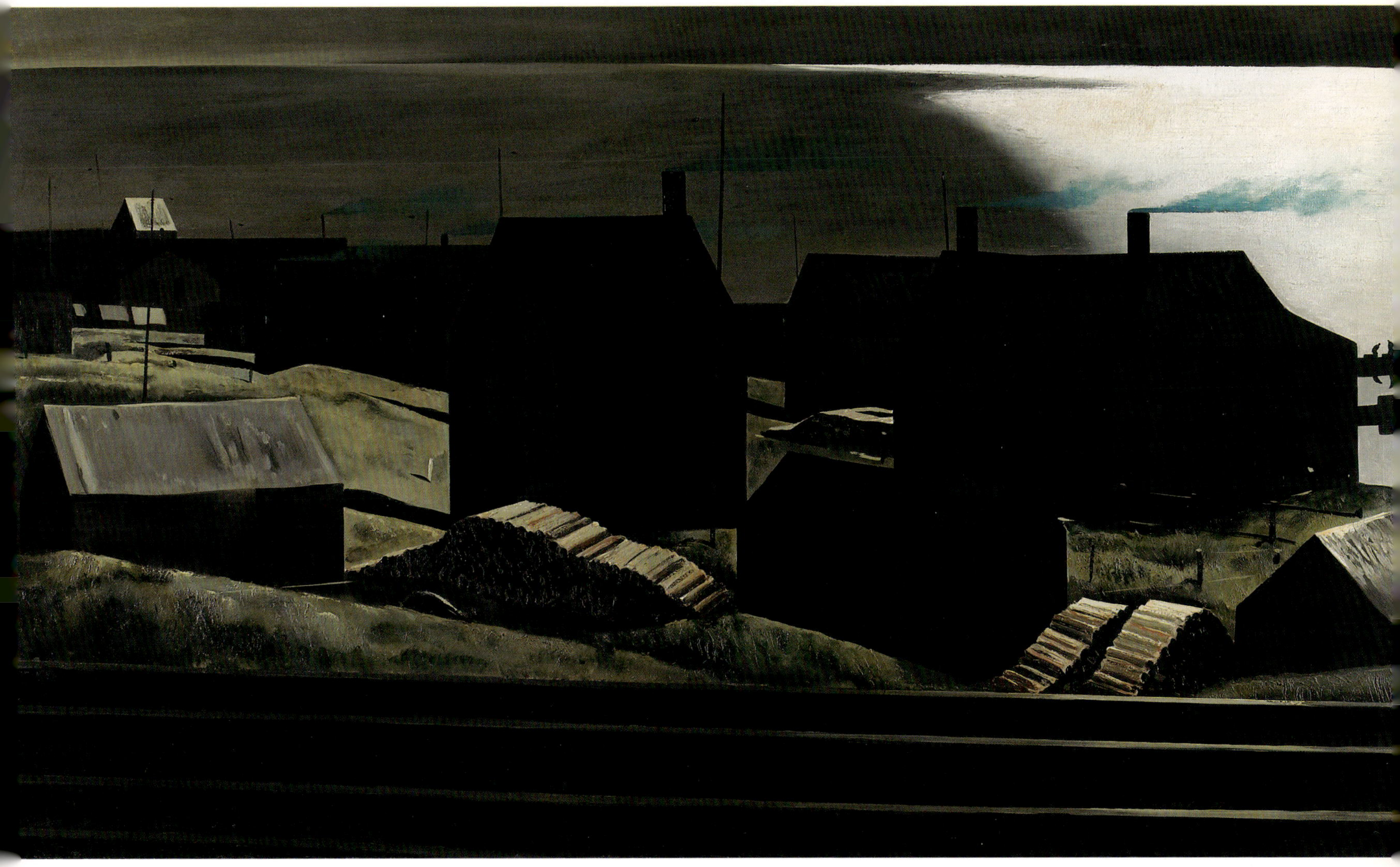

35. **Lake Superior Village**, 1937

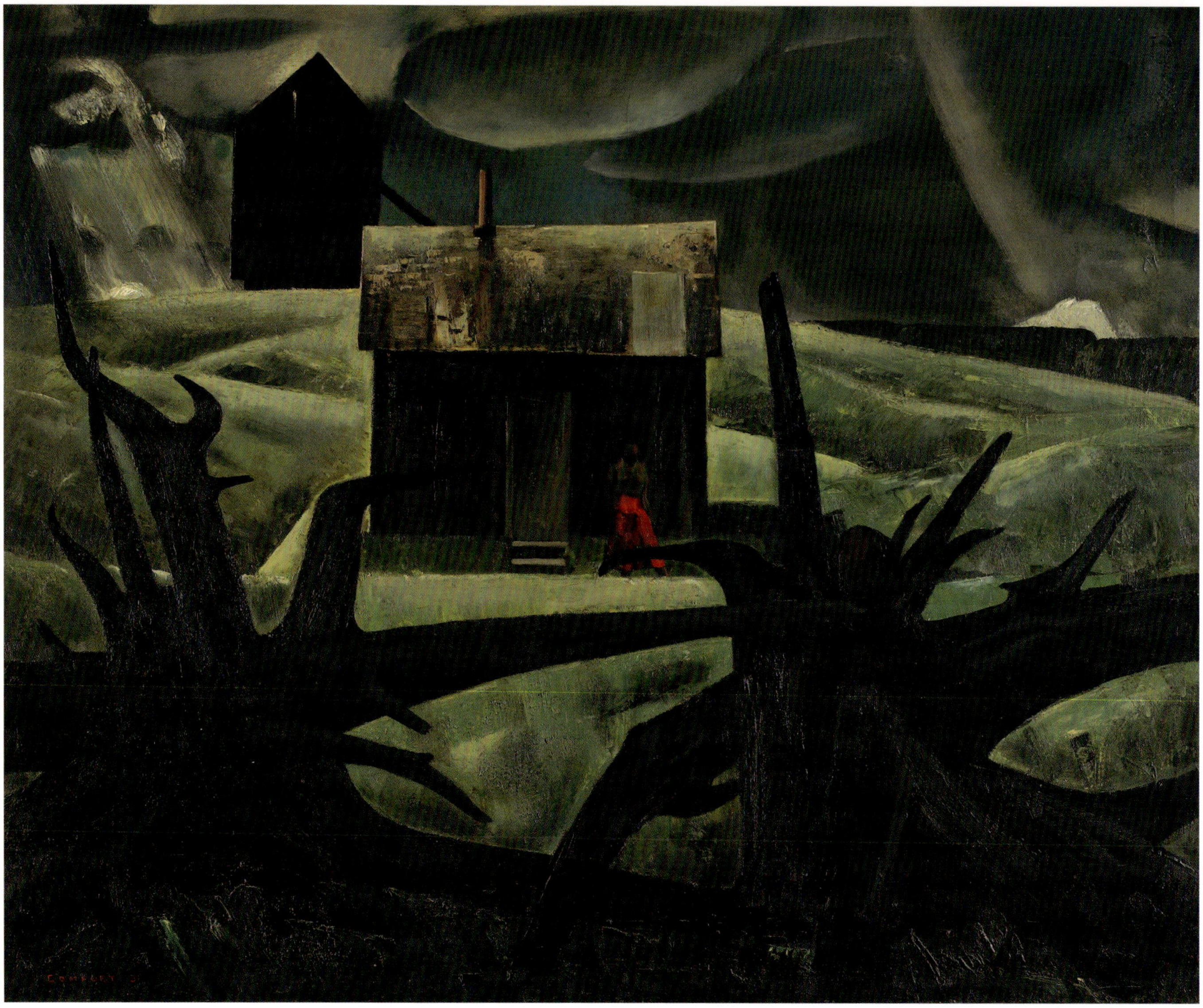

36. **Pioneer Survival**, 1938

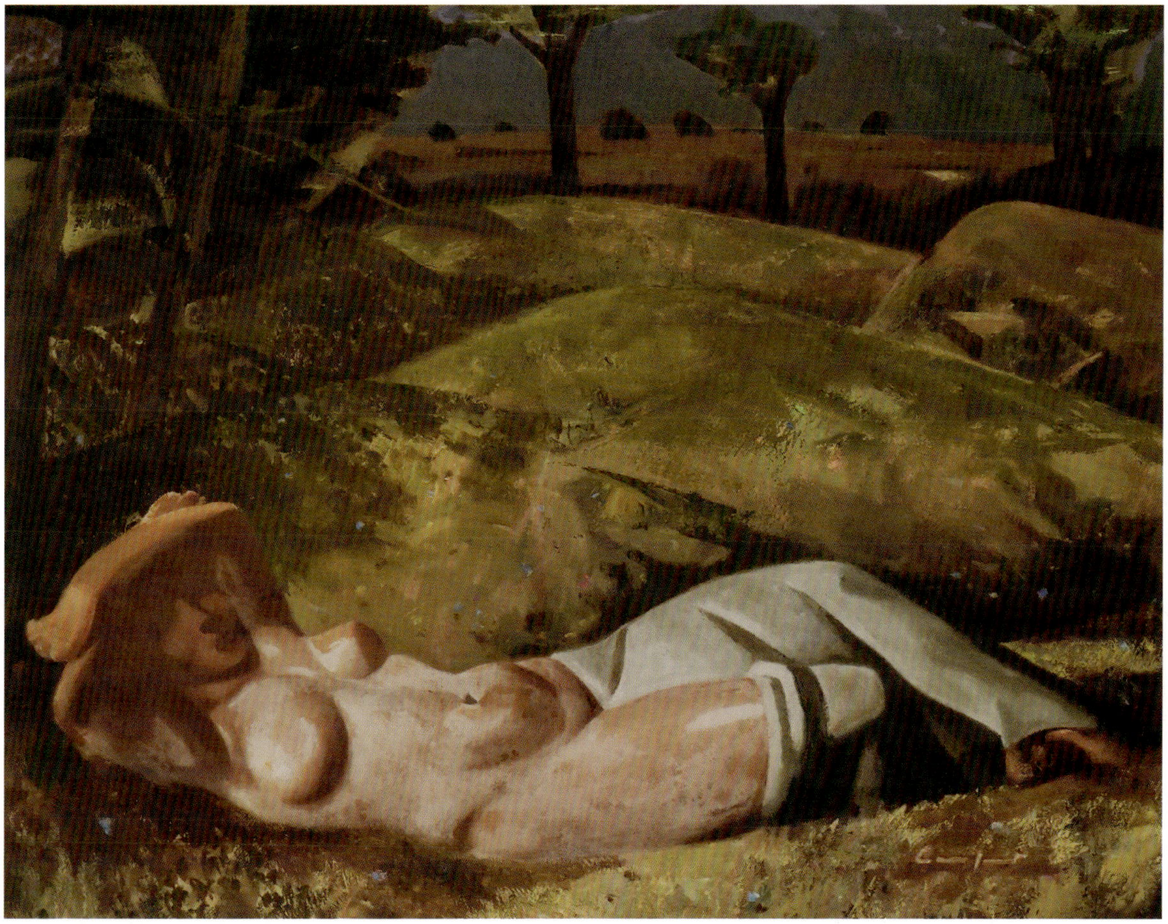

38. **Primavera II**, 1941/1972

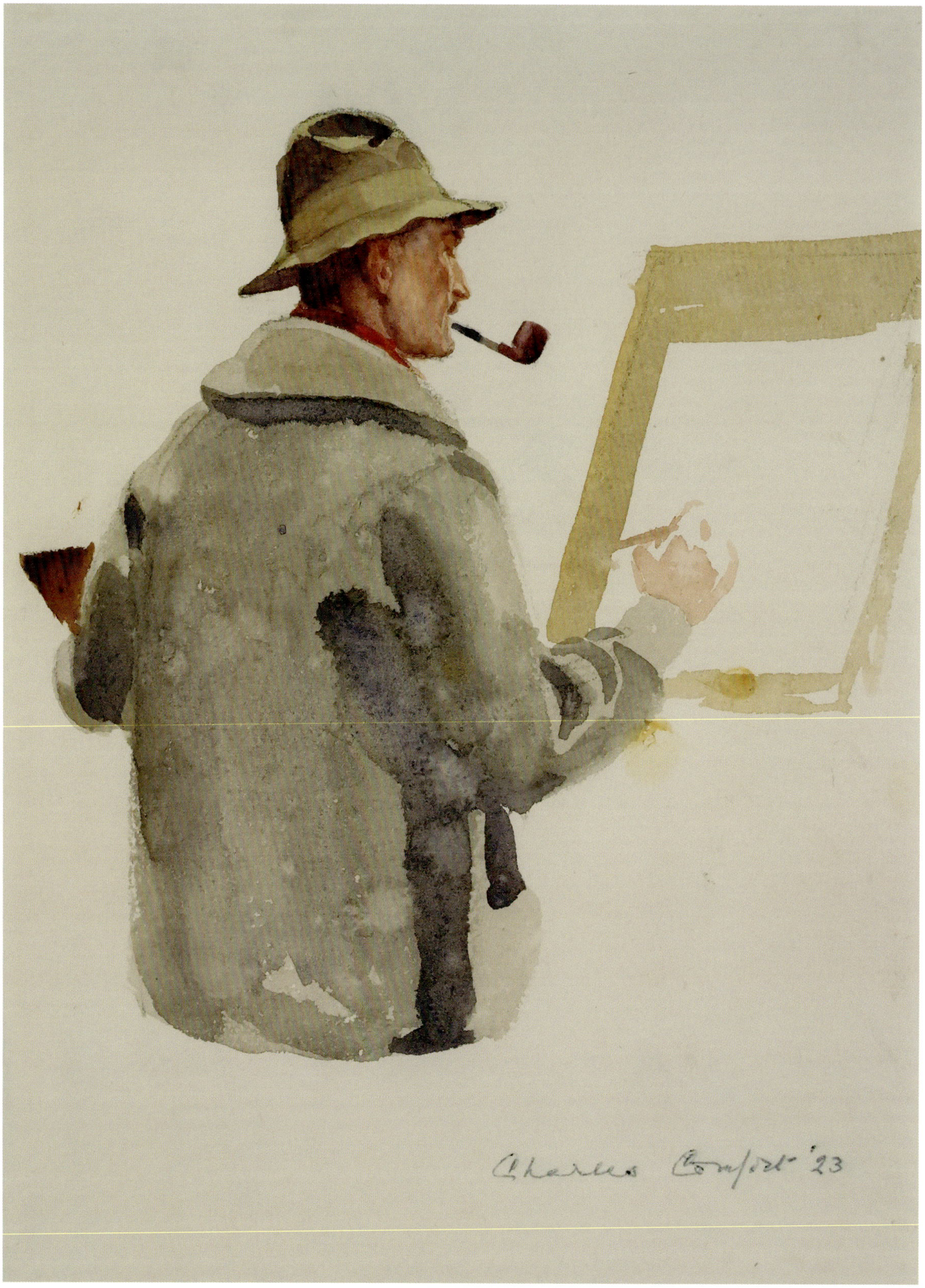

42. **H. Eric Bergman**, 1923

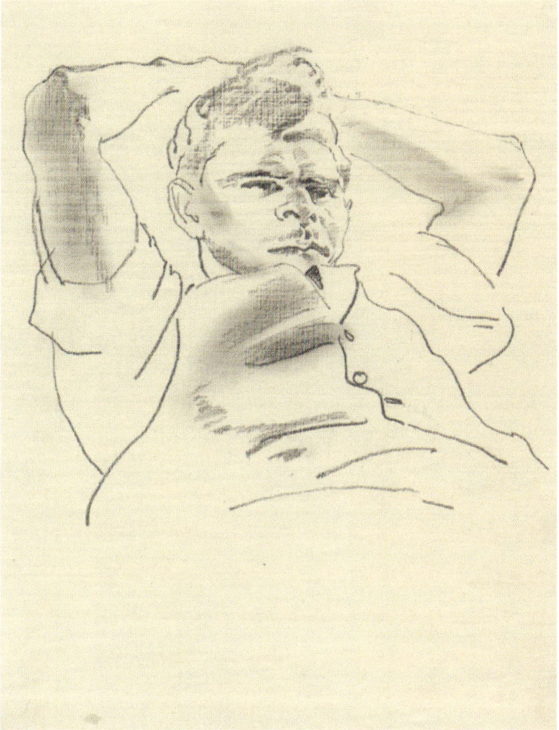

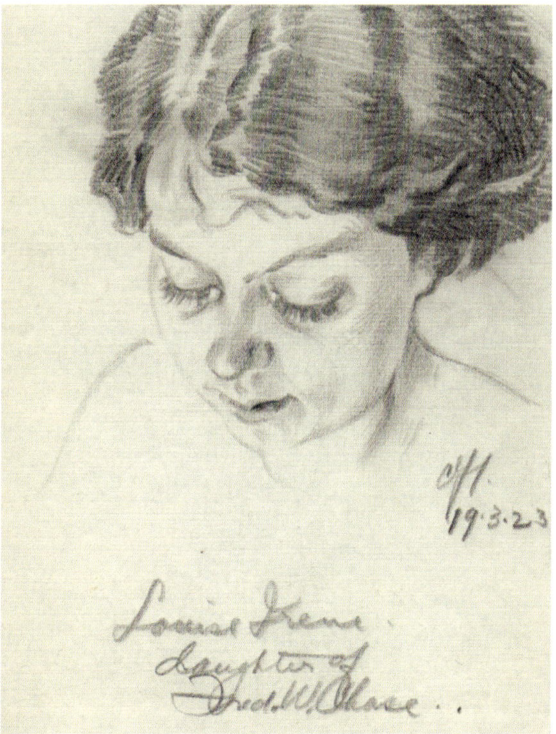

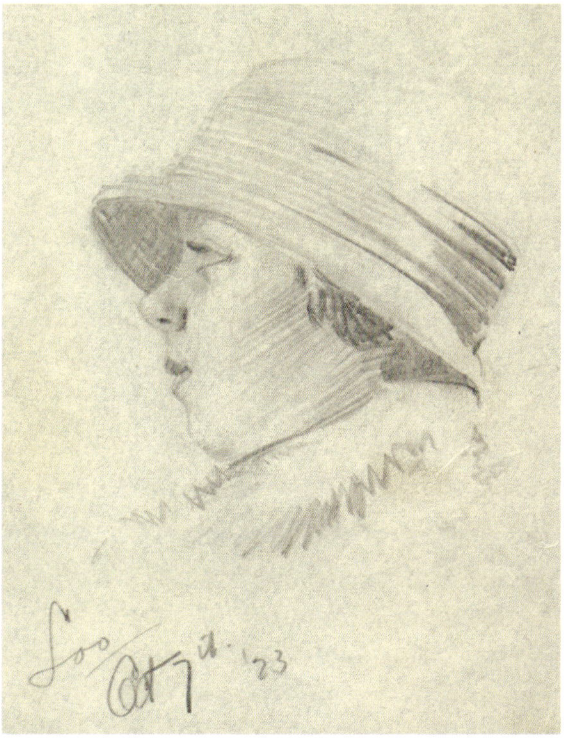

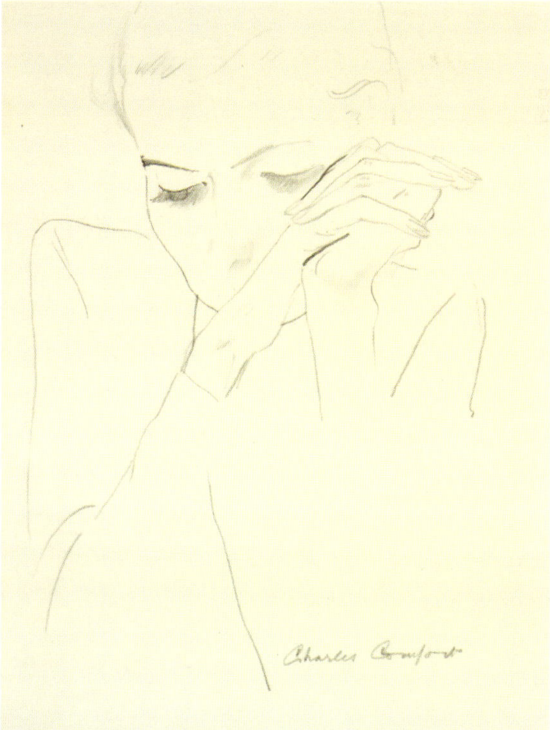

45. **Will Olgilvie**, 1931 | 41. **Louise Irene, daughter of Fred W. Chase**, 1923
40. **Loo (Head of Louise Comfort)**, 1923 | 49. **Untitled (Louise)**, 1933

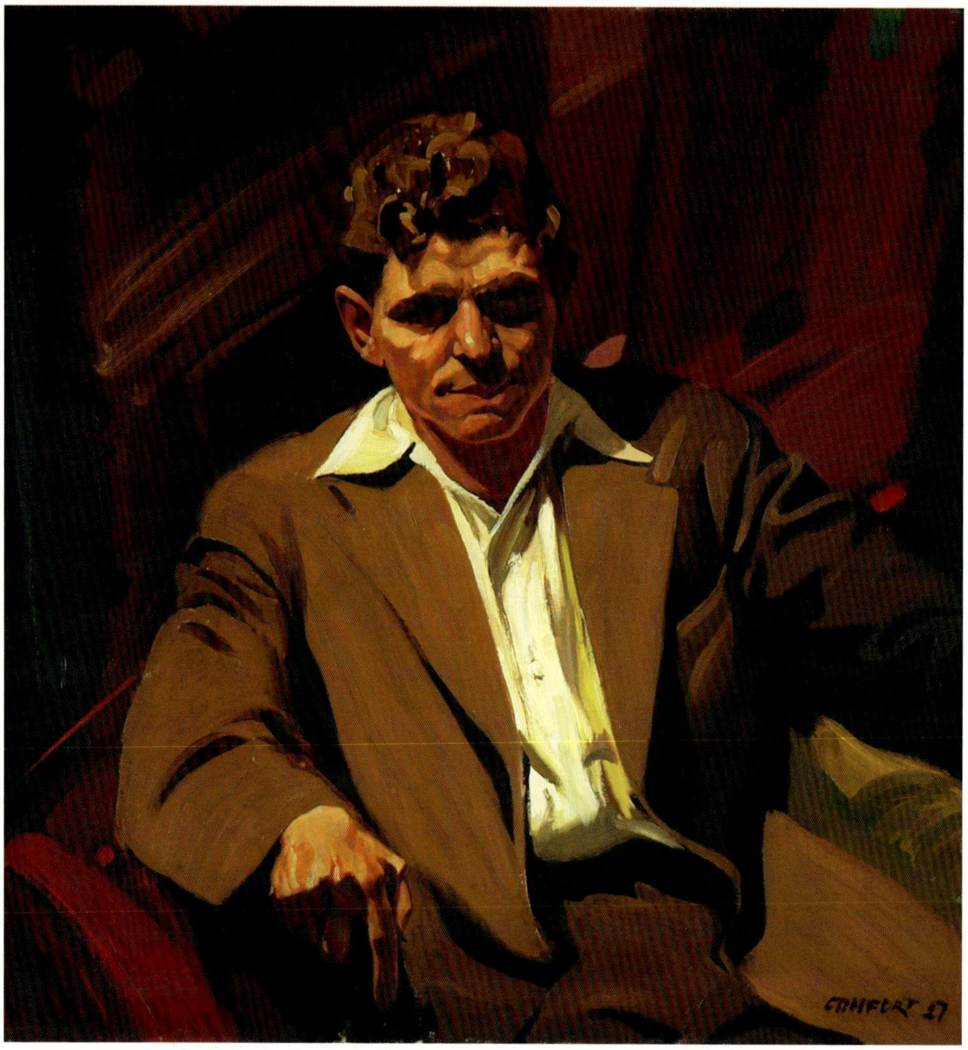

44. **Portrait of Will Ogilvie**, 1927 | 43. **Louise**, 1927

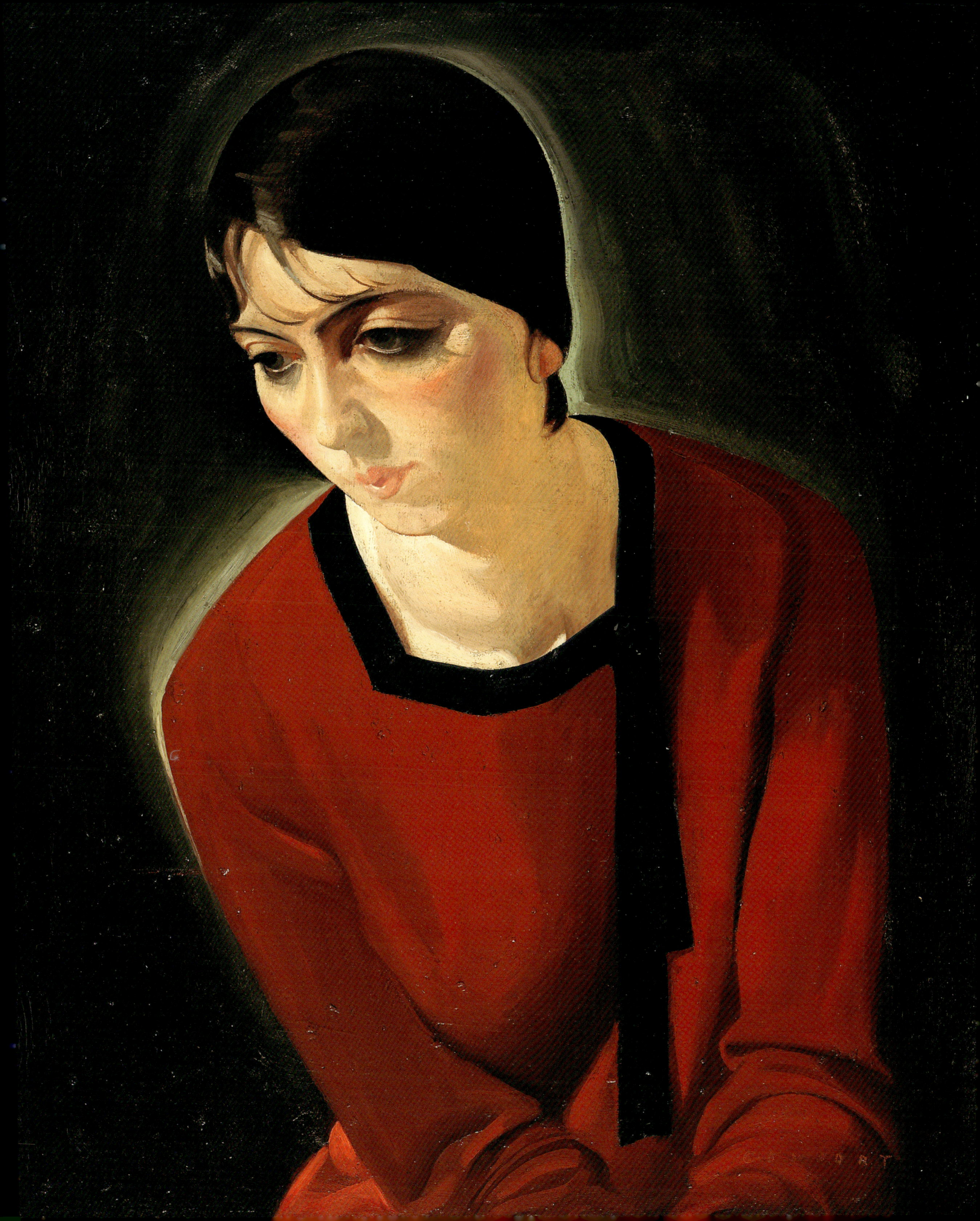

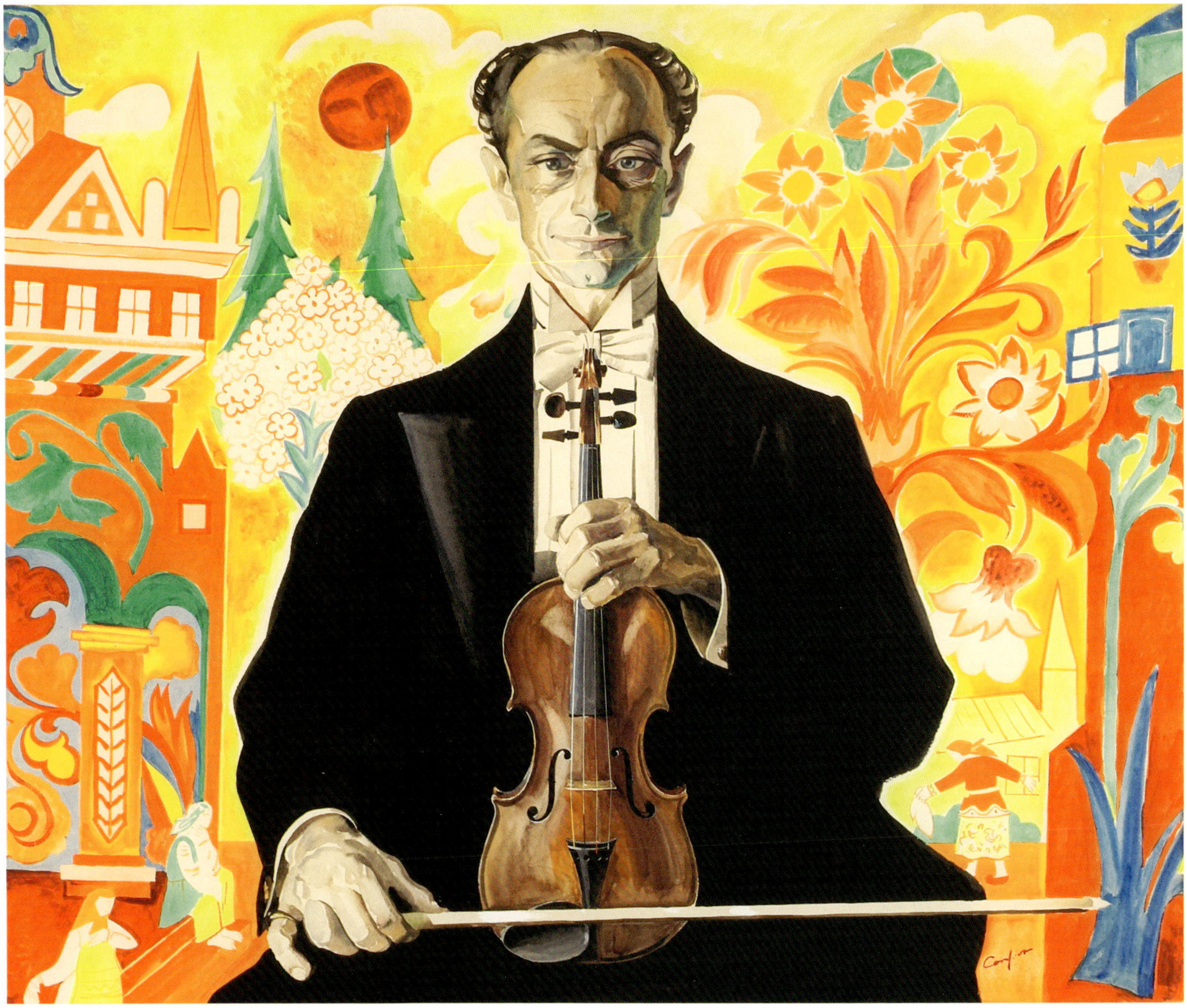

47. **Chuhaldin**, 1931

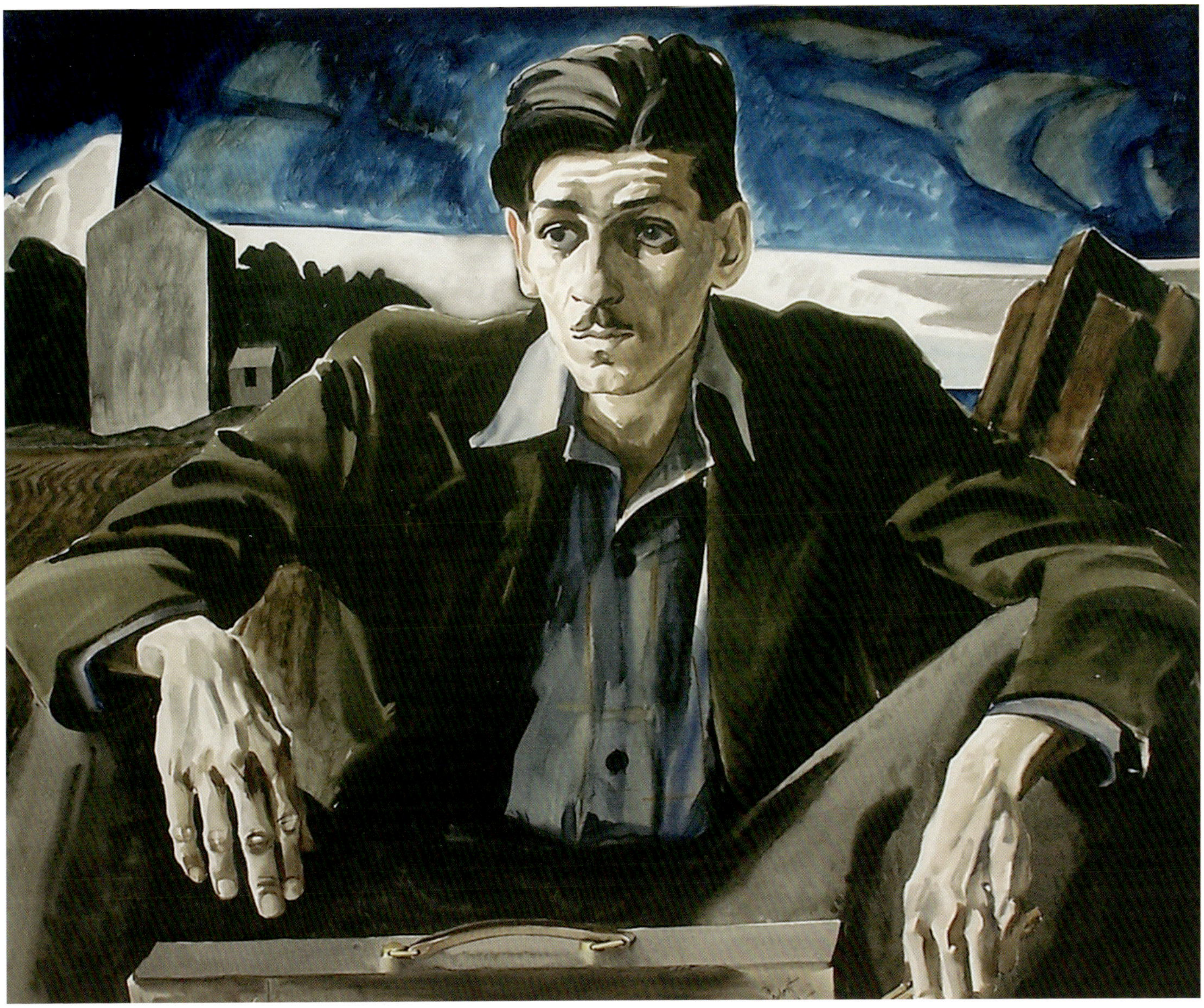

48. **Young Canadian**, 1932

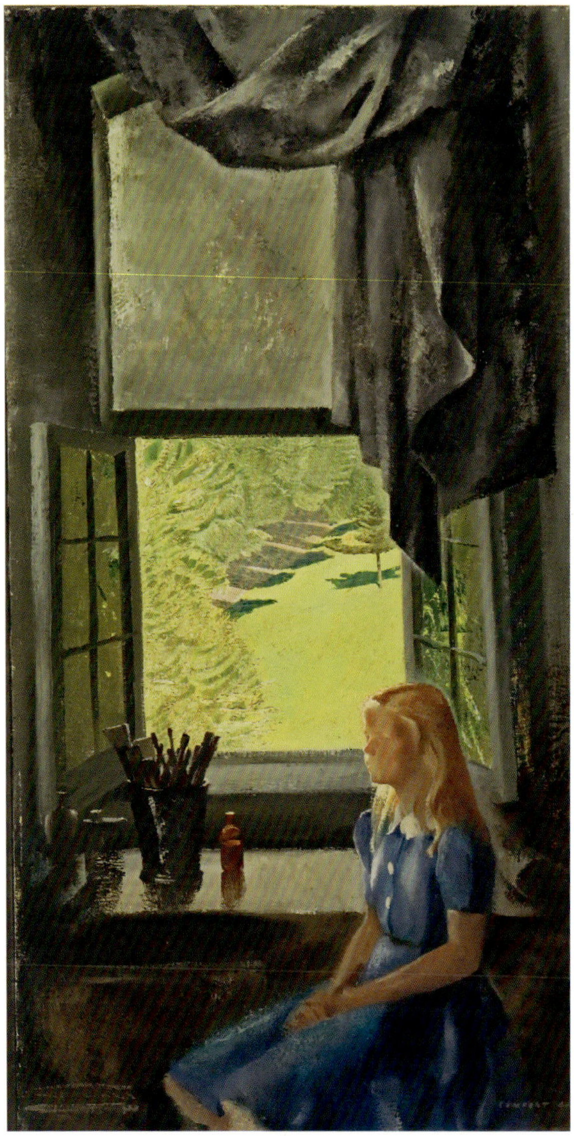

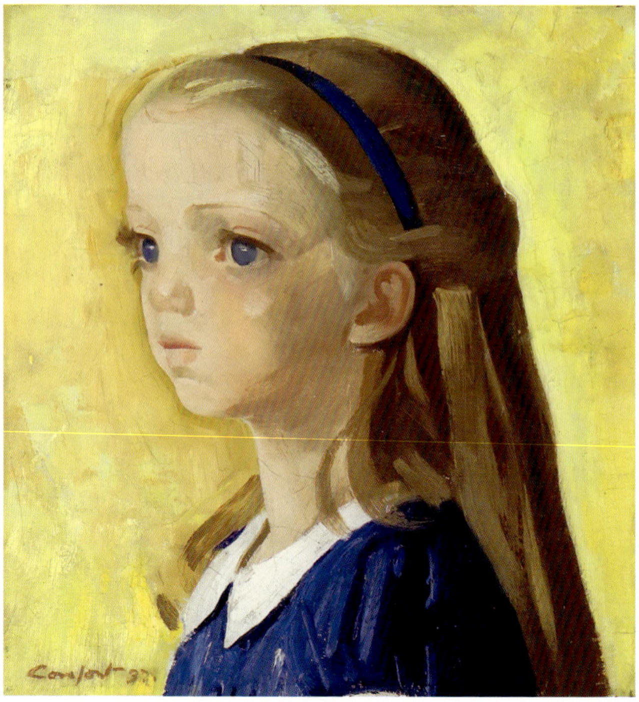

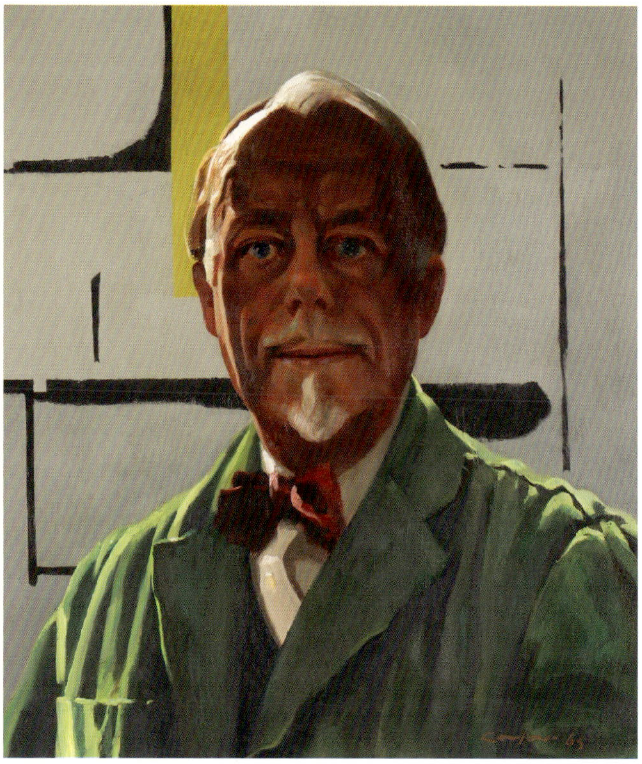

53. **Ruth at Studio Window**, 1940 | 52. **Portrait of Anne**, 1937 | 54. **Self-portrait**, 1965

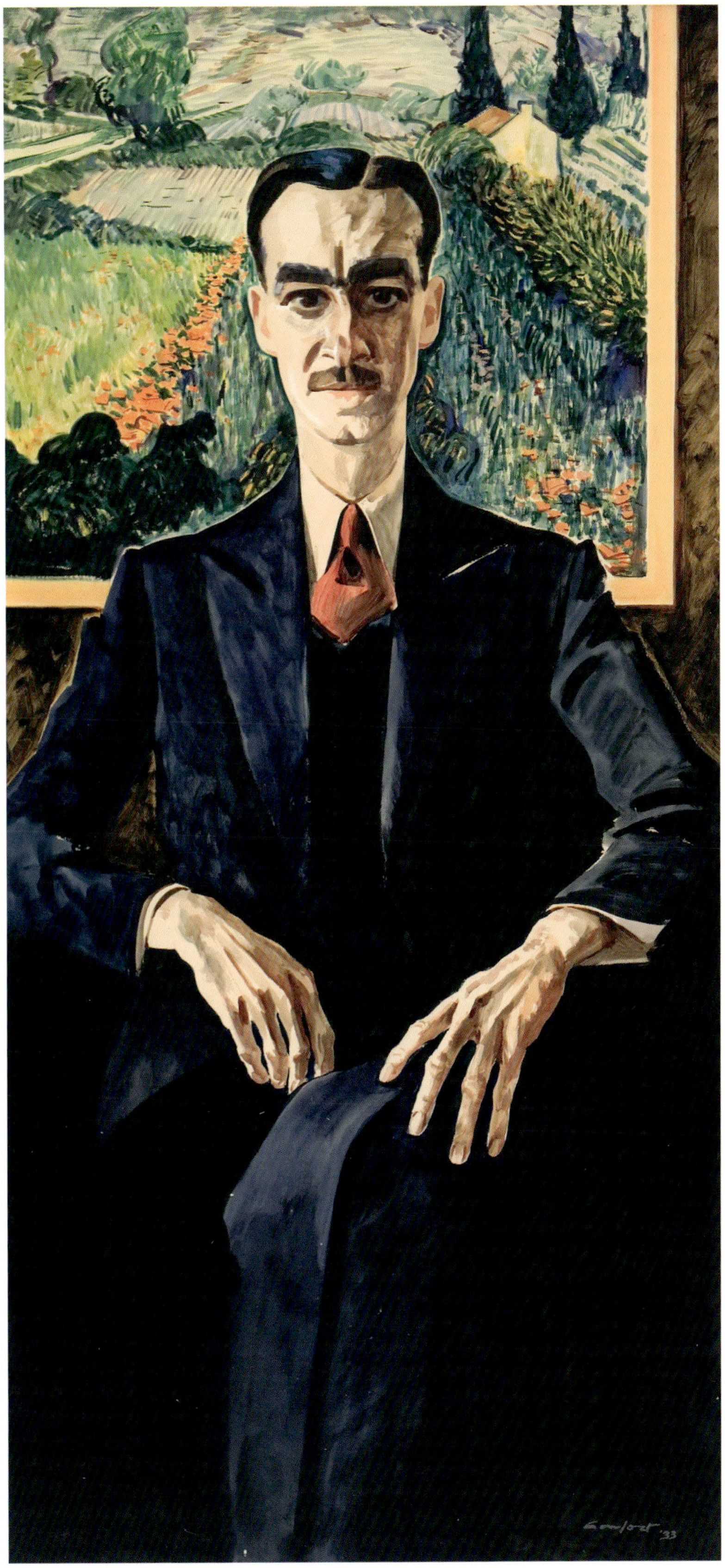

50. **Prof. Felix Walter**, 1933

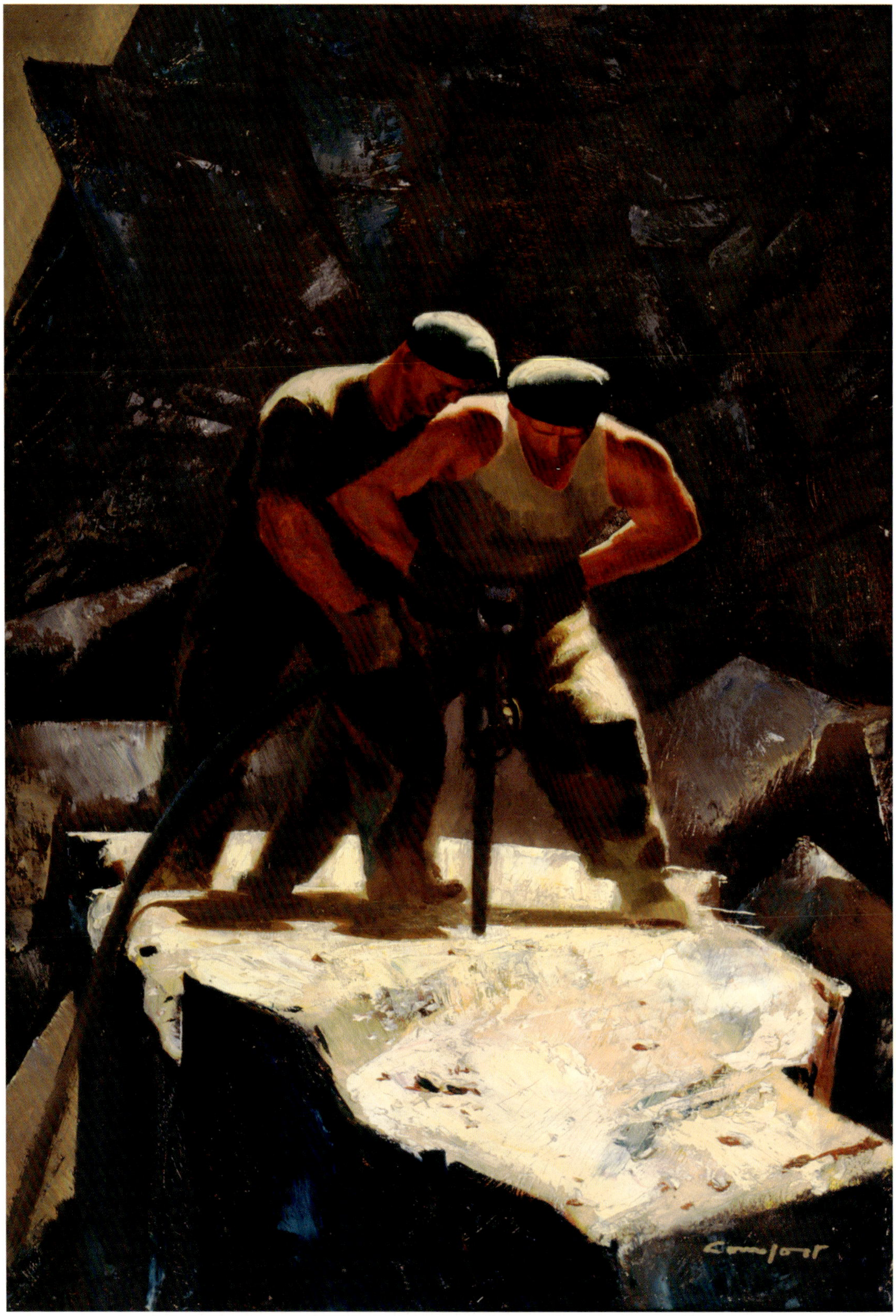

59. **Sappers Drilling in Preparation for Secondary Blasting**, 1943

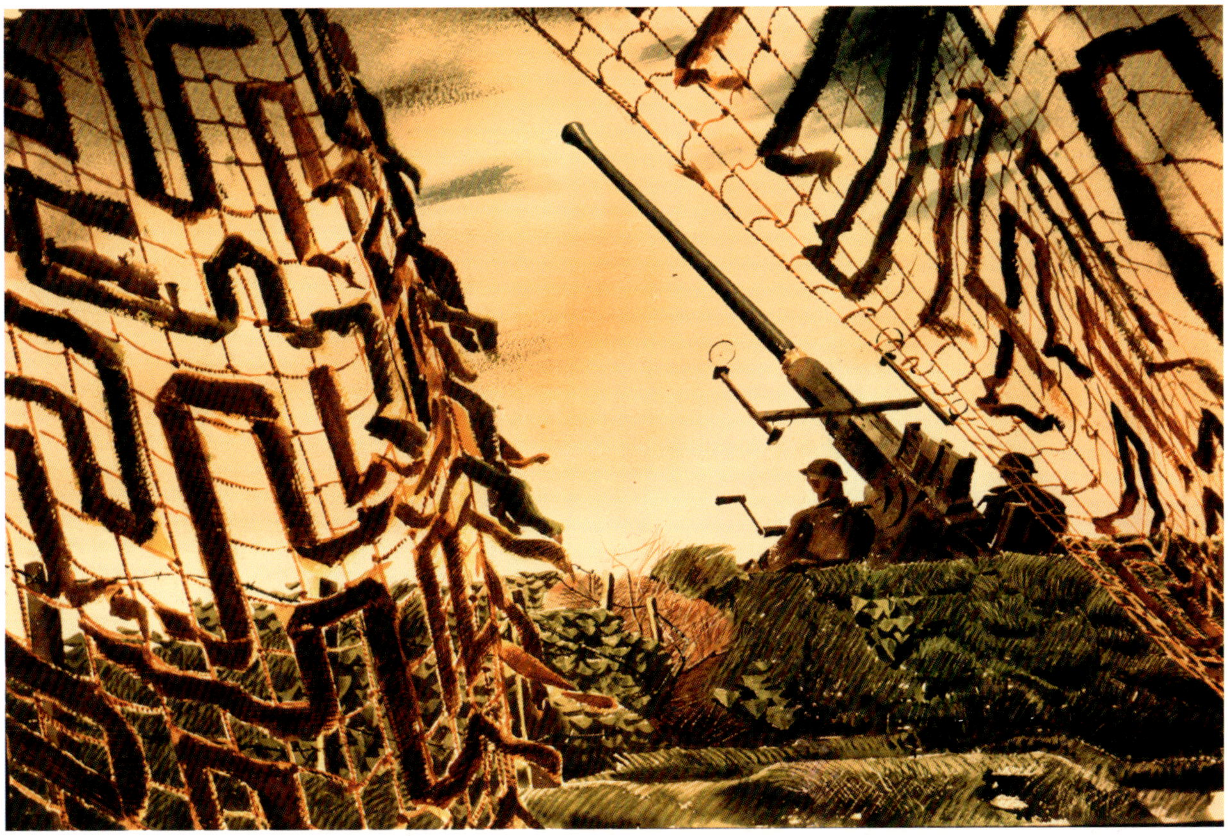

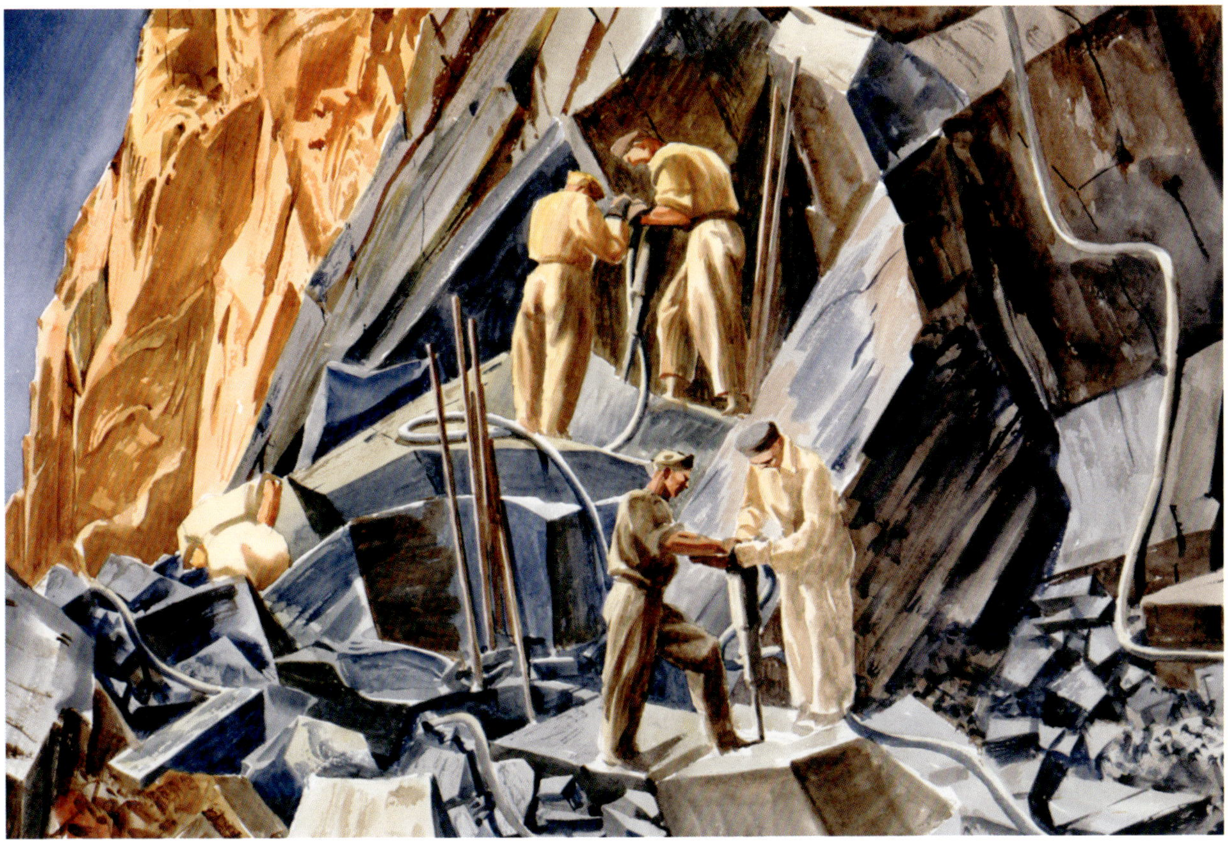

56. **Bofors Gun Site in a Field**, 1943 | 58. **Sappers Quarrying Stone**, 1943

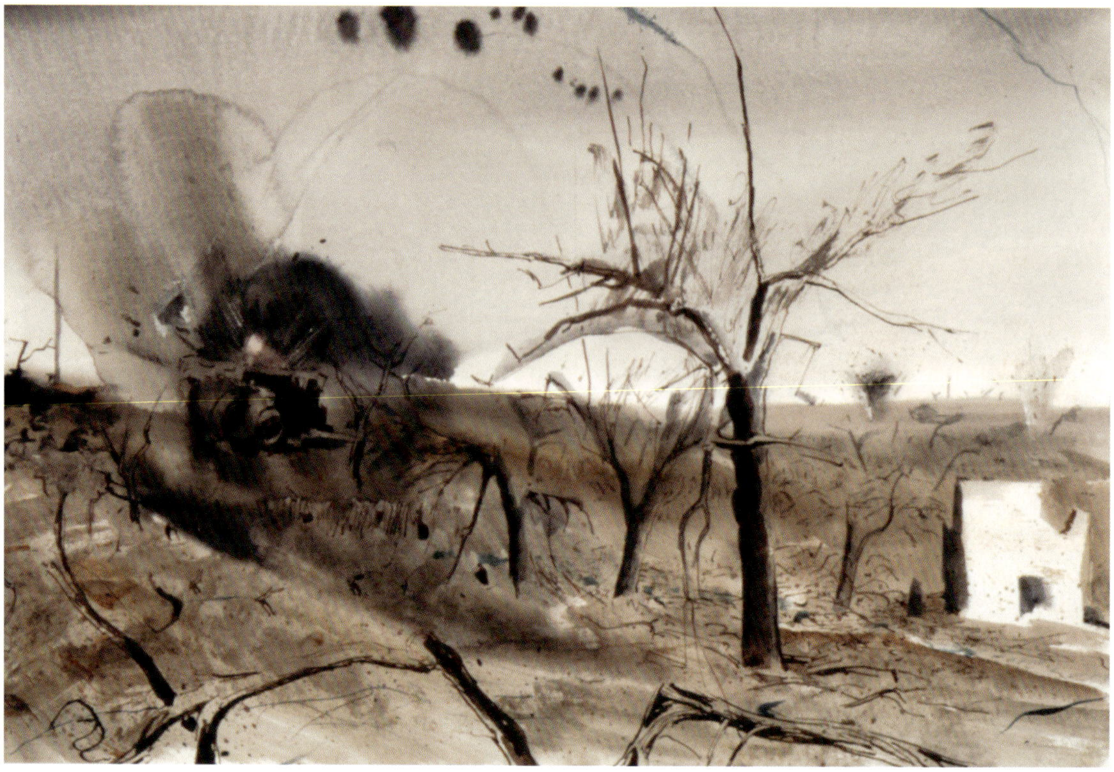

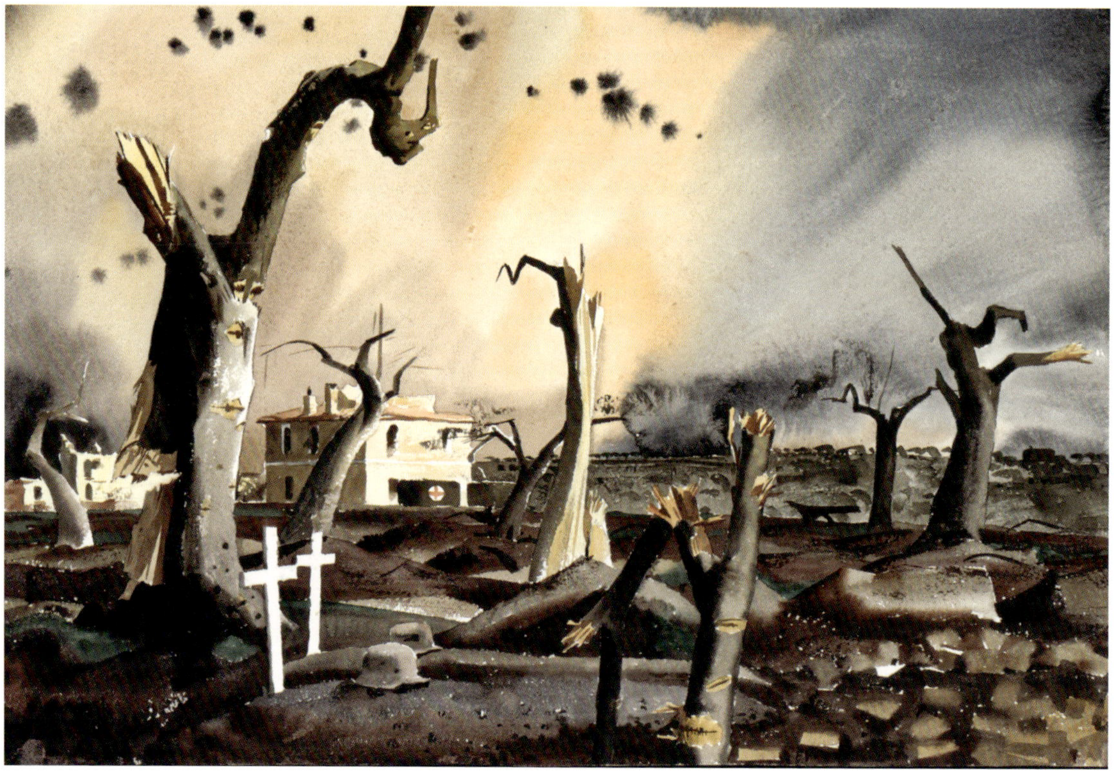

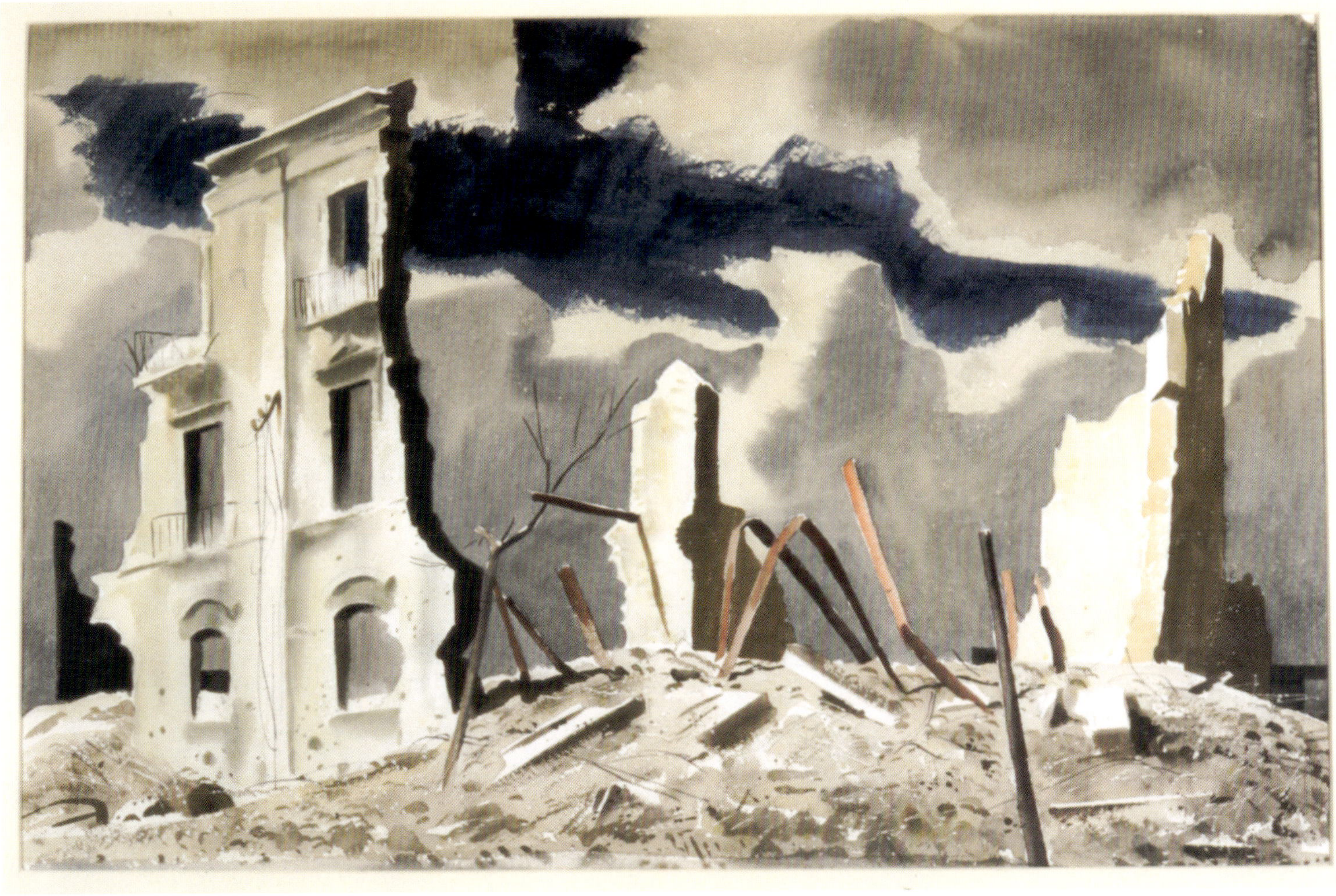

60. **Battle Scene (Fantasy)**, 1944 | 61. **Battlefield Near Berardi Crossroads**, 1944 | 62. **Wrecked Buildings, Ortona, Italy**, 1944

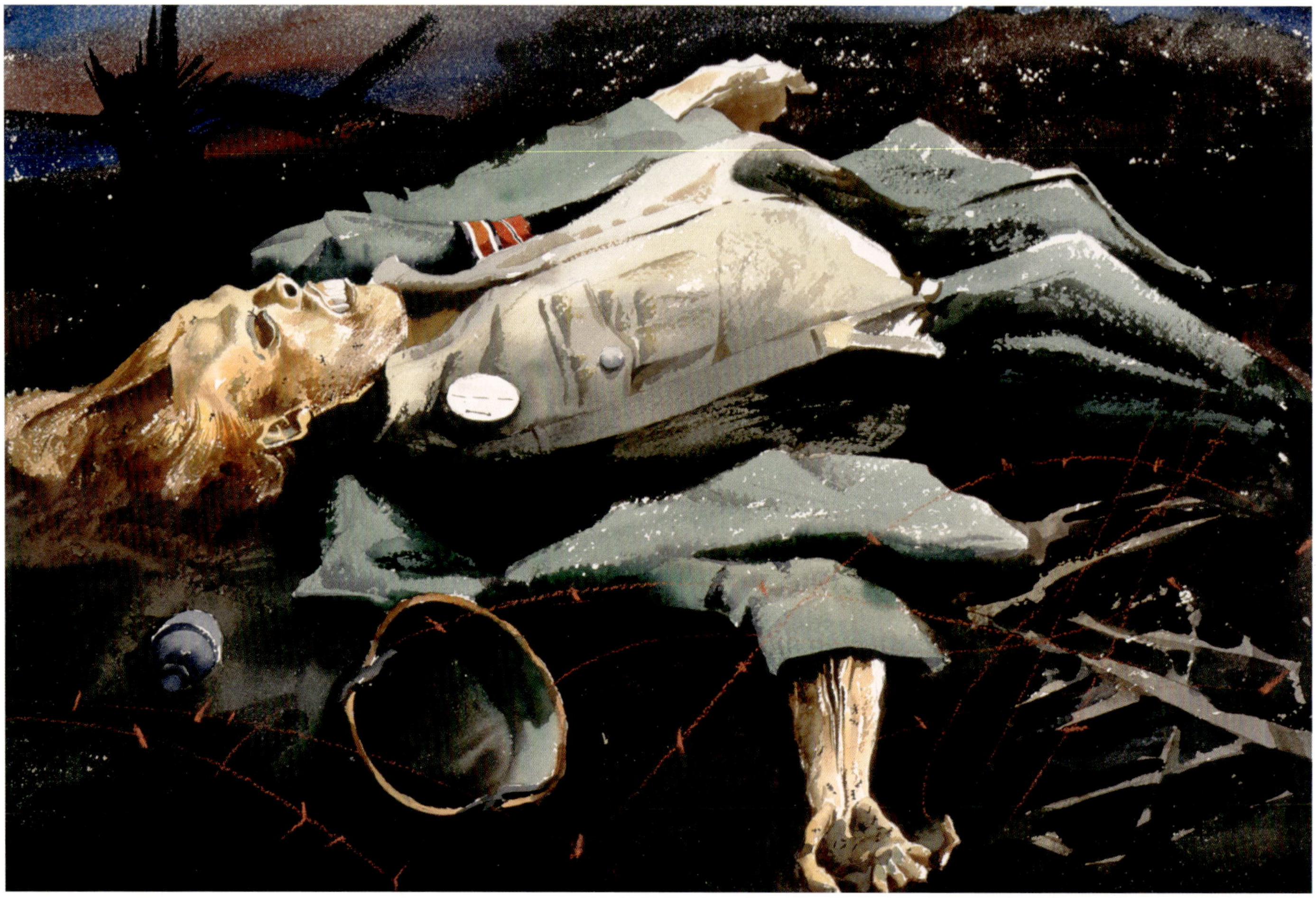

63. **Dead German on the Hitler Line**, 1944

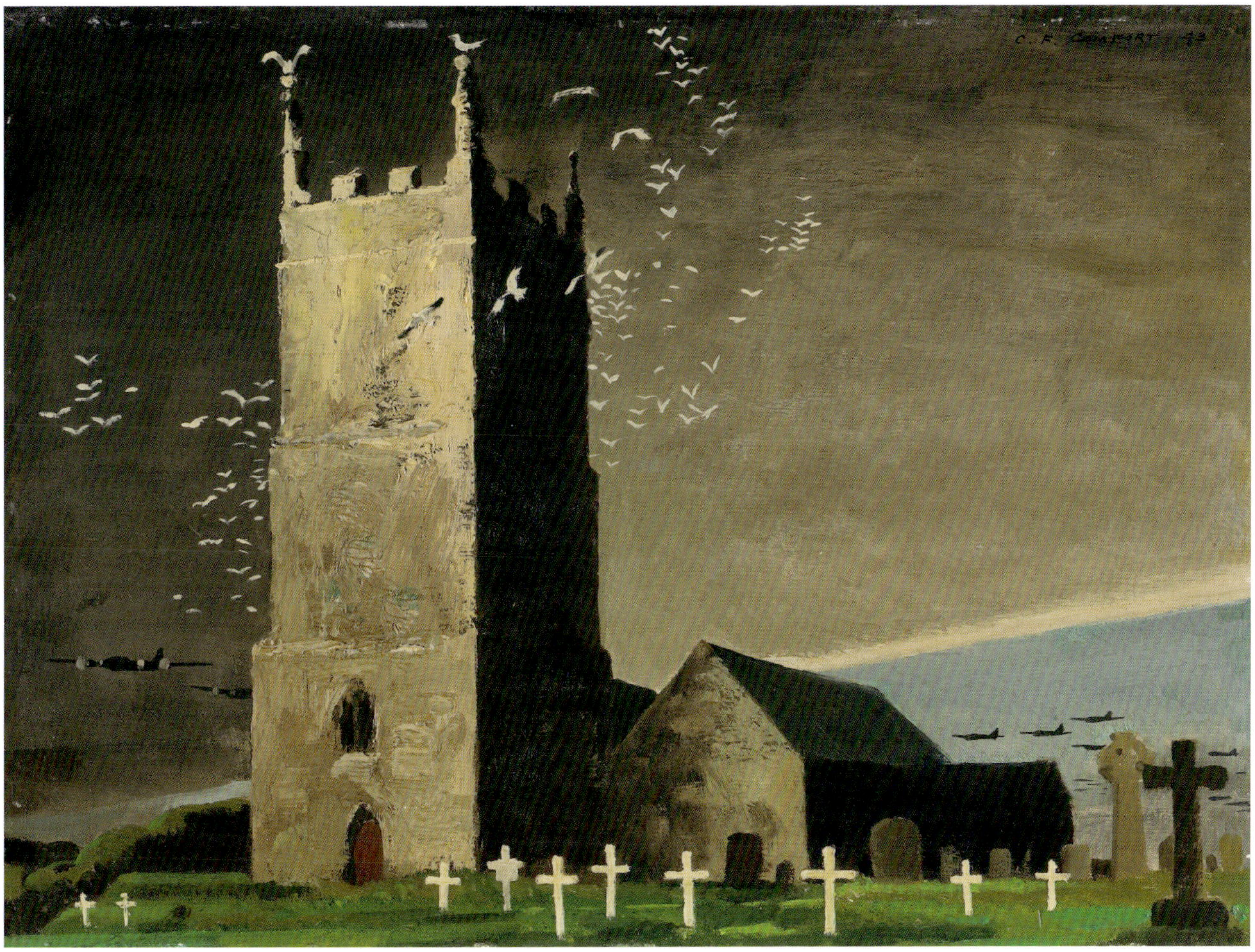

57. **St. Eval Church, Cornwall**, 1943

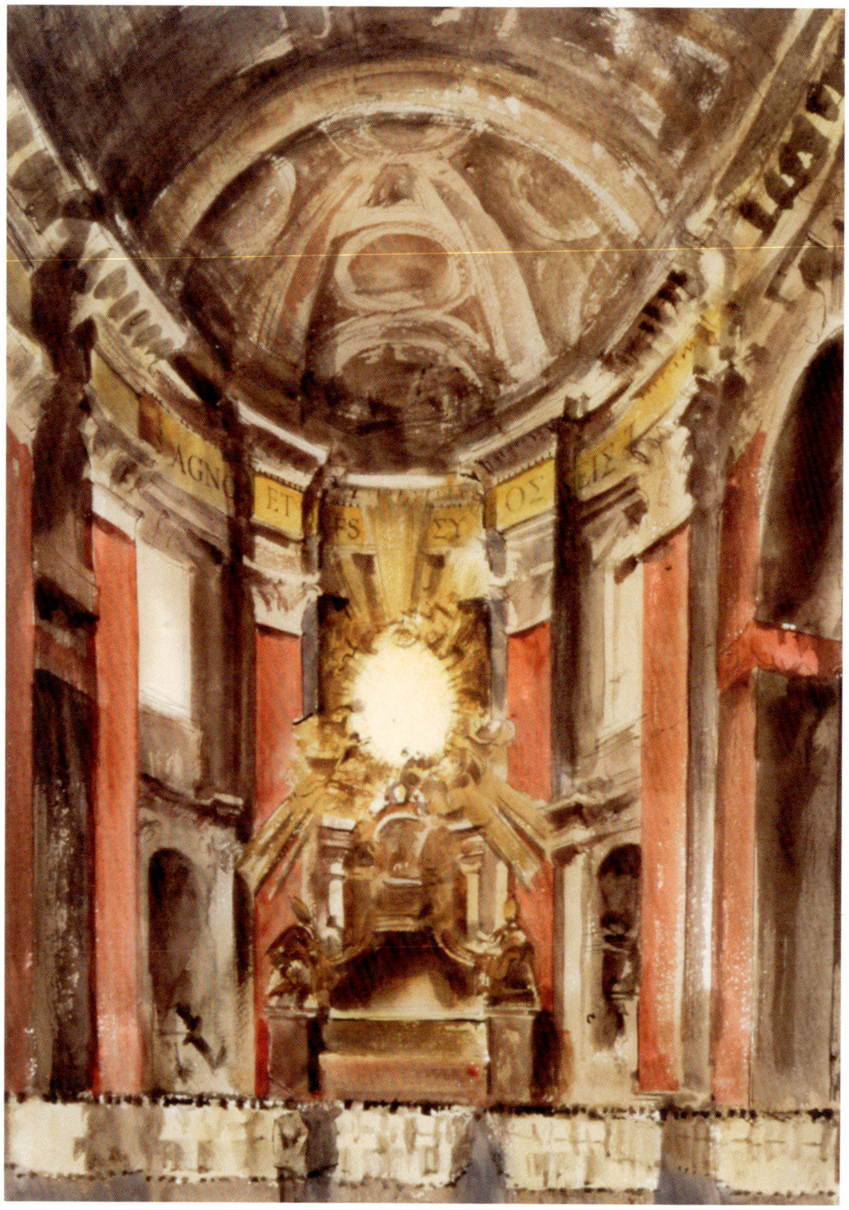

65. **San Pietro in Vaticano, Rome**, 1944

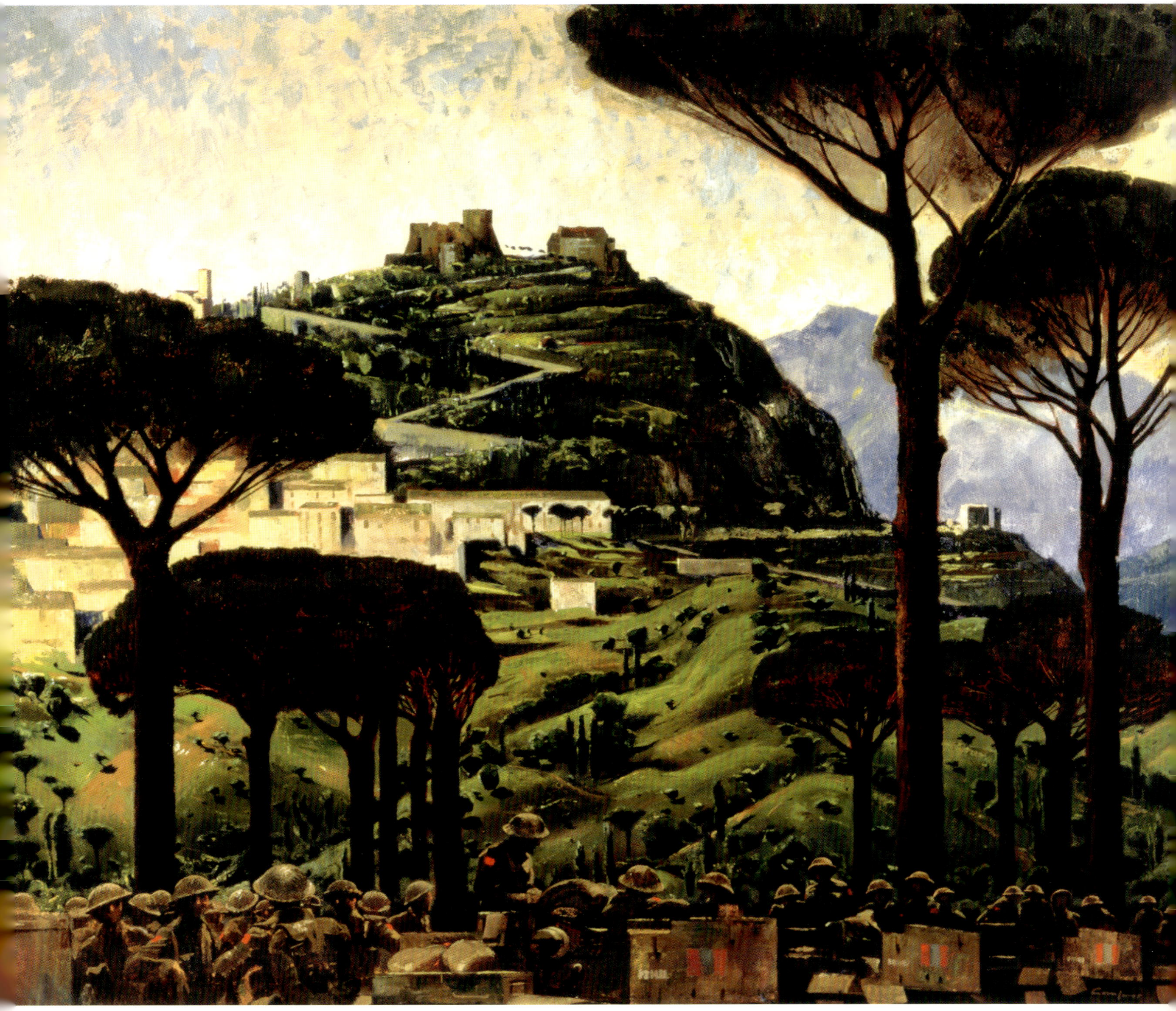

67. **Campobasso**, c. 1945

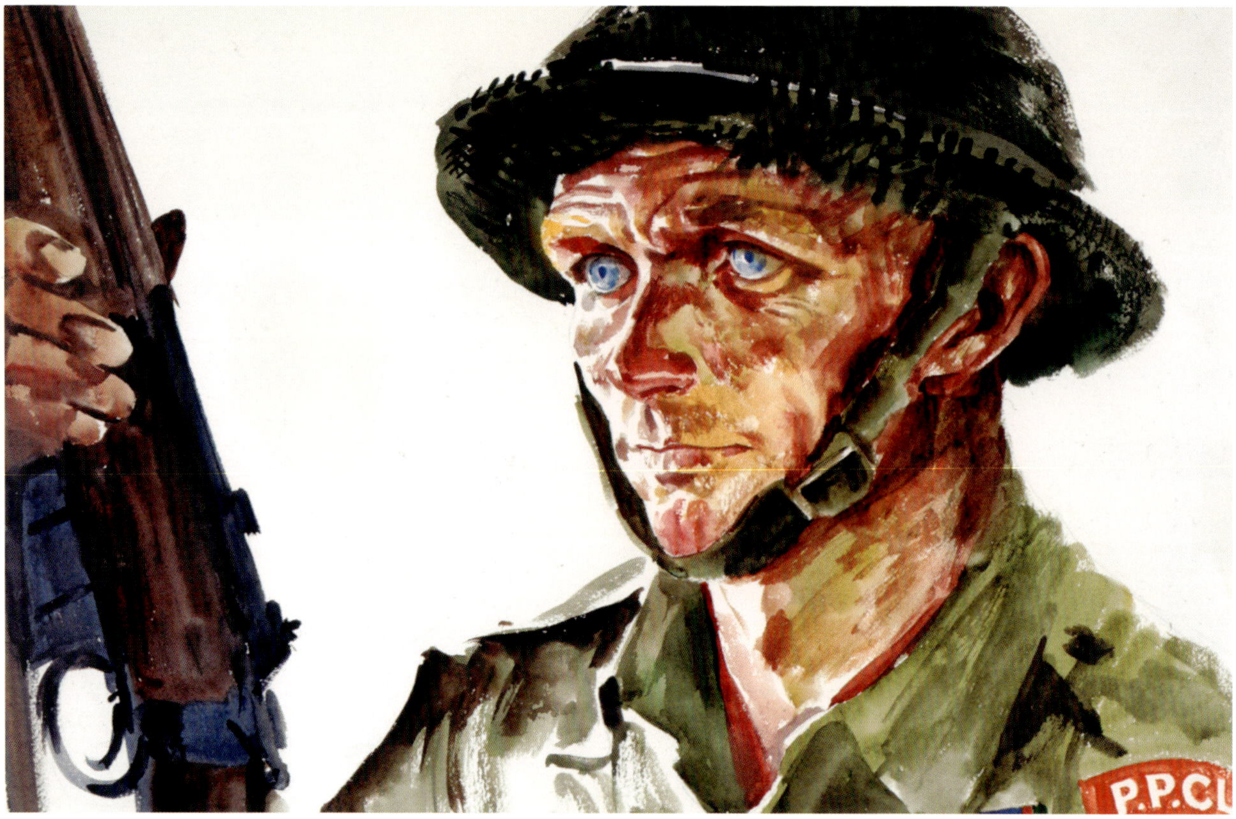

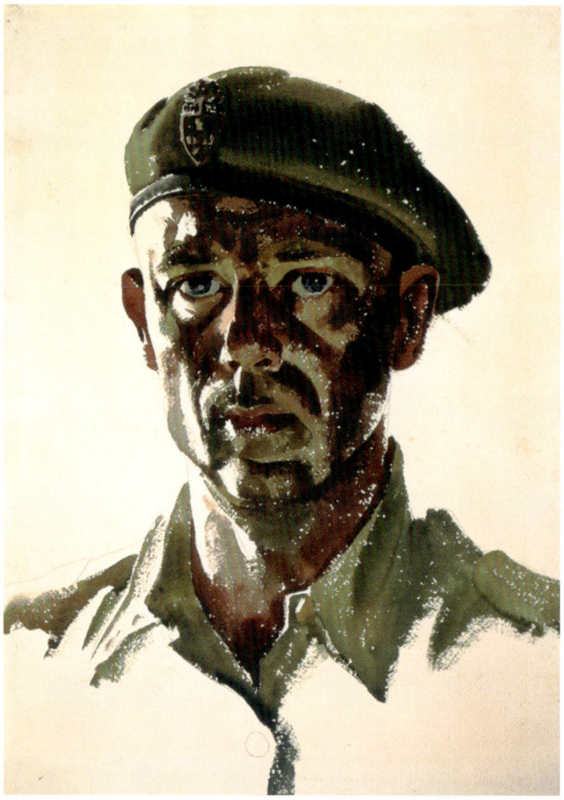

66. **Sergeant P.J. Ford**, 1944 | 64. **Major C.F. Comfort**, 1944

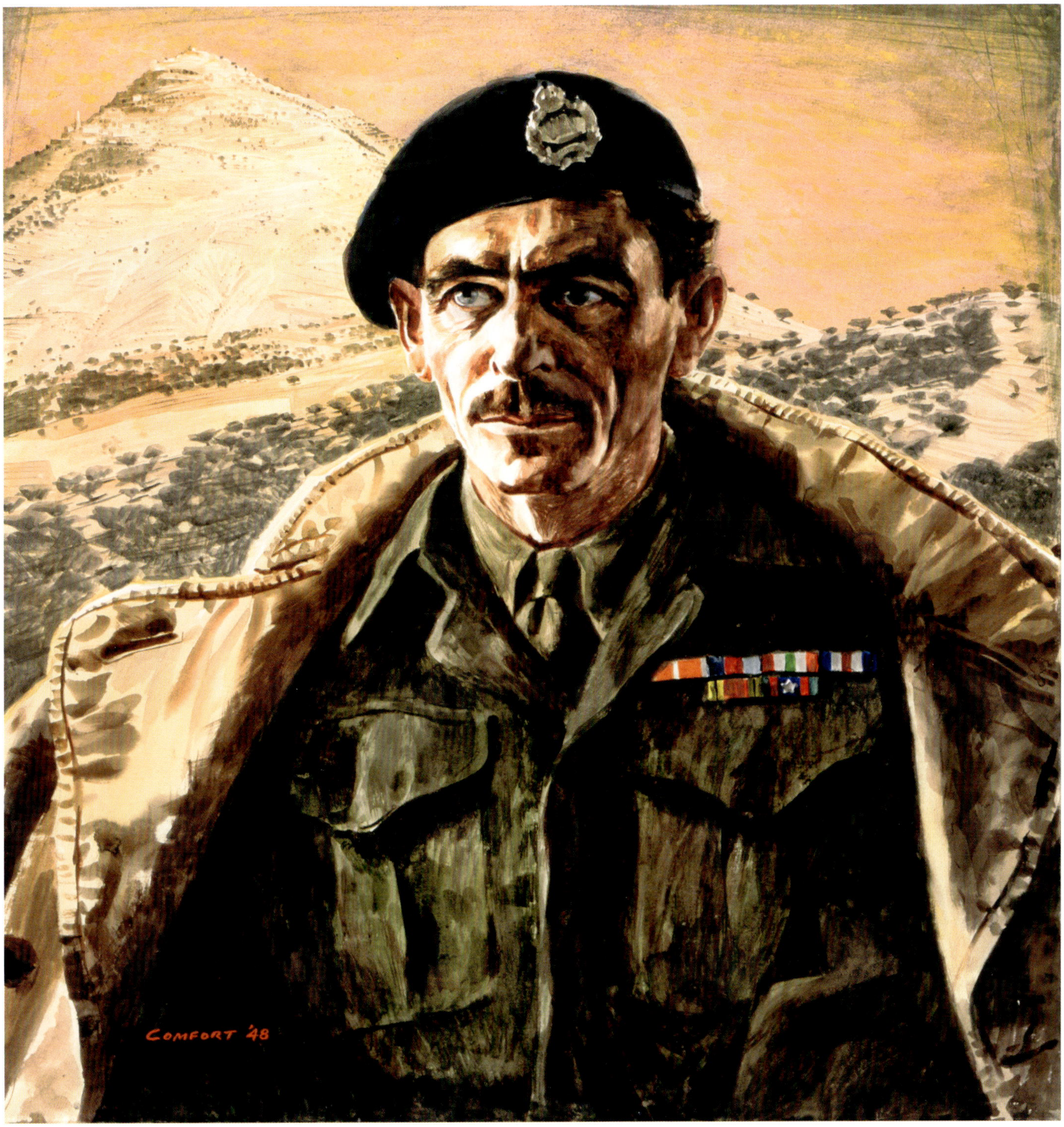

68. **Major W.A. Ogilvie**, 1948

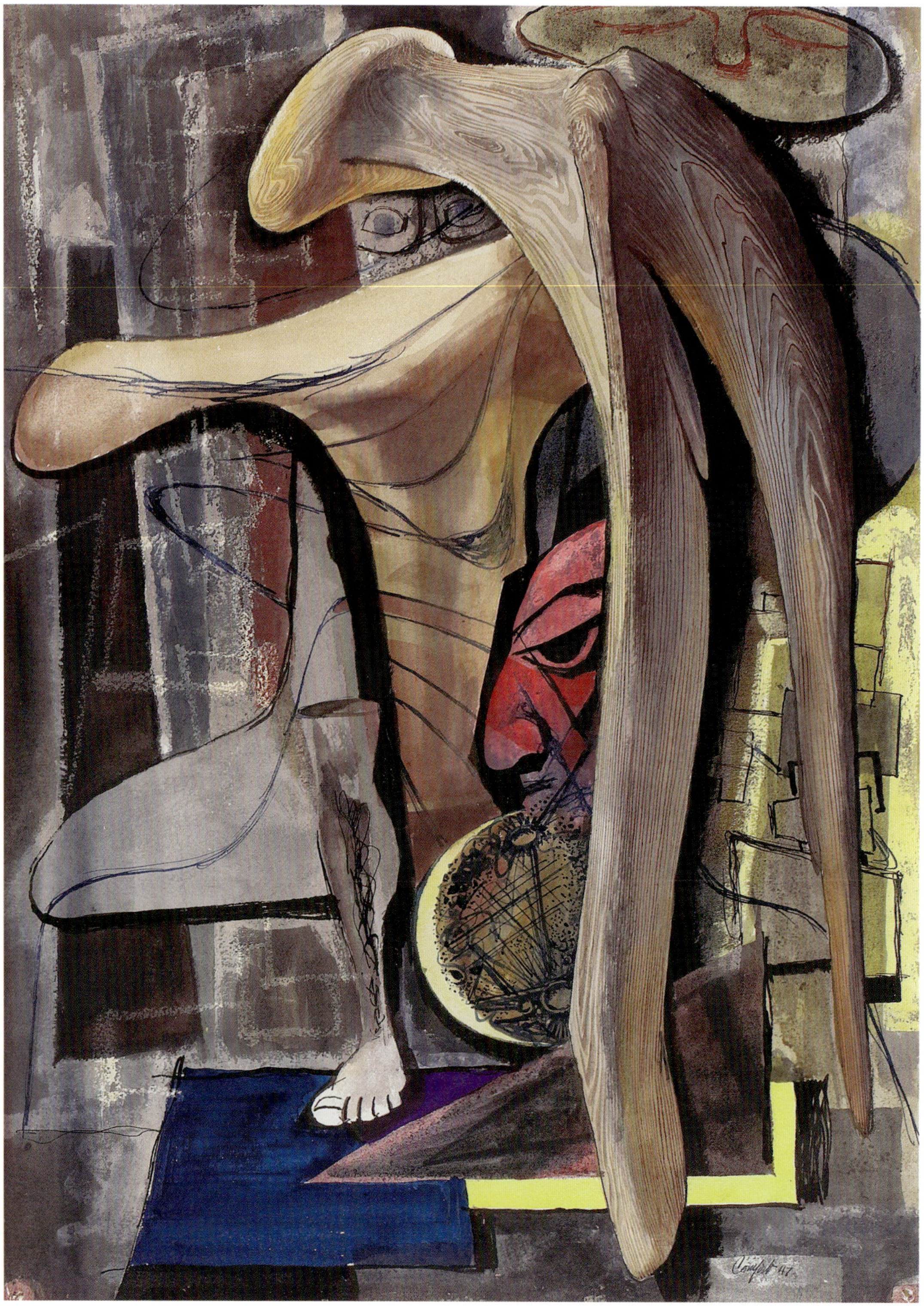

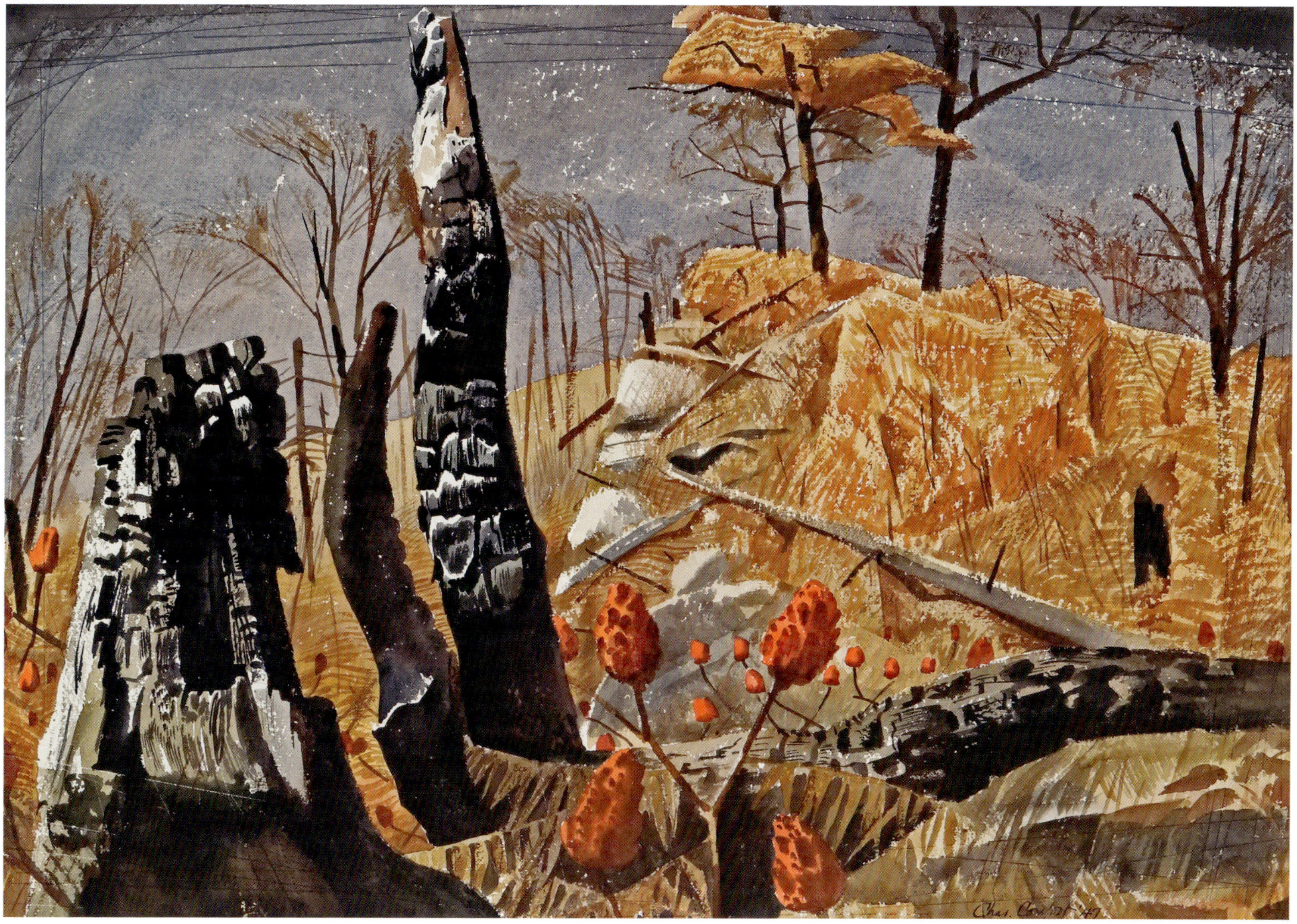

70. **Aeons Ago**, 1947 | 71. **Transfiguration**, 1947

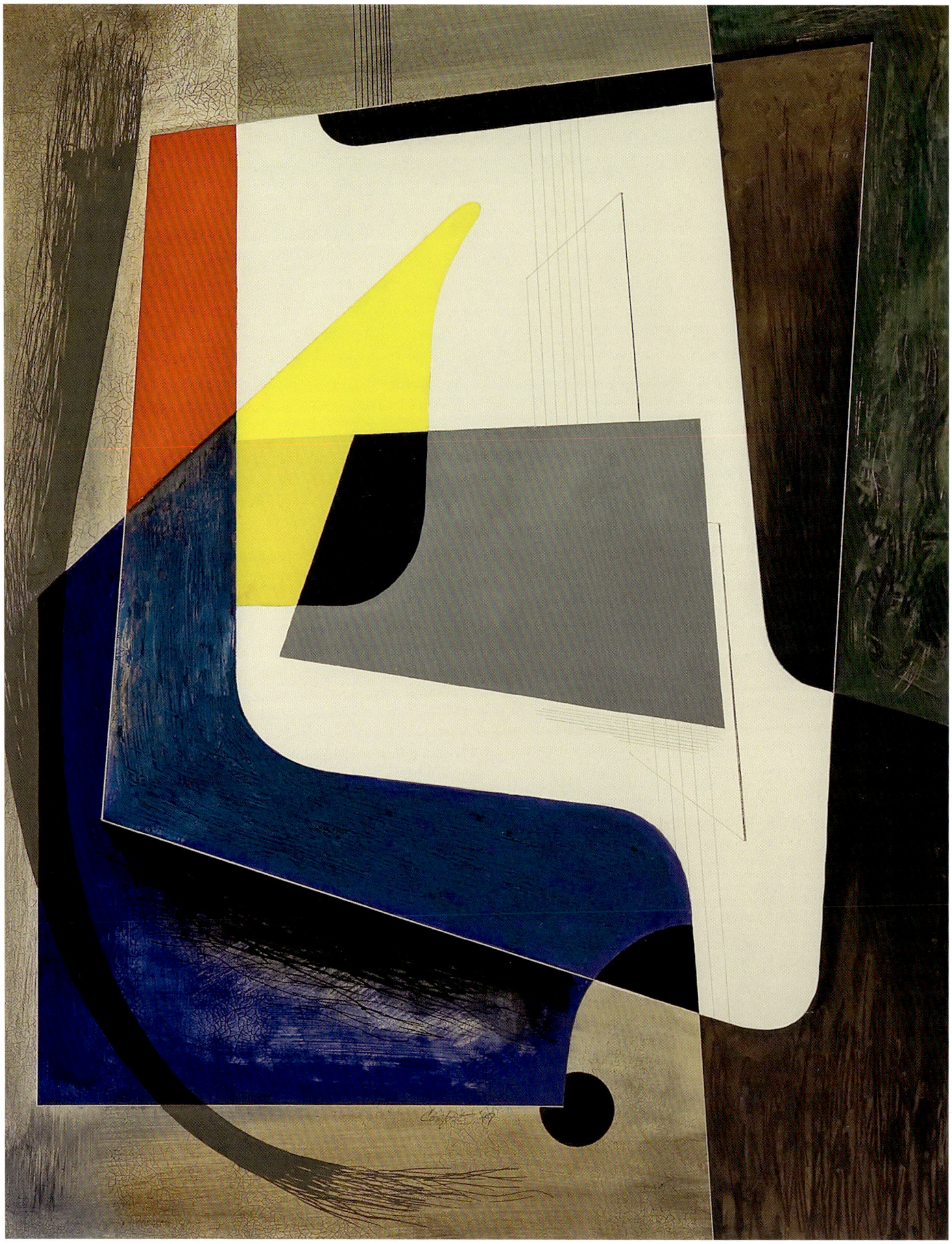

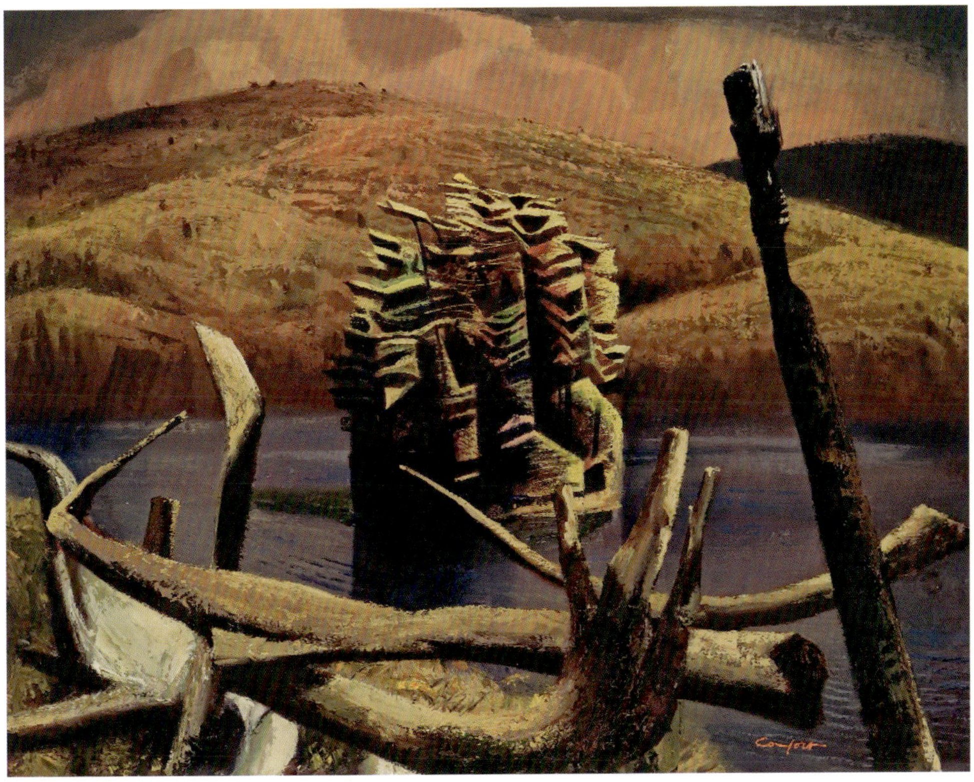

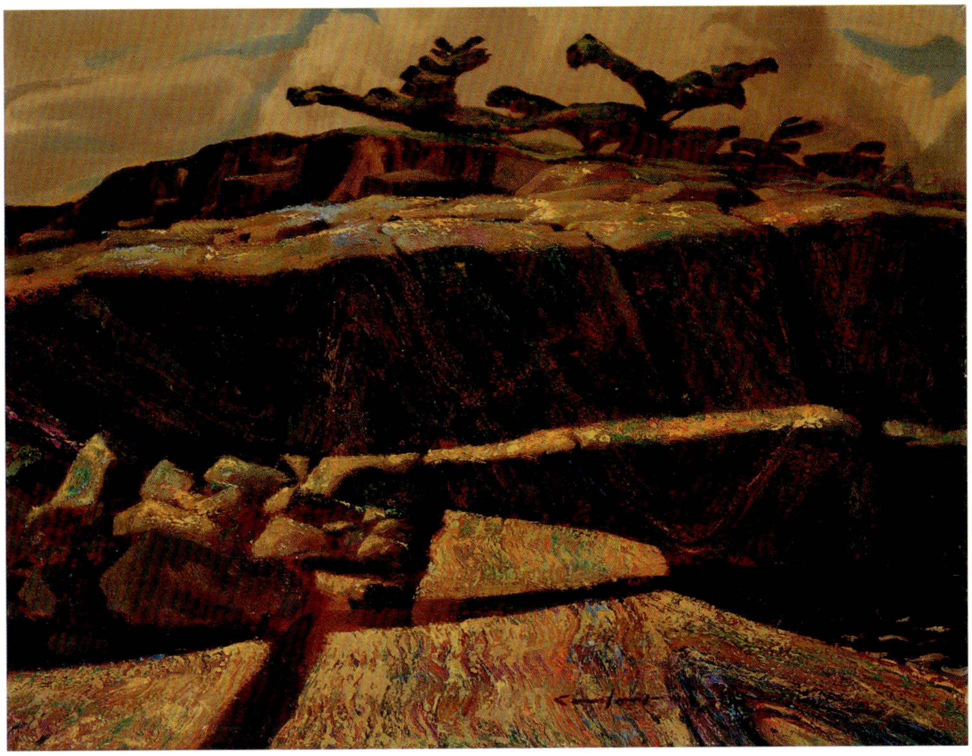

72. **Thrush Song**, 1949 | 73. **Aura Lee**, 1949/1950 | 74. **Rocky Site**,1952

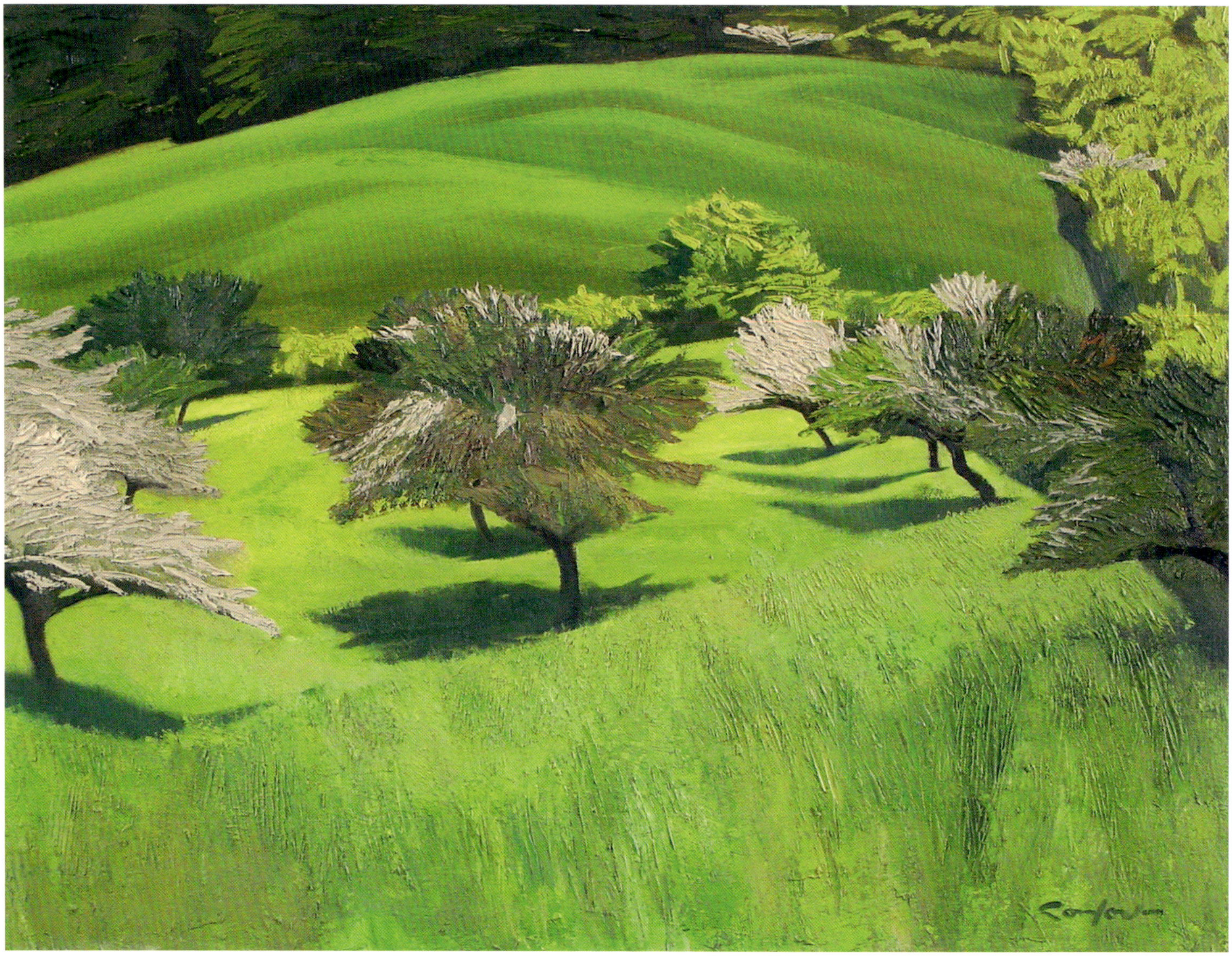

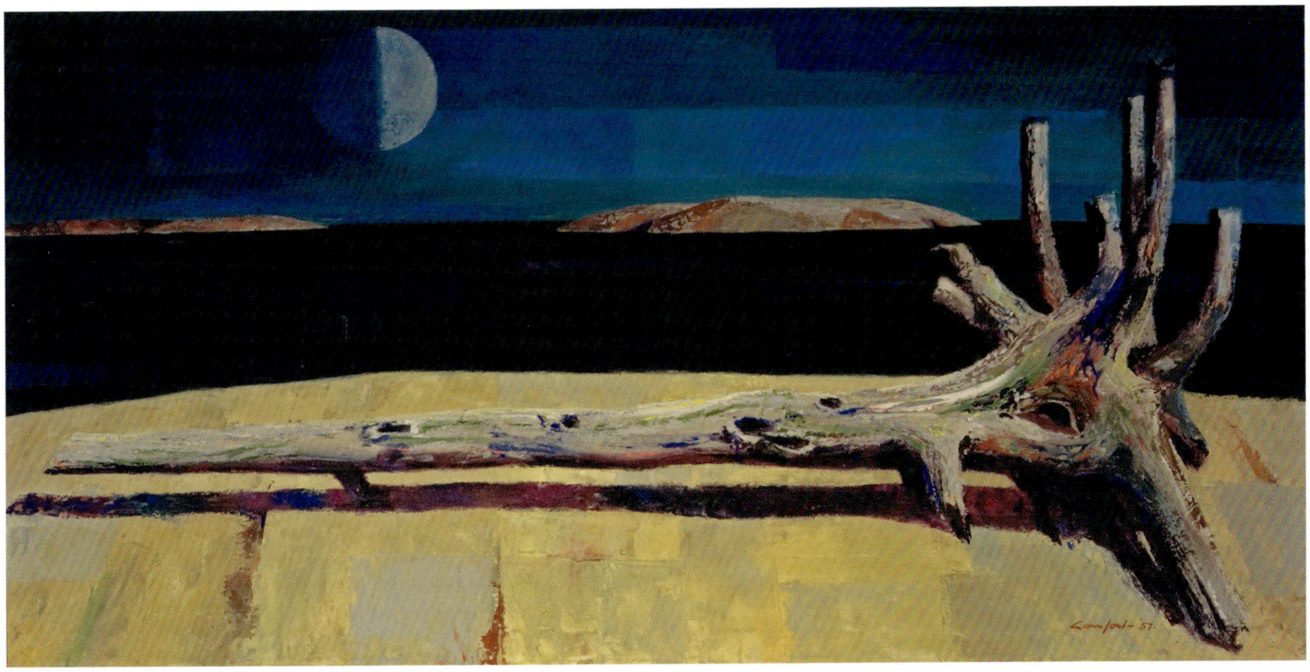

75. **Orchard in Albion**, 1957 | 76. **Wherewhen**, 1957

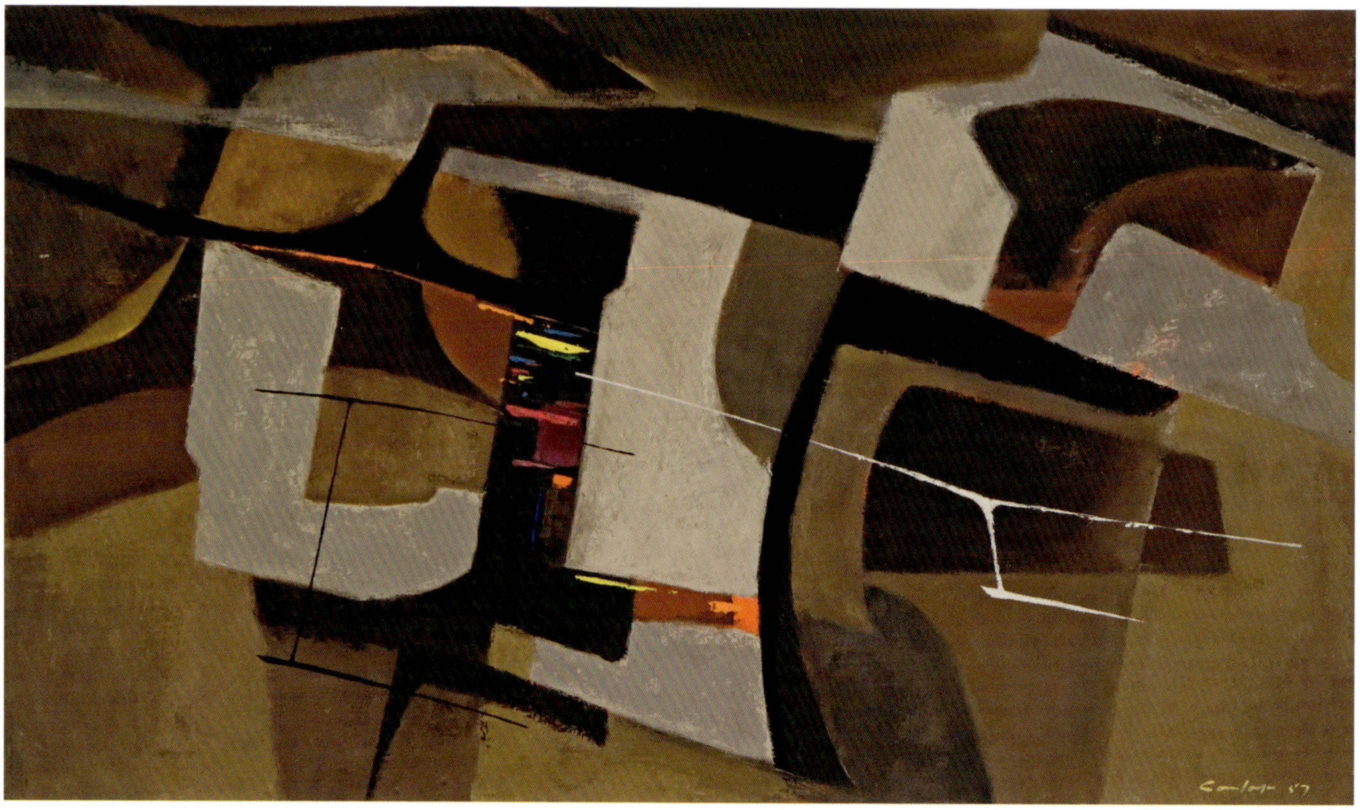

77. **Pre-Cambrian Legend**, 1957

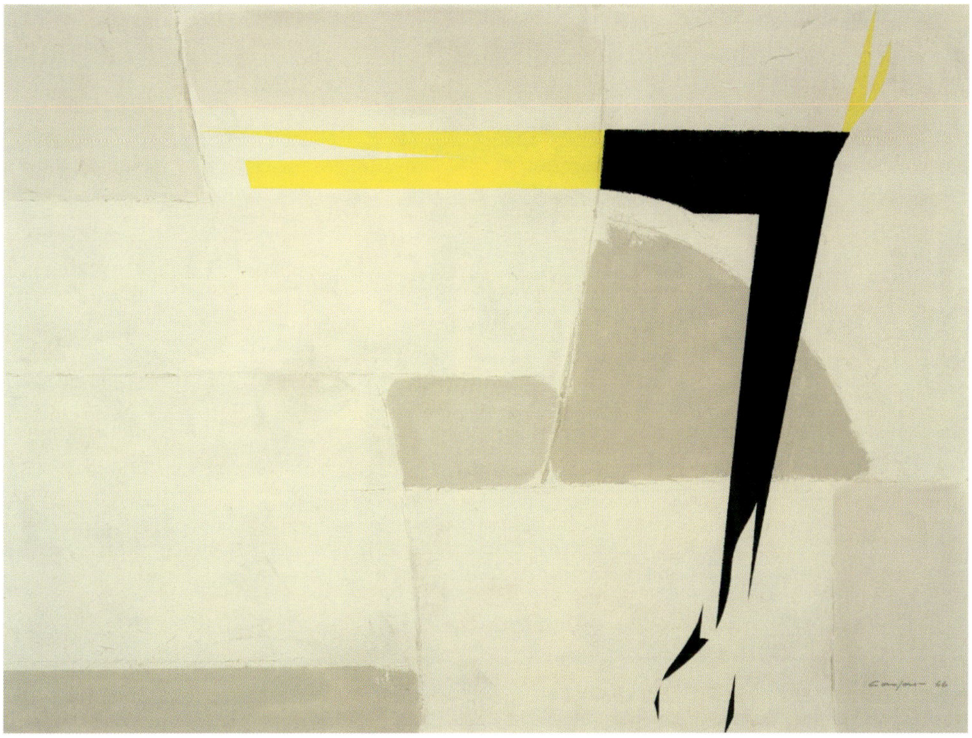

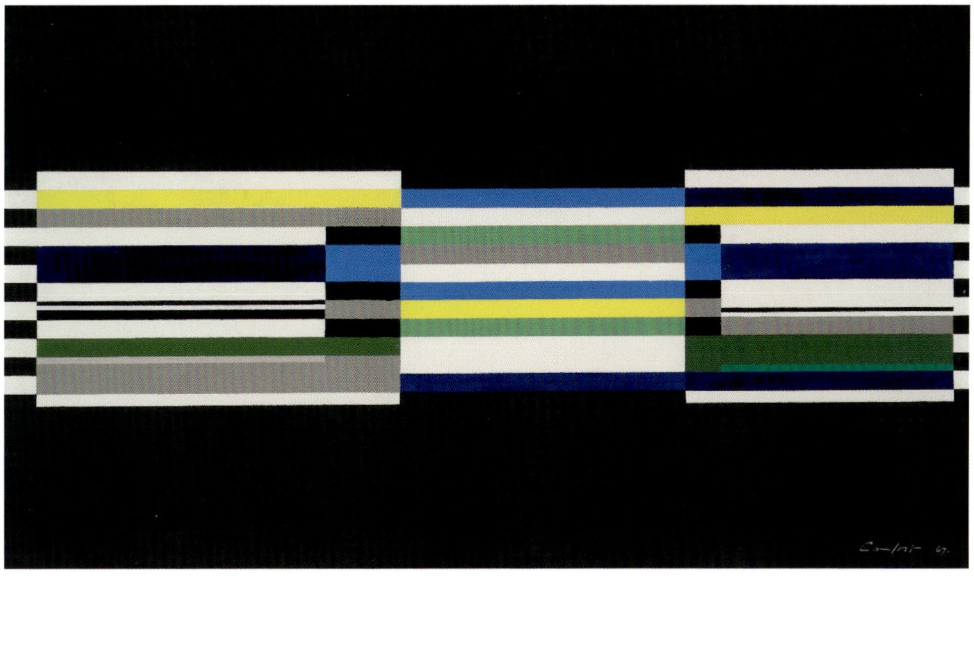

78. **Epic Theme**, 1966 | 79. **Horizontal Event II (Newspeak Series)**, 1967

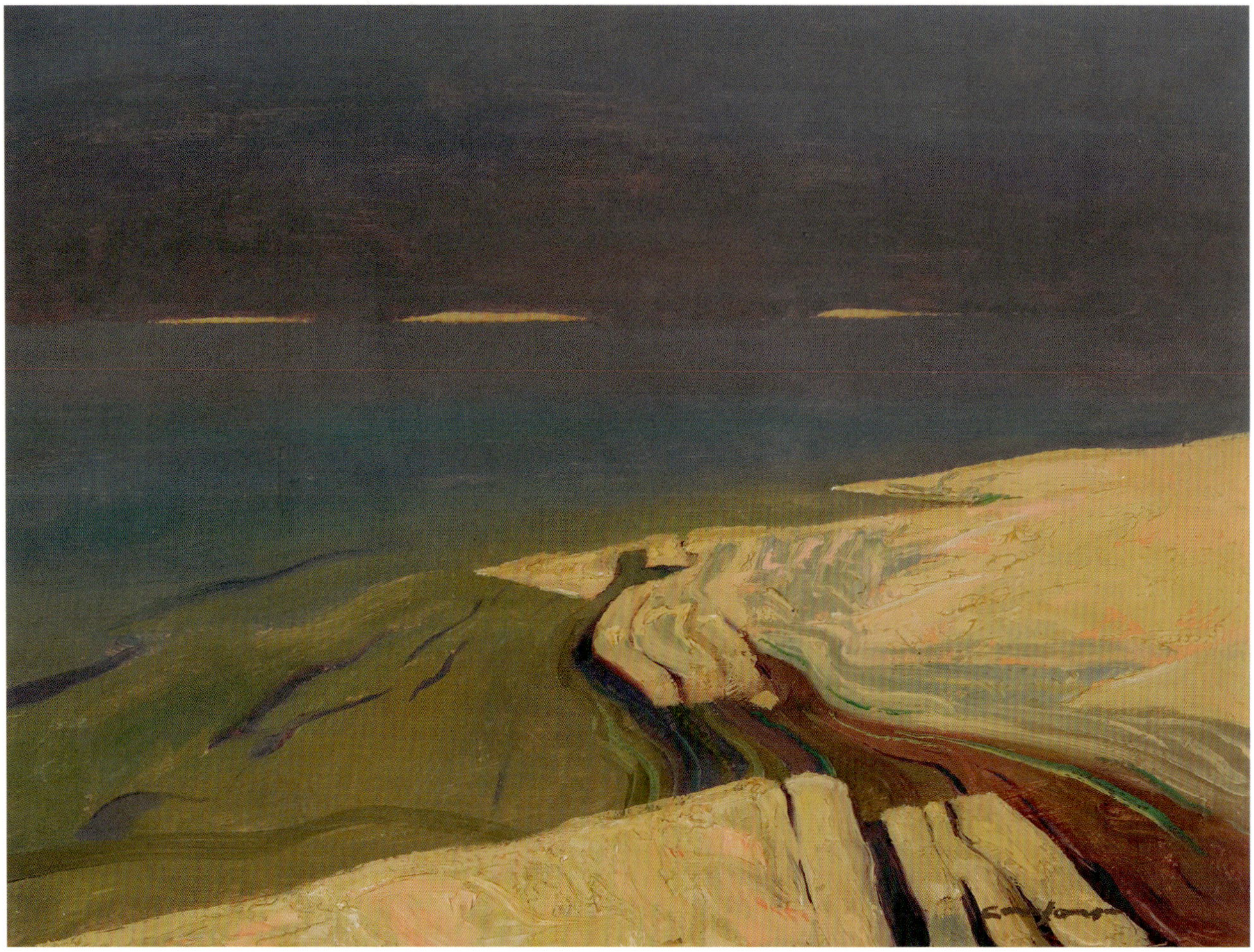

81. **Edge of the World, Georgian Bay**, 1972

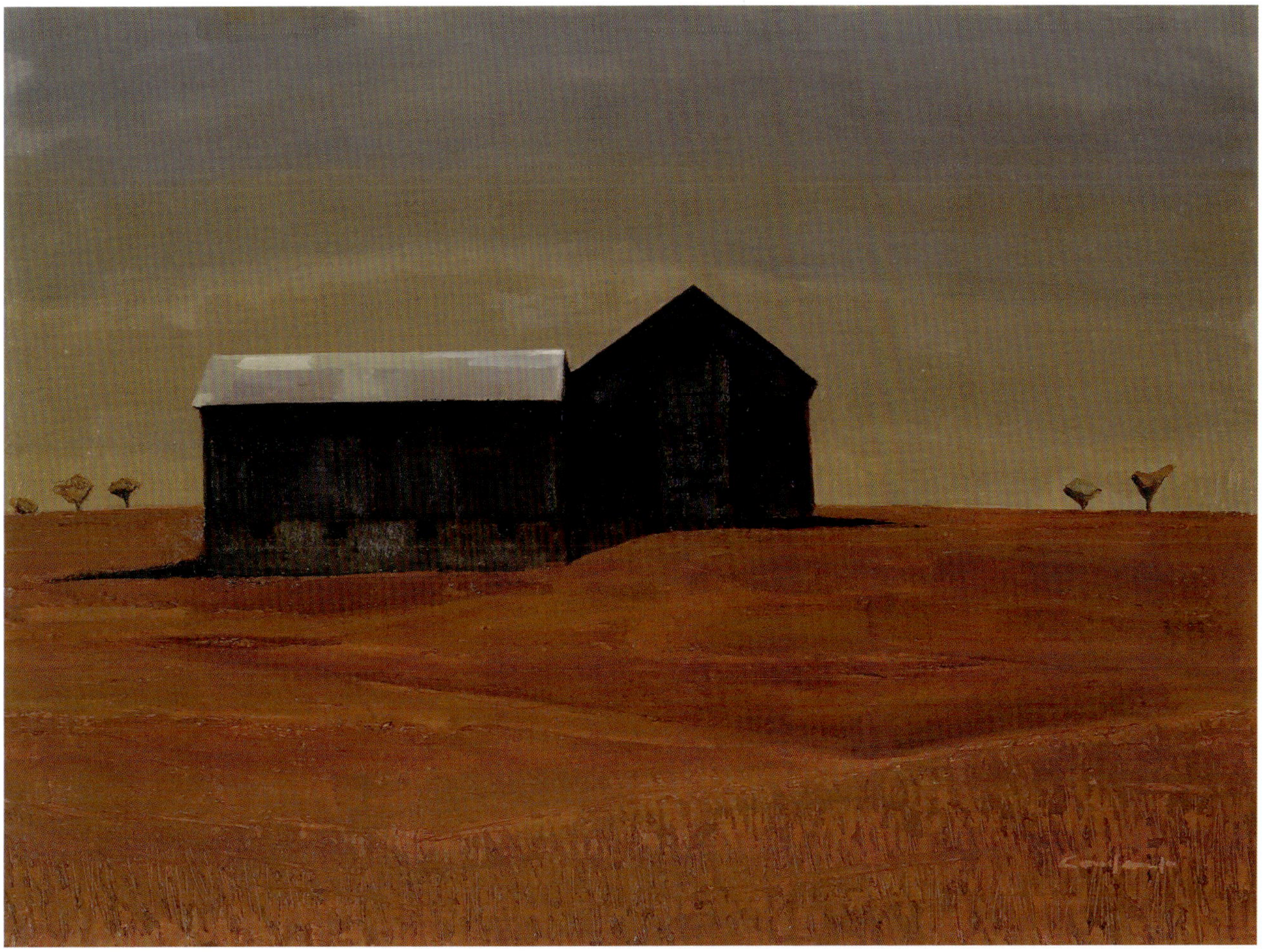

82. **Wichman's Barn**, 1976

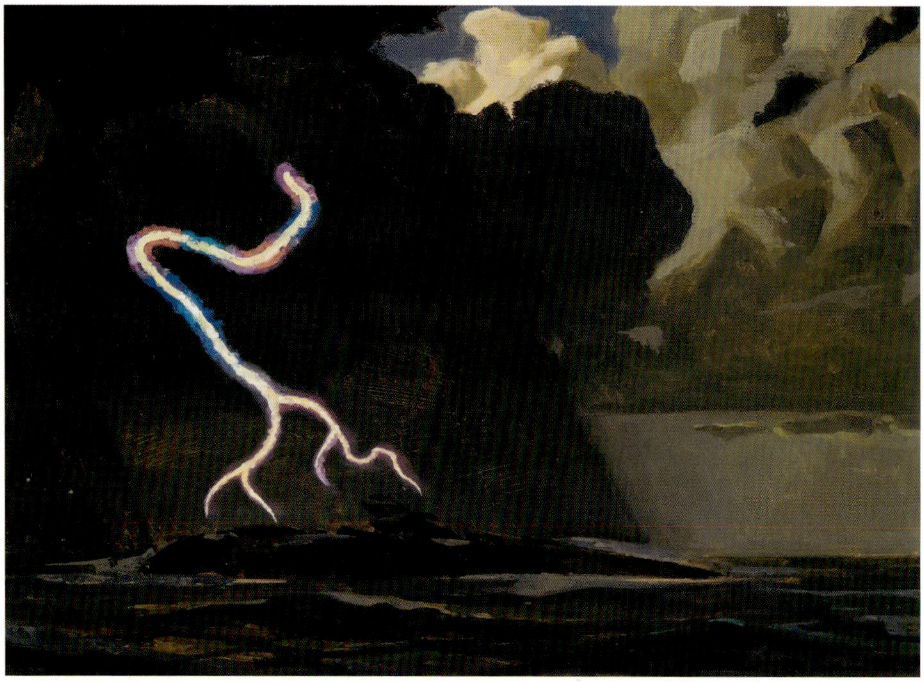

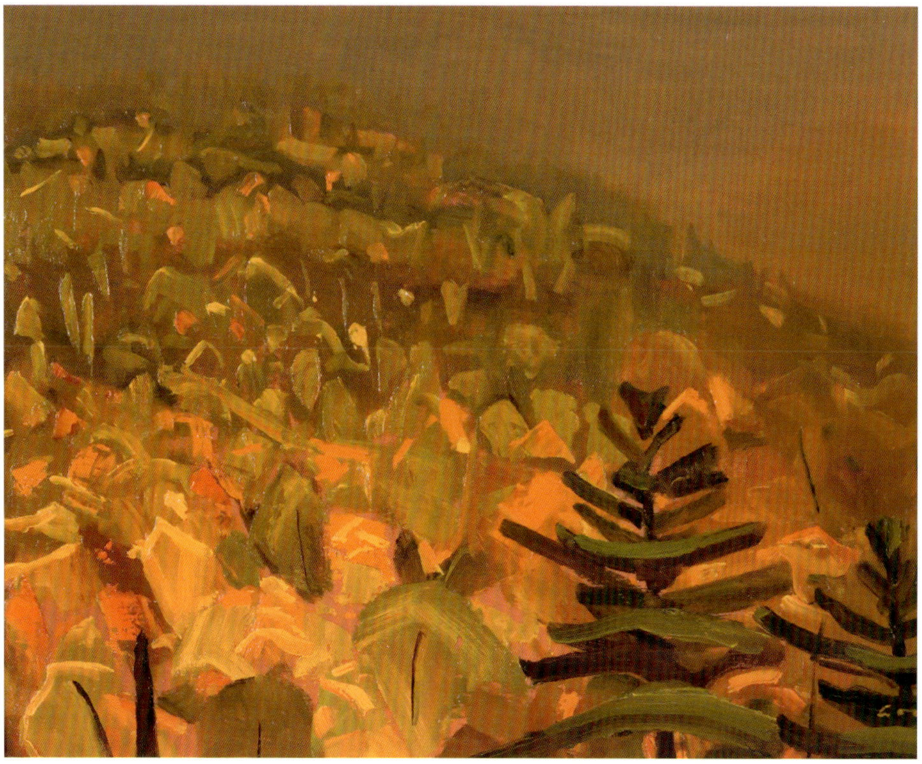

83. **Aspects of Nature 4, Thunderstorm, Georgian Bay**, 1978 | 84. **Rain, Mont St. Marie**, 1981

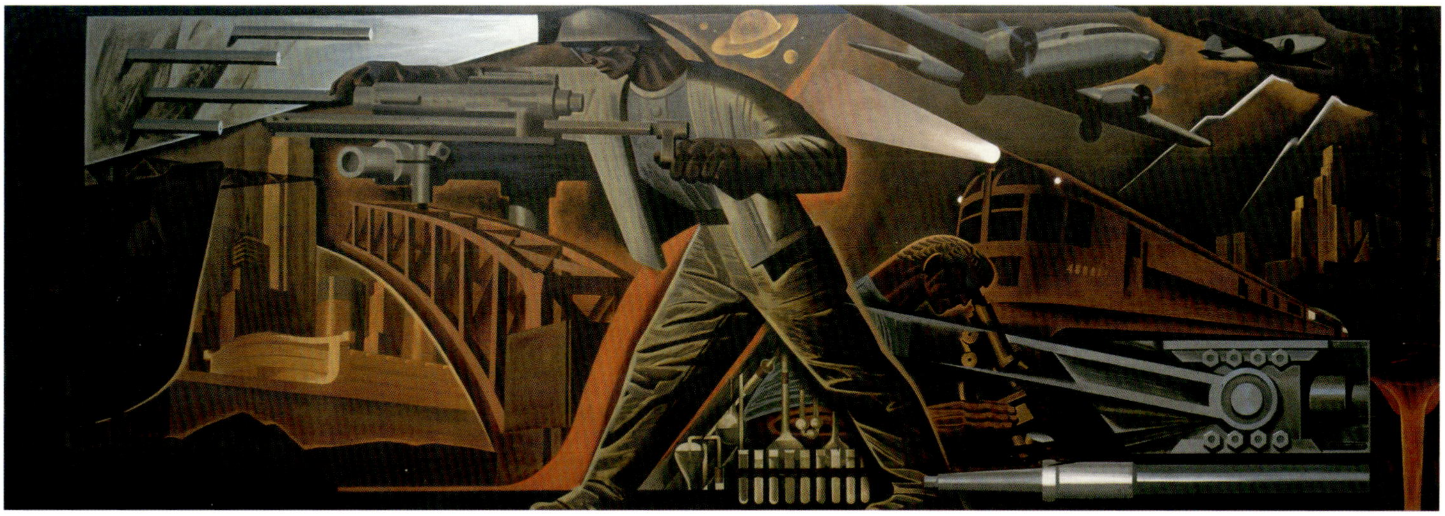

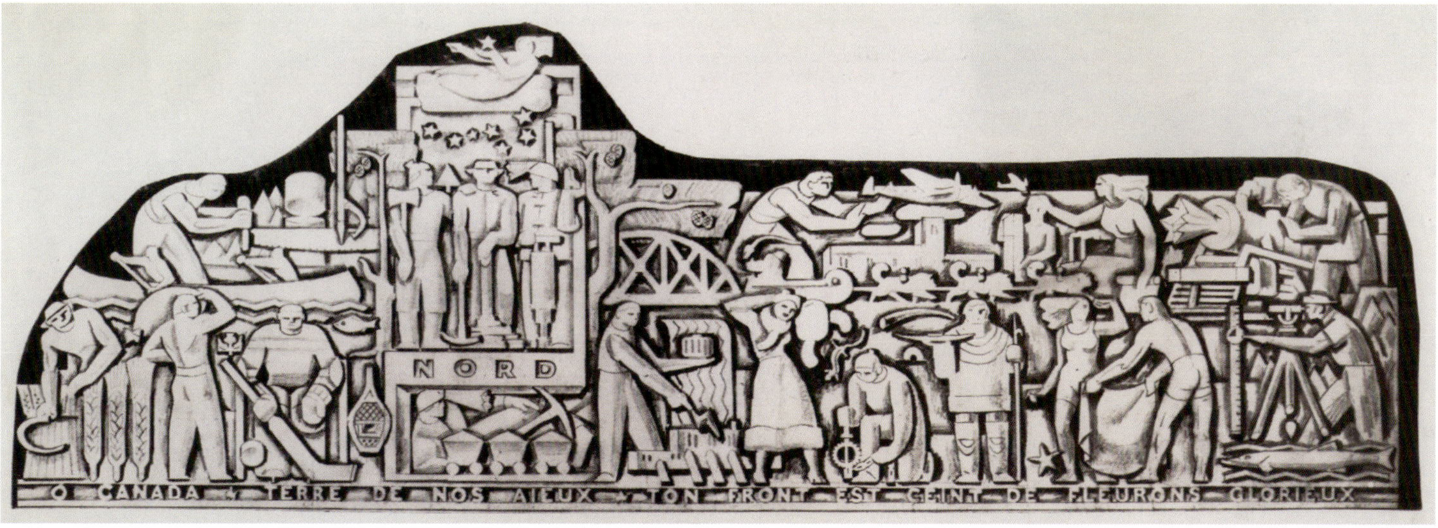

85. **The Romance of Nickel**, 1937 | 86. **Montreal Central Station relief–nord**, 1940–1941

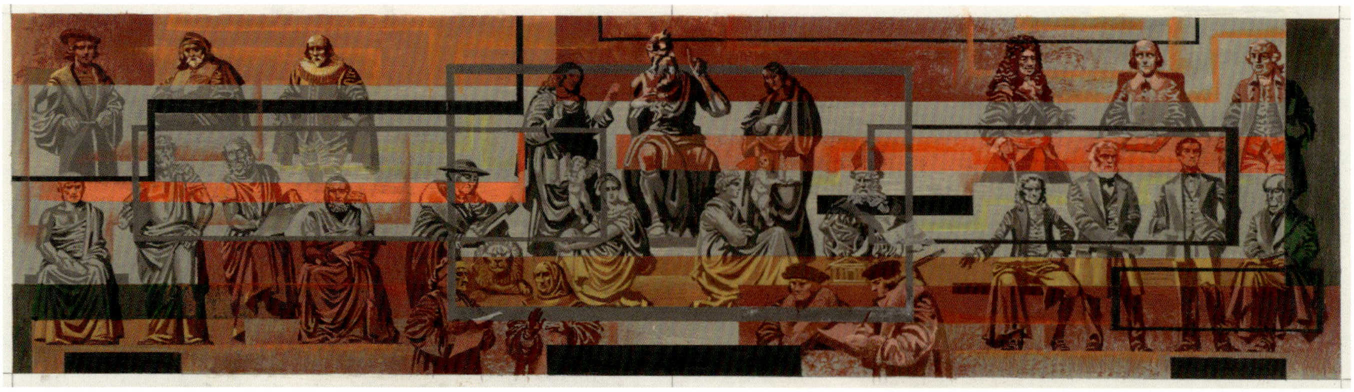

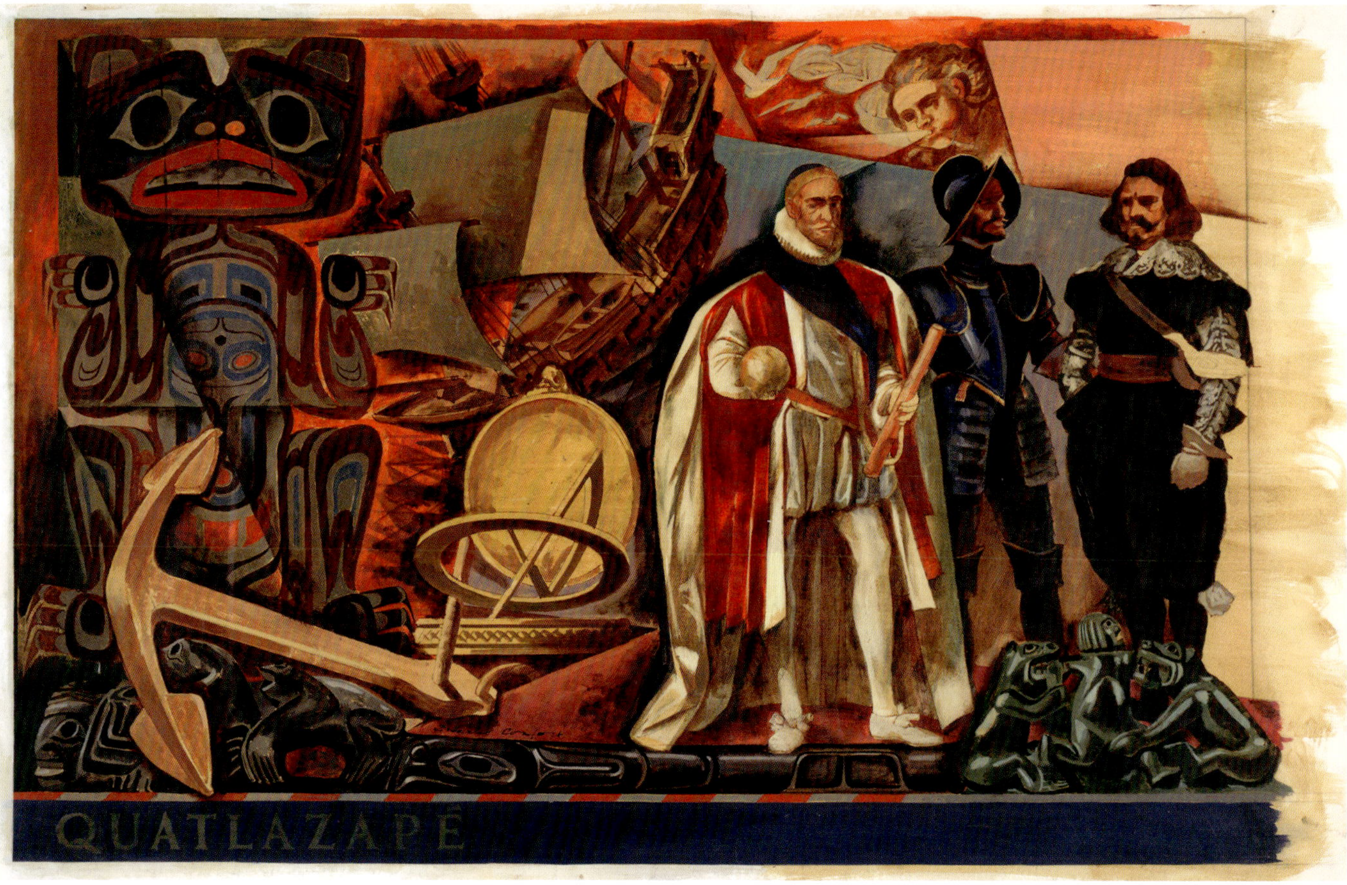

88. **Heritage – National Library Mural study**, 1965–1966 | 87. **British Columbia Pageant mural study**, 1951

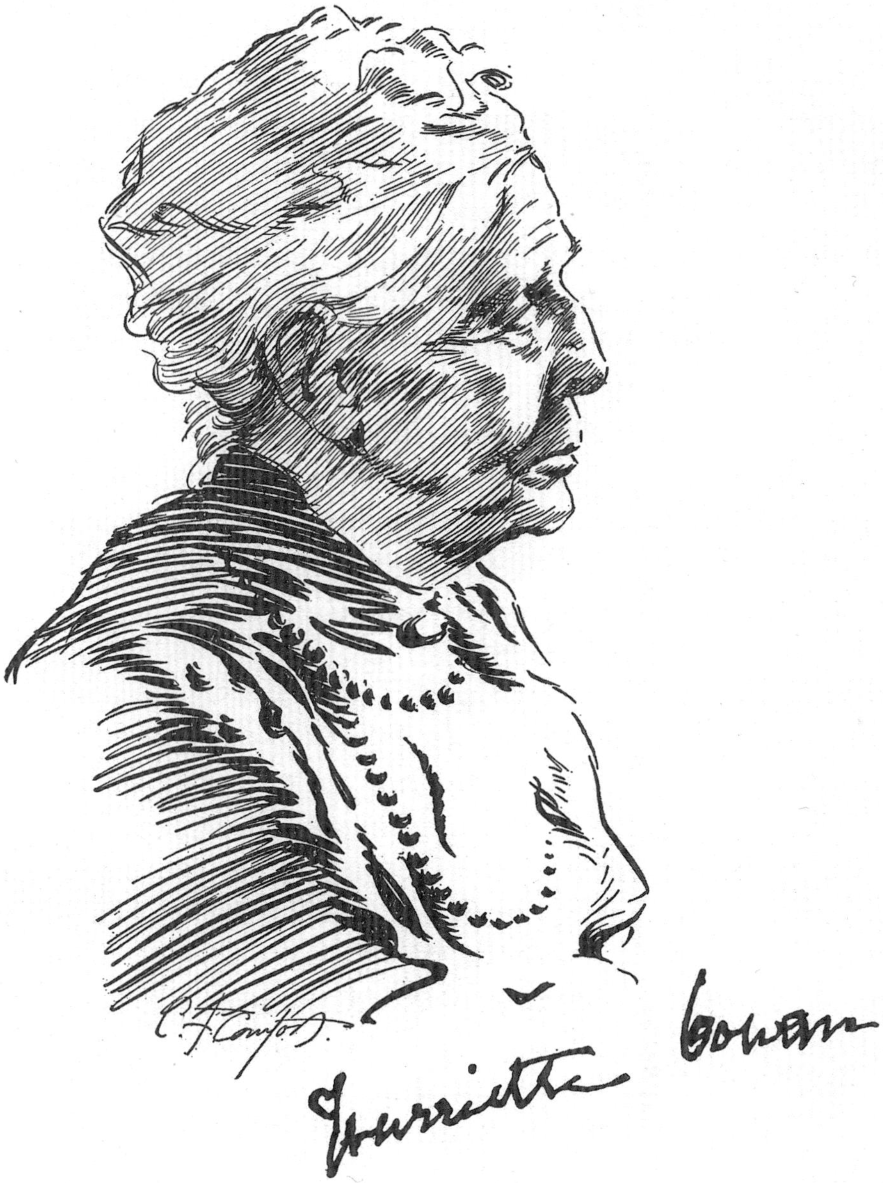

89. **Harriet Cowan – Women of Red River**, 1923

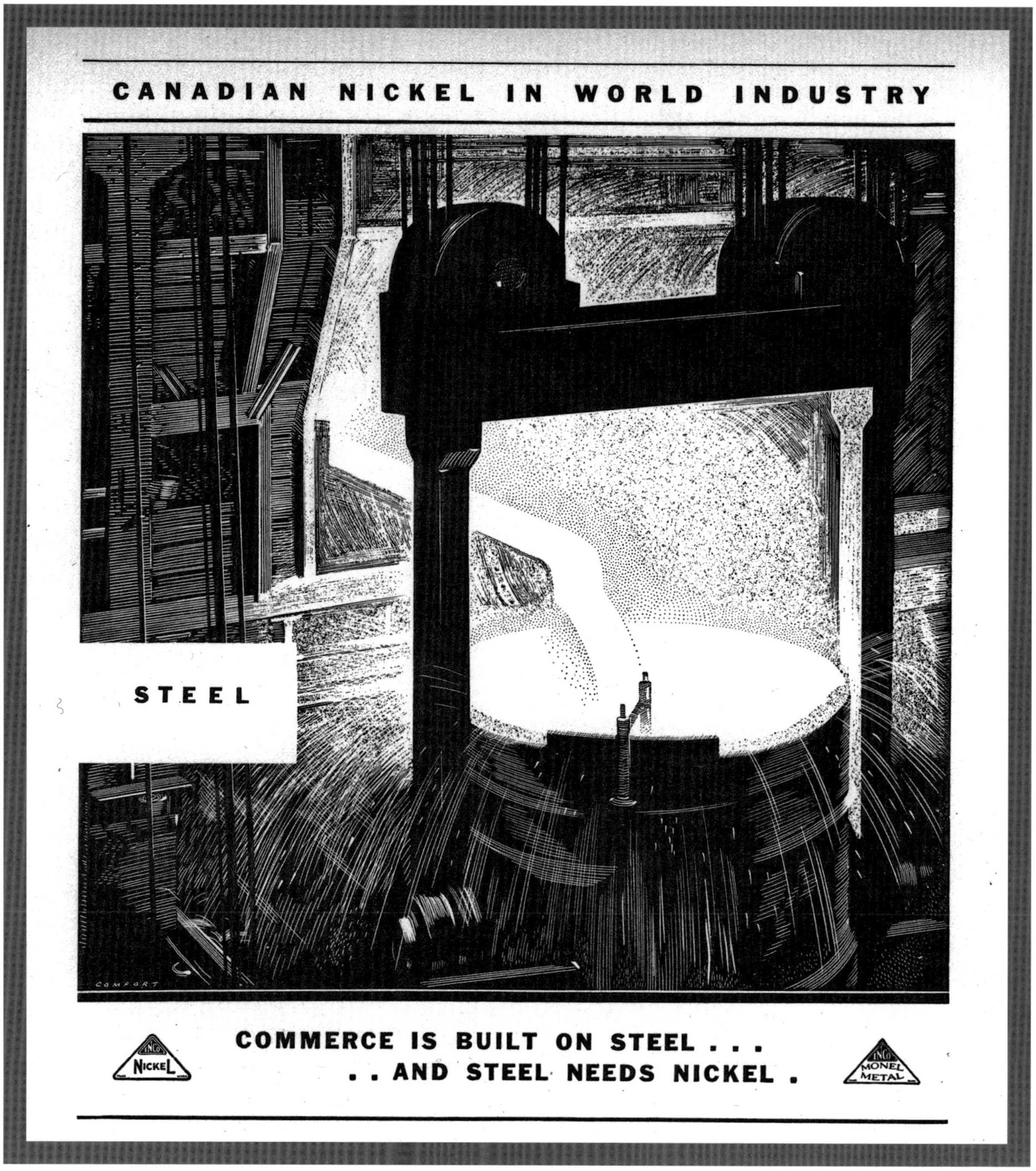

95. Images from **Nickel: A Vital Factor in the Economic Life of Canada**, c. 1940

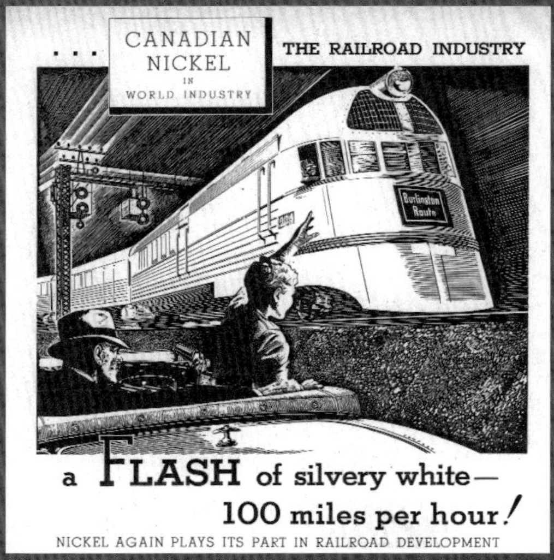
. . .
CANADIAN NICKEL IN WORLD INDUSTRY
THE RAILROAD INDUSTRY
Burlington Route
a FLASH of silvery white—
100 miles per hour!
NICKEL AGAIN PLAYS ITS PART IN RAILROAD DEVELOPMENT

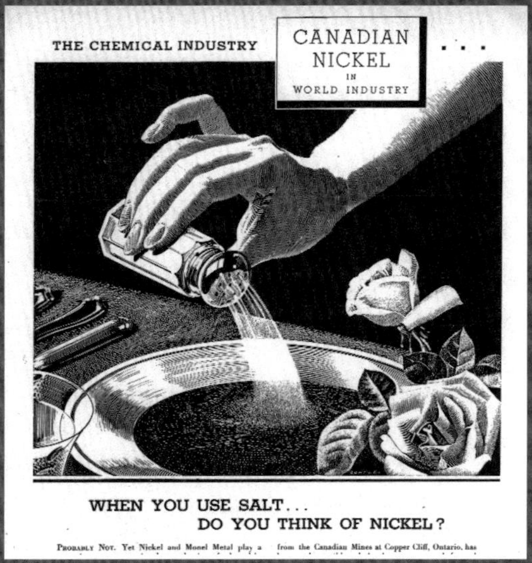
THE CHEMICAL INDUSTRY
CANADIAN NICKEL IN WORLD INDUSTRY
. . .
WHEN YOU USE SALT...
DO YOU THINK OF NICKEL?
PROBABLY NOT. Yet Nickel and Monel Metal play a
from the Canadian Mines at Copper Cliff, Ontario, has

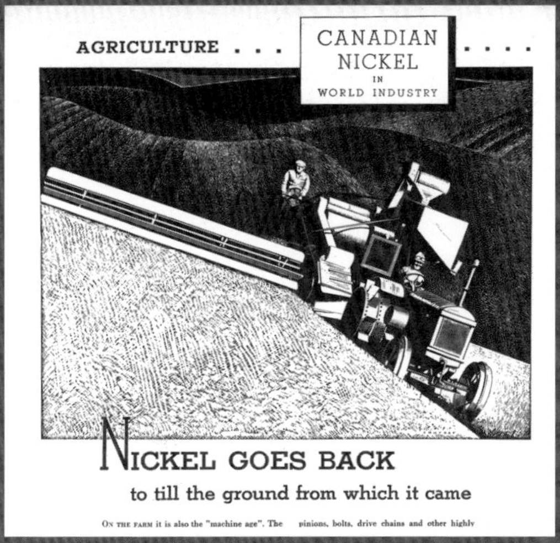
AGRICULTURE . . .
CANADIAN NICKEL IN WORLD INDUSTRY
. . . .
NICKEL GOES BACK
to till the ground from which it came
ON THE FARM it is also the "machine age". The
pinions, bolts, drive chains and other highly

MARY JO HUGHES

La vie et la carrière de Charles Comfort
Une rare célébration

La vie et la carrière de Charles Comfort. Cette exposition attire notre attention sur un artiste dont la contribution à la culture canadienne a été considérable. C'est dans les décennies de 1930 et 1940 que se révèle l'importance de Charles Comfort qui se situe entre les deux courants qui ont créé des ruptures dans l'art traditionnel du Canada, le courant très célébré du Groupe des Sept et celui très excitant de la génération d'après qui a fait de l'abstraction la forme dominante. Dans la foulée, Comfort et ses contemporains ont souffert d'une absence au niveau de l'analyse critique.[1] Les buts qu'ils poursuivaient en commun ont été trop souvent occultés, parce qu'ils ont graduellement et amicalement émergé du Groupe des Sept sans qu'il y ait eu, de leur part, un rejet déclaré de leurs prédécesseurs. S'ajoutant à cette attitude il y a aussi une sorte de condescendance qui s'attache à l'art commercial et qui a surtout visé Comfort dont la carrière, comme chez plusieurs personnages de son temps, a pris naissance dans un milieu qui pratiquait cette forme d'art, avec des œuvres qui ont souvent brouillé les pistes. Dans son cas particulier, l'art commercial lui a fourni des éléments qui ont servi à sa création artistique, surtout quand il s'est efforcé d'instaurer de nouvelles façons d'amener l'art à s'adresser aux gens. Mal comprises, ses intentions ont eu parfois pour effet de banaliser son œuvre. Et comme sa carrière s'est prolongée dans le temps, qu'il n'a simplement pas disparu après les années 1940 mais qu'il a continué à essayer diverses manières de communiquer ses préoccupations artistiques, on l'a souvent moqué en le traitant d' « éclectique ».

Notre but dans cet exercice consisterait dans une tentative d'encourager les débuts d'une meilleure, et plus grande compréhension de cette considérable carrière qui embrasse près de sept décennies. Dans tous les domaines d'activités que Comfort a abordés, que ce soit l'art commercial, l'art public, la peinture de portraits et de paysages, l'éducation artistique, la mise en œuvre et l'administration des politiques culturelles, il s'est toujours senti concerné par un dessein humaniste au service de la société. Comme il l'a lui-même déclaré : « les arts comptent parmi les plus importantes manifestations d'une culture, pour autant qu'ils contribuent à enrichir l'esprit humain. »[2]

> « Je suis né dans ce qui semblait être un monde civilisé et pondéré, un monde dont les défauts étaient discrètement dissimulés sous ses évidentes réalisations. J'achève mes jours utiles dans un monde plein de violence et de confusion qui, ouvertement et effrontément, fait état de ses intentions révolutionnaires en dépit de l'ampleur de ses accomplissements. Si cependant m'était offerte la possibilité de choisir le siècle et la période de l'histoire dans lesquels j'aimerais passer ma vie, je choisirais sans hésitation les premières huit décennies du vingtième siècle. »[3]

Charles Fraser Comfort (1900–1994) avait pleinement conscience du lieu et de l'époque dans lesquels son existence s'était déroulée. Il était également conscient de l'amplitude de sa durée de vie grâce à laquelle il avait traversé le vingtième siècle presque d'un bout à l'autre, ayant connu l'évolution des moyens de transport depuis les calèches et les chevaux jusqu'aux voyages en fusée. Il a vécu l'expérience de deux guerres mondiales, subvenant, durant la première, aux besoins de sa mère et de ses sept frères et sœurs pendant que son père accomplissait son devoir, puis servant à son tour son pays, durant la deuxième, à titre d'artiste militaire. Entre les deux, il survécut comme artiste commercial pour subvenir à son tour aux besoins de sa propre famille. Et pendant qu'il faisait de son mieux pour profiter de ses chances dans divers domaines de la culture canadienne, jamais rien ne lui fut aisément acquis. Du fait que ses racines appartenaient à la classe ouvrière, il avait acquis un grand sens de l'éthique professionnelle qu'il appliquait à tous les aspects de sa vie et qui nourrissait son penchant pour la conscience sociale.

Régulièrement impressionné par les scènes dont il était témoin et qu'il désirait ardemment exprimer par le biais de l'art, Comfort relate dans son journal personnel et sa biographie encore inédite comment il a constamment cherché à situer son expérience dans le contexte du monde extérieur. Scrupuleusement rédigés au jour le jour, ses notes, ses récits de voyage et sa correspondance font de Comfort l'artiste sans doute le mieux documenté de tous les Canadiens de sa catégorie au cours du vingtième siècle. De surcroît, on trouve dans son autobiographie inédite, *Sketches from Memory*, des détails sur son enfance en Angleterre, ses années de formation à Winnipeg et les prémices de sa vie adulte à Toronto. Dans l'avant-propos de cet ouvrage, il décrit son obsession pour la documentation : « J'ai été, toute ma vie, un preneur de notes compulsif et j'ai rempli des carnets de notes sans fin... une journée qui passerait sans une page qui soit lisible et confiée au papier aurait été une journée perdue. Il fallait absolument que je le fasse... »[4] Ces réflexions sur soi sont précieuses en ce sens qu'elles font revivre tout un passé modeste mais riche qu'il colorait de son humour auto-dénigrant.[5]

Débuts

Les débuts de Comfort laissent prévoir le personnage qu'il allait devenir : l'artiste acharné au travail et l'indéfectible militant de la cause culturelle. Né à Édimbourg, en Écosse, le 22 juillet 1900, il était le fils aîné de Charles Comfort Sr. (1879–1945) et de Jean Comfort (née Annan) (1879–1949). À l'âge de trois ans, on l'envoie vivre en Angleterre chez sa grand-mère maternelle et ses tantes célibataires, en raison de maigres ressources familiales. Il assure que les six années passées auprès de sa grand-mère furent les plus heureuses et les plus insouciantes de sa vie, lui inculquant les bases de son intérêt pour la culture et lui procurant des expériences qu'il n'aurait jamais pu avoir s'il avait continué à vivre au foyer paternel appauvri.

Sa grand-mère, Christina Annan, était veuve et dirigeait la blanchisserie de Hadham Hall, un manoir élisabéthain situé entre Londres et Cambridge. C'est dans ce cadre que s'éveilla l'intérêt de Comfort pour les questions d'esthétique et d'histoire. Quatre adultes devaient parfaire son éducation avec une attention et une considération extrêmes : « Elles ont nourri ma pensée... (et elles) étaient déterminées à cultiver en moi un respect pour les choses de l'esprit. »[6] À la différence de ses frères et sœurs, Charles avait sa propre chambre; on lui faisait la lecture et on l'emmenait voir les galeries d'art et les monuments architecturaux.

À l'automne 1909, il dut rentrer à Édimbourg et quitter une famille qu'il connaissait bien pour retrouver une autre dont il n'avait qu'un vague souvenir. Il en fut perturbé; non seulement il se trouvait plongé dans une maisonnée encombrée, mais l'environnement physique de la ville lui causait des difficultés : « Désappointé et même choqué, je découvrais que Spring Valley Gardens ne laissait place à rien qui pousse, pas un brin d'herbe, pas de fleurs, pas un seul arbre. »[7] Dans les semaines qui suivirent son retour chez son père, celui-ci lui fit comprendre qu'il devait se trouver un travail pour aider à l'entretien de la famille. Comfort soupçonnait que son retour au sein de sa famille était motivé par le besoin d'alimenter la caisse familiale et c'était probablement la vraie raison, mais il n'en fit jamais état.

Winnipeg

En avril 1912, sans ressources, la famille s'embarque pour Winnipeg où elle espère trouver meilleure fortune. Dans les semaines suivant de son arrivée, Comfort déniche un petit boulot provisoire dans la livraison d'échantillons de levures et quand arrive l'été, il transporte de l'eau pour une équipe d'asphaltage, toujours pour subvenir aux besoins de la famille. À l'école, il se fait beaucoup d'amis, parmi lesquels Robert Ayre qui devait devenir critique d'art et qui demeure un ami quand tous deux se retrouveront, adultes, à Toronto. Winnipeg, à cette époque, est encore une ville frontière cherchant à mettre sur pied des institutions officielles visant à promouvoir la culture.[8] Des dirigeants de la communauté encourageaient la formation d'un milieu parfait sous tous ces angles avec une scène artistique vigoureuse et une économie dynamique. L'année où Comfort débarqua dans la ville vit l'ouverture du Musée des beaux-arts de Winnipeg, alors appelé The Winnipeg Art Gallery, qui était logé à l'Industrial Bureau, organisation vouée au mieux-être de la communauté pour attirer les artisans du développement industriel. La « Gallery » était alors considérée comme le principal symbole culturel public de la ville. Chaque fois qu'il en avait l'occasion, Comfort allait y faire un tour pour examiner sa collection encore modeste et ses expositions itinérantes. L'emphase placée sur l'importance des activités culturelles dans le contexte civique eut une grande influence sur le jeune Comfort pour toute son existence car il continua à s'intéresser aux diverses galeries d'art qu'il considérait d'ailleurs comme des institutions sociales de grande valeur.

La création de la Winnipeg School of Art en 1913 offrit à la ville l'occasion de pousser les artistes du cru à y puiser des idées pour leurs projets de design, d'art commercial ou de beaux-arts. Cette année-là, Comfort remporta le premier prix dans la section peinture lors d'une exposition qui se tenait au YMCA sous l'appellation de « Boy's Hobby Exhibition. » L'artiste torontois Frederick Brigden était juge de l'exposition et il se trouvait à Winnipeg où il mettait sur pied la succursale ouest de la compagnie Brigdens Limited, entreprise familiale d'art commercial. Impressionné par le talent du jeune homme, Brigden se rendit chez les parents de Comfort pour leur demander l'autorisation de prendre le jeune garçon comme apprenti l'année suivante.

Un prodige dans l'art

Fondée à l'origine à Toronto, Brigdens Limited était l'une des plus anciennes compagnies d'art graphiques au Canada. La branche qu'elle avait ouverte à Winnipeg était spécifiquement destinée à produire la version pour l'Ouest du Canada du catalogue Eaton de commandes par correspondance. Brigdens of Winnipeg offrait à des artistes de talent une bonne raison de s'installer à Winnipeg tout en œuvrant dans un domaine qui près de l'art et en tirant parti d'un milieu stimulant, entourés de collègues créatifs. Son programme d'apprentissage offrait une formation artistique préliminaire complétée par des cours que les employés étaient incités à suivre en soirée à la School of Art. Du fait que Brigdens était l'un des employeurs d'artistes les plus importants de la ville, l'entreprise jouait un rôle considérable dans le développement de la scène artistique dans l'intervalle entre les deux guerres mondiales.

Les historiens de l'art ont dressé des parallèles dans le développement de deux formes d'art au Canada, l'art publicitaire et les beaux-arts.[9] L'historienne Angela Davis voyait en Brigdens « une pépinière de talents » pour de nombreux artistes qui ont beaucoup contribué à la scène culturelle non seulement à Winnipeg, mais aussi à l'échelle nationale. Voici ce qu'elle écrivait : « ...l'industrie des arts graphiques occupe, dans l'histoire socioculturelle du Canada, une place qu'on ne peut comparer à nulle autre dans l'industrie. Les gens que celle-ci mit à l'œuvre et le matériel qu'elle produisit devinrent des ingrédients essentiels autant dans la formation de « l'art canadien » que dans l'expansion de la communication de masse sur le plan populaire. »[10]

Il est certain que lorsque Comfort déménagea à Toronto, nombre d'artistes avec lesquels il s'était lié d'amitié étaient aussi liés à l'art commercial, y compris des membres du Groupe des Sept. Sortant d'un tel milieu chez Brigdens de Winnipeg, plusieurs artistes acquirent une réputation nationale, notamment Charles Comfort, Caven Atkins, Philip Surrey et Fritz Brandtner, tandis que d'autres, tels que le maître graveur Eric Bergman, connaissaient une fructueuse carrière à l'échelon local. Nul doute que dans le cas de Comfort, ses travaux de dessinateur toujours chez Brigdens à Winnipeg, puis à Toronto chez Rapid, Grip & Batten Ltd., et à son propre studio commercial au cours des années 1930 lui permirent d'entretenir sa famille pendant que sa carrière dans les beaux-arts prenait son essor. Par ailleurs, le rigoureux calendrier de production de catalogues chez Brigdens devait lui inculquer de la discipline et, comme on le verra plus loin, influença le style et l'iconographie de sa peinture murale et sur chevalet.

En Octobre 1914, Comfort entame sa carrière artistique chez Brigdens de Winnipeg, travaillant sous les ordres de Thomas McLean et d'Arnold Brigden, cousin de Fred et directeur de la branche. Le fait qu'il suit sérieusement les conseils de Frederick Brigden – pratiquer le dessin tous les jours et assister aux cours du soir – fera de lui, en peu d'années, l'un des meilleurs dessinateurs de la compagnie. Il commence par étudier à la Kelvin Technical School (1914–1916), sous la direction de Valentine Fanshaw, puis à la School of Art, de 1916 à 1919 sous celle d'Alexander Musgrove. «Le résultat de tout ceci fut que le don très naturel que j'avais pour le dessin fut raffermi et poli pour déboucher sur un accomplissement prometteur qui pouvait se révéler bien utile professionnellement. »[11] Mais tout en reconnaissant ce qu'il devait à ses instructeurs sur le plan technique, Comfort estima qu'aucun des deux n'avait été très utile pour l'aider à produire une véritable œuvre d'art.

Néanmoins, les interactions qui se produisaient chez Brigdens entre Comfort et les autres artistes eurent pour effet de le pousser à considérer sérieusement une carrière artistique : « Ces nouveaux et multiformes contacts qui se passaient, comme c'était le cas, dans un cadre cérébral et émotionnel tellement à l'écart de la simplicité domestique de notre foyer et des grossières vulgarités de l'usine d'asphalte opérèrent une transformation quasi magique... (et) éveillèrent en moi un intérêt constant pour la pensée réflexive avec l'irrépressible désir de me perfectionner et de cultiver une attitude de questionnement à l'égard de l'art sous toutes ses formes. »

Il assista donc, durant son adolescence et autant qu'il le put, à toutes sortes d'événements, des concerts, des opéras et des pièces de théâtre, entretenant ainsi une insatiable passion pour tout ce qui se rattache à la culture. Arnold Brigden l'amena à s'intéresser à ses collections privées d'estampes japonaises et européennes, notamment aux eaux-fortes de Rembrandt et aux gravures de William Blake, ce qui lui fit découvrir l'art historique. Les randonnées de dessin qu'il entreprit en compagnie d'autres artistes dans des coins sauvages du Manitoba et du Nord-ouest de l'Ontario aiguisèrent son goût pour la nature et sa capacité de peindre des paysages.[12] Mais la Première Guerre mondiale surgit dans ce décor et en octobre 1916 son père embarque pour se battre outre-mer. Le jeune Charles, désormais chef de famille, doit pourvoir aux besoins de sa mère et de sept autres enfants. Il participe quand même à un entraînement militaire en espérant qu'il sera recruté, mais il est régulièrement écarté.

Se faire des relations

« J'ai l'habitude de dire que je suis né physiquement en Écosse, mais ma naissance spirituelle a eu lieu au Arts and Letters Club de Toronto. C'est là que j'ai reçu mon éducation dans les circonstances les plus favorables, car cela m'a permis de rencontrer des poètes, des écrivains, des gens qui lisent, des professeurs d'université et des peintres. »[13]

C'est en 1919, au retour de son père, que Comfort accepta d'être brièvement transféré au bureau Brigdens de Toronto. Son directeur artistique, Tom McLean, l'aida à s'y faire des relations en l'emmenant à ce Club des arts et des lettres, un club pour hommes dont les membres qui s'intéressaient ou participaient à des activités de théâtre, de littérature, d'art visuels, d'architecture ou de musique se réunissaient pour échapper au banal train-train quotidien du monde des affaires. De nos jours, ce club est sans doute mieux connu pour le rôle qu'il joua à promouvoir la carrière des artistes du Groupe des Sept. Mais c'est là que Comfort rencontra des personnages de divers horizons, des artistes de la jeune avant-garde comme ceux qui feraient partie du Groupe des Sept et d'autres, plus âgés, du genre conservateur, comme George A. Reid, directeur du Ontario College of Art. Il suivit également des cours de dessin d'après nature parrainés par la l'Académie royale des arts du Canada (ARAC) avec Frederick Challenger, Charles W. Jefferys et Gustav Hahn.

Ce court séjour aida Comfort à prendre une décision : il allait devenir peintre.[14] Avant de rentrer chez lui, il alla d'abord rendre visite aux musées de Chicago et de Minneapolis et rencontra le conservateur des dessins et gravures avec lequel il s'entretint à propos des eaux-fortes de Rembrandt. De telles initiatives prouvent sa véritable passion pour l'art et son sincère désir de rencontrer des personnes de grande culture capables d'assouvir sa soif de connaissances.

Vers la fin du printemps, il reprit le chemin de Toronto et il y resta pendant toute une année grâce, en partie, à une somme de 100$ qu'il avait gagnée dans un concours lancé par Eaton pour la plus belle couverture de son catalogue.[15] Presque tous les jours de la semaine, il déjeunait au Arts & Letters Club et tout juste à la veille de son 20ième anniversaire, on lui demanda s'il voulait bien en devenir membre sous le parrainage de Frederick Brigden et Tom McLean. Il se joignit également à la Canadian Society of Graphic Art où il prit encore des cours libres de dessin d'après nature et put s'entretenir avec d'autres artistes.[16]

Vers la fin du printemps 1920, eut lieu à Toronto l'exposition inaugurale du Groupe des Sept, événement-clé dans la vie de Comfort. Dans les travaux de ces artistes, il discerna les premiers signes de vitalité qu'il avait jamais perçus dans l'art canadien et il entrevit la possibilité de transmettre une image du Canada au moyen d'un style plus moderne.[17] En 1921, il revint à Winnipeg, prit une chambre en location et travailla nuit et jour à des dessins pour catalogues, tout en aspirant ardemment à pouvoir appliquer son talent à des projets plus créatifs. En dépit d'un horaire qui ne lui laissait pas de répit, il parvint, dans les débuts de 1922, à exposer quatre aquarelles à l'exposition annuelle du Winnipeg Sketch Club. L'une de ces quatre était *The Green Canoe*. (cat. n° 2).[18]

Comfort se sentit encouragé par les événements qui se produisaient à Winnipeg. En 1922, Franz Johnston, membre du Groupe des Sept, avait pris en charge la direction du Musée des beaux-arts de la ville et de la School of Art. Il offrit à Comfort de monter une exposition de ses œuvres au Musée conjointement avec F. T. Moore Beatty, au courant de l'automne,[19] ce qui lui valut sa première attention publique sérieuse : « ...l'exposition, qui vient de se terminer de deux élèves de l'école d'art (la Winnipeg Art School) ... est un glorieux reflet des progrès de l'art dans le Canada de l'ouest et se traduit par un grand éloge s'adressant autant aux élèves eux-mêmes qu'à leur école... quelques centaines de visiteurs se sont rendus chaque jour au musée, mais à notre avis l'exposition méritait d'en recevoir un plus grand nombre... M. Comfort a, de même, accroché une quarantaine de peintures, qui vont des paysages aux tableaux de genre et aux portraits. Nous estimons que M. Comfort est à son fort dans le portrait. Ceux qu'il a réalisés font preuve d'un grand tempérament et d'ampleur avec une harmonie de couleurs qui suscitent instantanément l'intérêt et l'attention... »[20]

Un autre intéressant projet fut réalisé dans l'année quand Arnold Brigden recommanda Comfort comme illustrateur pour un livre sur la vie des pionnières de la région qui s'intitulait *Women of Red River*.[21] J. Healy, bibliothécaire de la province, interviewait des femmes d'un certain âge et, pendant ce temps, Comfort dessinait leurs portraits à l'encre à main levée, portraits qui étaient ensuite reproduits dans l'ouvrage (cat. n° 89).[22] Ces portraits révèlent son habileté à saisir les expressions et les caractères dans les visages et les attitudes, et ceci dans de rapides croquis exécutés apparemment sans effort.

En dépit du succès qu'il rencontrait, Comfort se rendait compte qu'il lui fallait recevoir une formation plus avancée. C'est ainsi qu'avec les encouragements de Tom MacLean et Walter Huntley, il se fit admettre au New York Arts Students' League où il espérait poursuivre des études avec Robert Henri, le plus respecté des professeurs de son temps, un homme qui s'était lancé dans la carrière en tant qu'illustrateur. Quelque temps avant son départ, en octobre 1921, Comfort avait rencontré Louise Irene Chase à une soirée et, comme il le relève dans ses notes, elle ne tarda pas à devenir « un élément indispensable de mon existence. » Louise appuya son désir quitter Winnipeg pour fréquenter cette école; son absence ne fit que renforcer leurs liens.

New York

En octobre 1922, Comfort entre au New York Arts Students' League pour un bref mais intense stage d'apprentissage formel. La transition s'opère sans problème. Sa grande-tante maternelle vit dans les parages et il entretient des rapports avec George Fawcett et son fils Robert, tous deux de Winnipeg. Les Fawcett étaient des artistes commerciaux de la ville et George lui proposait de temps à autre d'exécuter un travail commercial. À l'école, le rythme rapide des ateliers bondés, en ville les musées et galeries, le théâtre et l'opéra, tout cela maintenait Comfort en état de ravissement complet.

À l'école, Robert Henri l'exhorta à étudier plus attentivement les Maîtres anciens tels que Franz Hals et Velásquez, enflammant ainsi sa passion pour l'analyse des techniques. Son autre professeur, Euphrasius Tucker, avait participé à l'organisation de la fameuse Armory Exhibition de 1913, ce qui encouragea Comfort à produire un art vivant en contact avec l'expérience moderne. Tucker l'invita à lire les œuvres du critique d'art Clive Bell pour bien se pénétrer des principes modernes. Comfort écrira également que dans sa propre carrière d'enseignant il avait été marqué par les théories pédagogiques de Tucker qui mettaient l'accent sur l'analyse formelle de l'œuvre. Tucker se guidait sur cet énoncé de principe : « L'art doit être appris, on ne peut pas l'enseigner. »[23] La seule œuvre qui nous reste de cette période est une aquarelle de la ligne d'horizon de New York (cat. n° 3) où la dominante grisaille du smog noircissant les immeubles est égayée par la neige en touches blanches qui semblent sautiller presque comme un motif abstrait.

L'installation

En mars 1923, Comfort quitta l'euphorique ambiance de New York et revint chez Brigdens à Winnipeg. La tranquille atmosphère de la ville fut compensée par ses retrouvailles avec Louise. C'est au printemps de 1924 qu'ils se marièrent et leur lune de miel se passa rustiquement dans la région de Minaki au bord du fleuve Winnipeg. Cet été-là, ils allèrent également visiter Point au Chênes, le cottage de la famille de Louise sur Lake of the Woods.[24] Comfort prenait plaisir lors de randonnées en compagnie d'amis artistes comme Eric Bergman et il réalisa une série d'aquarelles. Ces œuvres (voir cat. n° 5 et 6) nous portent à croire que le séjour à New York avait fait naître un nouvel intérêt formel qui faisait avancer son œuvre au-delà d'une approche traditionnelle et pittoresque. L'artiste cherche maintenant à exprimer l'imprévu dans sa composition d'un paysage. Ainsi par exemple, dans *Lake of the Woods, Route Bay* (cat. n° 6) la tension entre le premier plan et le fond installe une ambiguïté par l'effet de contrastes entre la forme, la lumière et l'espace. Un rocher pyramidal, au bord de l'abstraction, domine le premier plan et fait contraste avec le paysage pastoral que l'on voit dans le fond.

Toujours soucieux d'élargir le champ de ses expériences, Comfort dessine les costumes et les décors pour la troupe du Winnipeg Community Players au cours de la dernière année qu'il passe au Manitoba. C'est là qu'il rencontre L.L.Fitzgerald et W.J. Phillips, deux artistes renommés pour leurs créations scéniques. C'est probablement à cette époque qu'il se met à l'étude de la gravure sur bois avec Phillips.[25] Le vif désir de conduire une voiture incite le jeune couple à quitter Winnipeg en avril 1925 pour s'installer à Toronto.

Toronto : Le peintre se lance dans la carrière

Installé à Toronto, Comfort reprend son travail chez Brigdens. Il passe de plus en plus son temps à dessiner en compagnie de Harold Ayres et Will Ogilvie. Ce dernier vient d'arriver d'Afrique du sud cette année-là, 1925. Demeuré célibataire – il ne se mariera que des décennies plus tard -, il va devenir l'ami le plus cher de Louise et Charles et passera d'innombrables soirées et jours de vacances dans leur foyer.[26] Plus tard, la même année, Comfort commencera à élaborer ses premières grandes tentatives de peinture à l'huile, dont *Prairie Road* auparavant intitulé *Out West* (cat. n°19). Il expérimente dans l'utilisation de couleurs intenses et d'amples coups de pinceau, sans doute inspirés par le traitement souple et les pigments crus relevés dans la peinture du Groupe des Sept. Lawren Harris va pousser Comfort à soumettre cette œuvre à l'exposition de l'Académie royale des arts du Canada présentée à l'Art Association of Montreal à la fin de 1925. Quand le tableau sera de nouveau présenté au public lors de l'exposition de Groupe des Sept en 1928, il sera l'objet de critiques dithyrambique saluant l'émergence de Comfort à titre d'artiste. Voici ce qu'écrit la critique Jeanne Adeney : « En dehors du Groupe des Sept, le peintre canadien le plus doué est sans conteste Charles Comfort. D'un modernisme qui ne cède en rien au leur, son œuvre véhicule un vivant message et est chaudement appréciée autant par le public que par la critique. Comme c'est au Groupe des Sept qu'il incombait de rompre avec l'ancienne tradition au Canada et que Charles Comfort s'est mis à peindre après cette rupture et en dehors du Groupe, il peut se faire que son destin soit de recueillir les fruits de ce qu'ils ont semé. De toutes façons, il semble que la voie soit claire devant lui, dégagée de tout doute, et sa peinture est une joie pour qui la regarde. Que peut-on dire de cette route aride qui s'étend là-bas à l'ouest à part que le soleil s'y couche, et qu'elle s'est changée en une bouffée de gloire? »[27]

Sur la recommandation de Fred Brigden, Comfort fut admis à la Canadian Society of Painters in Water Colour (CSPWC) en 1926 dans le cadre de laquelle il exposait régulièrement. Il se joignit également au comité des expositions qui se rendit à Ottawa en vue d'organiser une exposition d'aquarelles pour la Galerie nationale, exposition dans laquelle il fit figurer quatre de ses œuvres dont *Stoney Lake* et *Mountain Lake*. (cat. n° 11 et 12) L'année suivante il devint membre de L'Ontario Society of Artists (OSA), autre société organisatrice d'expositions dans laquelle il remplit activement un rôle administratif au cours des décennies suivantes.

Le printemps 1927 fut, à Toronto, une période essentielle pour l'art moderne.

Katherine Dreier avait fondé la *Société Anonyme* dans le but de promouvoir l'art moderne. Grâce à elle, Lawren Harris mit sur pied une exposition qui se déroula à l'Art Gallery of Toronto (AGT), et qui choqua les placides amateurs d'art de la ville découvrant les œuvres d'artistes modernes, notamment celles de Wassily Kandinsky, Kazimir Malevich, Joán Miro, et Piet Mondrian, tandis qu'elle excitait vivement Comfort et le cercle de ses relations. Ce dernier, et tout un groupe comprenant Hortense Gordon, Edna Taçon, Bertram Brooker, Gordon Webber, Lawren Harris et Lowrie Warrener se sentirent très honorés lorsque le président du Conseil d'administration Albert Robson les pria d'agir en qualité de spécialistes-conférenciers tout le temps que dura l'exposition.

Innovatrice comme elle l'était, cette exposition eut des répercussions sur la pratique artistique de Comfort sous différents aspects. Il soutint avoir été très frappé par le Brooklyn Bridge de Joseph Stella. Il est certain que dans nombre de ses projets commerciaux ainsi que dans sa murale *Romance of Nickel* (cat. n° 85), ses arrière-plans abstraits partagent avec Stella son intérêt pour les structures créée par la main de l'homme. La première preuve directe de cette influence sur sa peinture sur chevalet paraît dans *Louise* (cat. n° 43) qu'il acheva à l'automne de 1927. Dans cette œuvre, l'élégante figure féminine est assise devant un fond aux teintes imprécises de vert qui irradient de son corps comme des émanations d'énergie, rappelant la manière des Futuristes, et communiquant non seulement le mouvement, mais aussi cette énergie spirituelle virtuelle. De plus, la légère inclinaison de la tête de Louise et le grain lisse de sa peau font manifestement référence à la *Muse* de Brancusi qu'il avait eu l'occasion d'admirer dans le cadre de l'exposition de la Société Anonyme. Ce lien iconographique permet d'évoquer le rôle de muse que Louise, sa femme, jouait auprès de lui à cette époque. Il fit d'elle des centaines de croquis. (cat. n° 40-41 et 49) tout au long des sept décennies que dura leur mariage, elle fut son plus solide appui mais aussi son meilleur critique. L'appui qu'elle lui apporta, tant sur le plan administratif et pratique que sur le plan moral permit à Comfort de réaliser cette série d'accomplissements : « Louise n'est pas seulement mon épouse et la mère de mes enfants, elle est le chef de la circulation, le vice-président et le trésorier, tout autant que secrétaire. Elle me débarrasse de tous les aspects « affaires » de ma carrière d'artiste professionnel. Pour parler franc, je ne pourrais pas fonctionner sans elle. »[28]

Ce tableau représente la première incursion majeure de Comfort dans l'art du portrait, domaine qu'on verra se développer plus à fond au cours de la décennie suivante. La toile lui valut de recevoir le deuxième prix à la prestigieuse Willingdon Arts Competition et c'est elle que choisit Bertram Brooker pour la mettre en lumière dans le *Yearbook of the Arts in Canada 1928–29* à titre d'exemple d'un art canadien original.

De la fin des années 1920 au début des années 1930, les esquisses à l'huile que Comfort exécute dans des randonnées aux alentours de Toronto trahissent son admiration pour le Groupe des Sept. Il se consacre à des paysages où la nature est à l'état sauvage qu'il peint à amples coups de peinture épaisse appliquée rythmiquement sur toute la surface pour produire des formes simplifiées vigoureuses. Ainsi par exemple *Tawny, (York Mills)* (cat. n° 20) rappelle cette configuration de neige et de terre qu'on retrouve dans les esquisses de A.Y. Jackson. Comfort attire l'attention sur le caractère bidimensionnel de la toile en plaçant hardiment un tronc vertical qui coupe en deux visuellement la composition et incline le flanc de coteau parallèlement à la surface. Dans *Winter Woods* (cat. n° 24), nous avons une démonstration du jeu abstrait de lumière et d'ombre, qui est un hommage rendu par le peintre à d'autres membres du Groupe des Sept, notamment J.E.H. MacDonald; l'effet d'écran décoratif était devenu célèbre grâce à Tom Thomson, un précurseur du Groupe.

Vers la fin des années 1920, on voit Comfort changer de direction et s'intéresser à d'autres expérimentations dans le paysage. Dans son étude pour *Wilderness* (cat. n° 21), il s'engage dans une vision plus monumentale que dans ses précédents intérieurs dans le bois. Du sommet d'une colline, il peint une vaste étendue d'eau dans laquelle se réfléchissent un nuage et le ciel. L'aspect plat de la surface qui se reflète fait contraste avec le modelé des arbres qui semble se découper vers l'arrière dans un espace profond et éloigné. Dans la grande toile achevée qui porte le même titre (cat. n° 22), « la platitude » du reflet du plan d'eau est mise en évidence; la surface peinte plus lisse contraste avec l'impasto du rocher au premier plan. La forêt dans laquelle s'insinue la rivière se présente comme une seule masse solide dans l'œuvre finie, à la différence de l'indication picturalement moins importante des arbres dans le croquis. Dans cette œuvre, Comfort introduit un côté plus tranchant dans les formes organiques qui annoncent sa minutieuse peinture de paysages des années 1930 où les formes naturelles sont encore plus simplifiées jusqu'à devenir des éléments lisses et bien ordonnés.

Innovation

La grande Crise eut pour effet de pousser davantage Comfort à s'intéresser à diverses questions autant pratiques que philosophiques. Au début de la décennie 1930, on comptait plus d'un million et demi de Canadiens qui dépendaient de l'aide sociale du gouvernement ou qui étaient itinérants. La crainte de plans ourdis par les communistes allait croissant, se traduisant par des contrôles sur la liberté de pensée, les rassemblements et la critique politique qui dérangeaient considérablement les artistes. Les sources du travail commercial se tarirent, les collectionneurs privés cessèrent d'acheter, les budgets d'acquisition des collections publiques subirent de sombres coupures et les artistes en ressentirent économiquement les effets. Tout juste avant que la Bourse ne s'effondre, Comfort quitta Brigdens pour signer un lucratif contrat de deux ans avec Rapid, Grip & Batten Ltd, contrat que ceux-ci honorèrent en dépit de la baisse générale de l'économie.[29] Mais comme, en 1931, aucune occasion de travail n'était en vue, il lança sa propre affaire d'art commercial en compagnie de Harold Ayres et Will Ogilvie.[30]

Travailler comme illustrateur indépendant exigeait davantage des capacités de Comfort que celles qui étaient requises chez Brigdens. Les images qu'on y produisait pour le catalogue de Eaton's devaient nécessairement avoir une certaine uniformité. Les artistes ne pouvaient se distinguer à titre personnel, mais le travail qu'il accomplissait en indépendant pour des clients tels que Inco portaient sa signature et pouvaient lui valoir d'être reconnu pour ses talents en art commercial. Dans cette masse de travail, il put se livrer à des expériences sur la ligne et la texture, appliquer des éléments de design qu'il découvrait dans l'art contemporain pour créer une émotion, créer des personnages et développer un récit, tout ce qui peut plaire à un public populaire.

Comme Rosemary Donegan l'explique dans son essai, Comfort mit en pratique les leçons apprises dans sa pratique de l'art commercial sur la manière dont il faut s'adresser à un public ciblé et il appliqua ces leçons à sa production de peintures murales. Il s'était engagé dans cette aventure en 1932 avec la murale exécutée à Toronto pour la North American Life Assurance Company, murale qu'il installa avec l'aide de l'artiste Carl Schaefer. Avant la fin de la décennie, il avait mené à terme une série de projets, dont la murale et les frises extérieures de la Bourse de Toronto (1936-1937), *Romance of Nickel* une commande de Inco pour l'Exposition Universelle de Paris de 1937 et la murale du voyage du Capitaine Vancouver au nord-ouest du Pacifique que la Canadian National Railway lui avait commandée pour l'hôtel Vancouver. En 1938, il étendit la pratique de cet art afin d'y intégrer un bas-relief en pierre pour le projet de la Gare centrale de Montréal.[31]

À la fin de 1935, étant devenu le muraliste le plus connu au Canada, Comfort se vit proposer le poste de chef du nouveau département de peintures murales à l'Ontario College of Art,[32] mais en 1937, totalement épuisé d'avoir travaillé si fort pour joindre les deux bouts, il commença à sentir le contrecoup de la Crise. Il envisagea l'idée de déménager aux États-Unis où son ami Robert Fawcett, illustrateur lancé dans sa branche lui avait fait parvenir 500$ en espérant le dissuader d'espérer réussir au Canada en tant qu'artiste. Il conseillait vivement à Comfort de s'installer à New York où il trouverait facilement un travail régulier dans l'art commercial.[33] Mais l'idée d'abandonner les beaux-arts pour se lancer dans la publicité le rebuta et il décida de rester dans son pays.

En dépit de sa faible rentabilité, la peinture sur chevalet semblait prometteuse. Comfort commença par peindre des portraits symboliques à grande échelle, s'intéressant non seulement aux personnages mais aussi à des questions sociales. Dans *The Dreamer*, 1929 il a peint Norman Robinson et, durant les séances de pose, ce dernier, ami personnel, lui parlait littérature, citant André Gide et Aldous Huxley, deux humanistes concernés par les tendances morales de la société contemporaine. Le personnage que représente ce portrait est un homme délirant vêtu d'un pyjama sur un arrière-plan abstrait au-dessus duquel flottent les mots « GIDE » et « HUXLEY ». Ce portrait qui se dérobe aux conventions incite à croire que c'est Comfort lui-même qui se pose des questions sur l'état moral de la société.[34]

Comfort alla plus loin dans ses tentatives de capter l'essence d'un personnage et de son environnement. Ces essais se traduisent par des portraits tels que *Chuhaldin*, 1931 (cat. n° 47), *Young Canadian*, 1932 (cat. n° 48) et *Professor Felix Walter*, 1933. (cat. n° 50) Vu leur taille peu commune – chacun atteint presque un mètre de hauteur – ces portraits lui valurent une certaine attention. Les aquarelles étaient en vogue chez Comfort et ses contemporains à l'époque de la Crise parce qu'on pouvait en produire à peu de frais et qu'elles offraient des possibilités d'expression en permettant de travailler rapidement, ce qui tenait alors de la nécessité. Quant à *Young Canadian*, portrait de son ami et artiste Carl Schaefer, il fit l'objet de plusieurs expositions tout au long de la décennie et a passé l'épreuve du temps en tant qu'image type du combat de l'artiste durant les années de crise. Les trois tableaux en question mettent l'accent sur les têtes et les mains des personnages, l'arrière-plan ou le décor reflétant les domaines d'intérêt du « poseur ».

Vers la fin des années 1920 et au cours de la décennie suivante, alors que périclitait la domination du Groupe des Sept et que le Canadian Group of Painters (CGP) se développait sur les mêmes bases, Comfort se situait à cheval sur les divers courants de la peinture de paysages. L'engouement populaire lui était acquis alors qu'il poursuivait les thèmes qui l'intéressaient dans des œuvres telles que *The Great Rock* (cat. n° 23), *Black Spruce, Pickerel River* (cat. n° 26), *Clearing, Big Stone Bay, Lake of the Woods* (cat. n° 28), *Saugenay River* (cat. n° 29), and *Distant View of Manitoulin*, 1936 (cat. n° 33). Toutes ces œuvres renvoient une image de la vie sauvage et une esthétique rurale à la manière du Groupe des Sept,[35] mais du même coup, à l'instar de nombreux artistes de sa génération, son iconographie révèle qu'il prend conscience des questions sociales exprimant cette préoccupation dans des paysages bien ordonnés, tout en soulignant les traces portées par leurs habitants. La Crise avait altéré le climat social et causé des ravages tant sur le plan local qu'international.[36]

Comme l'a noté Robert Ayre dans sa critique de la première exposition du CGP : « Non seulement nous nous dirigeons vers l'expression de la vie humaine, délaissant des paysages qui, à la longue se révèlent stériles mais, allant vers la maturité nous commençons à exposer les effets du profond bouleversement des rapports humains qui a ébranlé le monde; les répercussions sociales s'inscrivent en nous. » Il distinguait Comfort des autres artistes pour avoir fait les progrès les plus marquants dans ce sens.[37]

Dans des œuvres comme *Tadoussac* (cat. n° 36), *Smelter Stacks* (cat. n° 34), *Lake Superior Village* (cat. n° 35) et *Pioneer Survival* (cat. n° 36), Comfort réussit parfaitement à réaliser un paysage ordonné reflétant l'aspect humain du Canada. Tadoussac est la claire démonstration d'un paysage dépouillé, effet attribuable à l'influence qu'eut sur l'artiste l'Américain Charles Sheeler, féru de précision, que Comfort avait rencontré en 1933, lors de sa visite à Robert Fawcett dans la demeure de celui-ci à Ridgefield (Connecticut).[38] *Smelter Stacks* et *Lake Superior Village* nous confirment que Comfort s'intéressait de plus en plus à des sujets d'un caractère moins pittoresque. L'imagerie industrielle n'était pas uniquement son apanage, car Lawren Harris et Bess Housser s'intéressaient aussi à de pareils sujets. Mais pour Comfort, cela dut être la conséquence naturelle de ses travaux pour Inco et les chemins de fer s'agissant de créer des images pour leur publicité. En fait, il rassemblait déjà des esquisses pour de futurs tableaux pendant qu'il se rendait à Sudbury travailler pour Inco. À l'heure où il mettait la dernière main à ce genre de travaux, il se trouvait engagé dans le projet des murales et des frises pour la Bourse de Toronto qui comportait des sujets axés sur les mines et le bois de construction.

Dans *Smelter Stacks*, l'artiste nous offre une vue à distance des opérations de fonderie avec un ciel qui domine dans la partie supérieure de la toile, l'imagerie industrielle étant reléguée à la partie inférieure, comme il l'avait fait dans ses compositions champêtres à l'aquarelle. (cats. 1 et 7) À l'instar des structures créées pour *Tadoussac*, les bâtiments et les cheminées fumantes ont une solidité géométrique simplifiée. Cependant, la tuyauterie dont s'échappent des volutes de fumée se charge d'une vie propre à elle, vomissant ces fumées dans le ciel bleu tout brillant où elles vont se fondre dans la mince couche de nuages. Visuellement dérangeante, la ligne droite de l'échappement qui s'élève en continu le long du côté gauche de la tuyauterie souligne le désir de Comfort de mettre de l'ordre dans cette opération chaotique. Ici l'artiste ne cherche pas à mettre en valeur l'opération industrielle comme il le faisait dans ses activités commerciales; il présente plutôt ces sujets non traditionnels en peinture comme esthétiquement valables et symbolisant la vie contemporaine. Au lieu de critiquer ses tableaux comme étant trop commerciaux – ce qui s'est produit fréquemment – je propose que l'on considère valable ce que fait Comfort quand il applique résolument les sujets et tendances stylistiques de sa pratique commerciale au domaine des beaux-arts, comme il nous arrive de le faire pour certains artistes contemporains dont le style et l'iconographie ressortent visiblement d'emprunts faits à la publicité et à la culture pop.

Lake Superior Village, 1937, tableau réalisé à partir d'esquisses datant de 1935 à Rossport, Ontario (cat. n° 32) représente la synthèse du talent de Comfort et sa consécration comme peintre sur la scène internationale.[39] Ce tableau fit partie de l'exposition Great Lakes Exhibition qui fut présentée en tournée dans des villes du Canada et des États-Unis. Il remporta le premier prix et attira l'attention du public sur son auteur.[40] Parlant de cette œuvre et du lauréat, Robert Ayre écrivit : « J'estime que c'est l'essence du Canada et c'est le plus important, parce que ce n'est pas le très-peinturé Canada des tourbillonnantes Laurentides, des monumentales Rocheuses ou de la flamboyante parade des forêts de l'automne...c'est solidement construit, bien ordonné et la petite taille des personnages humains révèle la grandeur d'échelle que doit toujours être le Canada... »[41] œuvre que l'on peut comparer à d'autres de la même année, *The Observatory* (cat. n° 37) conserve ce style très précis, très tranché, tout en réintroduisant une texture plus tactile de la pâte. Le tableau fut retenu comme le premier exemple de la peinture moderne au Canada[42] et son succès fit que son auteur reçut de la Albright Gallery de Buffalo l'offre de monter en 1939 une exposition consacrée uniquement à sa peinture. Par malheur, le déroulement des événements qui menèrent à la guerre obligea Comfort à annuler son engagement à ce qui aurait été sa première exposition internationale en solo.[43]

Enseignant et activiste culturel

En 1936, Charles Comfort fut élu membre associé de la Royal Canadian Academy et, ainsi encouragé, il put obtenir un atelier dans le célèbre Studio Building où il eut pour voisin A.Y. Jackson. Les efforts disparates entrepris jusqu'alors commençaient à être payants. Il fut nommé professeur associé de l'Université de Toronto, en charge d'enseigner l'histoire des techniques picturales, sujet qui l'avait passionné durant toute sa vie. Autre avantage, il pouvait désormais abandonner la pratique commerciale et se concentrer sur la peinture et les questions académiques.[44] Il conserva cette fonction sans interruption jusqu'en 1960, à l'exception des années de guerre à laquelle il participa de 1943 à 1946.

En mai 1939, à la fin de sa première année universitaire, il se rendit en Italie pour étoffer son bagage culturel en absorbant le plus d'art possible et en prenant des photos qu'il devait utiliser dans ses conférences. Il étudia des œuvres murales, comme les fresques de Michel-Ange à la Chapelle Sixtine et celles de Cimabue et Giotto à Assise ainsi que les mosaïques de Pompéi. Il scruta l'art et l'architecture italiens contemporains, notant la manière dont les artistes modernes avaient réussi à s'inspirer des traditions et à utiliser d'anciennes techniques.[45] Dans son journal personnel de cette période, il note son enthousiasme pour ces nouvelles expériences et le fait que sa passion pour l'art n'a pas décru. Il décrit sa réaction devant la Chapelle Sixtine : « Devant une telle œuvre, tout jugement critique fait défaut. Je savais que je me trouvais en ce lieu et sa la formidable beauté m'a immédiatement possédé. Je me suis trouvé dans la même extase spirituelle que celle qui présida à la Renaissance ...J'en suis ressorti tel que j'y étais entré, aveugle à tout le reste... »[46]

Pour les deux années suivantes, l'enseignement allait monopoliser tout son temps à l'université. Il y donna toute une série de cours en atelier, comprenant la peinture murale et les fresques, la peinture à l'huile, la détrempe, le dessin, le design, la création architecturale, l'anatomie et jusqu'à la peinture de camouflage. Outre les sessions ordinaires, il alla donner des cours d'été à Banff en 1941. Au fil des années, sa philosophie pédagogique méthodique devait comprendre la même approche bidimensionnelle : d'une part il encourageait l'étude et la compréhension des anciennes méthodes de travail, de l'autre il faisait suivre à ses élèves des travaux pratiques répétés.[47] Et parmi ces derniers, on peut citer quelques personnalités des plus remarquables, dont des historiens et des administrateurs, notamment Russell Harper, conservateur de l'art canadien, le Dr Gerald Finley, historien de l'art, Université Queen's et Jean Sutherland Boggs, spécialiste de Degas qui prit la suite de Comfort à la tête de la Galerie nationale.

La fin des années trente et les années quarante furent, pour Comfort et le cercle de ses relations, une période marquante dans l'activisme en faveur de l'art. Pendant que la Deuxième guerre mondiale battait son plein, les artistes canadiens firent entendre leurs réclamations au sujet du statut de l'artiste dans la société. Lors de la Conférence de Kingston qui se tint à l'Université Queen's en juin 1941, ils firent front commun avec les directeurs de musées et les historiens de l'art. Ayant eu connaissance du programme instauré par Roosevelt, la Works Progress Administration qui avait procuré du travail à de nombreux artistes américains dans des projets publics d'art au cours des années 1930, nos artistes voulaient présenter au gouvernement des recommandations visant à établir un programme de soutien. Ils tinrent également des ateliers de perfectionnement professionnel en techniques.[48] Comfort fut amené à participer à l'organisation de la conférence et c'est lui qui présenta l'orateur chargé du discours-programme, l'Américain Thomas Hart Benton, peintre de murales. La conférence accueillit le plus grand rassemblement public d'artistes canadiens et fut le point culminant de toutes les réclamations et rencontres informelles des années trente. L'objectif du rassemblement était d'établir et renforcer la notion d'artiste en tant que travailleur de plein droit dans la société. Au cours de la conférence, les artistes décidèrent de fonder la Fédération des artistes canadiens (Federation of Canadian Artists – FCA), élirent Andre Biéler comme président avec, pour mission, de promouvoir les idées avancées dans la conférence au moyen d'actions concrètes visant à améliorer la situation des arts. La première rencontre de la fédération eut lieu à l'automne et se tint dans l'atelier de Comfort. L'une des recommandations formulées fut la mise sur pied d'un programme gouvernemental d'art militaire visant à employer les artistes. À court terme, ce programme fut mis sur pied, mais d'autres objectifs visaient le plus long terme. L'appel pour le soutien aux artistes allait exiger du travail des comités et des tractations en coulisses pour bon nombre d'artistes et en particulier pour une bonne amie des Comfort, Elizabeth Wyn Wood. Leurs démarches, ainsi que celles de groupes de pression liés à d'autres intérêts culturels aboutirent à la création de la commission Massey en 1949 qui déposa le Rapport Massey de 1951. La commission faisait état de ses inquiétudes face au danger pour le Canada de s'aligner sur la culture des États-Unis ainsi que de la nécessité de protéger l'identité culturelle nationale en mettant le développement de la culture sous le patronage de l'État. De la défense de cette cause naquit le Conseil des Arts du Canada qui est toujours, pour les artistes, le gage d'un soutien vital.

En raison de son engagement constant en faveur de la culture canadienne tout au long de ces années et de sa capacité de s'entretenir sur des sujets touchant à l'art dans ses fonctions d'enseignant, de conférencier invité et de membre exécutif de diverses associations artistiques, Comfort fut prié de rédiger pour le rapport Massey un essai traitant de la situation de la peinture au Canada. Il en appela à un soutien gouvernemental plus ou moins calqué sur celui du British Arts Council afin « d'assurer des normes et un cadre de production en arts visuels dans l'intérêt de l'unité et de la conscience nationales. »[49] Il se fit aussi le champion de l'ouverture à l'égard des divers modes d'expression esthétique, en expliquant les raisons pour lesquelles l'art était en droit de se tourner vers l'abstraction dans un monde qui, depuis la Première Guerre mondiale, évoluait à une vitesse exponentielle. Tout en faisant l'apologie du Groupe des Sept qu'il présentait comme une force positive pour l'identité culturelle du pays en train de se forger, il souligna le fait qu'il faut laisser à l'expression de l'art le pouvoir de changer et de croître en considérant l'abstraction comme une forme d'art canadien valide. L'image conservatrice qu'il donna de lui au cours des années soixante où il exerça ses fonctions à ce qui s'appelait encore la Galerie nationale fait contraste avec l'ensemble des écrits des années trente à cinquante. Dans le document précité, il semble être un solide partisan du modernisme à l'esprit ouvert. Il en va de même des articles qu'il rédigea et qui sont souvent cités « The Painter and his Model (1931) » et « 1938–48 : Observations on a Decade » (1948).[50]

L'artiste militaire

Pour Comfort, la guerre marque en quelque sorte un sommet dans sa carrière, en dépit du fait qu'il se trouvait séparé de sa famille et qu'il était témoin forcé de destructions et de souffrances humaines pires que ce qu'il avait jamais imaginé. Son art militaire et le livre qui s'ensuivit *Artist at War* connurent un grand succès, tant sur le plan personnel que professionnel. Quand il rentre au Canada en 1946, il était un artiste canadien hautement respecté. Quand son livre parut, Robert Ayre, réagissant en ami et en critique d'art commenta brièvement ses activités de guerre dans ces lignes : « Il aurait pu faire un soldat efficace, peut-être même se distinguer au combat, mais le Canada a fait preuve de sagesse en se rendant compte qu'il lui serait bien plus utile d'en faire un observateur et un mémorialiste plutôt qu'un combattant. »[51]

Bien qu'officiellement ses instructions fussent « d'enregistrer » les activités des soldats canadiens en temps de guerre, la plupart de ses œuvres font penser à un subtil expressionnisme tissé d'émotions, les élevant ainsi à un niveau qui dépasse la simple documentation. À partir de croquis faits sur place, il produisait ensuite des huiles achevées, telles que *Campobasso* (cat. n° 67) qui semble être, au départ, l'agréable vision d'une ancienne cité vue à travers des arbres qui forment écran; en l'examinant plus à fond, on remarque des tanks et des soldats avançant le long du premier plan.

Certains de ses plus puissants tableaux sont des aquarelles directement réalisées sur le terrain, comme c'est le cas pour *Wrecked Buildings, Ortona* (cat. n° 62), qui nous montre des bâtiments déchiquetés réduit à un état squelettique, entraînant de ce fait une réflexion sur l'état de notre civilisation. On y remarque l'influence de l'artiste britannique John Piper que Comfort avait rencontré en 1943 lors d'une réception que donnaient Sir Kenneth et Lady Clark.[52] Ce séjour en Italie eut des à-côtés marqués d'une ironie douce-amère, car cela lui fournit l'occasion d'examiner – et dans certains cas de réexaminer les chefs-d'œuvre de l'art italien sur lesquels il lui arrivait de tomber au cours de ses diverses campagnes. En fait, on encourageait les soldats à admirer les œuvres-témoins de la culture des régions dans lesquelles ils étaient stationnés. On leur distribuait même des dépliants intitulés « Soldiers Guide to Rome» pour leur permettre d'apprécier les beautés de l'art.[53]

L'après-guerre

À son retour au pays, Charles Comfort fut posté à Ottawa le temps de compléter ses grands tableaux d'art militaire. Pendant plusieurs mois, il profita du climat d'après-guerre où on s'intéressait à tout ce qui s'était passé durant ces années-là. Une exposition sur l'art militaire eut lieu à Ottawa à la Galerie Nationale et une autre se tint à Toronto au Hart House ce printemps-là. Comfort y donna une série de conférences. En juillet, l'armée lui rendit sa liberté et il retrouva sa famille à Toronto. Cet été-là, il passa énormément de temps avec les siens et avec Will Ogilvie et ses amis Doris et Gordon Davies à Cedar Lake, dans le parc Algonquin. Pour la première fois de sa vie, son journal personnel ne fait étrangement aucune mention de quoi que ce soit qui touche à la peinture. Il décompressait de son expérience militaire : « Je n'éprouve aucune urgence de peindre et ne désire rien d'autre que de vivre dans l'oisiveté sans interruption.»[54]

Quand il reprit son poste d'enseignant, Comfort dut faire des efforts pour s'adapter à une vie régulière sans le tapage associé à sa qualité d'artiste militaire. Comme il le note dans son journal, l'humeur générale est à la baisse, les gens tournent le dos au passé et vont de l'avant dans une société en pleine mutation. Pour aggraver son cas, il était près de se retrouver sans ressources. En fait, lors du décès de sa mère en 1947, il envisagea de ne pas assister aux funérailles parce qu'il était sans le sou.[55] La dernière phrase de son journal, cette année-là (1947) est : « Je n'ai jamais été si pauvre, si déguenillé, depuis l'époque de mon enfance. »[56]

Les deux décennies suivantes, il continua à se débattre avec le manque d'argent, mais il se trouva très vite incroyablement occupé. Il continuait à enseigner tout en poursuivant ses recherches dans le domaine technique lorsqu'il remporta une bourse de la Royal Society pour suivre des études aux Pays-Bas en 1955. Louise et lui passèrent une année à voyager et à étudier les peintres flamands et hollandais. Il accepta également plusieurs commandes d'entreprises au cours des années cinquante. Dans le cadre d'une série axée sur les grandes villes du Canada, les Distilleries Seagram lui commandèrent de peindre Edmonton; le Canadian Club de New York lui commanda une peinture sur les édifices du Parlement. Parmi les commandes publiques, on note une murale massive pour la banque Toronto Dominion de Vancouver en 1951 (cat. n° 87); une murale plus réduite de la vallée Bow au parc national de Banff pour l'intérieur de l'une des voitures du Parc du Canadian Pacific Railway en 1954;[57] une murale pour le ministère des Anciens Combattants à Ottawa en 1955 et une murale sur l'histoire de la médecine pour le service de neurochirurgie de l'Hôpital général de Toronto en 1958. Et ceci sans compter le fait que pendant cette période et jusqu'au milieu des années 1970, il exécuta le portrait officiel de plusieurs hauts fonctionnaires politiques et militaires.

Comfort était aussi activement engagé dans des activités concernant des galeries d'art et des associations artistiques. Depuis le jour où il avait déménagé à Toronto, il s'était consacré à l'Art Gallery of Toronto. En 1946, il fut élu membre du conseil d'administration et siégea ensuite au comité des collections canadiennes de l'AGT (service des acquisitions) de 1949 jusqu'à la fin de 1959. Il fit ensuite partie de son comité des expositions de 1946 à 1949.[58] Il fut également membre du comité consultatif du Hart House Gallery pour l'achat d'œuvres d'art. En 1950, il fut élu président du Canadian Group of Painters tout en occupant simultanément la charge de président de la Canadian Society of Painters in Watercolors. Il fut aussi, de 1957 jusqu'à la fin de 1960 président de l'Académie royale des arts du Canada. En 1958, l'université de Mount Allison lui décerna le titre de docteur *honoris causa* en reconnaissance de ses accomplissements; en 1963, l'université de l'Alberta le récompensa d'une médaille d'or pour son œuvre picturale et enfin, la même année il reçut la *Medaglio al Merito Culturale* pour sa contribution aux échanges culturels entre l'Italie et le Canada.

Tout de suite après la guerre, Comfort exposa ses tableaux un peu partout : à l'OSA, à l'ARAC, à la CSPWC et au CGP. Au début, il soumettait des œuvres qui faisaient état de son expérience militaire ou des œuvres plus anciennes, telles que *Tadoussac* et *Young Canadian*. Et il participa également à des expositions à l'étranger, en France, en Nouvelle-Zélande et aux États-Unis.

Si, à l'échelon privé, ses ventes de tableaux furent modestes, à l'échelle publique il y en eut d'importantes qui aidèrent à placer ses principales œuvres dans différents centres du pays : *Lake Superior Village* fut acquis par l'Art Gallery of Ontario en 1950, *Aura Lee* par la Winnipeg Art Gallery en 1952; *Chuhaldin* et *The Dreamer* à l'Art Gallery of Hamilton en 1954 et 1957 et *Smelter Stacks* à la National Gallery également en 1957. À cette époque, Comfort était enfin parvenu au statut respecté d'artiste « sénior ». En conséquence, l'éditeur Ryerson Press estima qu'il méritait une monographie et chargea Robert Ayre de la rédiger pour l'inclure dans une série consacrée aux artistes canadiens, ce qui plaçait Comfort en compagnie de Cornelius Krieghoff, Tom Thomson, A.Y. Jackson et autres artistes renommés. Mais il se sentit insulté par Ayre qui le décrivait comme « un drôle de petit bonhomme qui écrit son journal personnel »[59] et, du coup, il refusa de laisser paraître l'ouvrage en question. À cause de sa mésentente avec Ayre, une étude synoptique de son œuvre ne fut pas publiée avant les années 1970, ce qui a peut-être compromis en partie la reconnaissance que sa peinture aurait obtenue plus tôt, dans les années intermédiaires.

Avec un renouveau de vigueur, Comfort reprit sa production de tableaux dans les deux années suivantes. De nouveaux portraits en sortirent, comme celui d'Ogilvie (cat. n° 68) et de Schaefer, rendant hommage à leur service dans l'armée. À la fin des années 1940, il exposa de nouveaux paysages, basés, pour la plupart, sur des études qu'il mettait au point chaque été soit à Cedar Lake ou, plus tard, à Go Home Bay où il se trouvait invité par les Jackman qui avaient récemment acquis le fameux chalet MacCallum. Pendant quelques décennies, les Comfort y passèrent des week-ends chaque été, souvent rejoint par A.Y. Jackson et Will Ogilvie. Intéressé à mener son travail vers de nouveaux terrains d'investigation, Comfort entreprit de combiner dans ses paysages des éléments symboliques avec divers niveaux d'abstraction. *Aeons Ago* (cat. n° 70), mené à terme pour faire partie d'une série réalisée à Cedar Lake, dénotait une sensibilité surréaliste : s'entremêlant avec un arrière-plan abstrait, on y voit des éléments figuratifs disparates – du bois à la dérive, un masque primitif, une lune balsamique dans son déclin (qui symbolise le temps de mourir et de renaître) et le pied désincarné (qui rappelle Guernica, le tableau de Picasso dénonçant la guerre). Dans cette œuvre, l'artiste s'efforce d'exprimer des idées concernant l'histoire de la civilisation, son passage par des périodes d'obscurantisme et sa foi dans l'avenir. D'un point de vue stylistique, Comfort reprend ici à sa manière l'influence d'Henry Moore et de John Piper, deux artistes britanniques qu'il avait eu l'occasion de rencontrer outre-mer.

Au cours des deux décennies suivantes, l'élaboration d'une iconographie symbolique qui ressort périodiquement dans l'œuvre de Comfort la rend particulièrement intéressante. Comme Anna Hudson le relève dans son étude, Comfort et ses contemporains tentaient dans leur peinture de mettre à l'épreuve des éléments symboliques courants.[60] Divers artistes de Toronto, à commencer peut-être par Bertram Brooker, utilisèrent comme symboles, la racine des arbres avec l'image rebattue du bois flottant qui part à la dérive. Inspiré par L.L. Fitzgerald au début des années 1930, Brooker commença par dessiner des arbres « biomorphiques ». En 1945, il peignit une huile représentant un morceau de bois flotté, la base d'un tronc d'arbre avec ses racines tronquées qui se transforme en visages animaliers, tableau qui devait être familier pour Comfort, vu qu'ils étaient amis. Dès 1938, avec *Pioneer Survival* (cat. n° 36) Comfort utilise des souches d'arbres déracinés prédominantes au premier plan, pour symboliser l'esprit humain qui, déplacé, se débat pendant la Crise. Il continuera à utiliser l'image des souches déracinées et du bois flottant à travers de nombreux tableaux, en explorant méthodiquement les significations formelles et symboliques des tronçons d'arbres. Dans *Transfiguration* (cat. n° 71) 1948, il poussera le symbolisme jusqu'à montrer des souches brûlées à la suite d'un incendie de forêt avec, autour d'elles une nouvelle végétation prometteuse de régénération. *Aura Lee* (cat. n° 73), une toile peinte deux ans plus tard, présente une pile de bois en dérive masquant l'îlot qui semble flotter comme un bateau au milieu du paysage de Cedar Lake. L'artiste ne se contentait pas de peindre un paysage en tant que tel, mais faisait passer dans son œuvre sa préoccupation de la condition humaine – en l'occurrence, la déchéance, la mort et la promesse d'un renouveau.

La surface rocheuse du Bouclier canadien est un autre élément récurrent de transformation symbolique et itératif adopté par

Comfort. Dans *Rocky Site* 1972 (cat. n° 74), nous assistons au résultat du mouvement de plaques tectoniques formant des débris épars à la partie inférieure et des pans exposés de rochers à la partie supérieure, au-dessus desquels s'accrochent des pins battus par les vents. L'application d'épaisses couches de peinture traduit son intérêt pour les effets techniques. Il étendait de brillants pigments, des oranges, des bleus, des jaunes et des verts – par dessus les teintes plus naturelles de brun et de beige du rocher. On reconnaît ce traitement au fait qu'il rappelle certaines des huiles du temps de guerre, telles que *La Ligne Hitler* ou transparaît l'influence de John Piper qui s'exerçait à de pareils effets dans ses toiles du début de 1940. Tout au long des années cinquante, la surface des tableaux de Comfort est un luxuriant impasto appliqué à la hâte qui dénote non seulement la texture mais même une transformation littérale. *Wherewhen* (cat. n° 76) représente peut-être le point culminant de cette tendance; c'est une œuvre monumentale qui nous montre ce qu'il appelait « une épave d'arbre », rejeté sur le rivage. Ce rivage simplifié, quasi abstrait, le lac et les îles rocheuses de la baie Georgienne dégagent une morne aridité évocatrice de solitude et d'abandon, compensée par la riche application d'une pâte texturée. Avec ses diverses teintes de bleu dans des plans qui s'entrecoupent, le ciel rappelle certaines formations du Bouclier canadien. Prédominantes, les couleurs « terre » de l'écorce de l'arbre sont égayées par des touches éclatantes de bleu, rouge et jaune. Enfin, le premier quartier de la lune là-haut dans le ciel, symbolisant l'évolution de nouvelles formes en dépit de la résistance, nous laisse penser qu'il y a dans ce tableau comme un présage d'espoir.

S'entremêlant avec ses expériences dans le domaine du symbolisme figuratif au cours de cette décennie, on assiste, chez Comfort, à de nouvelles incursions dans l'abstraction. Dans ses tentatives d'égaler les collages en techniques mixtes du milieu des années trente de John Piper, il réalise *Thrush Song*, 1948/1949 (cat. n° 72) qui est l'exemple le plus littéral de son admiration pour l'art moderne britannique. Bien qu'abstraite, cette œuvre utilise le Bouclier canadien comme source d'inspiration permettant à ses formes d'émerger. En 1957, il ira plus loin dans son exploration du paysage jusqu'à atteindre un nouveau degré dans des œuvres telle que *Pre-Cambrian Legend* (cat. n° 77).[61] Comme pour *Wherewhen*, ce qui l'inspire, c'est le paysage de la baie Georgienne et il y introduit d'audacieux éclaboussements de couleur à la manière expressionniste. Dans cette œuvre, toutefois, il rejette le lourd impasto de pigments à l'huile multicolores au profit d'une articulation plus uniforme de plans rocheux en interaction.[62]

C'est en 1959 que Comfort sera encouragé à soumettre sa candidature pour le poste de directeur de la Galerie nationale, et il lui est alors nécessaire de suspendre toute activité picturale sérieuse jusqu'en 1965.

L'administrateur d'art

Le fait que l'on ait pressenti Charles Comfort pour occuper un poste aussi prestigieux confirmait la direction qu'avaient pris ses travaux et ses efforts en faveur de la culture canadienne pendant plus de quatre décennies. Les liens qu'il avait tissés avec la Galerie dès le début des années vingt, les diverses tâches accomplies au sein de comités d'associations et de galeries d'art où il s'occupait d'expositions, d'acquisitions et de politiques l'avaient parfaitement préparé pour une telle fonction. Il avait, de plus, des rapports personnels et professionnels avec les trois directeurs qui l'y avaient précédé, Eric Brown, H.O. McCurry et Alan Jarvis. Néanmoins ce n'est pas sans inquiétude que Louise et lui devaient envisager cet nomination. Il en parle dans son journal comme d'un moment où il fit son examen de conscience et où il fut pris d'angoisse à l'idée d'être affilié à une institution dont le dernier directeur avait essuyé des critiques pour avoir mis l'accent sur l'art moderne. Quand, au bout du compte, il accepta d'assumer cette charge, il prit note d'une remarque de Louise : « Bon, jusqu'à présent, notre vie a été faite d'heureux moments et d'adaptations. Je ne puis m'empêcher de penser que nous avons définitivement tourné la page et que, dorénavant, nous serons harcelés par l'hostilité et les pressions. »[63] Même Harry Jackman qui était membre du conseil d'administration de la GNC tenta de le dissuader d'accepter ce poste.[64] Malgré ces désolantes prédictions, Comfort alla à l'encontre de son instinct et donna son accord à la proposition, espérant qu'avec lui ce serait différent, vu qu'il serait le premier artiste à accepter un tel poste.

Dans le rôle d'ambassadeur et de porte-parole de la Galerie où il avait à prononcer une allocution lors d'un vernissage et à escorter des hauts personnages qui venaient en visite, il se montra à la hauteur. La grande passion qu'il éprouvait pour l'art et sa connaissance de la pratique pertinente au Canada et à l'échelle internationale, au plan historique comme au contemporain, faisaient de lui une excellente figure de proue pour l'institution. Mais avant la fin de sa première année en exercice, des doutes devaient faire surface quent à ses rapports avec le personnel, plusieurs personnes-clés ayant donné leur démission. Au bout de l'année, les responsabilités de sa charge avaient sérieusement ébranlé sa vision enthousiaste des premiers temps : « Après une année de présence active, j'en suis au point d'être plus triste et aussi plus sage... ce fut une année d'incessant labeur sans que rien d'intéressant en ressorte encore, mais quand on travaille sérieusement, consciencieusement, cela ne peut rester indéfiniment sans récompense. »[65] Un journaliste relève que : « Une période de calme s'est installée à la Galerie nationale, faisant espérer qu'il y a eu divorce entre la politique et la peinture... en tous les cas, la Galerie a été libérée de toute controverse depuis sa nomination. »[66]

Mais en 1962, on ne pouvait plus en dire autant. Une exposition ironiquement intitulée « Un siècle de controverses : 1850-1950 » qui devait comprendre les œuvres prétendument signées d'artistes tels que Degas, Renoir, Cézanne et Van Gogh de la collection de Walter Chrysler souleva une controverse internationale. Un mois avant que l'exposition n'arrive à la GNC, Comfort reçut un appel d'Evan Turner, directeur du Musée des beaux-arts de Montréal, lui annonçant que lorsqu'il se trouvait à New York, il avait entendu dire que plusieurs tableaux de la collection Chrysler avaient été dénoncés comme étant des faux. L'ADAA (Art Dealers Association of America), association nouvellement constituée, était en train d'enquêter sur cette collection à Provincetown (Massachussetts) pour tenter d'éliminer du marché les contrefaçons. Comme il n'avait pas vu les pièces en question, Comfort faisait confiance à William Dale, son directeur adjoint qui, chargé de la recherche, avait négocié ce qui semblait être une rare occasion. Quant à Comfort, même s'il se rendit au ministère de la justice pour discuter de l'affaire, il en minimisa l'importance en l'attribuant à une rumeur, et ceci d'autant plus que l'ADAA n'avait jamais communiquer directement avec lui.

Lorsque cette association, l'ADAA, apprit que l'exposition était présentée au Canada, elle divulgua l'information dans la presse. Comfort fut submergé d'appels téléphoniques de la part des revues américaines *Time Magazine*, *Newsweek* et *Life Magazine*. John Canaday, critique d'art du *The New York Times*, désavoua les articles chaleureux qu'il avait fait paraître au lancement de l'exposition. Et quand ce fut le tour de la presse locale, Judy LaMarsh, députée libérale de l'opposition, ameuta le Parlement à ce sujet et Comfort fut prié de justifier son attitude devant le conseil d'administration du musée. Au bout du compte, le conseil vota en réitérant sa confiance dans l'intégrité professionnelle de Comfort, mais toutes ces épreuves l'avaient laissé meurtri et déprimé : « Une dépression sombre et inconsidérée remplit mon esprit... Personne ne semble comprendre ou reconnaître que j'ai fait tout ce qu'il était possible de faire sauf annuler l'exposition quand elle commençait à prendre de l'importance. »[67] Le fait que l'incident reçut une grande couverture médiatique jeta une ombre sur le restant de sa charge de directeur, comme il l'avait prédit : « cette exposition restera comme un épouvantable incident tant sur le plan personnel que dans l'histoire de la Galerie. »[68]

Épuisé par cette affaire et par l'incessante impression que le personnel et le conseil d'administration lui avaient manqué de respect, Comfort envisagea de partir. Peu de mois avant que ça se produise, une autre controverse vint le hanter, toujours claironnée par les médias. En sa qualité de directeur d'une institution nationale, il avait à signer les documents d'importation permettant à des œuvres d'art de passer la frontière exemptées de toutes taxes lorsqu'elles pénètrent dans le cadre d'une exposition. Mais il refusa de signer une décharge pour les fameuses boîtes à soupe (Campbell) et les « Brillo pads » d'Andy Warhol parce qu'il ne pouvait pas qualifier un « multiple » d'œuvre d'art originale, il fut brocardé et traité d'artiste vieux jeu.[69] On ressortit une de ses phrases : « Il m'est impossible de classifier ces cartons traités et ces boîtes de fer blanc dans la catégorie de sculptures. »[70] Quand on le critiqua à propos de ce genre d'objet il devait affirmer que la Galerie nationale avait déjà présenté deux expositions de Pop Art américain dans les années précédentes. Pour justifier la mesure qu'il avait prise, il raconta qu'il désirait discuter en priorité des questions concernant le statut de ce récent phénomène qu'on appelle des œuvres à tirages multiples. Il sentit cependant que la manière opportuniste avec laquelle les médias avaient tourné en ridicule un directeur en instance de départ avait éclipsé son argumentation.

La retraite lui fut à la fois douce et amère. Sur le plan positif, il laissait un héritage qui se traduisait par une augmentation du nombre de visiteurs à la Galerie grâce à des expositions de grande qualité. Le programme des expositions itinérantes fut également en hausse et la collection du Musée devait s'enrichir d'œuvres majeures historiques de grands maîtres européens tout autant que des peintres canadiens contemporains, tels que Jean-Paul Riopelle, Paul-Émile Borduas et Harold Town. Comfort apporta également sa pierre à l'édification du Laboratoire national de conservation et de recherches et à la fondation de l'ODMAC (Organisation des directeurs de musées d'art du Canada) qui est toujours en actif. Cet organisme joue un grand rôle dans la valorisation professionnelle des musées d'art au Canada. En dépit de tous ces accomplissements, Comfort eut de la difficulté à se libérer des noirs nuages le laissant penser qu'il avait perdu la respectueuse considération dans laquelle on le tenait auparavant. Dans son allocution adressée au personnel avant de quitter, il établit une comparaison entre ce départ et le moment où il quitta le service militaire : « J'abandonne mon rang, je rends les armes que j'avais appris à utiliser dans ce que Sir John Rothinstine a décrit comme « l'imprévisible, l'impitoyable, le cruel combat de jungle du monde de l'art. Je l'abandonne pour être rapatrié, pour retrouver mon identité et ma réputation en tant que Charles Comfort. »[71]

Le retour

Comfort se concentrant sur le côté positif devait reconnaître, qu'il aurait enfin l'occasion, pour la première fois de sa vie, de faire de la peinture à temps plein. Aussi accepta-t-il immédiatement des commandes de portraits et se lança-t-il dans la murale destinée à la salle de lecture de la Bibliothèque nationale.

Au cours des deux décennies suivantes, il continua à expérimenter avec l'abstraction à des degrés croissants. Dans cette partie plus tardive de sa carrière, il nous prouve qu'il s'est consacré à tenter d'approfondir sa quête et à chercher l'inspiration dans un monde en perpétuelle mutation où il occupa une place aléatoire. À titre d'humaniste autoproclamé, sa vision du monde se concentre sur la vie qu'il perçoit comme une chance exceptionnelle d'accéder à la connaissance et de faire de nouvelles découvertes. En 1974, il rédige sa profession de foi et il le fait comme suit, en parlant de lui à la troisième personne :

« En sa qualité d'artiste, il se présente comme un réaliste à tendance humaniste dont la peinture se caractérise par un esprit de liberté bien réglée et de conservatisme technique. Pour lui, le monde visible constitue un point de départ valide pour une œuvre d'art. Cela ne veut pas dire que son objet soit de copier la nature, mais plutôt de la recréer, d'en faire un nouveau moulage et de l'harmoniser pour la faire concorder avec son maniérisme idiomatique et ses concepts personnels propres. Il envisage son monde comme une source d'inspiration et de signifiance inépuisables. »[72]

Dans son œuvre figurative, Comfort a exploité à fond des thèmes correspondant à la quête épique d'un sens à donner à la vie. Ses œuvres de ces années-la, la décennie 1970, *Seventh Line, Tecumseh Township* (cat. n° 80) et *Edge of the World, Georgian Bay* (cat. n° 81) tendent à nous indiquer que ce qui l'intéresse dans la vie, c'est l'idée d'un voyage où l'on s'interroge sur ce qui vient après. Ces deux tableaux sont d'une belle facture. Sa façon de traiter le médium, élégante et à stratifiée, son sens très sûr de la couleur, sa simplification et son agencement des formes, qualités à travers lesquelles il traquait le paysage en tant que métaphore, tout cela devait se perpétuer dans son œuvre.

Mais en même temps, on voit Comfort revenir à l'abstraction pure, peut-être dans l'idée de casser l'image conservatrice qu'il avait acquise dans sa fonction de directeur de la Galerie nationale. Des œuvres telles que *Epic Theme* (cat. n° 78) nous montrent la sûreté avec laquelle il traitait l'abstraction et nous fait part de son admiration pour Borduas et ses premières œuvres en blanc et noir peintes au couteau. Comme il l'avait fait dans *Pre-Cambrian Legend* une dizaine d'années plus tôt, Comfort introduit une audacieuse tache de couleur sur une structure quadrillée à dominante monochrome. Dans ce tableau, les formes qui se chevauchent dénotent la constance de son intérêt pour traduire dans l'abstrait les aspects naturels du Bouclier canadien et, pour explorer, comme son titre l'indique, les prodigieux thèmes de la vie. Son besoin de réaffirmer son identité de peintre moderne est révélateur. Dans son autoportrait, (cat. n° 54) qui lui a été commandé par la Galerie nationale, il se peint vêtu d'un sarrau de peintre avec, à l'arrière plan, un tableau semblable à *Epic Theme*.

La même année, il produit la « Newspeak Series », abstraits horizontaux à bords tranchés qui représente son écart le plus marqué d'une morphologie naturelle (cat. n° 79).[73] Dans cette œuvre, la grille expressionniste devient, à l'instar des formations rocheuses de ses tableaux précédents, plus carrément géométriques. La manière dont il explique ce changement d'approche trahit sa quête persistante de nouvelles façons d'exprimer ses constantes préoccupations à travers les aspects formels de sa peinture : « Ma *Newspeak Series* est un nouveau développement dans mon travail en tant qu'organisation rectiligne et mûrement réfléchie, qui se présente en parallèle à la nature et dans lequel le mot-clé est « équivalence ». Le monde du naturalisme solide et spatial a toujours, pour moi, une signification vitale, mais mes « événements horizontaux » m'offrent un nouveau dispositif à travers lequel j'exprime des aspects de l'ordre dans une phase critique de l'évolution de notre société.»[74]

Pareille déclaration témoigne de son engagement dans l'art au service de la société. Cet engagement fur publiquement reconnu en 1972 lorsqu'il fut fait Officier de l'Ordre du Canada. Des décennies auparavant, il avait parlé du rôle de l'artiste qui est de : « ...contribuer à la vie culturelle de la communauté avec honnêteté, sincérité et profonde intégrité à l'égard de son œuvre et en rapport avec sa génération. »[75]

Dans ce contexte, nous pouvons déterminer une logique dans la démarche artistique de Comfort, démarche d'une grande diversité qui se fit jour sur plusieurs décennies. Ces œuvres tardives représentent la mise en ordre définitive du paysage, projet qu'il amorça vers la fin des années 1920 et exprima de façon plus évidente dans les années 1930. Jusqu'à la fin de sa carrière, il poursuivit avec ardeur ses expériences sur de nouvelles manières de traiter la configuration des paysages. Il eut le courage de laisser tomber ses méthodes de travail populaires et établies pour en aborder d'autres plus nouvelles et plus abstraites, ce qui lui permit de rechercher des équivalences visuelles donnant un sens plus profond au rendu des paysages. Après tout, l'objectif qu'il poursuivait dans l'art n'était ni de se forger une identité ni d'inventer un style reconnaissable auquel on aurait pu l'associer, mais plutôt de trouver, pour son art, de nouvelles façons d'explorer le monde et de nous rendre sensibles à sa nature fascinante et en perpétuelle transformation.

> Une vie humaine est un moment si bref, si éphémère à l'échelle du temps que, du moment qu'on m'a offert le privilège de vivre à travers ce qui pourrait bien être la « charnière » permettant de faire le lien entre une civilisation qui a mûri et l'étincelle qui mettra le feu d'où naîtra une identité culturelle totalement nouvelle et à ce jour inconnue, ayant donc eu ce privilège, je quitte la table et je m'adresse à mon hôte en lui disant « Merci pour cette rare célébration.»[76]

Notes

1. On trouvera dans les ouvrages suivants un tableau général de la période en question : *Peinture canadienne des années trente* (Ottawa : Galerie nationale du Canada, 1975) et Christine Boyanoski, *The 1940s : A Decade of Painting in Ontario*, (Toronto : Musée des beaux-arts de l'Ontario. 1984).

2. Charles Comfort, *Sketches From Memory*, manuscrit inédit, c 1984, Fonds Charles Fraser Comfort, (Fonds CFC) Bibliothèque et Archives Canada, Ottawa, MG30, D81 volume 8, V.

3. *Sketches*, III.

4. *Sketches*, I.

5. Nous avons accueilli les données de cette autobiographie avec précaution. Dans des documents de la sorte, il y a une naturelle tendance à la partialité, à la sentimentalité et à des erreurs de datation.

6. *Sketches*, p. 7.

7. *Sketches*, p. 37.

8. On trouvera un examen du développement de la scène culturelle à Winnipeg dans : Marilyn Baker, *The Winnipeg School of Art*, (Winnipeg : Les Presses de l'Université du Manitoba, 1984).

9. On en trouvera des exemples dans Angela E. Davis, *Art and Work : A Social History of Labour in the Canadian Graphic Arts Industry to the 1940s* (Montréal et Kingston: Les Presses de l'Université McGill-Queen's, 1995) dans Robert Stacey et Hunter Bishop, *J.E.H. MacDonald: Designer* (Ottawa: Archives de l'art canadien: Texte imprimé aux Presses de l'Université Carleton, 1996).

10. *Angela E. Davis, Business, Art and Labour : Brigden's (sic) and the growth of the Canadian Graphic Arts Industry 1870–1950* (Thèse de doctorat, l'Université du Manitoba, Winnipeg, 1986), p. 3.

11. *Sketches*, p. 111

12. Dans son essai inédit intitulé *The Walk*, 1917 Fonds CFC, il décrit une randonnée de croquis à Minaki, faite à pieds en compagnie de Walter Huntley.

13. Interview de Comfort par Charles Hill, 3 octobre 1973 (texte dactylographié, Archives du Musée des beaux-arts de Winnipeg, non paginé)

14. Interview par Hill.

15. Il a obtenu le dixième prix. Lettre de M. Leison à Comfort, 16 mars 1920. Fonds CFC, *Correspondence*, 1920–1938.

16. Cette Société fut une émanation du Graphics Art Club fondé en 1904/05 par des artistes professionnels oeuvrant dans le domaine commercial, tels que Frederick Brigden et C.W. Jeffreys dans le but d'encourager la création d'œuvres originales en gravure, dessin, art commercial et design du textile.

17. *Sketches*, p. 165.

18. Cette exposition eut lieu du 7 au 12 janvier 1922 au Musée des beaux-arts de Winnipeg.

19. Cette exposition débuta le 21 octobre. Il n'existe pas de liste des œuvres et Comfort n'indique pas ce qu'elle comprenait.

20. « Art Notes. » *The Winnipeg Free Press*, s.d. (1922), collage dans le Minute Book, Fonds CFC, vol. 22.

21. W.J. Healy, *Women of Red River: Being a Book Written from the Recollections of Women Surviving from the Red River Era* (Winnipeg: The Women's Canadian Club, 1923).

22. Comfort exposa certains de ces dessins à l'encre en 1924 lors de l'exposition du Canadian Graphic Art à l'Art Gallery of Toronto.

23. *Sketches*, p. 192.

24. *Portrait in August* (cat. N° 51). C'est là que ce tableau a été peint.

25. Voir l'essai de Tovell.

26. « J'ai rencontré un beau jeune homme d'Afrique du Sud qui venait de débarquer au Canada... ce jeune homme allait devenir un ami intime pour la vie... J'ai été immédiatement frappé par son charme et sa solitude. » *Sketches*, p. 210.

27. Jeanne Adeney. « The Group of Seven: Their 5th Annual Exhibition. » Citation de Charles Hill dans *The Group of Seven : Art for a Nation* (Ottawa: Musée des beaux-arts du Canada, 1995), p. 328.

28. Allocution prononcée à la Bibliothèque publique et Galerie d'art de Sarnia, 23 janvier 1976, *Lectures and Speeches Binder* « NG » 1972–1976, Fonds CFC.

29. Chez Grip, Comfort était très respecté et était autorisé à se libérer pour donner des cours sur l'art, « Je ne puis insister d'une façon assez insistante pour vous dire que vous allez travailler avec moi et non pour moi. » De Macnamara à Comfort, 5 décembre 1929, Fonds CFC, Vol. 31, *Correspondance* 1920–1938.

30. Ils obtinrent des comptes clients grâce à des agences de publicité telles que Cockfield, Brown et J.J. Gibbons chez qui Brooker travaillait. Interview par Hill.

31. Pour des détails sur ces projets, voir l'essai de Donegan.

32. Comfort enseignait déjà depuis 1928. Il donnait des cours sur l'art en dehors du cadre régulier, comme une

session de 10 semaines sur l'aquarelle aux employés des Architectes Darling et Pearson. Lettre de Comfort à Barry Cleveland, 29 octobre 1928, Fonds CFC, Vol. 31, *Correspondence* 1920–1938.

33. De Robert Fawcett à Comfort, 18 juillet 1938.Volume 31, *correspondance de* 1938–1940.

34. On trouvera une analyse de ce tableau dans Christopher Jackson, *The Dreamer*, (Art Gallery of Hamilton, 1996).

35. Bien que Jeanne Adeney ait démoli l'exposition de 1928 de l'OSA pour son manque de vitalité, elle avait été séduite par les paysages de Comfort : « Ayant erré sans intérêt dans trois des salles, j'ai été brusquement surprise par « The Great Rock » de Charles Comfort suspendu entre « Wilderness » du même artiste et « Waterfall » de Lawren Harris. Le premier choc dissipé, on commence à partager ce sentiment de crainte admirative suscitée par le majestueux rocher escarpé. » 56ième exposition de l'O.S.A., *The Canadian Bookman* (mars 1928), 79-80.

36. On trouvera un examen approfondi de la transition à des « paysages bien ordonnés » dans Anna Hudson, *Art and Social Progress : the Toronto community of Painters, 1933–1950*, Thèse de doctorat (Toronto : Université de Toronto, 1997).

37. Robert Ayre « Canadian Group of Painters, » *The Canadian Forum*, (14 décembre 1933), p. 100.

38. Interview par Hill.

39. Voir Christine Boyanoski, *Charles Comfort – Lake Superior Village*, (Toronto : Musée des beaux-arts de l'Ontario, 1991).

40. « Artist's Work Wins Acclaim, » *Globe and Mail* (29 octobre 1938); « Canadian Wins Prize for Art » *London Free Press* (29 octobre 1938).

41. Robert Ayre, «Tributes to Canadian Artist Who Achieved Wide Acclaim At Great Lakes Exhibition, » *Montreal Standard*, (12 novembre 1938).

42. Dans son exposé de 1947 sur la peinture moderne, Robert Hubbard, directeur adjoint de la Galerie nationale, choisit l'œuvre de Comfort comme son premier exemple d'un modernisme évident dans la peinture figurative « ... les paysages industriels et les murales de Charles Comfort... présentent une précision et une simplification des formes qui évoquent l'efficacité mécanique de notre époque. Et ces formes modernes sont inséparables de ses sujets bien concrets. » Robert Hubbard, *Modern Painting in Canada*, réimpression n° 48 (Ottawa: Galerie nationale du Canada, 1947), p. 1.

43. De Comfort à Edwin J. Wiess, 11 septembre 1939, Fonds CFC, vol. 31, *Correspondence* 1938–40.

44. Il continua également à enseigner la technique de la peinture murale dans ses cours à l'OCA en 1938.

45. « Un artiste de Toronto est impressionné par l'art de l'Italie moderne,» *Toronto Telegram*, (19 août 1939).

46. Journal de voyage, 25 mai 1939, Fonds CFC, Vol. 1.

47. Notes d'enseignement, Fonds CFC, vol. 5, 1938–1960.

48. Voir Michael Bell. *The Kingston Conference Proceedings-A reprint of the Proceedings of the 1941 Kingston Artists' Conference*. (Kingston,Ontario: Agnes Etherington Art Centre, 1991).

49. "Les arts visuels au Canada 1950," Fonds CFC, Vol. 42, *Commision Massey* 1949–51.

50. Voir « The Painter and his Model » dans William Arthur Deacon et Wilfred Reeves editors, *Open House* (Ottawa: Graphic Publishers Limited, 1931), 213-218 et "1938-1948:Observations on a decade," *Journal, Royal Architectural Institute of Canada* (janvier 1948), p. 3-9.

51. Robert Ayre « Charles Comfort-The Soldier's Eye » paru dans *The Montrealer*, décembre 1956, p. 61.

52. Voir Boyanoski, *The 1940s : A decade of Painting in Ontario, 23*. Les aquarelles de Piper ont été exposées au cours de cet événement. Assistaient également à la soirée Graham Sutherland, Henry Moore et Paul Nash.

53. « Ce dépliant a été rédigé à l'usage des troupes alliées par la sous-commission des Monuments et Beaux-arts de la commission de contrôle des Forces alliées. Elle a été conçue et produite par la Branche d'assistance psychologique, QGFA, Italie ». Introduction au « Soldier's Guide to Rome », Fonds CFC, Vol. 9, *War Art Printed Material : army n.d.* 1942/43.

54. *Journal*, 10 juillet 1946, Fonds CFC.

55. Ogilvie et Louise Comfort se sont associés pour lui acheter son billet de voyage.

56. *Journal*, 1947, page souvenirs.

57. Au départ, Comfort avait prévu de peindre une version moderne du tableau de Manet *Le Déjeuner sur l'herbe* en le situant dans les montagnes Rocheuses, mais son esquisse a été refusée et il se vit contraint de peindre un paysage conventionnel. Voir Ian Thom, *Murals from a Great Canadian Train* (Outremont, Québec: Libre Expression et Via Rail Canada, 1986). p. 115-123.

58. AGT/AGO: Liste des membres du comité, Bibliothèque du Musée des beaux-arts de l'Ontario.

59. Journal, 16 mai 1948.

60. Voir l'essai de Hudson.

61. En 1958, ce tableau sera inclus dans l'exposition *Australian-British-Canadian Art Exhibition* par l'entremise de la Women's Auxiliary de Vancouver.

62. Ayre a décrit en ces termes un exemple de cette série : « ...une recherche de la couleur et de la forme méticuleuse, presque scientifique... » il a également loué « ...la transition des couleurs qui se déplacent en diagonale à travers l'arrière-plan neutre – comme la paroi d'un rocher – une procession dans une parade. » Robert Ayre, « Canadian Group of Painters on Display at the Museum, » *The Montreal Star* (9 novembre 1957), p. 27.

63. *Journal*, 11 décembre 1959.

64. *Journal*, 21 décembre 1959.

65. *Journal*, 1er avril 1961.

66. Ralph Hyman, « Gallery of Canadians: Excellence the Only Standard », non daté, source non citée, Fonds CFC, Vol. 20, *Clippings* 1961.

67. *Journal*, 9 décembre 1962.

68. *Journal*, 6 novembre 1962. Il semblerait que ces œuvres étaient des faux. Elles n'ont jamais reparu depuis et ne faisaient partie des œuvres offertes plus tard par Chrysler au Musée Chrysler de Norfolk en Virginie. Voir le site web de l'AADA pour le récit de l'incident. Il y est affirmé que la controverse aurait coûté à Comfort son poste. http://www.artdealers.org/who.history.html

69. Gerald Waring, « Ottawa's Hunt for a New Art Czar." Date et source supprimés. Vol. 45, *Retirement National Gallery* 163-65.

70. Jay Walz, Canada Rules out Art-in-a-Can, *New York Times*, ? mars 1965, p. 34.

71. Observations adressées aux membres du personnel à l'occasion de son départ à la retraite, 21 juillet 1965. Fonds CFC, Vol 4, *Lectures and Speeches Binder, Octobre 1964 – Octobre 1965*.

72. *Curriculum Vitae* c. 1974, Fonds CFC.

73. « Newspeak » renvoie à Novlangue, langage fictionnel inventé par Orwell pour rendre impossible l'expression des idées subversives. (ref. traduction française de *1984*). Les mots y ont une signification tellement limitée et littérale qu'ils ne laissent aucune possibilité d'accéder à la pensée. On peut ici se demander si Comfort cherchait à critiquer l'idée que l'abstraction ne laissait aucune place à une réflexion profonde qui aille au-delà des questions de pure forme.

74. Prospectus d'Ottawa distribué à l'exposition de *Georgian Bay* et *Newspeak Series*, Robertson Gallery, du 5 au 20 mai 1967, Fonds CFC, Vol. 57.

75. Comfort, University of Toronto Extension Department Lecture, Art Gallery of Toronto (Musée des beaux-arts de l'Ontario), 23 octobre 1946, notes manuscrites au cours de la conférence, Fonds CFC, Vol.4, *Lectures and Speeches*.

76. *Sketches*, III.

ROSEMARIE L. TOVELL

Un talent prometteur : la formation d'un aquarelliste

La première apparition publique de Charles Comfort au Y.M.C.A. lors de l'exposition de l'été 1913 marque un tournant dans sa vie. Les aquarelles qu'il soumit attirèrent l'attention de l'unique membre du jury, F.H. Brigden, qui non seulement lui adjugea le premier prix, mais lui offrit de faire son apprentissage dans la succursale nouvellement inaugurée de Brigdens Limited à Winnipeg, qu'il dirigeait. S'il ne subsiste aucune de ces oeuvres, nous en avons des exemples dans les premières aquarelles qu'il peignit quelques années plus tôt, quand il n'était qu'un garçon de huit ou neuf ans. Ces études florales, bien qu'elles soient des oeuvres de jeunesse, témoignent de son aptitude naturelle pour ce médium, de son habileté pour la composition et pour la disposition de lavis de couleurs pures et brillantes.[1]

En acceptant la proposition d'apprentissage, Comfort pouvait s'attendre à être formé par Brigden lui-même, l'un des peintres et aquarellistes émérites du Canada. Mais Brigden, tout en se tenant au courant des activités de Comfort, confia son apprentissage à des tiers. Au département des arts l'entreprise, il travailla sous la supervision de T.W. MacLean, originaire de Toronto et membre de longue date du Graphic Arts Club, bien connu dans les cercles artistiques importants de cette ville, et aussi sous celle de T.G. Greene, artiste qui avait des relations de premier plan. Ces connaissances s'avérèrent utiles au début de 1919 lorsque Brigden lui-même affecta Comfort à diverses reprises à leur succursale de Toronto. Parmi les autres employés que Comfort fréquenta se trouvait H. Eric Bergman, graveur sur bois professionnel récemment arrivé d'Allemagne. En complément à sa formation chez Brigdens, Comfort suivit des cours de dessin avec Valentine Fanshaw au Kelvin Technical High School et par la suite avec Alexander Musgrove à la Winnipeg School of Art. À propos de ces activités, on notera avec intérêt que la formation de Comfort en matière de dessin mettait l'accent sur la technique et les procédés. Il y acquit fort peu ou presque pas de notions d'esthétique. En l'absence de véritable guide, Comfort comptait essentiellement sur sa propre intuition en observant les peintures et les aquarelles exposées au Musée des beaux-arts de Winnipeg et chez Richardson Brothers, l'unique marchand d'art en ville. L'art britannique contemporain régnait sur les murs des galeries, côtoyant les œuvres d'artistes locaux et les tournées d'exposition de l'Académie royale des arts du Canada. Cyril Barraud et Walter J. Phillips, deux aquarellistes de talent récemment immigrés d'Angleterre, étaient les figures les plus en vogue de la région à cette époque.[2] Au mieux, ce que Comfort découvrait pouvait être qualifié d'impressionniste et post-impressionniste conservateur et déjà démodé.

Comfort peignit son autoportrait *Self-Portrait* (cat. n°39) en 1920–21, pendant son deuxième séjour à Toronto, alors que son goût pour l'aquarelle s'affirmait. Pourtant, quand on connaît ses antécédents remontant à ses premières années à Winnipeg, il devient difficile de saisir l'influence que sa présence et ses interventions dans le milieu artistique foisonnant de Toronto eurent sur l'épanouissement de son art.[3] Les aquarelles de ses premiers maîtres à leurs débuts, Fanshaw and Musgrove, ne s'apparentent pas à son autoportrait ni du point de vue technique ni du choix de couleurs. Avec son format vignette et sa facture tendre et plutôt vieille école, cette œuvre se présente en couches superposées de lavis brun, vert, et mauve étendues à l'éponge et au pinceau. Cette palette de couleurs à laquelle il allait demeurer fidèle durant plusieurs années rappelle celle que préférait W. J. Phillips et donne sérieusement à penser que Comfort étudiait attentivement les aquarelles et les gravures sur bois en couleur de Phillips. Son emploi du vert pin, aujourd'hui décoloré en vert sauge, comme principale composante de la couleur du visage, est une probable indication de l'exaltation qu'il éprouvait devant ces couleurs et le dynamisme déployés lors de la première exposition du Groupe des Sept.[4] *Kildonan Skyline Across the Red River* de 1922 (cat. n° 1) met en oeuvre les vigoureux coups de pinceaux qu'il admirait dans les tableaux du Groupe des Sept tout en conservant les couleurs de *Self-Portrait*. Un an plus tard, Comfort peignit à New York une tempête de neige sur Manhattan (cat. n° 3) dans la tonalité quasi-monochromatique et abstraite dans le style impressionniste caractéristique de l'École de Glasgow,[5] sans avoir apparemment assimilé les derniers styles d'avant-garde, bien qu'il prétendît qu' Euphrasius Tucker, l'un de ses professeurs de l'Art Students League, avait éveillé en lui un goût pour des mouvements artistiques au-delà de l'impressionnisme et du post-impressionnisme.[6]

À son retour à Winnipeg en mars 1923, Comfort mit en pratique les leçons apprises de Tucker et analysa les récents travaux de ses collègues, notamment ceux de Bergman et de Phillips. Son meilleur ami et compagnon de croquis Eric Bergman s'était lancé dans l'aquarelle en 1922[7] et étudiait le potentiel technique de ce médium. En 1924,[8] Comfort prit des cours particuliers avec W.J. Phillips en gravure sur bois en couleur d'après la méthode japonaise, un procédé d'impression techniquement et plastiquement voisin de l'aquarelle. Comfort ne se contenta pas d'étudier les travaux de Phillips et Bergman, il collectionna aussi leurs gravures en couleurs sur bois et leurs aquarelles qui font actuellement partie des collections du Musée des beaux-arts du Canada. Si l'on compare *Near Blindfold Rapids, Lake of the Woods* (MBC 23891), aquarelle de Bergman, avec *Lake of the Woods, Route Bay* (cat. n° 6) de Comfort, toutes deux apparemment peintes pendant la même randonnée, nous les voyons expérimenter divers procédés techniques d'aquarelle sur la même feuille. Comfort utilise le buvard pour adoucir les couleurs et les contours des nuages; il applique la gomme arabique pour souligner la profondeur des verts sur les arbres situés à mi-distance; et, pour terminer, il appose rudement les lavis de marron sur pourpre pour reproduire la texture rocheuse au premier plan. Il semble cependant que *Lake of the Woods* (MBC 23539) de Phillips a servi de modèle à Comfort pour la composition, comme en témoigne la vaste étendue de terre nue produite par un lavis marron sur pourpre dominant la moitié inférieure de l'oeuvre.

Certes l'influence de Bergman sur les aquarelles de Comfort est moins marquée que celle de Phillips. L'inclination de Comfort pour des compositions rivalisant avec l'orientalisme de Phillips est apparente dans le style calligraphique des touches de pinceaux et la perspective en vol d'oiseau de *Blindfold Rapids, Lake of the Woods* (cat. n° 5), et dans l'horizon bas de *Suburban Cottages, Winnipeg* (cat. n° 7). Comfort rend hommage à Phillips dans cette dernière œuvre avec son ciel en bandes striées qui rappelle le traitement du ciel dans les gravures en couleurs sur bois de Phillips. Tel qu'indiqué plus haut, il y a peu de différences dans le choix des couleurs entre Comfort et Phillips.

Vers cette époque, Comfort fit la connaissance de L.L. FitzGerald en fréquentant le Winnipeg Little Theatre, mais sa réponse à l'oeuvre de ce dernier n'alla pas au-delà d'une certaine similitude dans le choix des sujets. Dans *Headingly, Manitoba*[9] (coll. AGO # 89/53), 1924, Comfort brosse la basse ligne d'horizon, le ciel chargé de nuages, les poteaux de téléphone bordant la route et s'allongeant à l'infini, qui sont des motifs courants dans l'œuvre de Fitzgerald.

Lorsque Comfort quitta Winnipeg pour Toronto au début de 1925, ses capacités d'aquarelliste et de graveur avaient de solides bases. Dès sa première année à Toronto, son style s'était affiné au point de lui appartenir en propre.

« Toronto était pour moi une ville attrayante, construite sur une forêt bordant un grand lac, sillonnée de ravins boisés menant à deux plaisants cours d'eaux qui à leur tour coulent en méandres face aux estuaires à travers des vallées romantiques, riches en fleurs et forêts. »[10] Tel fut le sujet qu'il choisit. *Don Valley Brick Yard* (cat. n° 10), peint en mai 1925 témoigne du fait que Comfort ne s'est jamais entièrement dégagé de sa façon de voir de Winnipeg ; nous retrouvons les mêmes couleurs et la même composition que dans *Suburban Cottages, Winnipeg*, mais inversées. Les effets de lumière sont une constante depuis ses débuts dans l'art. Dans *Bridge over the Don*, (cat. n° 8) il utilise une technique de tampon pour rendre de main de maître les taches éclatantes du soleil scintillant à travers les arbres invisibles dans la partie supérieure. *In the Valley* (cat. n° 9) constitue le point culminant de ses représentations de ravins de Toronto. Peinte en 1925, l'aquarelle saisit en un ton pourpre doux, les arbres du lointain, luisant dans la chaleur humide de l'été torontois.[11]

La visite aux lacs Kawartha en compagnie de Harold et Elisabeth Ayers constitua l'étape finale de cet art qui fit de lui un aquarelliste accompli. Comfort admira leurs aquarelles « traitées avec grandeur et richesse dans l'emploi des couleurs. »[12] Son propre travail au cours de ce voyage, *Kawartha Lakes*[13] (cat. n° 13) démontre une audace nouvelle dans le choix des couleurs et dans ses coups de brosse. Lorsqu'il retravailla ses esquisses à l'aquarelle de *Kawartha Lakes* dans la grande aquarelle *Stoney Lake*, qui défraîchie, retient le même style calligraphique et révèle des bleus éclatants. Nous ne pouvons que supposer qu'il employa d'autres couleurs de même intensité.

Membre fondateur de la Canadian Society of Painters in Water Colour à la fin de 1925, il rejoignit le rang des aquarellistes émérites du Canada. Il participa activement à la Canadian Society of Graphic Art dont il devint le secrétaire, et collabora brièvement à l'automne de la même année avec certains membres qui expérimentaient différents procédés d'impression tels que l'eau-forte et la gravure couleur sur linoléum. Il arrêta de produire des gravures sur bois en couleurs. Vers la fin de la décennie, Comfort était un artiste professionnel à la réputation bien assise. On pouvait admirer ses œuvres dans toutes les expositions importantes des grandes associations et son aquarelle *Stoney Lake* (cat. n° 11) fut acquise par la Galerie nationale du du Canada.

Notes

1. *Sketchbook, 1908–09*, Bibliothèque et Archives Canada (No 1991-306-142).

2. Comfort mentionne avoir vu une exposition d'aquarelles anglaises provenant de la collection de James McDiarmid au Musée des beaux-arts de Winnipeg. *Sketches*, p. 122 (i.e. *Sketches from Memory*, autobiographie non publiée). Il n'existe aucun trace de cette exposition pas plus qu'on ne sait quelles sont les aquarelles qui se trouvaient dans la collection de McDiarmid à cette époque. Les aquarelles de Barraud et Phillips devaient faire partie de l'exposition car McDiarmid avait été leur client à leurs débuts. Les rapports annuels du Fine Art Committe du Winnipeg Industrial Bureau (1913 à 1916) et plusieurs catalogues confirment que Comfort avait accès à un nombre impressionnant d'expositions canadiennes et internationales.

3. Comfort était membre du Graphic Arts Club (1919) et du Arts and Letters Club (1920) ce qui lai permit de rencontrer les plus importants artistes de Toronto.

4. Sketches, p. 164.

5. En septembre 1914 une exposition de peinture de picatre neodrnes écossais du Modern Scottish Artists eut lieu au Musée des beaux-arts de Winnipeg au Winnipeg Industrial Bureau. "Report of the Fine Arts Committee," Annual Reports (Winnipeg: Winnipeg Industrial Bureau, 1914) p. 37.

6 La datation des aquarelles de Comfort pose un problème : celle de New York est datée de janvier 1922 alors que son séjour dans cette ville s'établit entre octobre 1922 et mars 1923.

7. « Formulaire biographique H. Eric Bergman » reçu le 12 février 1927, Dossiers de documentation des artistes, Archives du Musée des beaux-arts du Canada.

8. Comfort parle des leçons privées prises dans la demeure de Phillips en juillet 1921 *Sketches*, 176-177. On peut s'attendre à ce que cette instruction aboutisse à la production et à la finition d'une gravure sur bois en couleurs. *At Headingly, Manitoba*, Bibliothèque et Archives Canada (No 1994-210-77), sa seule gravure sur bois en couleurs de qualité professionnelle a été exposée pour la première fois en février 1925 à l'exposition annuelle de la Canadian Society of Graphic Arts de Toronto. Comfort n'avait exposé que des dessins les années précédentes, et ses premières cartes de Noël produites en gravure sur bois ne furent exécutées qu'à partir de 1924. Ceci donne à penser que Comfort avait reçu sa formation par Phillips en 1924 et non en 1921. Cette même année, Bergman étudia la gravure sur bois japonaise en couleurs avec Phillips. (réf. « H. Eric Bergman Biographical form »).

9. La peinture de Fitzgerald des élévateurs de silos à grains de Headingly est semblable mais diffère de la gravure sur bois en couleurs de Comfort qui porte le même nom.

10. *Sketches* p. 207.

11. *Ibid*, 208. Lors de son premier été à Toronto, Comfort a éprouvé pour la première fois « la chaleur dévastatrice et une exaspérante humidité inhabituelle pour nous, gens de l'ouest.»

12. *Ibid*. 209.

13. Comfort a intitulé cette oeuvre *Lake of the Woods* et l'a datée de 1925 à une époque ultérieure, sans se rendre compte sans doute qu'il l'avait peinte aux lacs Kawartha. Il n'y a rien qui indique qu'il se trouvait au *Lake of the Woods* durant l'été 1925.

ROSEMARY DONEGAN

Travailleurs musclés, trains rapides, personnages composites : les murales de Charles Comfort

Tout au long des années 1920, Charles Comfort fit beaucoup d'efforts pour se faire reconnaître comme peintre indépendant, tout en gagnant sa vie comme artiste commercial. Il prit grand soin de se positionner entre ceux qui pratiquent l'art commercial et la communauté des artistes visuels, en exposant régulièrement avec les diverses associations d'artistes (voir autres textes). Toutefois, c'est grâce à la série de murales, qu'il créa dans les années 30, qu'il put consolider les différents éléments de son œuvre; il passa alors de l'art commercial aux beaux-arts en qualité de muraliste, de professeur et d'administrateur d'art, pour finalement être nommé, en 1960, directeur du Musée des beaux-arts du Canada.[1]

Lorsqu'en 1925 Comfort déménagea de Winnipeg à Toronto, il continua de travailler comme directeur artistique et chef de production pour Brigdens. Vers la fin de l'année 1929, il avait si bien fait sa place à Toronto qu'il était en mesure de quitter Brigdens et de négocier un contrat avec Rapid-Grip Ltd. pour un salaire annuel de 9 000 $, une forte somme pour l'époque.[2] Cependant, en raison du krach boursier de novembre 1929 et de ses répercussions au Canada au début de 1932, il se retrouva sans travail. Il essaya alors de retourner chez Brigdens, mais au plus fort de la Crise, il n'y avait aucun poste de salarié disponible. En 1932, il ouvrit un bureau avec Will Ogilvie et Harold Ayers dans le Studio Building, rue Severn et exécuta divers contrats d'illustration et de publicité. Il réussit ainsi à vivre en indépendant, en combinant le travail d'illustration, l'enseignement privé, la direction artistique, les contrats de peinture et les conférences publiques. Il parvint à s'attirer des clients et travailla entre autres pour *The Canadian National Railway Magazine*, le magazine *Saturday Night*, Imperial Oil et l'International Nickel Company of Canada (Inco).

Le fondement philosophique qui sous-tend l'œuvre de muraliste de Comfort découle de sa carrière publicitaire. Il estime en effet que l'artiste commercial ne doit jamais perdre de vue son client. Lors d'une conférence donnée en 1931, il déclare:

> « Il est bon d'être un peu en avance sur la foule mais pas trop, parce qu'on risque de se retrouver trop en avance par rapport aux acheteurs. Soyez original, mais pas à la limite de l'originalité. Certains s'emparent avec enthousiasme d'une nouvelle idée comme le modernisme et s'emballent là-dessus. Ils perdent alors de vue le but premier de la publicité et le fait primordial que l'art en publicité n'est après tout qu'un moyen en vue d'une fin, celle de vendre des produits. Photographies ou peintures, réalistes ou modernes. La question n'est pas ce que vous ou moi aimions dans l'art, mais l'efficacité de ce dessin à attirer le public et finalement le pousser à aimer et à acheter vos produits.[3]

Dans son oeuvre de muraliste, Comfort utilisa la même approche pragmatique, soit la compréhension de la publicité et du client. Il sût adapter atte approche à l'échelle architecturale et au rôle public de la peinture murale, en faisant la synthèse de la forme et du style.

II.

Son premier projet de murale réalisé en 1926, fut une décoration temporaire pour le Club des Arts et des Lettres de Toronto, qui présentait un côté humoristique et incongru de la capture du Général Wolfe à Québec.[4] En 1932, l'architecte F. Marani[5] lui commanda une peinture murale pour le hall d'entrée de l'immeuble de la North American Life Assurance. Dans ses premières murales, Comfort s'inspirait des anciennes traditions de peinture murale au Canada.[6] Au Québec, on voit souvent de grandes peintures murales ou sur chevalet dans les églises catholiques et les ordres religieux. Par contre, au Canada anglais, le mouvement *Arts and Crafts* avait fait entrer les peintures murales dans les maisons privées et les endroits publics, comme les hôtels, les bibliothèques, les théâtres, les grands magasins et les écoles. La plupart de ces murales sont descriptives, marouflées et installées sur les murs intérieurs; elles étaient habituellement de nature décorative.

Dans les années 30, ce sont incontestablement les fresques mexicaines de Diego Rivera, David Siqueiros et José Clemente Orozco qui donnèrent à la peinture murale la plus forte impulsion. Après les commandes de murales qu'il avait reçues de la Bourse de San Francisco, de l'Institute of Art de Detroit et après la fameuse destruction de sa murale du Rockefeller Center en 1934 à New York, Rivera était devenu une célébrité internationale du monde artistique. Les muralistes mexicains avaient créé une nouvelle histoire visuelle du peuple mexicain, en valorisant et en célébrant les populations autochtones conformément à la politique gouvernementale de *mexicanidad* (« mexicanitude »).[7] Le rendu narratif puissant et hautement symbolique de l'histoire nationale racontée en fresques, ainsi que l'organisation spatiale, la couleur et la vibration intenses de ces œuvres incitèrent nombre d'artistes canadiens et américains à aborder la peinture murale d'une autre manière.

Les nouveaux mouvements de la peinture murale adoptèrent l'idée de rapprocher la peinture et l'architecture, arts qui s'étaient séparées depuis le développement de la peinture sur chevalet à la Renaissance. Certains allèrent jusqu'à affirmer que la peinture murale épargnerait à l'artiste l'isolement de l'atelier, les limites des dimensions de la toile et le repli sur soi, ce langage privé de l'abstraction. On considérait que l'architecture moderne, et en particulier l'architecture institutionnelle moderne, offrait aux artistes une échelle et un lieu parfaits pour leur permettre de trouver un public plus vaste. La murale, comme expression sociale et politique, était vivement prônée et relevait d'une conception plus large du rôle de l'artiste dans la société.[8] Selon un commentaire d'Arthur Lismer dans un article publié dans le *Journal* de l'Institut royal d'architecture du Canada, daté de 1933, les murales « ...sont les signes que notre démocratie, qui est toujours au stade de l'adolescence, traverse lentement une nouvelle renaissance grâce à une plus grande activité de coordination dans la conception de la structure et de sa décoration. »[9]

C'est dans ce contexte de renouveau de la peinture murale que Samuel Maw, architecte associé chez George & Moorhouse et collègue du Club des Arts et des Lettres, demanda à Charles Comfort de concevoir une frise extérieure en pierre, pour la nouvelle Bourse de Toronto, rue Bay. L'objectif principal de cette dernière était de donner une image de stabilité et de ranimer la confiance dans la Bourse, après la désastreuse Crise de 1929. Dans cette frise extérieure, Comfort représenta donc une procession d'industries canadiennes qui avancent ensemble dans un puissant mouvement vers l'avant.[10] On y voit trente et un personnages grandeur nature qui se déplacent, de droite à gauche selon un dessin géométrique étroitement structuré, sur une élévation de vingt-deux mètres de long et plus d'un mètre et demi de hauteur. Comfort exécuta un dessin à l'échelle de l'œuvre qui fut ensuite fixé au mur et transféré par un procédé de perforation sur la surface au derrière; le motif présentant des personnages stylisés en bas-relief en contraste avec des détails gravés au trait pour obtenir ombres et profondeur. Le dessin fut découpé, plutôt que creusé, en combinant le travail à l'air comprimé et le burinage à la main du calcaire de l'Indiana.

Dans la frise de la Bourse, Comfort intégra de façon symbolique le capitaliste, représenté par le personnage de l'agent de change en tant qu'élément productif aux côtés de l'ouvrier, du vendeur, de l'employé de bureau, de l'agriculteur, du scientifique et du mineur, comme appartenant à *l'ordre naturel des choses* dans le monde du travail. Comme symbole de la sortie de la Crise, il offrit l'image publique de la puissance de l'industrie, en montrant le capital et la main-d'œuvre travaillant ensemble pour exploiter les ressources du Canada. Un détail plutôt ironique de la frise peut se voir au-dessus de la porte nord, c'est l'agent de change en haut-de-forme dont la main semble se glisser dans la poche du travailleur. Selon Comfort, il n'y avait aucune intention dans la juxtaposition des deux personnages.[11] Mais avec les années, cette image est devenue une blague pour initiés qui fait partie de la « mythologie » populaire de Toronto.

Même si à l'origine les murales de l'intérieur de la Bourse devaient être commandées à quatre artistes différents, c'est Comfort qui fut choisi lors de l'attribution du contrat en janvier 1937, pour dessiner et peindre les huit panneaux de la murale (chacun mesurant 11,2 x 4,9 mètres). L'œuvre représente les industries canadiennes dont les titres sont négociés sur le parquet de la Bourse : construction et ingénierie, mines, fonderies, raffinage, pétrolières, papetières, agriculture, transports et communications. Des travailleurs musclés, des trains rapides, des cuves se déversant, des pylones électriques et des bâtiments industriels donnent aux panneaux verticaux une unité d'ensemble très dense. Pour les personnages, Comfort réutilise les formes stylisées des murales extérieures produisant ainsi, dans la frise horizontale, un mouvement puissant vers l'avant. Sur les panneaux verticaux de l'intérieur, les forts tracés graphiques des personnages, la répétition de leur position, leur portée et les couleurs de terre chaudes et riches, tout cela sert à intégrer ces panneaux individuels de manière à former un tout. Dans l'espace global, les murales de Comfort parachèvent les dimensions et les détails du Parquet, sans les écraser, ni concurrencer le style architectural (qui s'appellerait maintenant l'Art Déco). Comme les murales verticales furent conçues pour être vues d'en bas, les panneaux individuels tendent à se présenter détachés en plans et formes purs, lorsqu'on les observe individuellement.

À l'automne 1936, pendant que Comfort se trouvait à compléter les murales extérieures et intérieures de la Bourse, la compagnie Inco lui commanda la réalisation d'une murale, pour son exposition sur les travaux de la mine au Pavillon canadien de l'Exposition universelle de 1937, qui allait se tenir prochainement à Paris.[12] La *Romance of Nickel* (cat. n° 85), qui fait 6,1 mètres de longueur, présente l'opération de production et transformation du nickel du cuivre sur fond de paysage de l'Ontario nouveau. La murale est dominée par la forme inversée du Y d'un mineur de fond héroïque, dont la posture agressive souligne la puissance des machines et le dynamisme des mineurs. Un autre personnage, un scientifique sérieux observe au microscope entouré de l'iconographie de la vie moderne : gratte-ciels, ponts, grues, trains et automobiles profilés, tours de radiodiffusion et avions représentant les objectifs rationnels de la technologie et de l'industrie. La murale combine les symboles de la technologie et du design français *moderne*, avec des éléments que certains qualifieraient de réalisme héroïque stalinien, représentant le futurisme industriel et les « bienfaits » de l'entreprise. Cette murale nous parle de progrès, d'avenir et d'emplois à une époque où le Canada et l'industrie minière que le Krach de 1929 avait frappée particulièrement fort, émergeaient tout juste de la pire période de la Crise.

III.

Même si les murales de la Bourse et la commande de l'Inco pour le Pavillon du Canada à l'Exposition universelle de Paris connurent un vif succès, Comfort éprouvait de graves difficultés financières à la fin des années 1930. Il n'arrivait pas à reprendre une activité commerciale régulière et s'intéressait davantage aux murales et à l'enseignement. L'argent était devenu un tel problème qu'il démissionna du Art & Letters Club, parce qu'il lui était impossible de payer ses cotisations arriérées. Cette situation était d'autant plus embarrassante pour Comfort qu'il avait été membre actif du Club depuis le début des années vingt. Bon nombre de ses contacts pour obtenir du travail professionnel lui avaient été fournis par les membres du Club qui, dans ces années-là, était devenu le centre de la vie culturelle et intellectuelle de Toronto. C'est à cette période qu'il se mit à enseigner la décoration murale et d'autres activités similaires, en soirée et les samedis à l'Ontario College of Art. En 1938, il commença à enseigner à temps partiel à l'Université de Toronto, ce qui lui permit de rester au Canada et de ne pas être obligé d'accepter un poste en art commercial à New York. Du fait qu'il était autodidacte, Comfort fut un professeur consciencieux qui consacrait beaucoup de temps à des recherches sur l'histoire des murales, des techniques de peinture et plus tard sur histoire de l'art.[13]

Au cours des vingt-cinq années suivantes, Comfort continua à vouloir peindre des murales. Au début de 1939, par une voie plutôt indirecte, le CN l'engagea pour créer une murale destinée à l'entrée du nouvel Hôtel Vancouver, avec des émoluments de 1 800 $.[14] Le dessin approuvé par le CN met principalement en scène le capitaine Vancouver et ses subalternes recevant des dons Potlatch des mains de trois autochtones au premier plan. Comfort commenta ironiquement le fait que sur la murale le capitaine Vancouver « ...est reçu de façon pacifique et cérémonieuse par les autochtones du district (situation qui paraît bien douteuse). »[15] Une fois terminée en 1939, la murale fut installée bien en vue et appréciée dans l'entrée de l'Hôtel Vancouver et y resta jusqu'en 1968, date à laquelle l'hôtel fut rénové. En 1942, Comfort reçut une importante commande publique pour dessiner les bas-reliefs extérieurs en pierre et les murales intérieures destinés à la gare centrale de la rue Dorchester à Montréal. Le thème devait porter sur l'histoire des transports.

En 1951, Comfort devait peindre une murale de presque vingt mètres de long, intitulée *British Columbia Pageant*, pour la banque Dominion, au coin de Granville et Pender, au centre-ville de Vancouver. Cette allégorie plutôt héroïque de l'histoire de la Colombie-Britannique débute avec les explorateurs espagnols en incluant le capitaine Vancouver et son équipage, divers personnages autochtones et euro-canadiens, ainsi qu'Emily Carr. L'espace de la murale a été organisé en utilisant divers motifs autochtones de la côte Ouest, tels que les totems Tlingit et les mâts Haïdas. En 1951, lors du dévoilement de la murale, Paul Duval décrivit Charles Comfort « comme le plus grand muraliste du pays... » et le vit jouer « un rôle de leader dans ce champ vital et pourtant négligé de l'art architectural ».[16]

En 1955, le ministère des Anciens combattants invita Comfort et deux autres anciens combattants, Will Ogilvie et Andre Bieler, à créer trois murales pour le nouvel édifice des Anciens combattants situé rue Wellington, à Ottawa. Dans sa murale, Comfort dépeint les trois branches de l'armée canadienne durant la guerre : la Marine au milieu d'une bataille navale de nuit, l'Armée de terre engagée dans un combat terrestre entre tanks et soldats et l'Aviation avec les bombardiers Lancaster dans des raids de nuit sur l'Europe centrale. Cinq petits panneaux posés au-dessus des grandes scènes, au bas de la murale, accompagnent cette œuvre. Pouvant se lire comme des capsules photographiques, ces vignettes exposent le rôle que jouaient les Anciens combattants dans les années 50 : soldats démobilisés, portrait d'un groupe de militaires incluant une religieuse infirmière, une réunion de la commission des pensions des anciens combattants et la classique image publicitaire du père de famille de retour à sa maison de banlieue où il est accueilli par sa femme et son enfant, avec sa nouvelle voiture garée dans l'allée.

La murale des Anciens combattants, bien que fort méconnue, offre un certain nombre de caractéristiques intéressantes : Comfort surmonte la difficulté de représenter le temps et l'abstraction en créant une série de scènes et de vignettes flottantes, tout en étant contraint par les limites qu'impose l'espace architectural. Le style de la murale est très figuratif et narratif. Plutôt que de placer des personnages hautement symboliques comme dans ses murales historiques, il recourt au cadrage photographique et aux références visuelles tirées de la vie des années 50, ce qui ajoute des éléments intrigants à une œuvre extrêmement formelle.

Sa dernière commande pour une importante murale fut pour la nouvelle Bibliothèque nationale du Canada qui fut inaugurée en 1967. Les deux fresques, *Legs et Héritage*, situées à chacune des extrémités de la salle de lecture, devaient être discrètes et ne pas distraire les lecteurs, tout en leur offrant un contexte historique avec un regard sur l'histoire des arts et des lettres au Canada. Les murales mettent en valeur une série de personnages historiques, ombrés selon la technique de la grisaille, flottant dans un champ visuel d'un doux vert/gris.

IV.

Comme forme d'art public, les murales associent l'art à l'idéologie, en raison, d'une part, de leur contenu et de leur style et, d'autre part, de la vision du client qui a commandé l'œuvre. Bien que la renaissance de la peinture murale dans les années 20 et 30 fût saluée comme une nouvelle forme d'art public et dans bien des cas, comme un instrument d'éducation politique, la réponse du public à leur égard fut, au cours des ans, quelque peu contradictoire et invariablement compliquée.[17]

Au Canada, comme aux États-Unis, les murales abordent surtout les thèmes historiques de penseurs célèbres, d'explorateurs, de pères fondateurs, de politiciens décédés, de héros classiques, du début des transports, etc. Presque toutes les murales commandées au Canada évitent les questions d'actualité, en particulier les conséquences désastreuses de la crise économique et agricole des années 1930.[18] Les murales à thème futuriste telle que la prospérité économique grâce à l'invention technologique, comme dans l'œuvre de Comfort, il y en a peu. Ces murales figuratives étaient surtout conçues pour être lues comme on lirait un récit. Vers le milieu des années 1950, les murales figuratives historiques seront éclipsées par l'attrait de l'abstraction. On en trouve un exemple dans la murale expressionniste dynamique que Harold Town réalisa en 1958, pour la centrale électrique St Lawrence, qui est située à Cornwall en Ontario et fait partie du projet de la Voie maritime du Saint-Laurent.

Comme bien des artistes canadiens des années 20 et 30, Comfort chercha par ses murales à construire une culture symbolique canadienne. Tout comme les muralistes mexicains tentèrent de créer une *mexicanitude* (une histoire nationale du peuple), Comfort et ses amis du Groupe des Sept s'efforcèrent de créer une iconographie moderne du paysage canadien. Les antécédents de Comfort en publicité lui permettaient d'être à l'aise dans ses commandes ; ses décorations murales étaient pour lui des allégories, plutôt que des documentaires que le public devait lire dans une perspective historique.[19]

À leur époque, les murales de Comfort furent presque toutes bien reçues, et leur contenu peu discuté car leur sens était évident. Plus récemment, le contenu symbolique de ses murales historiques, en particulier celle du capitaine Vancouver à l'Hôtel Vancouver et la murale intitulée *British Columbia Pageant* de la banque Dominion, a fait l'objet de débats houleux.[20] Les figures historiques et les personnages génériques composites des peuples autochtones créés par Comfort, et qui nous montrent ses efforts pour bâtir une histoire symbolique, sont contestables à l'heure actuelle où l'on aborde maintenant de façon différente les Premières Nations et l'histoire postcoloniale.

Les murales les plus frappantes de Comfort – la frise extérieure et les murales intérieures de la Bourse de Toronto et la *Romance of Nickel* – qui présentent l'industrie contemporaine, la technologie et l'avenir, font montre de cohérence sur le plan visuel, de maturité au niveau du style et de clarté en termes d'idéologie. Par contre, ses murales historiques sont aujourd'hui perçues comme des rouleaux de peintures didactiques, des clichés dépassés des figures de l'histoire. Dans ses images industrielles, il adopta une approche cubiste bidimensionnelle de l'espace qui est beaucoup plus ambitieuse dans la forme et dans le style. En utilisant des formes superposées, des plans flottants, des lignes et des couleurs, il se soustrait à l'obligation de la perspective exacte de la peinture figurative traditionnelle, tout en se permettant d'adapter la dimension des objets et des personnages aux limites narratives et spatiales de la composition. Ces murales sont une glorification tout à fait normale de l'industrie, un effort pour créer de nouveaux symboles, ceux de l'homme d'affaires, du chercheur et de l'ouvrier. Elles symbolisent la puissance de l'industrie moderne et implicitement du capitalisme, en particulier du secteur de l'extraction des ressources, s'élevant tel un phénix des cendres de la grande Crise. Dans les années 30, l'apport de Charles Comfort à ces murales, c'est la clarté de sa vision de l'industrie et sa foi dans l'avenir : toutes deux correspondaient fondamentalement à la recherche d'une image du Canada industriel moderne et d'une certaine façon, c'est encore le cas aujourd'hui.

J'adresse mes remerciements à David Wallace, Charles Hill, Scott James, Dot Tuer et Jerry Zaslove.

Annexe : les murales de Charles Comfort

1932 North American Life Assurance Co., Toronto (détruite)

1936 Bourse de Toronto, rue Bay, bas-relief extérieur en pierre (in situ au Design Exchange, Toronto)

1936 *Romance of Nickel*, Pavillon du Canada, Exposition universelle de Paris, 1937 (en prêt aux Musées des beaux-arts du Canada, Ottawa)

1937 Bourse de Toronto, peinture murale intérieure (in situ au Design Exchange, Toronto)

1938 Gare centrale, rue Dorchester, Montréal (en partie détruite, remnants réinstallés dans la gare ferroviaire de Montréal, Place Ville-Marie)

1939 Hôtel Vancouver/murale du Capitaine Vancouver (maintenant au Centre des Arts de la Confédération, Charlottetown, Î.-P.-É)

1948 Hôpital Sunnybrook, Toronto (détruite)

1951 *British Columbia Pageant*, Banque Dominion, rues Granville et Pender, Vancouver (maintenant dans la collection de l'Université Simon Fraser, Burnaby)

1955 *The Canadian Armed Forces*, Ottawa (in situ au ministère de la Justice, dans l'ancienne aile Est de l'édifice commémoratif des Anciens combattants, Ottawa)

1958 Division neurologique, Hôpital général de Toronto (maintenant dans la collection du réseau de santé de l'Université, Toronto)

1967 Édifice de la Bibliothèque et des Archives du Canada, Ottawa (in situ dans la salle de lecture de la Bibliothèque) (anciennement la Bibliothèque nationale du Canada et les Archives nationales du Canada)

1968 Académie de médecine, Toronto (présumée détruite)

Notes

1. Comfort est le premier artiste nommé directeur de la Galerie nationale; après sa nomination, il élimina toute mention de sa carrière artistique commerciale dans son curriculum vitae.

2. Contrat entre Charles Comfort et Rapid-Grip Corporation, Toronto, 28 nov. 1929, Fonds CFC, *Correspondance* 1920–1938, boîte 31.

3. Comfort, « A Value for Art in Advertising » 1931, Fonds CFC, vol. 34.

4. Voir le *Journal* de l'Institut royal d'architecture du Canada, (nov.-déc. 1926), p. 252.

5. Voir le *Journal* de l'Institut royal d'architecture du Canada, (juillet 1926), p. 132.

6. Voir Marylin McKay, *A National Soul: Canadian Mural Painting 1860s –1930s* (Montreal/Kingston : Les Presses de l'Université McGill-Queen's), 2002.

7. Voir Laurance P. Hurlburt, *The Mexican Muralists in the United States* (Albuquerque : University of New Mexico Press, 1989).

8. Voir Christine Boyanoski, p. 10-19.

9. Arthur Lismer, « Mural Painting », *The Journal Royal Architectural Institute of Canada* (juillet 1933), p. 127-135.

10. Comfort adopta une conception très semblable de l'espace, dont la forme du Y inversé et la structure narrative, à la fois pour la frise extérieure en pierre et les huit murales verticales intérieures de la Bourse de Toronto et pour la murale *Romance of Nickel*. Voir Rosemary Donegan, « Legitimate Modernism: Charles Comfort and the Toronto Stock Exchange », *Designing the Exchange: Essays Commemorating the Opening of the Design Exchange* (Toronto : The Design Exchange, 1994) et « Mural Roots: Charles Comfort and the Toronto Stock Exchange », *Canadian Art*, vol. 4, no 2 (été 1987), p. 64-69.

11. Irvin Lutsky (Tr) « Le concepteur nie que la frise montre un travailleur détroussé », *Toronto Star*, 19 oct. 1977. Il est intéressant de noter que Comfort, bien qu'il vécut à Toronto jusqu'en 1960 ne vit pas les murales intérieures de la Bourse installées avant 1977.

12. Après l'Exposition universelle de 1937, la murale de Comfort, intitulée *Romance of Nickel*, semble avoir été roulée et envoyée au ministère des Mines à Ottawa où elle fut entreposée pendant de nombreuses années. Elle fut présentée en public au Canada pour la première fois en 1987, à l'exposition *Images industrielles/Industrial Images* de l'Art Gallery de Hamilton. La murale fait actuellement l'objet d'un prêt à long terme au Musée des beaux-arts du Canada.

13. Voir Fonds CFC, classeur Murals in *Teaching Notes*, dossier 1938–1951.

14. Voir la lettre du 13 février 1939, Fonds CFC, vol. 60, *Vancouver Mural*, dossier 1939–1975.

15. Voir la lettre du 7 février 1939, Fonds CFC, vol. 60, *Vancouver Mural*, dossier 1939–1975.

16. Paul Duval, « BC Mural: Sixty Feet of Progress », *Saturday Night* (6 oct. 1951).

17. Voir : Karl Ann Marling, *Wall-to-Wall America: A Cultural History of Post Office Murals in the Great Depression* (Minneapolis : University of Minnesota Press, 1982) où l'auteure étudie les difficultés et les complications de la commande de murales, de la production de peintures *in situ* et de la réaction du public aux peintures dans les bureaux de postes aux États-Unis.

18. D'autres grandes murales historiques, comme la commande exécutée par Edwin Holgate pour l'Exposition universelle de New York en 1939 ou la murale de Orville Fisher, Paul Goranson et E.J. Hughes pour l'exposition du Golden Gate de 1939, à San Francisco, (de nature célébratoire) ne furent pas exposées au Canada. Seules font exception les murales de Miller Brittain pour le sanatorium de St John qui furent conçues au début des années 40, mais jamais produites. Brittain y examinait certaines des causes et des conséquences de la tuberculose dans la société contemporaine. Voir Barry Lord, *The History of Painting in Canada: Towards a People's Art* (Toronto : NC Press, 1974), p. 183-189. Voir aussi la thèse à paraître de Kirk Niergarth, « Art and Democracy: New Brunswick Artists and Canadian Culture between the Depression and the Cold War », Université du Nouveau-Brunswick, 2007.

19. « Notes re : Vancouver Hotel Mural, 3 mars 1939 », Fonds CFC, vol. 60, dossier *Vancouver Mural*.

20. En 1972, quand la murale de l'Hôtel Vancouver fut offerte en donation à l'Université de Colombie-Britannique, ce fut le commencement d'une série d'échanges houleux au sujet du traitement historiquement inexact et stéréotypé des autochtones s'agenouillant servilement aux pieds de Vancouver dans les murales. Pour éviter d'autres controverses, la murale fut par la suite offerte en donation au Centre des Arts de la Confédération de Charlottetown, à l'Île-du-Prince-Édouard. La murale de la banque Dominion, *British Columbia Pageant*, récemment offerte en donation à l'Université Simon Fraser, a également été sévèrement critiquée dans des discussions publiques, pour leur inexactitude et insensibilité aux peuples des Premières Nations. Cette question sera le sujet d'un prochain numéro de *West Coast Line*, en 2007.

ANNA HUDSON

Le Moment psychologique de Charles Comfort dans le rapport entre l'art et la vie, 1935–1945

Tadoussac, 1935, (cat. n° 31) : bleu, lisse, immobile et gracieux. Charles Comfort a fait de ce village du Saguenay, célèbre destination touristique estivale, un point de mire hallucinant. Bourré de mescaline, un Aldous Huxley halluciné voyait le monde sans inhibitions. Notre perception de *Tadoussac* est pareillement euphorique.

Huxley, un écrivain britannique qui s'est installé en Californie en 1937, recourait à des drogues psychédéliques pour « ouvrir les portes de la perception. »[1] Ces portes étaient comme des portes d'Eden, écrivit-il, derrière lesquelles : « je voyais ce qu'Adam avait vu à l'aube de sa création – le miracle, d'un moment à l'autre, de l'existence toute nue. »[2] Comfort peignit *Tadoussac* pour obtenir un violent contraste avec l'aveuglement dont nous témoignons ordinairement dans notre vie quotidienne. Nous avons tendance à oublier ce que nous voyons. En comparaison, une expérience visuelle mémorable, recèle une quantité de significations. La quête de Huxley pour recouvrer la pleine potentialité de la vision était en fait une quête de la signifiance dans sa propre vie. Ses efforts sont parallèles à la démarche suivie par un artiste visuel tel que Comfort. Comme Herbert Read l'a noté:

> Aldous Huxley a récemment montré que sous l'influence de la drogue appelée mescaline, une sensation accrue de la réalité, de l'essence des choses (« *isness* ») était provoquée: les formes sont plus nettes, les couleurs plus intenses, etc. Selon sa théorie, cette sensation accrue de la réalité est due, non à une augmentation des facultés normales mais plutôt à un relâchement des inhibitions qui ramènent normalement la conscience à des proportions raisonnables.[3]

Read, un philosophe de l'art britannique, dont les œuvres ont été largement publiées au Canada anglais, a pris soin de faire une différence entre l'« *isness* » (l'essence des chose) et la réalité distincte de l'art. Voir, précisa-t-il, « c'est révéler ou créer un monde objectif et non en représenter un. »[4]

Le rapport entre l'isness et la figuration définit une génération obsédée par l'union de l'art et de la vie. L'artiste et critique anglais Roger Fry l'a cerné en employant les termes de « *Vision and Design* », tel qu'il titra son influente collection d'essais publiée en 1920. On peut déceler les prémices de cette pensée chez John Ruskin, William Morris et les membres du mouvement *Arts and Crafts*. Au Canada, cette tradition britannique s'est incarnée dans le Groupe des Sept, qui envisageait de promouvoir délibérément l'art dans la vie nationale par l'entremise de paysages sauvages peints au cours des années 1920. Charles Comfort compta parmi les jeunes artistes que le Groupe invitait à participer à ses expositions. L'un des principaux membres d'une des communautés de peintres torontois qui aurait émergé à la suite de la formation du Canadian Group of Painters (CGP), à Toronto, en 1933. Cette communauté, qui incluait entre autres, Comfort, Paraskeva Clark et Carl Schaefer, visait, selon une déclaration de principes incluse dans son premier catalogue, à : « pousser la faculté créatrice au-delà du sens professionnel de l'art pour en faire un langage plus courant d'expression… »[5] Le problème, rendu criant par la crise économique, était de savoir comment y parvenir. Comment faire pour unir l'art et la vie?

Paraskeva Clark ne manquerait pas de rappeler à ses confrères de Toronto le soutien que l'état accordait aux arts à Leningrad (à nouveau Saint-Pétersbourg), où elle avait grandi et où elle avait été formée dans les « ateliers libres ». En outre, la New Deal en matière d'arts du Président Roosevelt aux États-Unis donnait un exemple dans l'immédiat d'arts qui prospéraient au sein d'une vie nationale. En contraste, l'idée erronée selon laquelle l'art était un luxe, dont les connaisseurs torontois se plaignaient, était peut-être symptomatique de la société moins éclairée dont elle émanait. Comfort a qualifié *Young Canadian* (cat. n° 48), portrait à l'aquarelle de Carl Schaefer, qu'il devait peindre en 1932 de : « symbolique de la futilité et du découragement dont les jeunes de cette mémorable décennie ont souffert pendant la Crise économique; c'est un document qui a consigné le désespoir ressenti […] par toute une génération… »[6] Schaefer est assis au premier plan du tableau, et il regarde fixement la maison de son enfance, de son point d'observation situé dans un champ d'une ferme typique de la région de Hanover (Ontario). Il semble fasciné par l'ordre essentiel et le motif formé par les sillons. Comme l'a fait remarquer Comfort : « la régularité dans un paysage est toujours une marque laissée par les hommes. »[7] Schaefer isolait l'essence (« *isness* ») de la sensation communiquée par le paysage rural dans ses tableaux des années 1930. Comfort soulignait l'importance de la communication visuelle et il cherchait ses propres « idiomes formels par l'entremise desquels un contenu renouvellé pourrait être plus largement appréhendé ».[8]

Charles et Louise Comfort célébrèrent leur treizième anniversaire en achetant *Années*, roman à succès de 1937 de Virginia Woolf. Et à l'intérieur de la couverture, ils devaient inscrire :

> De notre part
> à
> nous-mêmes
> après 13 ans de vie commune
> le 22 mai 1937[9]

L'histoire des membres de la famille Pargiter, telle que la raconte Virginia Wolf, situe tous les faits de leur existence ordinaire dans le contexte social en transition rapide de la Grande-Bretagne de 1908 aux années 1930, en passant par la Première Guerre mondiale. « Aucun fait n'est trop futile pour qu'on le laisse se déverser à travers nos doigts » disait Virginia Woolf.[10] Les journaux méticuleux qu'a tenu Comfort pendant toute sa vie sont, eux aussi, l'expression d'un être tout aussi obsessionnel.

Comme chez tant d'écrivains de l'entre-deux-guerres, sa description de « *tout* ce qui se produisait » révélait une scission entre le moi intérieur et la vie extérieure.[11] Cette scission en psychologie moderne, telle que décrite à l'époque, était profondément ressentie alors qu'un individu devait vivre un « moment psychologique. »[12] Dans *Les Années*, Virginia Woolf suscite de tels moments au début de chacun des onze chapitres de son livre, saisissant les années au moyen de descriptions vivantes de la nature, qui interrompent le cours autrement banal des évènements quotidiens. Ainsi en 1911 :

> Le soleil se levait. Très doucement il apparut au dessus de l'horizon déversant de la lumière. Mais le ciel était si vaste, si dépourvu de nuages, que l'emplir de lumière a pris du temps.[13]

Tadoussac de Comfort illustre puissamment cette même incroyable contradiction sur laquelle repose le roman de Virginia Woolf. Une intense sensation visuelle tient le temps en otage. Dans la suite perpétuelle de scènes qui traverse quotidiennement notre vision, il arrive bien trop rarement qu'une image devienne un moment fort, prolongé. Même dans la mémoire, la sensation présage un élargissement du champ de la conscience. Quand le temps s'arrête ainsi, les limites humaines – comme la famille Pargiter le prouve de façon si convaincante dans le roman de Virginia Woolf – sont abolies pour révéler la grandeur d'être, ou ce qu'Huxley a appelé son essence des chose (« *isness* »). Les précisions relatives au temps et au lieu deviennent donc hors de propos, au niveau spirituel. « Si l'on nettoyait les portes de la perception, toutes choses apparaîtraient à l'homme telles qu'elles sont: infinies » a repris Huxley citant *Le Mariage du Ciel et de l'Enfer* (1790–1792), poème de William Blake.

Dans la confusion entraînée par la guerre mondiale et la rupture de l'ordre religieux dans la société occidentale, la vie séculière – le sujet en vogue dans les arts des années 1920 à 1950 – est devenu un impératif spirituel. Les êtres prévoyant anxieusement une nouvelle remise en cause de l'ordre social et politique, leurs *moments [psychologiques]* se sont raréfiés. Lady Kitty Lasswade, un personnage de Virginia Woolf en savoure un :

> Un profond murmure bourdonne dans ses oreilles – c'est la terre, qui se chante un refrain pour elle seule. Elle se tenait là pour écouter. Elle était pleinement heureuse. Le temps s'était arrêté.[14]

En 1938, Comfort mit carrément sa peinture à contribution pour ce que Fred Housser, l'auteur de *A Canadian Art Movement : The Story of the Group of Seven*, avait qualifié en 1926 de besoin de « replanter des légumes dans nos champs afin que nous puissions récolter des aliments pour nourrir nos esprits et nos corps. »[15] Dans un monde à l'orée d'une deuxième guerre mondiale, les enjeux spirituels propres à « un mode d'expression commun et partagé » étaient élevés. Aucun artiste de Toronto ne pouvait manquer de répondre à l'appel passionné lancé par Paraskeva Clark aux membres du Groupe des Sept pour les enjoindre de « sortir de derrière le bouclier précambrien. » Mais la question de l'importance de la peinture en tant qu'un des beaux-arts demeurait.[16] « L'art et le rôle de l'artiste sont des sujets très difficiles à débattre dans un esprit de compréhension et de simplicité » constatait Paraskeva Clark, qui exhortait ses confrères à mettre leur art en prise avec la société. Par l'entremise du Canadian Group of Painters, à la différence de l'Académie royale des arts du Canada (ARAC), plus ancienne et collet monté, ainsi que de l'Ontario Society of Artists (OSA), la communauté torontoise cherchait à trouver une pertinence contemporaine à la tradition occidentale en matière de peinture (héritée de la Renaissance et perfectionnée par l'entremise des académies européennes). Selon Walter Abell, un éducateur et philosophe de l'art américain, qui a exercé au Canada de 1928 à 1943, le design était la clé de cette pertinence.[17]

Comme l'a déclaré Abell dans sa publication de 1936 intitulée *Representation and Form: A Study of Aesthetic Values in Representational Art*, une analyse sur le design dans l'art à toutes les époques de l'art occidental révèle la présence « de liens ultra-picturaux avec la pensée et la sensibilité actuelles, des liens que nous percevons à peine nous-mêmes parce qu'ils font intimement partie de l'existence telle que nous l'acceptons. »[18] Dans son estimation un artiste recourt au design pour maîtriser la psychologie de la vision.[19] Comme Virginia Woolf et Huxley le croyaient, il y a un lien dans notre mémoire entre ce que nous voyons et ce que savons. D'ailleurs, Herbert Read l'a confirmé en déclarant : « L'art est un mode de connaissance et le monde de l'art est un système cognitif aussi précieux pour l'homme que celui de la philosophie ou de la science.»[20] L'artiste anticipe cette connexion et il chorégraphie notre réaction. Ce niveau de maîtrise inquiétait le critique d'art montréalais Robert Ayre, méfiant à l'égard de la touche de Comfort, parfaitement exercée grâce à des années de dessin publicitaire chez Brigdens Limited, à Winnipeg et à Toronto, qui lui semblait travailler « trop facilement. »[21] Mais Comfort avait parfait sa sensibilité au design grâce à son travail de création publicitaire. Il avait maîtrisé des représentations symboliques qui étaient, essentiellement, des distillations retentissantes de moments psychologiques d'*isness*. Comfort a mis en avant la combinaison de la conception symbolique et de la pratique de la peinture académique dans *Pioneer Survival* de 1938 (cat. n° 36) son oeuvre de réception à l'Académie royale du Canada.

Il s'agit d'un nouveau travail sur le thème du paysage rural, qui caractérise les expositions du CGP des années 1930 et sur l'œuvre de Carl Schaefer en particulier. Comfort a repris, en les isolant comme son confrère, les rythmes et les motifs généreux des terres agricoles du sud de l'Ontario. Mais l'équilibre ensoleillé d'un paysage ondoyant à motifs, enveloppé dans un grand pan de ciel, est devenu orageux sous le pinceau de Comfort. Paraskeva Clark avait, plus d'un an auparavant, retravaillé les motifs de paysages campagnards signés par Schaefer. L'exposition simultanée des images parallèles de champs de blé de Paraskeva Clark et de Schaefer conférait un remarquable synchronisme à l'exposition de 1937 du CGP. Les artistes se parlaient davantage et un langage de symboles émergeait de leur dialogue visuel. Quand Comfort se mêla à leur conversation picturale, en plaçant de façon proéminentes des souches déchiquetées au premier plan d'un paysage « pionnier » historique, le langage des beaux-arts devint académique. Le crédit accordé à sa peinture augmenta parce qu'il faisait référence à l'histoire de l'art du Canada. Les images de la vie des pionniers en Ontario peintes par Homer Watson, le président de l'Académie royale du Canada de 1918 à 1922, étaient aussi des évocations dramatiques du passé de l'Ontario. La référence délibérée faite par Comfort à son prédécesseur était conforme à la tradition et découlait de l'intérêt de plus en plus soutenu du public pour l'histoire de l'art. Quand Comfort se mit à enseigner au Département des beaux-arts de l'Université de Toronto, il conféra un caractère sacro-saint à sa peinture. *Pioneer Survival* introduisit la rigueur académique dans la conception d'un tableau. En cela, le moment psychologique approcha la connaissance de l'*isness* [l'essence] de l'art.

En 1938, Comfort resta à Toronto pour y enseigner la peinture muraliste ainsi que des techniques historiques au lieu de prendre un emploi plus lucratif en art commercial aux États-Unis. Cette décision, expliqua-t-il, lui permettrait d'avoir plus de temps pour peindre. Mais il dut se battre pour avoir droit à la sécurité de son emploi et à une rémunération adéquate en contrepartie de son enseignement de chargé de cours à l'Ontario College of Art et à l'Université de Toronto. Ce n'est qu'en 1946, après la guerre, quand il revint une fois accomplis son devoir d'artiste militaire officiel au sein de l'Armée canadienne, que l'université l'engagea dans son corps enseignant à titre de professeur adjoint au Département des beaux-arts et d'archéologie nouvellement fusionné. L'artiste de 46 ans dut alors étoffer ses cours pratiques pour y inclure l'étude de l'histoire de l'art. Depuis qu'il avait atteint les débuts de la trentaine, Comfort avait élargi son réseau professionnel pour y inclure des historiens de l'art. John Alford, un diplômé de l'Institut Courtauld et le fondateur, en 1934, de la chaire des beaux-arts de l'Université de Toronto, que Comfort considérait comme un ami, ainsi que Peter Brieger, un historien de l'art formé en Allemagne que l'Université engagea en 1936, guidèrent l'artiste dans son étude de l'histoire de l'art.[22] Juste avant que la guerre n'éclate, en 1939, Alford et Brieger organisèrent le long voyage de Comfort en Italie, prévoyant aussi des séjours plus courts à Paris et à Londres.[23] Comfort consomma les œuvres iconographiques de l'histoire de l'art occidentale en même temps que sa nourriture, son vin et ses modes d'hébergement, sachant pertinemment qu'une guerre imminente détruirait beaucoup d'œuvres d'art et d'architecture. Seule sa mémoire préserverait son expérience.

L'histoire de l'art est la mémoire collective des arts visuels. La pensée de Comfort sur son rôle dans la société a évolué parallèlement au développement de l'histoire de l'art en tant que discipline au Canada, sous l'égide de l'Université de Toronto. Il considérait la valeur de l'enseignement des beaux-arts, qu'Arthur Lismer, membre du Groupe des Sept, avait institué comme prérogative de l'Art Gallery of Toronto. Comfort devait « favoriser un respect pour la culture occidentale qui constitue le fondement même du mode de vie démocratique en occident. »[24]

> L'art en tant que manière de penser et que conception humaine n'a jamais joué un rôle plus inspirant, plus utile, oui plus salutaire dans la vie qu'aujourd'hui.[25]

Dans le contexte de la citation qui précède, du romancier allemand Thomas Mann, extraite du catalogue de l'exposition du CGP de 1942, le tableau *Primavera* de Comfort est une peinture humaniste. La meilleure façon de comprendre l'humanisme du XXe siècle est de le considérer comme un idéalisme intellectuel qui a uniformément attiré des artistes, écrivains, philosophes et même des scientifiques dans les pays alliés – de 1920 à 1950. Certes, tout humaniste avoué avait, semble-t-il, des opinions personnelles, mais les humanistes en général craignaient le fascisme, le communisme et le nazisme qu'ils tenaient pour des idéologies anti-démocratiques. Plusieurs d'humanistes à l'époque avaient une vie spirituelle mais ne croyait pas en une religion. Ils admettaient à quel point les théories sur l'évolution opposaient l'art et la science. Les humanistes croyaient surtout aux bienfaits de l'instruction et à la nécessité d'accroître nos connaissances sur les fondements de l'histoire humaine. Ainsi, l'histoire de l'art étant une des sciences humaines, elle trouva sa place en tant que domaine d'étude humaniste, et la reprise par Comfort dans son *Primavera* de la *Vénus d'Urbino*, peinte par Titien au XVe siècle, évoque les sources culturelles que constitue la Renaissance italienne.

Dans *Primavera* Vénus prend une pose décontractée dans les champs vallonnés d'une campagna italienne. Elle est indubitablement une œuvre d'art, plus en pierre qu'en chair, exemple manifeste pour Comfort d'un héritage culturel démocratique. Cependant, son avenir semble en péril. Dans la version originale de la peinture de Comfort,[26] des moyettes de blé se transforment en chars d'assaut qui avancent dans la campagne italienne. *Primavera* représente la réalité de la destruction culturelle que craignait Comfort. Son art suscite l'action avec un prescient appel aux armes, lancé dans un esprit d'humanisme afin de protéger la civilisation occidentale. Comme l'écrivain et philosophe britannique Bertrand Russell l'a déclaré avec passion : l'art naît quand « un sentiment de toute l'espèce humaine se percevant comme un ensemble qui coopère » remplace l'identité nationale, et plus encore l'identité individuelle.[27] Comfort accédait à une communauté culturelle internationale imaginaire.

Imaginez trente ans d'insécurité, d'« incertitude anxieuse et pessimiste » a écrit le philosophe américain John Dewey au sujet des séquelles de la Première Guerre mondiale.[28] « Notre monde est un monde fou, a écrit Russell, depuis 1914 il a cessé d'être constructif. » Pour les Nord-Américains comme Comfort le problème était compliqué par l'absence d'« un sentiment instinctif de communauté qui existe dans les vieux pays. »[29] Dans sa quête d'une union entre l'art et la vie qui devait renforcer la civilisation, Herbert Read devait découvrir la théorie de Jung. Il a exploré des archétypes et des modèles junguiens collectifs, héréditaires, de perception qui façonnent notre perception de la réalité.[30] Read découvrit que ces modèles étaient imbriqués dans les œuvres d'art. Comfort fit des essais pour déterminer dans quelle mesure les symboles enrichis par des références à l'histoire de l'art fournissent un langage d'expression plus courant ou archétypal. Il jouait avec le feu. Il risquait de tomber dans le cliché. En effet, si l'on pense que les formes d'art ne sont importantes qu'en raison de leur caractère archétypal et donc de leur signification figée, prédéterminée, est-ce qu'on ne rend pas l'art pédant?[31]

La différence entre l'art et la publicité ou la propagande, qui a contrarié les artistes et les écrivains de 1920 à 1950, se résume à la question de la liberté d'expression et d'interprétation. Le souvenir d'un contact avec l'art devrait conserver quelque chose de ce moment d'euphorie psychologique au cours duquel l'on communie inexplicablement avec l'universel. Pour la philosophe américaine de l'art Susanne Langer, qui a publié *Philosophy in a New Key* en 1942, « il faut que les signes et les symboles abrégés soient étayés par une vaste structure intellectuelle afin qu'ils opèrent avec une telle douceur que nous ne nous rendions pas compte de leur présence… »[32] « Une fois exhumé de l'ensemble de nos connaissances enfouies » ce langage de l'art constitue un jeu intellectuel qui opère de façon énigmatique. Cette idée concordait bien avec l'objectif du Département des beaux-arts et de l'archéologie de l'Université de Toronto, qui était d'« enseigner à l'étudiant un vocabulaire lui permettant de s'exprimer. » La pratique de Comfort a montré comment cela pouvait fonctionner.

Susannne Langer a parlé de notre besoin de partager « quelques symboles historiques 'chargés'de sens qui ont à peu près la même richesse de signification pour tout le monde. » Elle a aussi constaté le manque de ces symboles dans le monde moderne, qui est de plus en plus fragmenté.[33] La décision de Comfort de miner l'histoire de l'art pour y trouver les vestiges de ce que Langer appelait l'« ancrage mental » était très délibérée.[34] Pouvait-il investir des formes anciennes en recourant à « cette accumulation riche, confuse et historique » de significations décrite par Langer? Réussirait-il à recréer ces symboles chargés [de signification] « auxquels nous semblons réagir instinctivement? »[35] Le besoin impérieux d'un front uni pendant la Deuxième guerre mondiale devait pousser les artistes vers le symbolisme tant dans les pays alliés que dans les puissances de l'Axe. Comfort a joué le rôle d'un soldat culturel qui défend la démocratie. En 1945, à titre d'artiste militaire officiel, il paracheva *Canadian Armour Passing Through Ortona* [Blindé canadien traversant Ortona]. Dans ce tableau, la campagne vallonnée a été remplacée par des tas de décombres qui correspondent aux bâtiments détruits de la Piazza Plebiscito, à Naples. Les *putti* qui adressent des admonestations en bas du premier plan du tableau représentent l'Art qui nous rappelle notre histoire. Le char situé à gauche est un signe du présent.

Mircea Eliade, un historien des religions controversé de la génération de Comfort, a constaté que : « le monde *complètement* profane, le cosmos totalement désacralisé sont une découverte récente dans l'histoire de l'esprit humain. »[36] La scission entre le for intérieur et la vie extérieure, qui obnubilait les psychologues, évidente dans la séparation entre l'art et la vie, dénotait pour Eliade le simple fait de la perte de la foi. Le résultat en a été notre expérience singulière d'une époque séculière qui est passée dans une histoire irrécupérable avec l'angoisse existentielle. Par comparaison, le temps sacré décrivait un cercle pour relier le passé, le présent et le futur en une unité universelle. Oh que cela est près d'expliquer ce moment psychologique raréfié grâce auquel les écrivains et les artistes conféraient – symboliquement – une signification à la vie ordinaire! Le moment de la guerre peut difficilement mériter pareille vénération. Comme le conclut Eleanor Pargiter dans le roman de Virginia Woolf :

Il faut bien qu'il y ait une autre vie, pensa-t-elle, se laissant retomber sur sa chaise, exaspérée. Pas dans les rêves, mais ici et maintenant... Il faut bien qu'il y ait une autre vie ici et maintenant, répéta-t-elle. Celle-ci est trop courte, trop brisée. Nous ne savons rien, même sur nous-mêmes...elle voulait retenir le moment présent; pour qu'il demeure; pour le remplir sans cesse, de passé, de présent et d'avenir, jusqu'à ce qu'il brille, tout entier, de tous ses feux, d'une profonde compréhension.[37]

De 1935 à 1945, de *Tadoussac* à *Canadian Armour Passing Through Ortona*, Comfort a invité le spectateur à contempler de plus en plus délibérément les rapports entre l'art et la vie. Et dans sa quête pour trouver un langage d'expression plus courant, son art est devenu de plus en plus symbolique et donc autoréférentiel. Peut-être l'art et la vie se sont-ils éloignés davantage de ce fait. C'est, du moins ce que l'historien de l'art R.H. Wilenski prévoyait en 1927. « Après tout, expliquait-il, le mouvement moderniste est fondé non sur l'idée de rendre service à la religion mais sur celle de service à une idée consciemment entretenue de l'art. »[38]

Notes

1. « Si l'on nettoyait les portes de la perception toute chose apparaîtrait à l'homme comme elle est, infinie.» William Blake, *The Marriage of Heaven and Hell* (1790–1792) [Le Mariage du Ciel et de l'Enfer trad. André Gide], cité par Aldous Huxley, *The Doors of Perception*, (London: Chatto & Windus Ltd., 1954, p. 6.

2. Aldous Huxley, *The Doors of Perception*, (1954, Londres, réimp. London: Granada Publications Limited/Panther Books, 1977), p. 15.

3. Herbert Read, Icon and Idea: The function of art in the development of human consciousness, (London: Faber and Faber, 1955), p. 130.

4. *Ibid.*, p. 130.

5. « Foreword » Catalogue of an Exhibition of Paintings by [the] Canadian Group of Painters (Toronto: Canadian Group of Painters, 1933), non paginé.

6. « Three hundred years of Canadian art », Lecture III – The Twentieth Century: 1900-1950, Musée des beaux-arts du Canada, 2 mai 1967, CFC Fonds, Vol.2.

7. *Cartable de notes d'enseignement* : "Camouflage" 1942, CFC Fonds, Vol. 5.

8. «1929 marque la fin d'une période importante dans l'art canadien, déclara Comfort. De toute évidence, l'art n'est pas toujours le reflet direct et simple de la société ou d'évènements sociaux, mais même si son résultat entend être purement esthétique, l'art demeure un phénomène social. La crise fut un cataclysme économique qui eut une incidence sur les relations sociales et donc sur le rapport entre l'art et la société.» Traduction française d'un discours prononcé le 12 mai 1962, au Montreal Arts Club, lors d'un banquet célébrant le cinquantième anniversaire de ce club, Fonds CFC, Vol. 2.

9. Inscription se trouvant dans l'exemplaire de Charles et de Louise Comfort de *The Years* (Les Années) de Virginia Woolf, Londres, Hogarth Press, 1937. SCS1 COMF1 W66 1937, Bibliothèque et archives du Musée des beaux-arts du Canada, Ottawa.

10. Virginia Woolf, *The Common Reader*, p. 95, cité par C.E.M. Joad, *Guide to Modern Thought*, (1933, réimpression, Londres Faber and Faber, 1948), p. 246.

11. « On se rend de plus en plus compte que la vie intérieure" a écrit Joad – qui était célèbre en raison de sa participation à l'émission de guerre de la BBC Brain's Trust – est peut-être plus importante que la vie extérieure et que la lutte entre des éléments en conflit au sein d'une même personne peut être plus acerbe que celle entre deux personnes.» Joad, p. 244.

12. Selon Joad, qui s'est penché sur le rapport entre la psychologie moderne et la littérature contemporaine, la vie intérieure de la pensée et des sentiments devait primer tant et si bien que le vrai sujet du romancier c'est la matière psychologique. On ne peut trouver la vérité sur la vie, a-t-il poursuivi, ni dans une biographie, ni dans le contenu d'un esprit, ni dans son développement, ni même dans une humeur psychologique, « mais dans un moment psychologique.» C'est là que la psychologie moderne intervient car « un individu n'est nullement une personnalité quand on l'examine, il n'est qu'une succession de personnes fugaces, dont chacune fait l'objet d'un moment psychologique.» Joad, p. 249-251.

13. Virginia Woolf, *The Years*, (1937, réimp. Londres, The Hogarth Press, 1979), p. 206.

14. *Ibid.*, p. 300.

15. Fred Housser, *A Canadian Art Movement: The Story of the Group of Seven*, (Toronto: The Macmillan Company of Canada Limited, 1926) p. 32 et 33.

16. Paraskeva Clarke [sic] (comme on l'a dit à G. Campbell McInnes), « Come Out From Behind the Pre-Cambrian Shield » *New Frontier* 1 (avril 1937).

17. Abell arguait que le design était « une qualité si importante que l'on pouvait qualifier le fait de le comprendre de 'clé' de l'art. » Walter Abell, « A Key to Art : summary of a lecture,» Carnegie Corporation – Individuals: Abell, Walter (1934–1937), Boîte 296, dossier 13-7.4c, Bibliothèque et archives du Musée des beaux-arts du Canada, Ottawa.

18. Walter Abell, Representation and Form : A Study of Aesthetic Values in Representational Art, New York: Charles Scribner's Sons, 1936), p. 102.

19. Abell donna le nom de «forme figurative » à un design amélioré dans le domaine des beaux-arts. Il expliqua que la forme n'est pas essentiellement tangible ni physique ni plastique de par sa nature. « C'est plutôt une vie influençant un corps, un principe organisateur qui assemble des éléments pour créer un rapport important entre eux. Sa beauté résulte de la qualité de ce rapport plutôt que de la nature des éléments mis en rapport les uns avec les autres.» « Cette forme [figurative] peut, à elle seule, impartir le maximum de beauté formelle et de richesse auquel on puisse prétendre dans le domaine des arts visuels.» Walter Abell, p. 165.

20. Herbert Read, *Art and Society*, 3d ed. rev. (1936; Londres: Faber + Faber, 1956), p. 7.

21. Robert Ayre, « Canadian Art Series: Charles Fraser Comfort » RCA, manuscrit sans date, fonds CFC, Vol. 54.

22. E. Lisa Panayotidis, « The Departement of Fine Art at the University of Toronto, 1926–1945 – 'Institutionalizing the Culture of the Aesthetic', *Journal of Canadian Art History /Annales de l'histoire de l'art canadien* XXV (2004), p. 100-121.

23. Comfort quitta de New York pour l'Europe le 12 mai 1939. Il atterrit en Italie, puis se rendit en Espagne, en Suisse, à Paris et en Normandie avant de retourner à New York le 26 juin. *Journal de voyage* (Europe) 1939, Fonds CFC, Vol.1.

24. « En étudiant l'art du passé et du présent » ajouta Comfort en 1948 » on amène l'étudiant à comprendre le rôle joué par les arts dans la vie humaine. » Teaching Notes : University of Toronto. 1946–59, « Talk on Department of Art and Archeology – 20 Octobre 1948, » CFC Fonds Vol. 5.

25. Thomas Mann (1875–1955), citation extraite de l'avant-propos du catalogue *Canadian Group of Painters* (Toronto: Art Gallery of Ontario 1942), p.3.

26. Comfort a repeint *Primavera* en 1972. La dernière version du tableau se trouve dans la présente exposition.

27. Russell a déclaré que « cultiver le sentiment aigu de la nécessité d'une citoyenneté mondiale » était le besoin le plus essentiel. Bertrand Russell, *Education and the Social Order*, (1932; réimp. Londres: Unwin Paperbacks, 1977), p. 19.

28. John Dewey, *Reconstruction in Philosophy*, (1920; rpt. New York: Mentor Books, 1950), p. 8.

29. Russell, p. 152.

30. David Thistlewood, Herbert Read – *Formlessness and Form: An introduction to his aesthetics*, (Londres: Routledge & Kegan Paul, 1984), p. xiii.

31. Read a consacré beaucoup de réflexion à ce paradoxe au cours des années 1950. Selon lui, les archétypes étaient indubitablement « indispensables en tant que condensateurs sociaux,» mais ils étaient inefficaces si on s'en servait délibérément. *Guernica*, le tableau peint par Picasso en 1937 est un exemple d'œuvre dans laquelle la manière ou facture d'un artiste a empêché des formes archétypales de se démoder et donc de perdre leur attrait esthétique. Thistlewood, p. 153 et suiv.

32. Susanne K. Langer, *Philosophy in a New Key: A Study of the Symbolism of Reason, Rite and Art*, 3rd ed. (1942; réimp. Cambridge, Mass.: Harvard University Press, 1957), p. 281.

33. Dans la civilisation moderne, il y a deux grandes menaces à la sécurité mentale : le nouveau mode de vie « qui a rendu les anciens symboles de la nature étrangers à nos esprits, et la nouvelle façon de travailler, qui rend les activités personnelles insensées...» Langer, p. 291.

34. «Si nous sommes en mesure d'envisager la tradition comme une expérience réussie, a déclaré Comfort en 1949, elle devient un élément vivant de notre travail créateur, vivant parce qu'elle change et croît constamment, et parce que son changement et sa croissance sont les nôtres.» Charles Comfort, « Painting: An Essay Prepared for the Royal Commission on National Development in the Arts, Letters, and Sciences, 1949–51, » p.414; CFC Fonds, Vol. 8.

35. Langer, p. 287-288.

36. Mircea Eliade, *The Sacred and the Profane : The Nature of Religion*, trans. Williard R Trask (1957; New York: Harcourt Brace Jovanovich, 1959), p. 13 [trad. française : Le Sacré et le Profane, Payot, Paris].

37. Woolf, *The Years*, p.461 et suiv.

38. R.H. [Reginald Howard] Wilenski, *The Modern Movement in Art*, (New York: Frederick A. Stokes Company, 1927), p. 51 et suiv.

LAURA BRANDON

Véracité et attentes dans l'art militaire de Charles Comfort de 1940 à 1948 : La ligne Hitler en rétrospective

La ligne Hitler (1944)[1] est un des tableaux les plus connus sur la participation canadienne à la Deuxième Guerre mondiale. Comfort le considérait comme son œuvre la plus réussie.[2] Cette toile d'environ un mètre carré, représente un groupe de soldats canadiens en Italie qui avancent dans un paysage embrasé, de collines, d'arbres fracassés, de pièces d'artillerie défoncées et de volutes de fumée noires. La composition de la scène est soignée. On remarque dans le tiers de la toile qui forme le premier plan une *panzerturm* dont le canon a été remplacé par un grand trou noir béant dans un morceau de métal rouillé et par un tronc d'arbre horizontal brisé dont les entrailles se déploient, telles des palmes sombres, sur le rouge orangé criard du tiers intermédiaire du tableau.[3] Dans cette partie, six hommes avancent en diagonale suivant une ligne qui traverse la largeur de la toile. Derrière eux, une montagne presque noire domine le tiers formant l'arrière-plan du tableau. Deux éléments verticaux divisent aussi le tableau en trois. À gauche, la base de l'arbre fracassé est reliée à de la fumée issue d'un incendie situé dans le plan moyen. À droite, une tourelle de char verticale découpe la toile. Plus loin une colonne de fumée grise et blanche souligne la construction verticale de l'œuvre.

Les figures sont bizarrement tracées. Les six soldats, sans expression, sont parfois dépourvus de visage. Leurs têtes, coiffées de casques d'acier, perchées sur de longs cous au-dessus de leurs corps musclés, brandissent des armes. Tels des robots, ce sont des êtres humains étrangement peu crédibles, dans un paysage autrement plausible. La raison de leur aspect étrange nous éclaire non seulement sur le problème posé par la représentation de la guerre en général, mais encore sur la démarche adoptée par Charles Comfort pour aborder l'art militaire.

De toute évidence, la composition de ce tableau était destinée à faire une forte impression sur le spectateur. La brèche ouverte dans la ligne Hitler en mai 1944 était, après tout, un important succès canadien qui méritait d'être reconnu.[4] Le gouvernement se servit presque immédiatement de cette œuvre d'art en la reprenant sous forme d'une affiche destinée à pousser les gens à souscrire au huitième emprunt de la victoire.[5] Quatre ans plus tard, l'influent historien militaire C. P. Stacey devait l'indure dans son livre de 1948 sur l'Armée canadienne, estimant que le soldat situé au premier plan était le chef de section.[6] En 1970, Comfort accepta de copier *La ligne Hitler* pour un soldat-ami qui avait participé à la bataille. C'est cette oeuvre qui figure dans la présente exposition (cat. n° 69).[7] Plus récemment, le tableau a servi à illustrer l'en-tête de chapitre de *Tableaux de guerre : Chefs-d'œuvre du Musée de la guerre* (2000).[8] Et il ne s'agit que de quelques exemples de ses nombreuses utilisations depuis sa réalisation initiale.

Il convient cependant de noter que *La Ligne Hitler* ne représente pas une scène observée avec soin peinte entièrement sur un champ de bataille. Il s'agit plutôt d'une œuvre faite en atelier. En effet, la violence de la bataille qui l'a inspiré exclut absolument que le tableau ait pu découler d'une esquisse de l'époque réalisée sur le terrain. Mais Comfort était sur place les 23 et 24 mai 1944. Il a écouté les comptes rendus de témoins oculaires de la bataille; il a entendu le bruit de l'affrontement et s'est ensuite rendu sur le champ de bataille. Il a noté dans son journal de guerre ce qu'il a ainsi appris, vu et entendu.[9] Un examen de ce document et une analyse de certains aspects du programme officiel d'art militaire de la Deuxième Guerre mondiale, dans le contexte de l'époque, nous aident à expliquer la démarche suivie par Comfort pour réaliser *La ligne Hitler*. Cela nous a conduits à nous poser une importante question au sujet de l'art militaire : la véracité d'une image que nous percevons est-elle fondée sur notre observation ou sur nos attentes?

Comme beaucoup de ses confrères, Comfort a peint des sujets militaires longtemps avant la création d'un programme officiel destiné à favoriser ce genre d'art. *Ontario summer, 1940* (cat. n° 55), œuvre fondée sur l'expérience qu'il a acquise de 1939 à 1943 à titre d'instructeur de tir au fusil dans le Corps-école d'officiers canadiens à l'Université de Toronto, a les mêmes dimensions que *La ligne Hitler*. Ce tableau représente des hommes de troupe qui se déplacent dans un paysage bucolique composé d'arbres verts et de volutes de nuages blancs. Son aspect militaire est presque fortuit tel un post-scriptum à un essai pittoresque sur la nature en été. Un peu plus de deux ans plus tard, en février 1943, le Comité canadien des archives de guerre (CWRC) a engagé Comfort en tant qu'artiste officiel de guerre affecté dans l'Armée. (Il a été rendu à la vie civile en juillet 1946). Ce comité sis à Ottawa, qui avait été officiellement institué en janvier 1943, était composé de H.O. McCurry, directeur de la Galerie nationale (l'actuel Musée des beaux-arts du Canada) et d'officiers supérieurs des trois armes.[10] Des artistes d'âge mûr et reconnus, dont Comfort, conseillaient les membres du groupe. À ce titre, ce dernier dressa une liste de fournitures pour artistes recommandées en se fondant sur les exigences en matière de production décrites dans les instructions que le Comité canadien des archives de guerre donnait aux artistes récemment nommés. En Grande-Bretagne, le Haut-commissaire Vincent Massey servait de guide; les officiers supérieurs des divers corps d'armée s'occupaient des aspects pratiques du programme.

Le Comité engagea trente-deux artistes militaires qui reçurent le grade d'officier, une rémunération en conséquence, ainsi que du matériel et des instructions. Le Comité les répartit entre les trois principaux corps d'armée. Les instructions reçues lors de leur engagement donnent à penser qu'ils n'avaient guère de marge de manœuvre dans le domaine artistique.[11] « Notre intention est de faire en sorte que vos réalisations soient dignes des plus hautes traditions culturelles du Canada, qu'elles soient fidèles à l'Histoire, enfin qu'en tant qu'œuvres d'art, elles méritent d'être toujours et partout exposées.»

Les instructions données précisaient la dimension et la quantité des tableaux ainsi que leurs sujets. Sur le terrain les artistes faisaient des esquisses du matériel, des véhicules, des uniformes, des machines, ainsi que des hommes et des femmes qui s'en occupaient. Les scènes de bataille étaient extrêmement rares. Les aquarelles les plus grandes étaient peintes sur le terrain mais aussi après la bataille. L'heure, la date, le lieu, la scène ou les noms des unités étaient soigneusement inscrits au dos des œuvres. Des officiers historiens affectés aux mêmes unités que les artistes évaluaient les compositions en termes de précision et de respect des exigences de la censure, avant l'envoi des tableaux au quartier général de Londres. À la fin de la guerre en Europe, les artistes furent renvoyés au Canada, où on leur procura un atelier pour achever un nombre prédéterminé de toiles d'après des aquarelles réalisées à Londres.

La plupart d'entre eux, qui avaient été formés en tant que peintres paysagistes, étaient mal placés pour rendre les réalités de la guerre sur la toile. De sorte que *Campobasso* (cat. n° 67),[12] le grand tableau spectaculaire de Comfort, œuvre fondée sur les expériences initiales du peintre en Italie, en dit plus, semble-t-il, sur l'appréciation par son auteur des paysages de Giovanni Bellini, artiste de la Renaissance, que sur son intérêt pour l'armée canadienne. Cela explique aussi pourquoi un artiste ayant une grande expérience de l'enseignement de l'histoire de l'art, mais qui n'avait pas fait de service militaire à l'étranger, a eu du mal à se dérober aux attentes des militaires qui s'attendaient justement à des scènes émouvantes de drame et d'héroïsme puisqu'il était question d'art de guerre, alors que ces scènes étaient contraire à ce qu'il voyait de ses propres yeux.

Comfort servit initialement en Angleterre, où il peignit des scènes à Selsey, sur la côte méridionale du Sussex occidental. Tout comme l'aspect boisé d'*Ontario Summer, 1940*, le sentiment de mise en scène qu'inspire le filet de camouflage entrouvert révélant la présence du canon plus loin dans *Bofors Gun Site in a Field* (cat. n° 56) montre à quel point pour Comfort l'équilibre de la composition de ses œuvres l'emportait sur le contenu militaire. Quelques mois plus tard, le peintre se trouve à Cornwall, où le Corps royal du Génie de l'Armée canadienne construit des pistes d'atterrissage en vue de l'invasion de l'Europe prévue pour l'année suivante. Saint Eval, dont il a représenté l'église (cat. n° 57), servait de base pour ce Corps. *Sappers Quarrying* (cat. n° 58) est l'aquarelle préparatoire de *Sappers Drilling in Preparation for Secondary Blasting* (cat. n° 59). Dans cette dernière composition, l'artiste s'est concentré sur les deux personnages situés au premier plan, les dotant d'une musculature et d'une pertinence qui ne se remarquent pas dans son esquisse à l'aquarelle. Ce style figuratif s'apparente à celui que le peintre avait adopté pour réaliser ses peintures murales durant décennie précédente.

Se fondant sur les preuves constituées par les aquarelles peintes en octobre 1943 en Italie, Comfort continue à chercher un moyen efficace de peindre ce qu'il voit et entend consigner sur la toile. Il commence par aller voir Casa Berardi, qui avait été la scène d'une importante bataille le 14 décembre 1943. Dans *Battle Scene (Fantasy)* (cat. n° 60), il lance littéralement la peinture sur le papier; son application gestuelle de l'aquarelle évoque une scène d'action imaginaire dans laquelle le feu de la défense anti-aérienne s'associe aux bombes qui explosent. *Battlefield near Berardi Crossroads* (cat. n° 61) pourrait bien se situer au même endroit, sinon tout à côté. Toutefois, en l'occurrence, les deux croix représentées à gauche de la composition, l'aspect statique des arbres et les explosions dans le lointain nous portent à croire que l'affrontement est terminé. À la suite de la bataille sauvage d'Ortona qui se déroule sur la côte Adriatique du 21 au 27 décembre 1943, Comfort s'applique à représenter, quatre mois plus tard, les conséquences de l'assaut réussi lancé par les Canadiens contre cette ville. Dans *Wrecked Buildings, Ortona* (cat. n° 62), il se sert des mêmes trois éléments verticaux et horizontaux auquel il aura recours plus tard dans *La ligne Hitler* pour élaborer sa composition. Dans *San Pietro in Vaticano*, (cat. n° 65) œuvre peinte après le 4 juin 1944, date à laquelle les Canadiens aidèrent à libérer Rome, Comfort minimise la portée militaire de son œuvre en faisant une frise qui contraste avec la remarquable beauté du *Triomphe de la Cathedra Pietri* du Bernin (1657) représentée au-dessus d'elle. Il devait construire des compositions semblables à des frises de ce genre dans *Ontario Summer* et *Campobasso*.

Dans une visite subséquente à la ligne Hitler, Comfort peint le fascinant *Dead German on the Hitler Line* (cat. n° 63). Les artistes militaires représentaient rarement la mort. À l'endos de son aquarelle, Comfort a inscrit : «Je ne suis guère porté à peindre des sujets lugubres de ce genre, mais en pareil cas on peut dire qu'une image d'horreur n'est pas déplacée.»

Ses sujets préférés étaient, en fait, les portraits des vivants, tel l'extraordinaire *Sergeant P. J. Ford* (cat. n° 66), dont les yeux d'un bleu intense trahissent les longues années de lassitude de la guerre. Deux semaines plus tôt, Comfort avait fait son autoportrait (cat. n° 64), mais sans l'arme qu'il avait fournie à Ford. Ici le peintre nous regarde, alors que Ford regarde dans une autre direction. Et il fallut attendre 1948 pour que Comfort, revenu à la vie civile, parachève le portrait de son camarade, l'artiste militaire Will Ogilvie, qui était peut-être son meilleur ami (cat. n° 68). Ici, le paysage de la campagne sicilienne, que Ogilvie a illustrée quand il était artiste militaire en 1943, encadre le portrait du soldat-peintre en uniforme, les deux aspects de cet homme étant liés à tout jamais et son regard n'exprimant ni sollicitude ni indifférence à l'égard du spectateur, mais seulement un peu des deux.

Comme nous l'avons vu plus tôt, les tableaux de Comfort prouvent que son intérêt pour la composition l'emportait sur celui qu'il aurait pu avoir pour les sujets militaires, sauf s'il s'agissait de personnages qu'il peignait la plupart du temps avec sympathie et sincérité. Il est incontestable cependant que l'artiste était un témoin de la guerre très sensible à ce qu'il voyait. Ses notes personnelles, méticuleusement tenues, attestent d'un sens aigu de l'observation. Ceci transparaît dans son rendu de la trouée dans la ligne Hitler. Familier avec le champ de bataille (il s'était rendu la veille reconnaître les lieux, d'une certaine distance). Il écrit le 23 mai 1944 d'un endroit situé à proximité : « Nous avons connu un drame après l'autre cet après-midi. Confrontés avec les obstacles insurmontables de 96 tanks, nous avons continué à nous frayer un passage en traversant la route d'AQUILO à PONTECORVO. Apparemment, nous n'avions pas assez d'infanterie pour protéger cette masse de blindés. »[13]

Le lendemain aux premières heures, Comfort note ceci : «Un fort tac-tac [fait par la défense anti-aérienne] m'a réveillé à 3 h 10 du matin. J'ai regardé dehors pour voir la nuit que les fusées éclairantes allemandes faisaient flamboyer...Le tir de la DCA était très nourri. Le ciel semblait plein d'avions, les étoiles pâlissaient derrière le stupéfiant ballet rouge feu de milliers d'obus tombant.» [14]

Plus tard ce jour-là, l'artiste écrit dans son journal: « La destruction d'arbres chargés de leur épais feuillage fait une impression encore plus sinistre que leur dépouillement total en hiver. Aucun arbre, arbuste ni buisson n'a été épargné. Ils sont dénudés, cisaillés et fracassés.»

Ajoutez à cela cette observation ultérieure extraite du journal de guerre publié de Comfort au sujet d'un canon planté à la verticale et comment il a soigneusement pris en compte les éléments nécessaires à *La Ligne Hitler* : « Un canon fiché perpendiculairement à la surface du sol, tel un gigantesque pylône commémorant les désastres de la guerre et se dressant dans les airs, constituait un spectacle fantastique. Un coup direct avait fait détoner son chargeur, et la conflagration qui en était résultée avait arraché toute la tourelle de son logement et l'avait lancée dans les airs. De sorte qu'il ne restait plus qu'une immense sonde d'acier, qui défiait aveuglément les cieux. »[15] Comfort a également fait une esquisse du canon.[16] Les descriptions de soldats au combat sont notablement absentes de ses documents. Comfort ne les voyait pas en action sur le champ de bataille et l'on suppose seulement qu'on lui a raconté leurs actes d'héroïsme et de pur stoïcisme. C'est sans doute en écoutant ces récits qu'il a imaginé les soldats de *La ligne Hitler*. En tous cas, il n'avait aucune expérience personnelle du combat. Comme il l'a fait remarquer lors d'une interview de 1977 : « Je ne suivais pas les troupes car les non-combattants n'avaient pas le droit d'aller dans les zones d'affrontements.»[17]

Il faut aussi tenir compte du contexte. Comfort savait qu'il assistait à d'importants événements et qu'en tant qu'artiste militaire officiel il lui incombait de capter leur nature par la peinture. Les hommes de son entourage et l'histoire elle-même lui faisaient comprendre que c'étaient les soldats qui comptaient. Quant à lui, toutefois, ce qu'il voyait et entendait, ce n'était pas des hommes se battant mais la puissance de la technologie. C'est la tension entre ce qu'il percevait et ce qu'il était censé représenter qui entraîne un décalage dans *La ligne Hitler* et constitue le manque d'humanité crédible dans tant d'autres œuvres. Ce n'est que récemment que des historiens militaires comme l'Australien Robin Prior ont argué que la guerre est une affaire de technologie et non d'hommes. Il écrit : « Toutes les vertus du guerrier – son courage, sa ténacité, sa capacité à garder le moral, son aptitude aux prouesses physiques – ne sert à rien face à une puissance de feu déchaînée. »[18]

Comme ses journaux et beaucoup de ses esquisses à l'aquarelle l'attestent, Comfort a été témoin de la puissance de feu lors de la Deuxième Guerre mondiale et de ses conséquences sur le champ de bataille. Voulant décrire le côté humain de la guerre, il a peint des portraits de soldats placés derrière les lignes, ou longtemps après leur mort. Dans *La ligne Hitler*, il était incapable de représenter l'évènement sans en profiter pour faire des soldats de l'infanterie les principaux acteurs, d'où leur inclusion dans son œuvre. Ce faisant, il a réalisé une œuvre d'art prisée qui répondait aux attentes les plus courantes du public quant à la nature de la bataille, mais il a minimisé sa propre expérience à ce sujet. En outre, en tant que documents historiques, ses réalisations ont prêté le flanc à la critique même si, en tant qu'œuvres d'art, elles dépassaient les attentes.

Notes

1. Charles Comfort, *La ligne Hitler*, 1944, huile sur toile, 101,6 x 121,7 cm, collection Beaverbrook d'art militaire, Musée canadien de la guerre, (nº 19710261-2203).

2. Joan Murray, entretien avec Comfort, p. 14.

3. La *Panzerturm* était une tourelle de char dotée d'un canon monté sur une base de béton, à laquelle les Allemands recouraient pour se défendre pendant la guerre.

4. Voir Daniel G. Dancocks, *The D-Day Dodgers: The Canadians in Italy, 1943–1945* (Toronto: McClelland and Stewart, 1991).

5. Charles Comfort, *They Also Buy Victory Bonds*, 1945, lithographie en offset sur vélin, Bibliothèque et Archives Canada no 1994-210-114). Quand le Quartier général de la défense à Ottawa a demandé d'utiliser ce tableau, celui-ci se trouvait exposé à la National Gallery, à Londres. E.T. Heathcote, *Weekly Progress Report* (1 Fév. 1945), Bibliothèque et Archives Canada, RG 24, vol. 20, p. 299, dossier 937.013 (D1).

6. C. P. Stacey, *The Canadian Army*, 1939–1945 (Ottawa, King's Printer, 1948), p. 140.

7. Il a été peint en 1970 à la demande d'Albert E. Shepherd, qui était chancelier de l'Université de Western Ontario. Au cours de ses séances de pose pour son portrait officiel peint par Comfort, il avait dit à l'artiste qu'il aimerait avoir sa propre version de *La ligne Hitler*.

8. Dean F. Olivier and Laura Brandon, *Canvas of War:Painting the Canadian Experience*, Vancouver: Douglas and McIntyre, 2000), p. 72 et suiv.

9. Les journaux de guerre de Comfort se trouvent dans le Fonds CFC, vol. 36, dossiers 6-12.

10. Pour de plus amples renseignements, voir Laura Brandon, *Art or Memorial? The Forgotten History of Canada's War Art* (Calgary : University of Calgary Press, 2006).

11. Ces instructions ont été intégralement reproduites dans *Art or Memorial?*

12. La ville de Campobasso a été conquise à la fin d'octobre 1943.

13. *Journaux de guerre*, Fonds CFC, vol.36, dossier 9, 23 mai 1944.

14. *Journaux de guerre*, 24 mai 1944.

15. Charles Comfort, *Artist at War*, 2nd. ed. (Pender Island, B.C.: Log House Books, 1995), p.134.On peut aussi voir ce canon en projetant la bobine 33 d'actualités de l'Armée canadienne, Bibliothèque et Archives Canada, Fonds J.P. Rigby, 1973-0162/33109.

16. Charles Comfort, *Destroyed Panzerturm, Hitler Line*, (Tourelle de char détruite, ligne Hitler), 21 juin 1944, aquarelle sur papier, collection Beaverbrook d'art militaire, Musée canadien de la guerre (nº 19710261-2182).

17. Interview de Murray, p.4.

18. Robin Prior, « The Heroic Image of the Warrior in the First World War,» *War and Society* 23 septembre 2005), p. 21.

TAKE COMFORT – THE CAREER OF CHARLES COMFORT

All works by Charles Comfort

All dimensions are centimetres, height by width.

EARLY WORKS OF ART ON PAPER

1. **Kildonan Skyline Across the Red**
June 18, 1922
watercolour on paper
19.8 x 23.5
The Winnipeg Art Gallery; Gift of A. Lorne Campbell, O.C., Q.C.
G-91-334

2. **Green Canoe**
1922
watercolour on paper
9.0 x 27.6 (sight)
Robert and Margaret Hucal, Winnipeg

3. **New York**
January, 1923
watercolour with traces of graphite, scraping out on wove paper
21.5 x 15.7 (sheet)
Art Gallery of Ontario, Toronto.
Gift of Louise and Charles Comfort, Ottawa, 1989
89/52
(Winnipeg and Charlottetown only)

4. **Red River and the St. Boniface Cathedral**
c. 1923
watercolour on paper
23.1 x 16.1
The Winnipeg Art Gallery
G-47-160

5. **Blindfold Rapids, Lake of the Woods**
August 22, 1923
watercolour, graphite on wove paper
23.7 x 26.2
Art Gallery of Ontario, Toronto.
Gift of Louise and Charles Comfort, Ottawa, 1989.
89/56
(Winnipeg and Charlottetown only)

6. **Lake of the Woods, Route Bay**
July 1924
Watercolour with traces of graphite on wove paper
22.9 x 25.2 (sheet)
Art Gallery of Ontario, Toronto.
Gift of Louise and Charles Comfort, Ottawa, 1989.
89/59
(Winnipeg and London only)

7. **Suburban Cottages, Winnipeg**
May 31, 1924
watercolour with traces of graphite on wove paper
20.5 x 22.5
Art Gallery of Ontario, Toronto.
Gift of Louise and Charles Comfort, Ottawa, 1989.
89/60
Winnipeg and (Charlottetown only)

8. **Bridge Over the Don**
July 1925
watercolour on paper
22.2 x 25.4
Art Gallery of Ontario, Toronto.
Gift of Sam and Ayala Zacks, 1970.
70/224
(Winnipeg and London only)

9. **In the Valley**
1925
watercolour on wove paper
23.3 x 26.0
National Gallery of Canada, Ottawa;
Gift of Louise Comfort, Ottawa, 1996
#38272
(Winnipeg only)

10. **Don Valley Brickyard**
1925
watercolour on buff wove paper
24.0 x 26.0
National Gallery of Canada, Ottawa;
Gift of Louise Comfort, Ottawa, 1996
#38274

11. **Stoney Lake**
1925
watercolour over graphite on buff wove paper
57.6 x 67.1
National Gallery of Canada, Ottawa;
Purchased 1927.
#3518

12. **Mountain Lake (Kawartha Lake)**
August, 1925
watercolour on paper
23.5 x 25.8
The Winnipeg Art Gallery; Gift from the Estate of Arnold O. Brigden
G-73-264

13. **Kawartha Lakes**
1925
watercolour
25.4 x 22.9 cm
The Winnipeg Art Gallery; Gift of Robert and Margaret Hucal
2005-69

14. **Wolf Collar**
1925
colour linocut on paper, 20/30
38.0 x 28.0
The Winnipeg Art Gallery; Gift of Robert and Margaret Hucal
2001-22

15. **Sounding Sky**
1925
colour linocut on paper, 20/30
38.0 x 28.0
The Winnipeg Art Gallery; Gift of Robert and Margaret Hucal
2001-23

16. **Andre Lapine**
c. 1925
linocut on paper
9.5 x 9.3
The Winnipeg Art Gallery; Gift of Robert and Margaret Hucal
2005-70

17. **Boschink**
c. 1925–1926
etching on wove paper
19.5 x 22. 5
The Winnipeg Art Gallery; Gift of Robert and Margaret Hucal
2005-68

18. **December**
c. 1926
colour linocut on paper
34.3 x 21.0
The Winnipeg Art Gallery; Gift of Robert and Margaret Hucal
2003–131

LANDSCAPES

19. **Prairie Road (Out West)**
1925
oil on canvas
116.9 x 86.4
Justina M. Barnicke Gallery, University of Toronto. Donated by the Graduating Year of 1931
31.01

20. **Tawny, (York Mills)**
March, 1927
oil on board
25.0 x 30.0
The Winnipeg Art Gallery; Acquired with the assistance of Mrs. Ethel Fanshaw in memory of Hubert L. Fanshaw and the Estate of Agnes Riehl
2004-86

21. **Study for Wilderness**
1927
oil on wood-pulp board
25.5 x 29.8
National Gallery of Canada, Ottawa;
Gift of Louise Comfort, Ottawa, 1996
38278

22. **Wilderness**
1927
oil on canvas
101.8 x 122.2
McMichael Canadian Art Collection; Gift of Mrs. Anne (Comfort) Andersen and the
Estate of Mrs. Ruth (Comfort) Jackson
#2002.1

23. **The Great Rock, Bon Echo**
1928
oil on canvas
127.0 x 152.4
Museum London; Gift of the Volunteer Committee, 1961
#61.A.22

24. **Winter Woods**
1928
oil on card
23.7 x 29.0
Agnes Etherington Art Centre, Queen's University, Kingston, Ontario; Gift of the Estate of Kathleen Ryan, 1995

25. **Pastoral, Duncan, Ontario**
May 21st 1929
oil on panel
25.2 x 29.6
Robert and Margaret Hucal, Winnipeg

26. **Black Spruce, Pickerel River**
1932
oil on board
30.5 x 25.5
George and Jessie Falconer, Sydney, B.C.

27. **Barns Near Wexford on the Lawrence Ave. Line**
June 5, 1932
oil on board
25.1 x 30.5
The Winnipeg Art Gallery; Gift of Vernon S. MacKelvie in memory of his parents, Charles W.L. MacKelvie and Josephine (Hibbard) MacKelvie and his brother, James A. MacKelvie, killed in action in World War II
G-88-375

28. **Clearing, Big Stone Bay, Lake of the Woods**
1934
oil on board
25.6 x 30.3
Art Gallery of Ontario, Toronto. Purchase, 1985.
85/253

29. **Saugenay River**
1935
oil on canvas
76.8 x 92.1
Justina M. Barnicke Gallery, University of Toronto;
Donated by the Graduating Year of 1935
15471

30. **Tadoussac**
1935
oil on plywood
24.7 x 30.0
National Gallery of Canada, Ottawa;
Purchased 1973
17613

31. **Tadoussac**
1935
oil on canvas
76.1 x 91.4
National Gallery of Canada, Ottawa; Vincent Massey Bequest, 1968
15471

32. **Rossport, Lake Superior**
1935
oil on board
31.5 x 37.5
John Clancy, Toronto

33. **Distant View of Manitoulin**
1936
oil on wood

25.2 x 30.5
Agnes Etherington Art Centre, Queen's University, Kingston, Ontario; Bequest of Herbert Clarke

34. **Smelter Stacks, Copper Cliff**
1936
oil on canvas
101.9 x 122.2
National Gallery of Canada, Ottawa; Purchased 1957
#6666

35. **Lake Superior Village**
1937
oil on canvas
108.0 x 177.8
Art Gallery of Ontario, Toronto. Gift from the Fund of the T. Eaton Co. Ltd. for Canadian Works of Art, 1950.
50/10
(Winnipeg only)

36. **Pioneer Survival**
1938
oil on canvas
102.0 x 122.0
National Gallery of Canada, Ottawa; Royal Canadian Academy of Arts diploma work, deposited by the artist, Toronto, 1945.
#4613
(Winnipeg only)

37. **Observatory**
1938
oil on wood panel
37.8 x 30.5
George and Jessie Falconer, Sydney, B.C.

38. **Primavera II**
1941/1972
oil on canvas
59.5 x 75.0
Anne and Clarke Andersen

PORTRAITURE

39. **Self-portrait**
1920–1921
watercolour on wove paper
25.2 x 23.2
National Gallery of Canada, Ottawa; Gift of Louise Comfort, Ottawa, 1996
#38276

40. **Loo (Head of Louise Comfort)**
1923
pencil on wove paper
13.4 x 9.9
Library and Archives Canada/1994-210-138
Photo Neg. #C-125834

41. **Louise Irene, daughter of Fred W. Chase**
1923
pencil on wove paper
20.4 x 12.7
Library and Archives Canada/1994–210–5
Photo Neg. #C-124463

42. **H. Eric Bergman**
August, 1923
watercolour on paper
22.8 x 14.6
The Winnipeg Art Gallery; Gift of the artist
G-69-57

43. **Louise**
1927
oil on canvas
67.2 x 52.0
National Gallery of Canada, Ottawa; Purchased 1981
#26541

44. **Portrait of Will Ogilvie**
1927
oil on canvas
91.8 x 86.7
Art Gallery of Hamilton; Gift of the artist, 1971
71.56.207

45. **Will Olgilvie**
1931
pencil on wove paper
26.2 x 20.4
Library and Archives Canada/1994–210–87
Photo Neg. #C–125347

46. **Comfort Guestbook: Signatures of visitors to the Comfort residence**
1931–1939
mixed media book
33.0 x 20.4
Collection of Library and Archives Canada/1992–692

47. **Chuhaldin**
1931
watercolour on paper
91.7 x 106.8
Art Gallery of Hamilton; Gift of the Women's Committee, 1954
54.56.K
(Winnipeg only)

48. **Young Canadian**
1932
watercolour on paper
91.9 x 107.3
Justina M. Barnicke Gallery, University of Toronto;
Purchased by the Sketch Committee
34.06

49. **Untitled (Louise)**
1933
graphite on paper
33.3 x 21.4
George and Jessie Falconer, Sydney, B.C.

50. **Prof. Felix Walter**
1933
watercolour on paper on stretcher
162.4 x 76.4
The Winnipeg Art Gallery; Gift of the artist
G-71-22

51. **Portrait in August**
1934
oil on plywood
50.7 x 60.5
Art Gallery of Ontario, Toronto. Gift of the Artist, 1991.
91/383

52. **Portrait of Anne**
August 22, 1937
oil on masonite
40.6 x 36.8
Anne and Clarke Andersen

53. **Ruth at Studio Window**
1940
oil on canvas
102.0 x 51.0
C. Fraser Jackson, Toronto

54. **Self-portrait**
1965
oil on plywood
65.5 x 54.8
National Gallery of Canada, Ottawa; Commissioned by the National Gallery of Canada in 1965, for the collection of official portraits of directors and of chairmen of the Board of Trustees
5659

WAR ART

55. **Ontario Summer**
1940
oil on canvas
101.6 x 121.9
Beaverbrook Collection of War Art, Canadian War Museum
19710261-1673

56. **Bofors Gun Site in a Field**
May 12, 1943
watercolour on paper
39.6 x 56.4
Beaverbrook Collection of War Art, Canadian War Museum
19710261-2147

57. **St. Eval Church, Cornwall**
July 1943
oil on canvasboard
30.5 x 40.3
National Gallery of Canada, Ottawa; Bequest of Norah Michener, Toronto, 1992.
#36830

58. **Sappers Quarrying Stone**
July 31, 1943
watercolour on paper
37.1 x 54.0
Beaverbrook Collection of War Art, Canadian War Museum
19710261-2283

59. **Sappers Drilling in Preparation for Secondary Blasting**
1943
oil on canvas
67.7 x 40.6
Beaverbrook Collection of War Art, Canadian War Museum
19710261–2282

60. **Battle Scene (Fantasy)**
January 29, 1944
watercolour on paper
37.0 x 53.8
Beaverbrook Collection of War Art, Canadian War Museum
19710261–2139

61. **Battlefield Near Berardi Crossroads**
1944
watercolour on paper
37.0 x 53.9
Beaverbrook Collection of War Art, Canadian War Museum
19710261–2137

62. **Wrecked Buildings, Ortona, Italy**
April 19, 1944
watercolour on paper
36.8 x 53.8
Beaverbrook Collection of War Art, Canadian War Museum
19710261-2312

63. **Dead German on the Hitler Line**
June 22, 1944
watercolour on paper
38.8 x 58.5
Beaverbrook Collection of War Art, Canadian War Museum
19710261-2179

64. **Major C.F. Comfort**
June 30, 1944
watercolour on paper
51.4 x 34.3
Beaverbrook Collection of War Art, Canadian War Museum
19710261-2172

65. **San Pietro in Vaticano, Rome**
July 3, 1944
watercolour on paper
55.8 x 37.5
Beaverbrook Collection of War Art, Canadian War Museum
19710261-2281

66. **Sergeant P.J. Ford**
July 15, 1944
watercolour on paper
38.8 x 57.1
Beaverbrook Collection of War Art, Canadian War Museum
19710261-2189

67. **Campobasso**
c. 1945
oil on canvas
127.5 x 153.2
Beaverbrook Collection of War Art, Canadian War Museum
19710261–2151

68. **Major W.A. Ogilvie**
1948
watercolour on paper
47.8 x 79.1
Beaverbrook Collection of War Art, Canadian War Museum
19710261–1672

69. **Hitler Line II**
1944/1970
oil on canvas
92.0 x 116.5
Private Collection, Winnipeg

POST-WAR ART

70. **Aeons Ago**
1947
watercolour, ink, gouache, wax resist on wove paper
57.4 x 39.1
Gallery of Ontario, Toronto. Gift of Mrs. Anne (Comfort) Andersen and the estate of Mrs. Ruth (Comfort) Jackson, 2000. 2000/58
(Winnipeg and London only)

71. **Transfiguration**
October 18, 1947
tempera on paper
39.2 x 56.0
The Winnipeg Art Gallery
L-34

72. **Thrush Song**
1949
mixed media on board
67.0 x 50.5
Suzanne F. Jackson and Richard K. Edwards, Toronto

73. **Aura Lee**
September 1949/1950
oil on canvas
60.9 x 76.6
The Winnipeg Art Gallery; Acquired with the help of the School of Art Fund, March, 1952
G-52-175

74. **Rocky Site**
1952
oil on canvas
50.8 x 66.0
McMichael Canadian Art Collection; Gift of the Artist
#1971.2

75. **Orchard in Albion**
1957
oil on canvas
51.0 x 65.5
Agnes Etherington Art Centre, Queen's University, Kingston, Ontario; James Ferres, Estate, 1985

76. **Wherewhen**
1957
oil on canvas
74.5 x 154.0
C. Fraser Jackson, Toronto

77. **Pre-Cambrian Legend**
1957
oil on canvas
61.3 x 102.3
Suzanne F. Jackson and Richard K. Edwards, Toronto

78. **Epic Theme**
May 1966
acrylic on canvas
127.3 x 170.7
George and Jessie Falconer, Sydney, B.C.

79. **Horizontal Event II (Newspeak Series)**
1967
oil on canvas
61.1 x 102.2
C. Fraser Jackson, Toronto

80. **Seventh Line, Tecumseh Township, Simcoe County**
1970
oil on canvas
51.0 x 66.5
Agnes Etherington Art Centre, Queen's University, Kingston, Ontario; Gift of Elizabeth Harrison, 2001

81. **Edge of the World, Georgian Bay**
1972
oil on wood panel
29.7 x 40.7
George and Jessie Falconer, Sydney, B.C.

82. **Wichman's Barn**
August, 1976
oil on wood panel
31.0 x 41.0
The Winnipeg Art Gallery; Gift of Vernon S. MacKelvie in memory of his parents, Charles W.L. MacKelvie and Josephine (Hibbard) MacKelvie and his brother, James A. MacKelvie, killed in action in World War II
G-93-94

83. **Aspects of Nature 4, Thunderstorm, Georgian Bay**
1978
oil on wood
30.6 x 39.7
George and Jessie Falconer, Sydney, B.C.

84. **Rain, Mont St. Marie**
October 1981
oil on board
31.4 x 41.1
Suzanne F. Jackson and Richard K. Edwards, Toronto

MURAL DESIGN

85. **The Romance of Nickel**
1937
oil on canvas
213.5 x 610.0
Collection of Natural Resources Canada
Winnipeg only

86. **Montreal Central Station relief – nord**
1940–1941
reproduction on paper
32.8 x 60.5
Library and Archives Canada/1994-210-249

87. **British Columbia Pageant mural study**
1951
oil on commercial board
51.0 x 76.0
Library and Archives Canada/1994–210–204
Photo neg. #e002712502

88. **Heritage – National Library Mural**
1965–1966
oil on commercial board
38.3 x 102.2
Library and Archives Canada/ 1994-210-216

COMMERCIAL WORK

89. **Harriet Cowan – tipped into book: Women of Red River**
1923
pencil on wove paper
20.5 x 15.2
Library and Archives Canada; Comfort Fonds/1995-143-1
Photo neg.# C-143437

90. **Last Dog Train Leaving Fort Garry, 1909.**
1931 Hudson's Bay Company calendar.
78.0 x 46.5
Hudson's Bay Company Archives, Archives of Manitoba

91. **Toronto's 100 Years: The Official Centennial Book, 1834–1934 Toronto: The Corporation of the City of Toronto,**
1934
29.0 x 17.5
Private Collection

92. **The Council of the Northern Department of Rupert's Land, meeting at Norway House. June 21st, 1836**
1936
Hudson's Bay Company calendar.
78.0 x 46.5
Hudson's Bay Company Archives, Archives of Manitoba

93. **McLoughlin Welcomes the Americans, Fort Vancouver, 1834**
1941
Hudson's Bay Company calendar.
78.0 x 46.5
Hudson's Bay Company Archives, Archives of Manitoba

94. **R.M. Ballantyne at Tadoussac, 1846**
1942/Hudson's Bay Company calendar.
78.0 x 46.5
Hudson's Bay Company Archives, Archives of Manitoba

95. **Nickel: A Vital Factor in the Economic Life of Canada**
The International Nickel Company, c. 1940
book
28.6 x 22.2
George and Jessie Falconer, Sydney, B.C.

96. **Nickel: A Review of Institutional Advertising**
The International Nickel Company, c. 1947
book
28.6 x 22.2
Private Collection

TAKE COMFORT – LA CARRIÈRE DE CHARLES COMFORT

Toutes ces œuvres sont de Charles Comfort

Les dimensions, hauteur par largeur, figurent en centimètres.

PREMIÈRES ŒUVRES SUR PAPIER

1. **Kildonan Skyline Across the Red**
18 juin 1922
aquarelle sur papier
19,8 x 23,5
Le Musée des beaux-arts de Winnipeg
Don de A. Lorne Campbell, O.C., Q.C.
G-91-334

2. **Green Canoe**
1922
aquarelle sur papier
9,0 x 27,6 (vue)
Robert et Margaret Hucal, Winnipeg

3. **New York**
Janvier, 1923
aquarelle, mine de plomb, grattoir sur papier vélin
21,5 x 15,7 (feuille)
Musée des beaux-arts de l'Ontario, Toronto
Don de Louise et Charles Comfort, Ottawa, 1989
89/52
(exposé uniquement à Winnipeg et à Charlottetown)

4. **Red River and the St. Boniface Cathedral**
c. 1923
aquarelle sur papier
23,1 x 16,1
Le Musée des beaux-arts de Winnipeg
G-47-160

5. **Blindfold Rapids, Lake of the Woods**
22 août 1923
mine de plomb et aquarelle sur papier vélin
23.7 x 26.2
Musée des beaux-arts de l'Ontario, Toronto.
Don de Louise et Charles Comfort, Ottawa, 1989.
89/56
(exposé uniquement à Winnipeg et à Charlottetown)

6. **Lake of the Woods, Route Bay**
Juillet, 1924
aquarelle, gouache et mine de plomb sur papier vélin
22,9 x 25,2 (feuille)
Musée des beaux-arts de l'Ontario, Toronto.
Don de Louise et Charles Comfort, Ottawa, 1989.
89/59
(exposé uniquement à Winnipeg et à London)

7. **Suburban Cottages, Winnipeg**
31mai 1924
aquarelle et traces de mine de plomb sur papier vélin
20,5 x 22,5
Musée des beaux-arts de l'Ontario, Toronto.
Don de Louise et Charles Comfort, Ottawa, 1989.
89/60
(exposé uniquement à Winnipeg et à Charlottetown)

8. **Bridge over the Don**
Juillet 1925
aquarelle sur papier
22,2 x 25,4
Musée des beaux-arts de l'Ontario, Toronto.
Don de Sam et Ayala Zacks, 1970.
70/224
(exposé uniquement à Winnipeg et à London)

9. **In the Valley**
1925
aquarelle sur papier vélin
23,3 x 26,0
Musée des beaux-arts du Canada
Don de Louise Comfort, Ottawa, 1996
(No 38272)
(exposé uniquement à Winnipeg)

10. **Don Valley Brickyard**
1925
aquarelle sur papier vélin chamois
24,0 x 26,0
Musée des beaux-arts du Canada
Don de Louise Comfort, Ottawa, 1996
(No 38274)

11. **Stoney Lake**
1925
aquarelle sur mine de plomb sur papier vélin chamois
57,6 x 67,1
Acheté en 1927
Musée des beaux-arts du Canada
(No 3518)

12. **Mountain Lake (Kawartha Lake)**
Août, 1925
aquarelle sur papier
23,5 x 25,8
Le Musée des beaux-arts de Winnipeg;
Don de la succession Arnold O. Brigden
G-73-264

13. **Kawartha Lakes**
1925
aquarelle sur papier
25,4 x 22,9
Le Musée des beaux-arts de Winnipeg;
Don de Robert et Margaret Hucal
2005-69

14. **Wolf Collar**
1925
gravure lino couleur sur papier, 20/30
38,0 x 28,0
Le Musée des beaux-arts de Winnipeg;
Don de Robert et Margaret Hucal
2001-22

15. **Sounding Sky**
1925
gravure lino couleur sur papier, 20/30
38,0 x 28,0
Le Musée des beaux-arts de Winnipeg;
Don de Robert et Margaret Hucal
2001-23

16. **Andre Lapine**
c. 1925
gravure lino sur papier
9,5 x 9,3
Le Musée des beaux-arts de Winnipeg;
Don de Robert et Margaret Hucal
2005-70

17. **Boschink**
c. 1925–26
eau-forte sur papier vélin
19,5 x 22,5
Le Musée des beaux-arts de Winnipeg;
Don de Robert et Margaret Hucal
2005-68

18. **December**
c. 1926
gravure lino couleur sur papier
34,3 x 21,0
Le Musée des beaux-arts de Winnipeg;
Don de Robert et Margaret Hucal
2003-131

PAYSAGES

19. **Prairie Road (Out West)**
1925
huile sur toile
116,9 x 86,4
Galerie Justina M. Barnicke, Université de Toronto.
Don des diplômés de la promotion 1931
31.01

20. **Tawny, (York Mills)**
Mars, 1927
huile sur panneau
25,0 x 30,0
Le Musée des beaux-arts de Winnipeg;
Acquis avec le concours de Mme Ethel Fanshaw en mémoire de Hubert L. Fanshaw et de la succession Agnes Riehl
2004-86

21. **Study for Wilderness**
1927
huile sur panneau de fibres
25,5 x 29,8
Musée des beaux-arts du Canada
Don de Louise Comfort, Ottawa, 1996
(No 38278)

22. **Wilderness**
1927
huile sur toile
101,8 x 122,2
Collection d'art canadien McMichael
Don de Mme Anne (Comfort) Andersen et de la succession Mme Ruth (Comfort) Jackson
(No2002.1)

23. **The Great Rock, Bon Echo**
1928
huile sur toile
127,0 x 152,4
Musée de London. Don du Comité des Volontaires, 1961
(No 61.A.22)

24. **Winter Woods**
1928
huile sur carton
23,7 x 29,0
Centre d'art Agnes Etherington , Université Queen's, Kingston, Ontario. Don de la succession Kathleen Ryan, 1995

25. **Pastoral, Duncan, Ontario**
21 mai 1929
huile sur panneau
25,2 x 29,6
Robert et Margaret Hucal, Winnipeg

26. **Black Spruce, Pickerel River**
1932
huile sur panneau
30.5 x 25.5
George et Jessie Falconer, Sydney, C.-B.

27. **Barns Near Wexford on the Lawrence Ave. Line**
5 juin 1932
huile sur panneau
25,1 x 30,5
Le Musée des beaux-arts de Winnipeg;
Don de Vernon S. MacKelvie en mémoire de ses parents, Charles W.L. MacKelvie et Josephine (Hibbard) MacKelvie et de son frère, James A. MacKelvie, mort au champ d'honneur durant la Deuxième Guerre mondiale
G-88-375

28. **Clearing, Big Stone Bay, Lake of the Woods**
1934
huile sur panneau
25,6 x 30,3
Musée des beaux-arts de l'Ontario, Toronto. Acheté en 1985.
85/253

29. **Saugenay River**
1935
huile sur toile
76,8 x 92,1
Galerie Justina M. Barnicke, Université de Toronto;
Don des diplômés de la promotion de 1935
15471

30. **Tadoussac**
1935
huile sur contre-plaqué
24,7 x 30,0
Musée des beaux-arts du Canada, Ottawa; acheté en 1973
(No 17613)

31. **Tadoussac**
1935
huile sur toile
76,1 x 91,4
Legs de Vincent Massey , 1968
Musée des beaux-arts du Canada, Ottawa
(No 15471)

32. **Rossport, Lake Superior**
1935
huile sur panneau
31,5 x 37,5
John Clancy, Toronto

33. **Distant View of Manitoulin**
1936
huile sur bois
25,2 x 30,5
Centre d'art Agnes Etherington, Université Queen's, Kingston, Ontario; Legs de Herbert Clarke

34. **Smelter Stacks, Copper Cliff**
1936
huile sur toile
101,9 x 122,2
Acheté en 1957
Musée des beaux-arts du Canada
(No 6666)

35. **Lake Superior Village**
1937
huile sur toile
108,0 x 177,8
Musée des beaux-arts de l'Ontario, Toronto.
Don de la Fondation T. Eaton Co. Ltd. pour Canadian Works of Art, 1950.
50/10

36. **Pioneer Survival**
1938
huile sur toile
102,0 x 122,0
Morceau de réception à l'Académie royale des arts du Canada, déposé par l'artiste
Toronto 1945
Musée des beaux-arts du Canada
(No 4613)
(exposé uniquement à Winnipeg)

37. **Observatory**
1938
huile sur panneau de bois
37,8 x 30,5
George et Jessie Falconer, Sydney, C.-B.

38. **Primavera II**
1941/1972
huile sur toile
59,5 x 75,0
Anne et Clarke Andersen

PORTRAITS

39. **Self-portrait**
1920–1921
aquarelle sur papier vélin
25,2 x 23,2
Musée des beaux-arts du Canada
Don de Louise Comfort, Ottawa, 1996
(No 38276)

40. **Loo (Head of Louise Comfort)**
1923
mine de plomb sur papier
13,4 x 9,9
Bibliothèque et Archives Canada/1994–210–138
No négatif C-125834

41. **Louise Irene, daughter of Fred W. Chase**
1923
mine de plomb sur papier
20,4 x 12,7
Bibliothèque et Archives du Canada/1994–210–5
No négatif C-124463

42. **H. Eric Bergman**
Août, 1923
aquarelle sur papier
22,8 x 14,6
Le Musée des beaux-arts de Winnipeg;
Don de l'artiste
G-69-57

43. **Louise**
1927
huile sur toile
67,2 x 52,0
Acheté en 1981
Musée des beaux-arts du Canada
(No 26541)

44. **Portrait of Will Ogilvie**
1927
huile sur toile
91,8 x 86,7
Art Gallery of Hamilton.
Don de l'artiste, 1971
71.56.207

45. **Will Olgilvie**
1931
mine de plomb sur papier
26,2 x 20,4
Bibliothèque et Archives Canada/1994-210-87
No négatif C-125347

46. **Comfort Guestbook: Signatures of visitors to the Comfort residence**
1931–1939
33,0 x 20,4
Collection Bibliothèque et Archives du Canada/1992–692

47. **Chuhaldin**
1931
aquarelle sur papier
91,7 x 106,8
Art Gallery of Hamilton; Don du Comité des femmes, 1954
54.56.K
(exposé uniquement à Musée Winnipeg)

48. **Young Canadian**
1932
aquarelle sur papier
91,9 x 107,3
Galerie Justina M. Barnicke, Université de Toronto;
Acheté par the Sketch Committee
34.06

49. **Untitled (Louise)**
1933
mine de plomb sur papier
33,3 x 21,4
George et Jessie Falconer, Sydney, C.-B.

50. **Prof. Felix Walter**
1933
aquarelle sur papier sur châssis
162,4 x 76,4
Le Musée des beaux-arts de Winnipeg. Don de l'artiste
G-71-22

51. **Portrait in August**
1934
huile sur contre-plaqué
50,7 x 60,5
Musée des beaux-arts de l'Ontario, Toronto.
Don de l'artiste, 1991
91/383

52. **Portrait of Anne**
22 août 1937
huile sur masonite
40,6 x 36,8
Anne et Clarke Andersen

53. **Ruth at Studio Window**
1940
huile sur toile
102,0 x 51,0
C. Fraser Jackson, Toronto

54. **Self-portrait**
1965
Huile sur contre-plaqué
65,5 x 54,8
Commandé en 1965 par le Musée des beaux-arts du Canada pour la collection de portraits officiels des présidents du Conseil d'administration et des directeurs du Musée des beaux-arts du Canada
(No 5659)

ART MILITAIRE

55. **Ontario Summer**
1940
huile sur toile
101,6 x 121,9
Collection Beaverbrook d'art militaire, Musée canadien de la guerre
19710261-1673

56. **Bofors Gun Site in a Field**
12 mai 1943
aquarelle sur papier
39,6 x 56,4
Collection Beaverbrook d'art militaire, Musée canadien de la guerre
19710261-2147

57. **St. Eval Church, Cornwall**
Juillet 1943
huile sur carton entoilé
30,5 x 40,3
Musée des beaux-arts du Canada
Legs de Norah Michener, Toronto, 1992
(No 36830)

58. **Sappers Quarrying Stone**
31 juillet 1943
aquarelle sur papier
37,1 x 54,0
Collection Beaverbrook d'art militaire, Musée canadien de la guerre
19710261-2283

59. **Sappers Drilling in Preparation for Secondary Blasting**
1943
huile sur toile
67,7 x 40,6
Collection Beaverbrook d'art militaire, Musée canadien de la guerre
19710261-2282

60. **Battle Scene (Fantasy)**
29 janvier 1944
aquarelle sur papier
37,0 x 53,8
Collection Beaverbrook d'art militaire, Musée canadien de la guerre
19710261-2139

61. **Battlefield Near Berardi Crossroads**
1944
aquarelle sur papier
37,0 x 53,9
Collection Beaverbrook d'art militaire, Musée canadien de la guerre
19710261-2137

62. **Wrecked Buildings, Ortona, Italy**
19 avril 1944
aquarelle sur papier
36,8 x 53,8
Collection Beaverbrook d'art militaire, Musée canadien de la guerre
19710261-2312

63. **Dead German on the Hitler Line**
22 juin 1944
aquarelle sur papier
38,8 x 58,5
Collection Beaverbrook d'art militaire, Musée canadien de la guerre
19710261-2179

64. **Major C.F. Comfort**
30 juin 1944
aquarelle sur papier
51,4 x 34,3
Collection Beaverbrook d'art militaire, Musée canadien de la guerre
19710261-2172

65. **San Pietro in Vaticano, Rome**
3 juillet 1944
aquarelle sur papier
55,8 x 37,5
Collection Beaverbrook d'art militaire, Musée canadien de la guerre
19710261-2281

66. **Sergeant P.J. Ford**
15 juillet 1944
aquarelle sur papier
38,8 x 57,1
Collection Beaverbrook d'art militaire Beaverbrook, Musée canadien de la guerre
19710261-2189

67. **Campobasso**
c. 1945
huile sur toile
127,5 x 153,2
Collection Beaverbrook d'art militaire, Musée canadien de la guerre
19710261-2151

68. **Major W.A. Ogilvie**
1948
aquarelle sur papier
47,8 x 79,1
Collection Beaverbrook d'art militaire, Musée canadien de la guerre
19710261-1672

69. **Hitler Line II**
1944/1970
huile sur toile
92,0 x 116,5
Collection privée, Winnipeg

ART D'APRÈS-GUERRE

70. **Aeons Ago**
1947
plume et encre, aquarelle, gouache et cire résistante sur papier vélin
57,4 x 39,1
Musée des beaux-arts de l'Ontario, Toronto. Don de Mme Anne (Comfort) Andersen et de la succession Mme Ruth (Comfort) Jackson, 2000.
2000/58
(exposé uniquement à Winnipeg et à London)

71. **Transfiguration**
18 octobre 1947
détrempe sur papier
39,2 x 56,0
Le Musée des beaux-arts de Winnipeg;
L-34

72. **Thrush Song**
1949
multimédia sur panneau
67,0 x 50,5
Suzanne F. Jackson et Richard K. Edwards, Toronto

73. **Aura Lee**
Septembre 1949/1950
huile sur toile
60,9 x 76,6
Le Musée des beaux-arts de Winnipeg;
Acheté à l'aide du Fonds de l'École des arts, en mars 1952
G-52-175

74. **Rocky Site**
1952
huile sur toile
50,8 x 66,0
Collection McMichael d'art canadien. Don de l'artiste
1971.2

75. **Orchard in Albion**
1957
huile sur toile
51,0 x 65,5
Centre d'art Agnes Etherington, Université Queen's
Kingston, Ontario; succession James Ferres, 1985

76. **Wherewhen**
1957
huile sur toile
74,5 x 154,0
C. Fraser Jackson, Toronto

77. **Pre-Cambrian Legend**
1957
huile sur toile
61,3 x 102,3
Suzanne F. Jackson et Richard K. Edwards, Toronto

78. **Epic Theme**
Mai 1966
acrylique sur toile
127,3 x 170,7
George et Jessie Falconer, Sydney, C.-B.

79. **Horizontal Event II (Newspeak Series)**
1967
huile sur toile
61,1 x 102,2
C. Fraser Jackson, Toronto

80. **Seventh Line, Tecumseh Township, Simcoe County**
1970
huile sur toile
51,0 x 66,5
Centre d'art Agnes Etherington, Université Queen's, Kingston, Ontario. Don d'Elizabeth Harrison, 2001

81. **Edge of the World, Georgian Bay**
1972
huile sur panneau de bois
29,7 x 40,7
George et Jessie Falconer, Sydney, C.-B.

82. **Wichman's Barn**
Août, 1976
huile sur panneau de bois
31,0 x 41,0
Le Musée des beaux-arts de Winnipeg;
Don de Vernon S. MacKelvie en mémoire de ses parents, Charles W.L. MacKelvie et Josephine (Hibbard) MacKelvie et de son frère, James A. MacKelvie, mort au champ d'honneur durant la Deuxième Guerre mondiale
G-93-94

83. **Aspects of Nature 4, Thunderstorm, Georgian Bay**
1978
huile sur bois
30,6 x 39,7
George et Jessie Falconer, Sydney, C.-B.

84. **Rain, Mont St. Marie**
Octobre 1981
huile sur bois
31,4 x 41,1
Suzanne F. Jackson et Richard K. Edwards, Toronto

ŒUVRES POUR MURALES

85. **The Romance of Nickel**
1937
huile sur toile
213,5 x 610,0
Collection des Ressources naturelles du Canada
(exposé uniquement à Musée Winnipeg)

86. **Montreal Central Station relief – nord**
1940–1941
reproduction de photogravure sur papier
32,8 x 60,5
Bibliothèque et Archives Canada/1994-210-249

87. **British Columbia Pageant mural study**
1951
huile sur support commercial
51,0 x 76,0
Bibliothèque et Archives Canada/1994-210-204
No négatif e002712502

88. **Heritage – National Library Mural**
1965–1966
huile sur support commercial
38,3 x 102,2
Bibliothèque et Archives Canada/1994-210-216

ŒUVRES COMMERCIALES

89. **Harriet Cowan Inséré dans un livre: Women of Red River.**
crayon sur papier vélin
1923
20,5 x 15,2
Bibliothèque et Archives Canada/1995-143-1
No négatif C-143437

90. **Last Dog Train Leaving Fort Garry, 1909.**
Calendrier 1931 de la Hudsons's Bay Company (La Baie)
78,0 x 46,5
Archives Hudson's Bay Company, Archives du Manitoba

91. **Toronto's 100 Years: The Official Centennial Book, 1834–1934 Toronto: The Corporation of the City of Toronto,**
1934.
29,0 x 17,5
Collection privée

92. **The Council of the Northern Department of Rupert's Land, meeting at, Norway House. June 21st, 1836**
Calendrier 1936 de la Hudsons's Bay Company (La Baie)
78,0 x 46,5
Archives Hudson's Bay Company, Archives du Manitoba

93. **McLoughlin Welcomes the Americans, Fort Vancouver, 1834**
Calendrier 1941 de la Hudson's Bay Company
78,0 x 46,5
Archives Hudson's Bay Company, Archives du Manitoba

94. **R.M. Ballantyne at Tadoussac, 1846,**
Calendrier 1942 de la Hudson's Bay Company
78,0 x 46,5
Archives Hudson's Bay Company, Archives du Manitoba

95. **Nickel: A Vital Factor in the Economic Life of Canada.**
Le livre de The International Nickel Company, c. 1940
28,6 x 22,2
George et Jessie Falconer, Sydney, C.-B.

96. **Nickel: A Review of Institutional Advertising.**
Le livre de The International Nickel Company, c. 1947
28,6 x 22,2
Collection privée

Credits

Curator and publication project manager: Mary Jo Hughes

Guest writers: Laura Brandon, Rosemary Donegan, Anna Hudson, Rosemarie L. Tovell

Editor: Sarah Yates

French translater and editor: Gérard Boulad

Copy editor: Heather Mousseau

Graphic designer: Frank Reimer

Printer: Friesens Corp.

This project has been made possible in part through a contribution from the Department of Canadian Heritage through its Museum Assistance Program. Supported by the Department of Canadian Heritage through the Canada Travelling Exhibitions Indemnification Program. Additional financial support is courtesy of The Winnipeg Art Gallery Foundation; the Heritage Grants Program, Manitoba Culture, Heritage and Tourism; Inco Limited, Princess Auto, Friesens Corporation, and Western Paint. Media Sponsor: Winnipeg Free Press.

Photo Credits:

Ernest Mayer: catalogue # 1-3, 12-8, 20, 25-27, 32, 37, 38, 42, 49, 50, 52, 53, 69, 71-73, 76-79, 81-84, 95.

© National Gallery of Canada/Musée des beaux-arts du Canada: 9, 21, 30, 31, 34, 36, 39, 54, 57, 85.

© Canadian War Museum/Musée canadien de la guerre: 55, 56, 58-68.

George Lobb: 19, 29, 48.

Cheryl O'Brien: 24, 33, 75, 80.

Crédits

Conservatrice et administratrice du projet et de la publication: Mary Jo Hughes

Collaboratrices invitées à la rédaction: Laura Brandon, Rosemary Donegan, Anna Hudson, Rosemarie L. Tovell

Révision: Sarah Yates

Traduction et révision en français: Gérard Boulad

Correction d'épreuves: Heather Mousseau

Conception graphique: Frank Reimer

Impression: Friesens Corp.

Ce projet a pu être réalisé en partie grâce à une contribution du ministère du Patrimoine canadien dans le cadre de son Programme d'aide aux musées. Avec l'appui du ministère du Patrimoine canadien par le biais du Programme d'indemnisation pour les expositions itinérantes au Canada. Un soutien financier supplémentaire a été gracieusement fourni par la Fondation du Musée des beaux-arts de Winnipeg; le Programme de subventions destinées au Patrimoine; Culture, Patrimoine et Tourisme du Manitoba; Inco Limited; Princess Auto; Friesens Corporation; et Western Paint. Commanditaires médiatiques: Winnipeg Free Press.

Canadian Heritage Patrimoine canadien

Manitoba Culture, Heritage and Tourism
Culture, Patrimoine et Tourisme

Inco

The Unique World of Princess Auto

Friesens

Western Paint and Wallcovering

The Free Press
We're there for you

The Winnipeg Art Gallery

The Comfort Guestbook, 1931–1939: The Artist's Circle

The Comfort Guestbook expands our knowledge of a pivotal decade in the career of Canadian artist Charles Comfort, during which time he excelled as a commercial artist and muralist, and established his painting and teaching careers, even while struggling financially. Visitors to the Comfort's Toronto home left signatures, drawings, or photographs in the Guestbook . Events such as Emma Goldman's 1934 lecture tour to Toronto, the 1935 earthquake, a visit by Norman Bethune, and the completion of the Toronto Stock Exchange murals are documented therein. Labels from the wine consumed recall parties enjoyed in Comfort's home. A large number of the visitors are significant figures in the history of Canadian culture including painters, writers, critics, collectors, and musicians. The Guestbook draws a picture of a lively social scene that provided the Comforts with entertainment, intellectual stimulation, and professional connections during the challenging years of the Depression. In this CD-ROM format, we can page through the otherwise inaccessible document and uncover information about the artist's circle during this rich period in Canadian intellectual and cultural life.

Le Livre d'or de Charles Comfort : Le cercle des relations de l'artiste

Le livre d'or de Comfort étend le champ de nos connaissances sur une décennie qui marqua un tournant décisif dans la carrière de cet artiste canadien, décennie durant laquelle il s'illustra comme artiste commercial et peintre de murales et assura sa position dans les domaines de la peinture et de l'enseignement, alors même qu'il se débattait dans des problèmes d'ordre financier. Tous ceux et celles qui rendirent visite à Comfort dans sa maison de Toronto laissèrent dans son Livre d'or soit leur signature, soit des dessins ou des photographies. On y trouve ainsi, bien documentés, des événements tels que la tournée de conférences d'Emma Goldman à Toronto en 1934, le tremblement de terre de 1935, une visite que lui fit Norman Bethune, ainsi que l'achèvement des murales qu'il réalisa pour la Bourse de Toronto. Des étiquettes de bouteilles de vin consommées au cours de soirées festives évoquent le souvenir de ces soirées passées dans la demeure de l'artiste. Nombre de ces visiteurs sont des personnages notables dans l'histoire de la culture canadienne, notamment des peintres, des écrivains, des critiques, des collectionneurs et des musiciens. Le Livre d'or dresse un tableau de la scène sociale de ce temps, scène très animée qui devait être, pour les Comfort, une source de divertissement et de stimulation intellectuelle, en même temps qu'elle leur procurait des connexions professionnelles durant les éprouvantes années de la Grande Crise. Par la grâce de ce cédérom, nous pouvons maintenant passer en revue des documents qui nous seraient autrement inaccessibles et découvrir ce qu'il importe de savoir sur le cercle des relations de l'artiste au cours de cette féconde période de la vie culturelle et intellectuelle au Canada.

For / Pour Microsoft Windows:
Windows 98, 2000, or / ou XP; Pentium IV or faster / ou plus rapide;
256 MB of installed RAM / 256 Mo de mémoire vive; 1024 x 768 or better display resolution / affichage en résolution 1024 x 768 ou supérieure

For / Pour Macintosh:
Macintosh OS 10.1.5 or later / ou plus récent; G3 or faster / ou plus rapide; 256 MB of installed RAM / 256 Mo de mémoire vive; 1024 x 768 or better display resolution / affichage en résolution 1024 x 768 ou supérieure